REPICTURING

THE RESTORATION

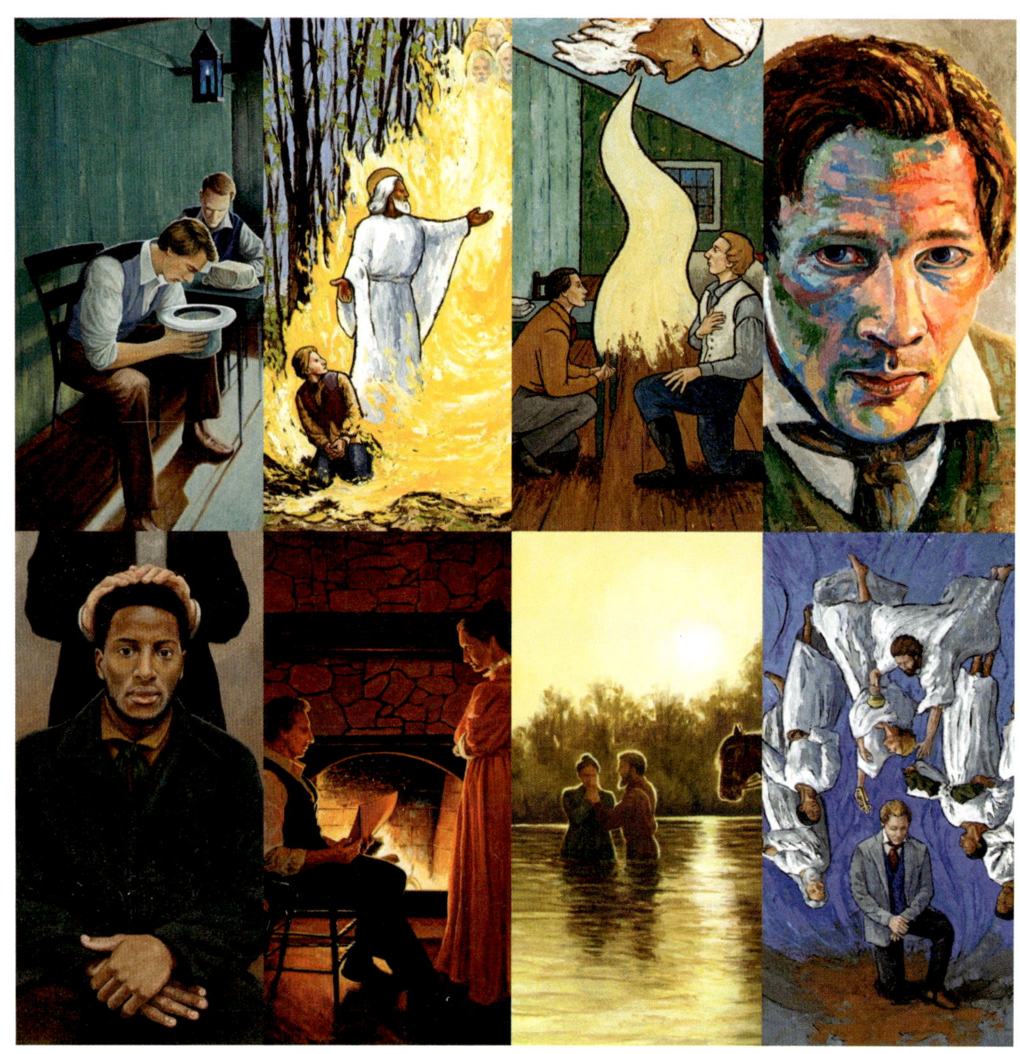

Scan this QR code with your phone to download images from *Repicturing the Restoration* for home use or classroom teaching.

REPICTURING THE RESTORATION

NEW ART TO EXPAND OUR UNDERSTANDING

ANTHONY SWEAT

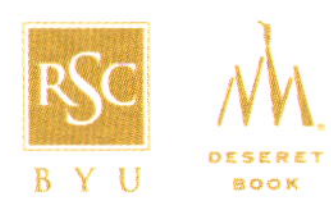

Art and text by Anthony Sweat

Published by the Religious Studies Center, Brigham Young University, Provo, Utah, in cooperation with Deseret Book Company, Salt Lake City, Utah.

Visit us at rsc.byu.edu.

Printed in the United States of America by Sheridan Books, Inc.

DESERET BOOK is a registered trademark of Deseret Book Company.
Visit us at DeseretBook.com.

Cover and interior design by Emily V. Strong

ISBN: 978-1-9443-9498-1

Library of Congress Cataloging-in-Publication Data

Names: Sweat, Anthony, author, illustrator.
Title: Repicturing the Restoration : new art to expand our understanding / text and paintings by Anthony Sweat.
Description: 1st. | Provo, Utah : Religious Studies Center, Brigham Young University : Salt Lake City, Utah : Deseret Book Company, [2020] | Includes index. | Summary: "Bringing together the author's artistic and academic training, this book offers twenty-five paintings of important events from the early Restoration that have either never been painted before or that have not had key elements depicted consistent with the historical record"-- Provided by publisher.
Identifiers: LCCN 2020015877 | ISBN 9781944394981 (hardcover)
Subjects: LCSH: Church of Jesus Christ of Latter-day Saints--History--19th century--Art. | Mormon Church--History--19th century--Art. | LCGFT: Illustrated works.
Classification: LCC BX8638 .S94 2020 | DDC 289.309--dc23
LC record available at https://lccn.loc.gov/2020015877

CONTENTS

Part 2: Ohio and Missouri

Part 3: Illinois

PROLOGUE

The Art of Belief

"Painting contains a divine force which not only makes absent men present . . . but moreover makes the dead seem almost alive."

—LEON ALBERTI, *ON PAINTING*[1]

My first prophets were painters.

The apostles who originally taught me the gospel were artists like Arnold Friberg, Minerva Teichert, Harry Anderson, Tom Lovell, Gary Smith, Del Parson, Greg Olsen, Liz Lemon Swindle, C. C. A. Christensen, James Tissot, Carl Bloch, Gustave Doré, and Rembrandt van Rijn, to name a few.

When I was young and the monthly *Ensign* magazine would arrive in our family mailbox, I would excitedly sit down with it on our flowered 1980s sofa, not to read the articles but to gaze at the art. The images were what captivated and instructed me. I visualized Joseph's vision because of Parson's painting. I comprehended that Christ was crucified because of Anderson's art. I empathized with the exodus from Nauvoo because of Christensen's canvas. These images embedded themselves in my mind and heart unlike any sermon or written word I can recall from my formative years.

Art has the power to do that, especially religious art, which is why Christianity has long deployed visual imagery for its purposes. In his classic 1897 work *The Ministry of Art*, Frank Bristol wrote:

> Art has glorified Christianity. It has set forth her doctrines, portrayed her saints, and even her very God and Savior. Limited only by the necessary restrictions of her powers, art has been a teacher of things divine. It has robed religion in loveliness, and crowned her white brow with jewels of beauty. It has reared the noblest structures that adorn the earth to her honor and service. Not to science, not to letters, not to philosophy, not to liberty, not to nature, not to art itself, but to religion has art dedicated its most glorious achievements, whether in painting, in sculpture, or in architecture.[2]

Although visual art has long been a major force in Christianity, it took about one hundred years for the restored Church of Jesus Christ of Latter-day Saints to regularly use artistic imagery in its institutional publications to perpetuate its founding events and doctrines. From the Church's organization in 1830 until 1900, there were fewer than three dozen images dealing with Church history or doctrine published in tens of thousands of pages of Church periodicals.[3] The first painting of the First Vision was not printed by the institutional Church until 1912.[4] Only in the mid-twentieth century did the Church begin to consistently publish artistic images in its printed pages. Those born after the turn of the twentieth century are the first Latter-day Saints who have been raised on an abundant visual Church curriculum.

It is highly likely that the religious images published by the Church since that time have impacted you also, teaching you the gospel visually, perhaps almost subconsciously. If I ask you to imagine Abinadi and King Noah, I can probably guess the scene that appears in your mind: Abinadi as a soft, doughy-faced youth, and King Noah holding a red rooster, right? No! You likely pictured Abinadi as an old man, shirtless, and rippled with muscles most anyone would envy. King Noah is overweight, sits on a throne, and has pet leopards. Two of them to be exact. How did I know?

You can thank Arnold Friberg for that. He created masterfully epic paintings in the mid-1950s that have since been redistributed millions of times in missionary copies of the Book of Mormon and in Church magazines. Friberg's paintings have almost become visual canon. So much so that if I asked you to list a dozen Book of Mormon stories off the top of your head in thirty seconds, your list would likely include many of the twelve that Friberg created: the two thousand stripling warriors, Ammon cutting off marauders' arms, the brother of Jared with the shining stones. Those may not be the most pivotal Book of Mormon events, but they are among the most dramatically portrayed. I have tried this experiment with people, and they rarely list stories such as Alma and Amulek's prison walls tumbling down (see Alma 14), Teancum killing Ammoron with a javelin (see Alma 62), or Nephi and Lehi being encircled by fire and conversing with angels (see Helaman 5). Something tells me that if Friberg had epically depicted those scenes, we might know them as well as we know Samuel the Lamanite on the wall.

REPICTURING THE RESTORATION

This leads me to the purpose of the present project, *Repicturing the Restoration*. I am a religion professor for the Department of Church History and Doctrine at Brigham Young University. I teach about Joseph Smith and the early Restoration as my profession. My PhD is in curriculum and instruction applied to religious education. I think and research and write about how people learn religiously and am driven by the quest to help Latter-day Saints have broad, deep, mature, abiding, and converting faith, and to learn what best helps in that process. I am convinced that visual art is one of the most potent tools. This is because, as art historian Herman Du Toit has written, "art has the capacity to create new meaning in the mind of the viewer, often by nondiscursive means."[5] As I have taught the Restoration and researched paintings that

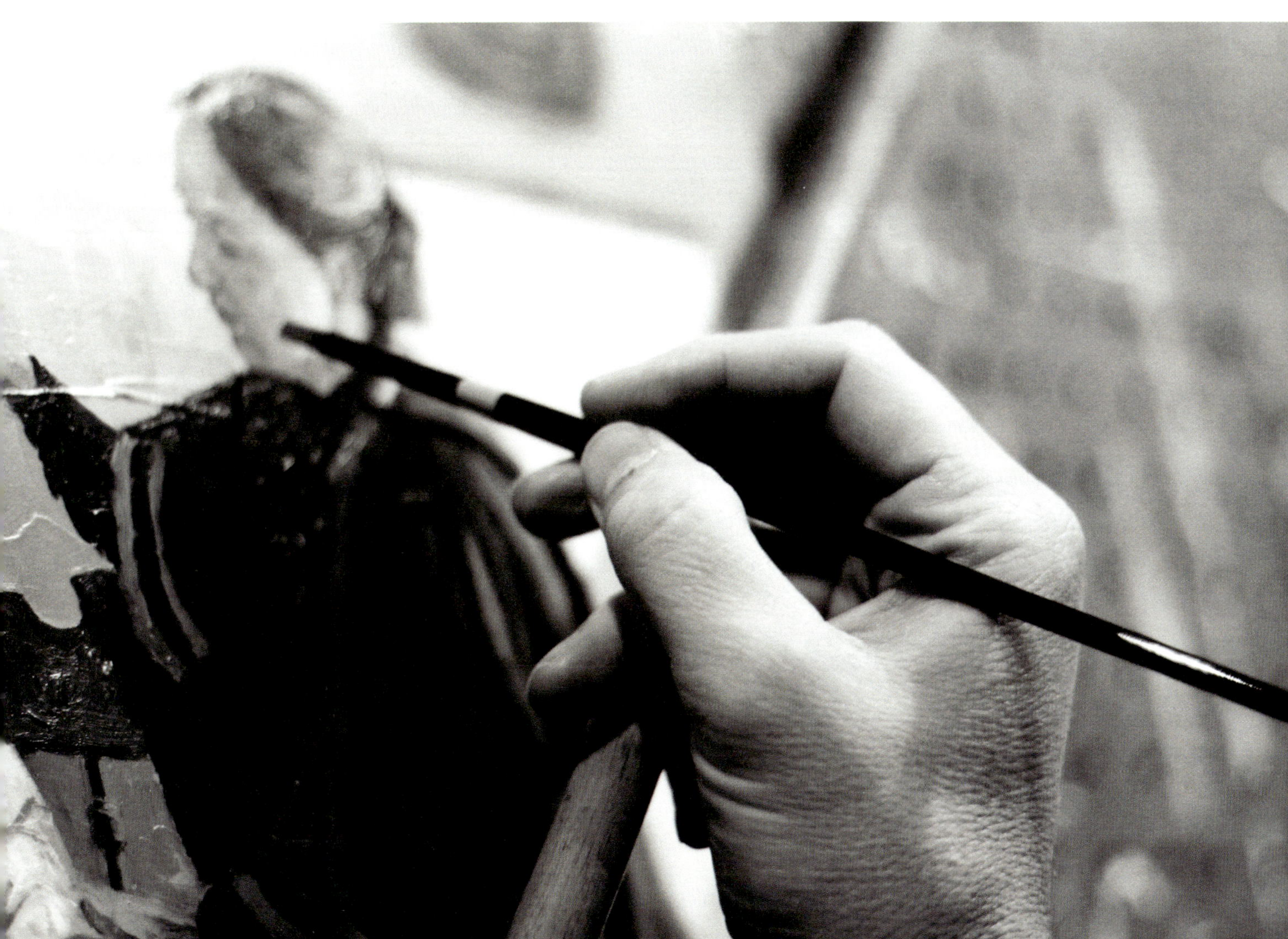

were associated with it, however, I have noticed that our Latter-day Saint imagery is sometimes lacking. Not in artistic quality, but sometimes in subject breadth, depth, historicity, and complexity. We have primarily shown the same Church history images over and over: the First Vision, Joseph with Moroni, Joseph and Oliver with John the Baptist or Peter, James, and John, and images of pioneers. It is for good reason that these scenes are repeatedly painted, since they are central to our founding Restoration narrative. But important and instructive Latter-day Saint history is often more diverse than these handful of events.

As I have taught about Church history, seeking to help learners develop a broad, deep, historically informed, and doctrinally mature faith, I have longed for paintings to visually accompany these types of discussions. Where are our images of Joseph Smith translating the Book of Mormon using a stone in a hat? Why don't we have a portrayal of the First Vision with "many angels" in the grove, as the 1835 account mentions? Oliver Cowdery may have used divining rods, according to early versions of Doctrine and Covenants 8. Where's that painting? Why do we not have any art that deals with plural marriage? Faithful women in the Church used to give healing blessings for more than one hundred years. Where are those women on canvas? Black men were ordained to the priesthood during Joseph Smith's tenure. Why haven't we painted that? Wouldn't images of these events help open wonderful knowledge and discussion and insights about the Restoration? Hence, this project.

Although I am a religion professor, I am also a practicing artist, having received my bachelor's degree in painting and drawing from the University of Utah.[6] Bringing together my artistic and academic training, herein are twenty-five chapters with paintings of important events from the early Restoration that either have never been painted before (or rarely so) or have not had key elements depicted consistently according to the historical record. Accompanying each image is a researched narrative called "A Background" that describes a history of the painting's content. Next, "An Image" gives some artistic insights into how and why the painting was created and composed. "An Application" provides a way to understand how this part of our history may inform our faith. Last, each painting write-up has "An Analysis" section offering potent questions that can be considered for further discussion. This book is not meant to be just a nice art book, although I hope it can be that. This is a pedagogical book using art as a launching pad to learn, evaluate, apply, and discuss important aspects of Latter-day Saint history and doctrine.

PAINTING HISTORY

Because the depictions in this book deal with historical subjects, a few words are in order about painting "history." First, I call the historical write-up for my images "A Background" for a reason. It's not "*The* History." The background I provide is one historical perspective, as I see it. Admittedly, I'm an academic pedagogue, not a professional historian. I strive to be scholastically sound with the sources I rely on to provide these backgrounds (there are about five hundred total sources cited in this book), but I readily acknowledge that others may interpret these historical sources differently than I do and therefore may come to alternate conclusions. I am perfectly comfortable with that, since there is no such thing as purely objective history. History isn't made by events; it is made by those who record and interpret events. "Historians do not discover a past as much as they create it," write the authors of *An Introduction to Historical Methods.* "They choose the events and people that they think constitute the past, and they decide what about them is important to know."[7] Thus, as historian Dean C. Jessee wrote, "The sources are not the past but only the raw materials whence we form our conception of the past, and in using them we inherit the limitations that produced them."[8] All history passes through individual lenses—the lenses of those who record it, the lenses of those who compile and propagate it, and the lenses of those who consume it. "A Background" is my lens based on the sources I've studied.

Additionally, some advocate that paintings that deal with important history must be "accurate," and they sometimes wonder aloud why artists do not have certain historical specifications correct in their paintings. To be clear, in this series I strive to be *historically accurate in concept* but not necessarily in detail. As I've written before,[9] true art and true history rarely, if ever, fully combine. Jacques-Louis David's *The Death of Marat* (1793) is a prime example of a historical painting that is not entirely accurate, for a reason. The painting depicts the death of the radical French Revolution journalist Jean-Paul Marat as he was murdered in his bathtub by a French loyalist. However, it is full of historical inconsistencies, artistic license, and idealizations intended to cause the viewers to sympathize with the martyr and the revolution. The painting was meant as a political piece of art, not a photographic re-creation of the actual murder scene. History and art are intertwined entities (history needs to be visually represented, and artists need meaningful history to create impactful images),

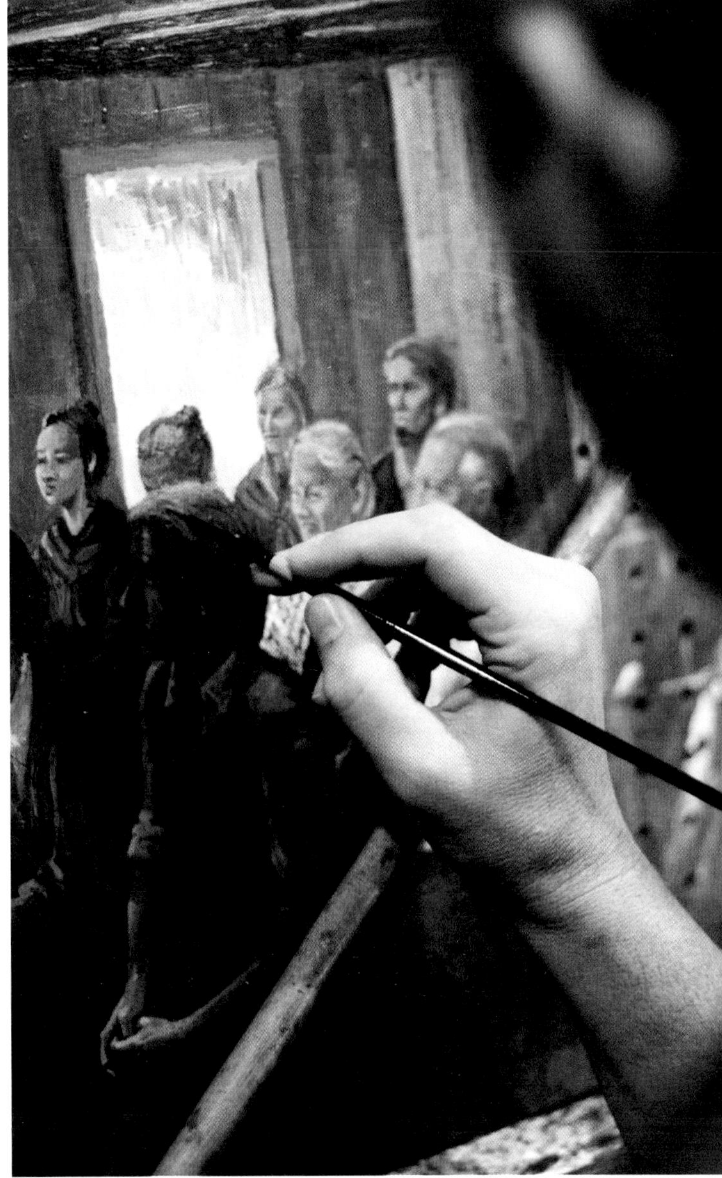

but their connection often creates difficult knots instead of well-tied bows that serve both art and history. These knots result because the aims of history and the aims of art are not aligned, often pulling in entirely different directions. History wants facts; art wants meaning. History wants to validate sources; art wants to evoke emotion. History is more substance; art is more style. History wants accuracy; art wants aesthetics. The

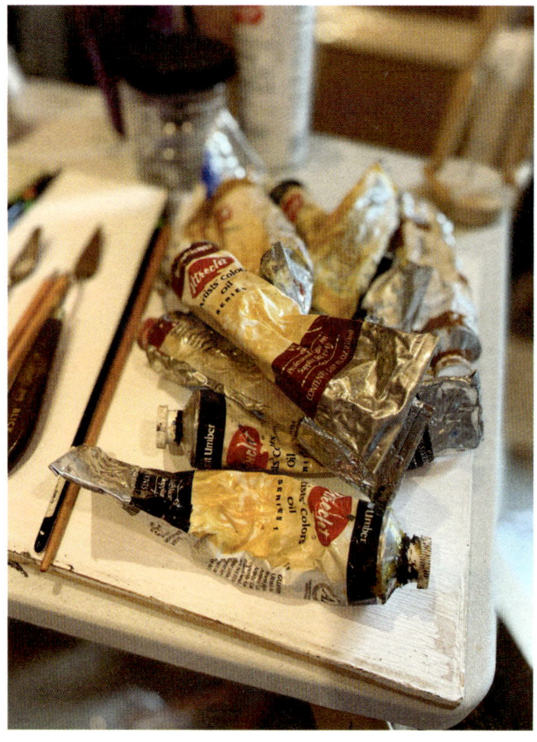

two disciplines often love, and hate, one another as they strive to serve their different masters.

Typically, those who call for absolute historical accuracy in art have likely never painted a historical scene themselves, for the moment you do, you quickly realize it is an impossible—and even an undesirable—ideal. Without photographs, how do we know how the subject posed? Did they stand over here or there? What exact clothing were they wearing that day? Is this how the light bounced and reflected in the room that morning? Did the event take place in *that* room? Was it even in the morning? Was their hairdo like that, that day? What did their facial expression look like in that moment? Who was everyone present? How do you *know* that? Thus, some artistic license is almost always taken in a historically based painting. As Arnold Friberg once said, "There is no tube of paint that says, 'Don't know.' I have to come to grips with it. You have to decide if [something] is going to be *this* big. Now I don't know any more than [the next person], but I have to paint *something*."[10]

Even if those details were known, would it correctly communicate the concept visually? It is vital to recognize that art speaks a different language than history. Art speaks through line, balance, contrast, color, texture, shape, rhythm, and other principles and elements of design to communicate with the viewer *without* words. History speaks through primary sources, contemporary accounts, consistency across claims, objectivity, context, and other tools to communicate *with* words. Sometimes, however, those historical realities run counter to the accomplishment of artistic aims. As artist Walter Rane once said to me: "Art is self-expression. Art is communication. That's what art is. If I'm trying to express something that is important to me, I'll do whatever I want. If it means putting Christ in contemporary clothing, or whatever, if it's important to the message I'm trying to make, then I'll do it."[11] Or as artist Kirk Richards said, "I've had people talk about what the 'correct' clothing is [of the First Vision] and so on and so forth. In reality, I don't care. I want it to portray what we feel when we think about the First Vision. And a lot of times historical details detract from getting that feeling across. So, very low on my list of considerations is historical detail. Sorry historians. Don't hate me. . . . I'm usually trying to present the principle of a spiritual truth rather than a historical truth."[12]

For my paintings in this project, I follow the basic advice that art historian Richard Oman observed: "That is not to say that simplification of style and visual elements is not possible. Most LDS folk art of this subject does just that. But it does mean that all the key elements must be depicted."[13] For didactic, historical, religious art (such as this project), I believe that is a good rule of thumb—*key elements must be depicted*. If the element isn't central or distracts from the main message, however, I feel it is open to adaptation to better communicate visually. In my paintings, facial features roughly resemble evidence of their subjects' features (if known). Their clothing is symbolic of the general period. Interiors are representative. But none of it is exact, nor am I trying to be precise in these particulars. This artistic approach may frustrate some detail-conscious viewers, but as Elder Jeffrey R. Holland once said when referring to a classic Latter-day Saint painting, it should be acceptable with an artistic interpretation to say, "It's close enough."[14] Again, my emphasis is on key concepts from the historical record that tell the primary narrative.

SOURCE AMNESIA

However, because art has such power to communicate concepts and embed itself in memory, for me "close enough" and "key elements" being correctly represented based on reliable historical sources are essential. In a discussion with a colleague about why art isn't always historically accurate, he said to me in frustration, "When are artists going to take responsibility for the falsehoods they perpetuate under the guise of artistic expression?" Because paintings have such power to propagate ideas, they can just as easily spread untruths and mere myths. For example, if I asked you to tell me about George Washington's prayer at Newburgh, New York, it is likely that you couldn't. But if I asked you to tell me about Washington's prayer at Valley Forge, suddenly you can, likely because of the dozens of famous artistic images depicting the event for the last two centuries. It's even on a stamp!

The problem, however, is that Washington's prayer at Valley Forge probably never occurred as portrayed in the paintings. It is more likely a folk legend perpetuated in the decades after Washington's death, validating our admiration of Washington as a religious man and providing a powerful symbol of God upholding the American nation. These reverential feelings embodied through the idea of the prayer at Valley Forge are so ingrained in our American psyche that reading these very words likely upsets some of you. Before casting nationalistic stones, however, ask yourself these questions: How did I learn about Washington's prayer at Valley Forge? Have I ever actually read a historical source that confirms this

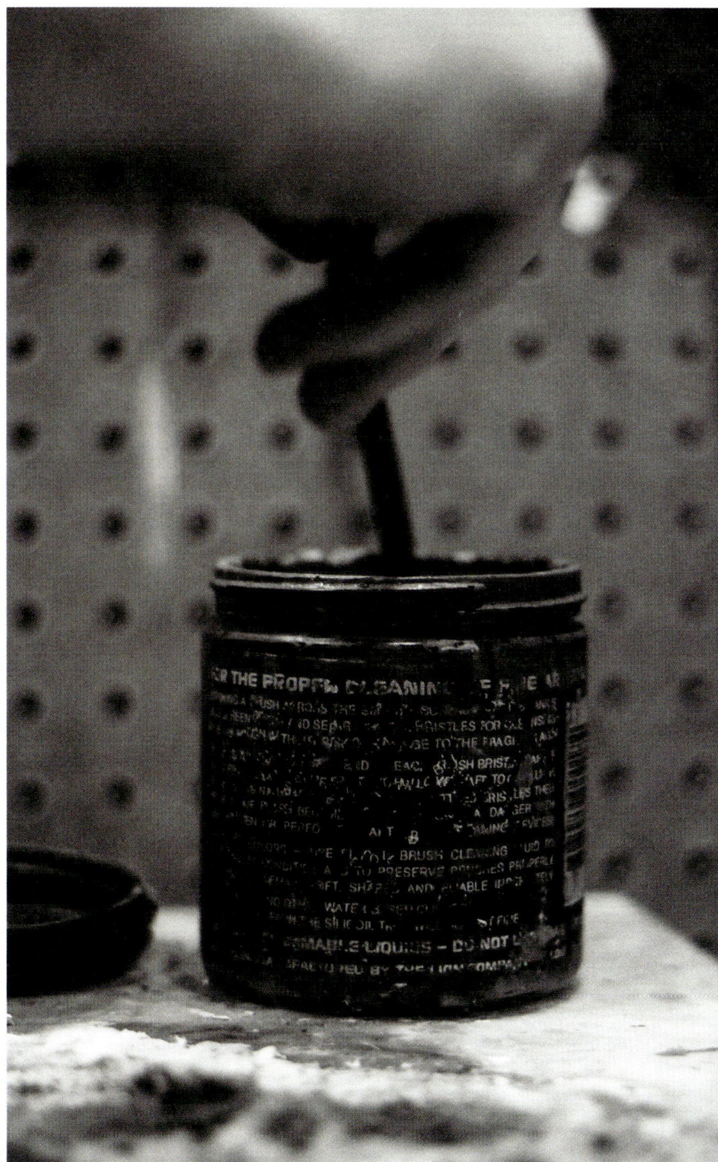

event? The sources for Washington's prayer at Valley Forge are not strongly reliable—they're even contradictory. One of them originated from the same man who started Washington's cherry tree fable. Another source places Washington praying in a barn.[15] As the 1918 Valley Forge Commission said when rejecting a proposed sculpture to be placed at Valley Forge, in its review of thousands of pages of contemporary historical documents from Washington and those who were at the Valley Forge camp, "In none of these were found a single paragraph that will substantiate the tradition of the 'Prayer at Valley Forge.'"[16] Ironically, however, there *is* a historically documented prayer of Washington at Newburgh, New York, [17] read every day at Mount Vernon at the wreath-laying ceremony at Washington's tomb.[18] The problem is, there's little if any famous art depicting it. Documented history dies while myth lives on in inspiring art. As the movie *The Man Who Shot Liberty Valance* so deftly summarized, "When the legend becomes fact, print the legend."[19]

The line between fact and fable also blurs through the lens of religious art because we can unconsciously consume artistic expressions as our sources for history or doctrine, especially if we have a bent toward literalism as opposed to symbolism. Art historian Jenny Champoux said, "[Art] has the power to shape belief, influencing the way Mormons tell scriptural stories and understand doctrinal lessons. . . . A literal interpretation of the scriptures has led to literal interpretations of religious art and vice versa."[20] Thus, sometimes Latter-day Saints can struggle when art isn't historically accurate, expecting it to be as much. Scholars Steven C. Harper and Elise Petersen call this phenomenon "source amnesia," saying, "When the Saints rely too heavily on visual or cinematic arts as the catalysts of their memory, the problem of source amnesia can be compounded. . . . It is common to hear Latter-day Saints talk about, even testify of, elements of [scripture, doctrine, or history] that are suggested by artistic or cinematic representations."[21] Some of us learn things, and we simply can't trace back where we learned them from. Was it from a historical or scriptural source, a painting or film? Epistemology isn't just a big intellectual word, it's also a large practical challenge.

REALISM VERSUS ABSTRACTION

One approach that some artists choose to help minimize visual source amnesia is to move away from realism. When we see a very realistic painting, our mind usually associates it with fact. Thus, sometimes *abstraction* is desirable in art, especially religious art. There are some who operate under the assumption that the best art is the most photo-realistic art. That may be the goal for some, but for many artists it isn't. In fact, some who could paint very detailed images purposely do the opposite. Abstraction (the distortion away from representation) is sometimes desirable because it leaves out distracting details, invites the viewer to complete the image mentally, and clearly sends the message, "This isn't a photo; it's art." Abstraction can also speak more broadly by being less specific. Recently the Church released a new version of the *Missionary Handbook*. In it, Church leaders chose some purposefully abstracted art of the Savior. Elder Richard Holzapfel said, "We wanted to warm it up, and we chose an artist who didn't depict Jesus in very much detail." The *Church News* article on the art in the handbook concluded, "The simple, detail-less and nonspecific imagery helps project a Savior 'any missionary can relate to.'"[22]

Richard Oman observed:

> Realism . . . has its potential problems. One of those problems is that realism can focus the viewers on the trivial instead of on the transcendent. For example, if the key element in realism is tight detail, we sometimes can become seduced into thinking that if we just know exactly what the bridge of the Savior's nose was like or whether his eyebrows were bushy or medium or thin then we will somehow know Christ better. We expect that we would somehow be able to pick him out if he were walking down the street.
>
> What is distinctive about Christ is not his physical appearance but his spiritual power. The question then arises, How does an artist communicate spiritual power?[23]

SYMBOLISM IN ART

One way artists attempt to communicate spiritual power in visual art is also another reason why visual art is not always historically accurate. Artists will employ the use of visual *symbols* to quickly and powerfully communicate a concept. In Christian art, a disciple holding keys tells the viewer it's Peter. Paint a man with a long beard who is holding a staff and wearing a red cloak with black and white stripes, and the viewer knows it's Moses. Skulls represent death, and snakes suggest Satan. Wings represent angels. Halos designate holy figures and glory. A

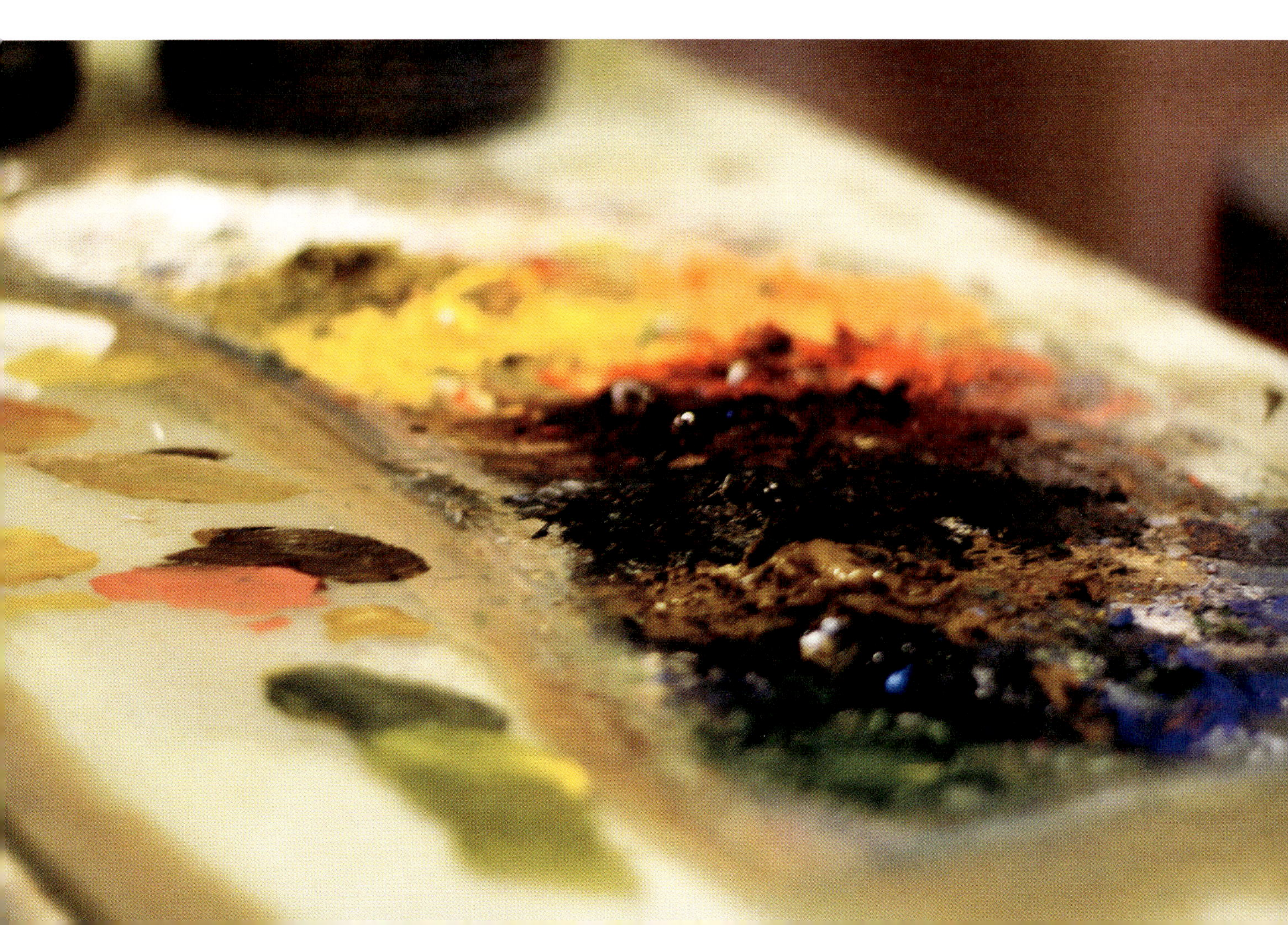

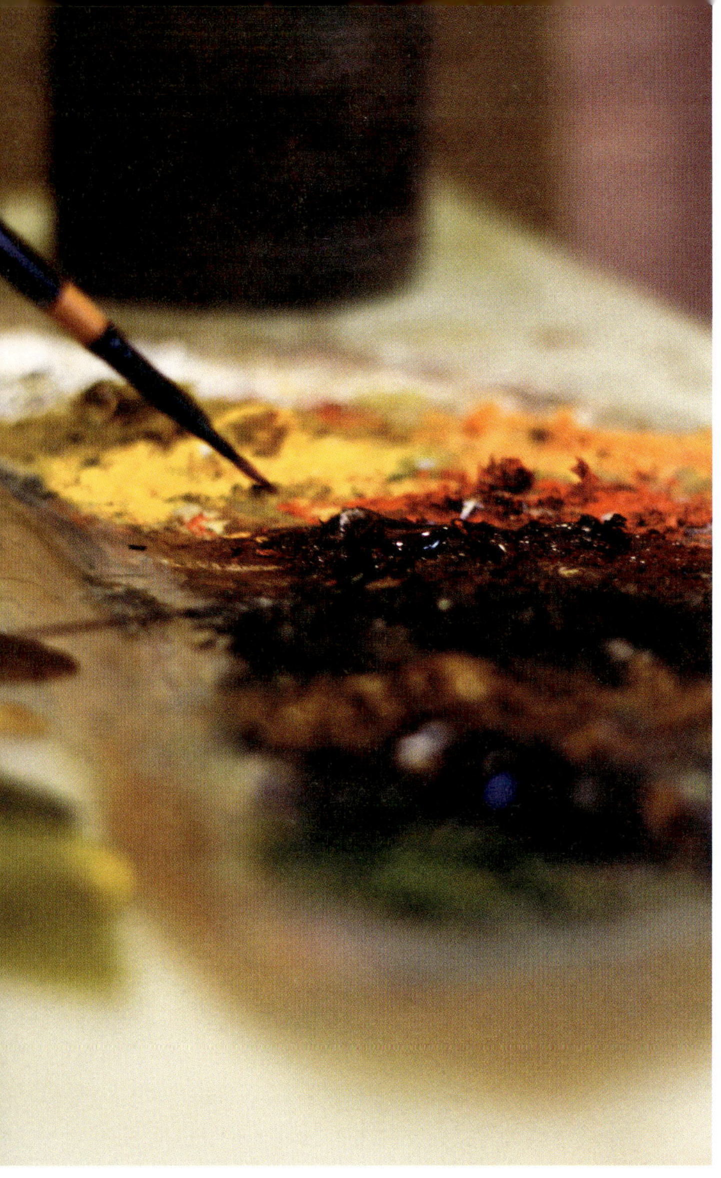

dove is the Spirit. We are not truly painting Jesus when we paint a man with high cheekbones and shoulder-length brown hair parted down the middle, with a full, forked beard, wearing a white robe. That is a *symbol of Jesus*. But it's likely not literally what historical Jesus looked like. The symbol is what speaks to us. Thus, as a report on Church temple art summarizes, "Added artistic elements, such as symbolism, can also add to the meaning of the image even if that means alterations to the historical accuracy."[24]

The Church has typically used realism in its institutional art and continues to emphasize this for its temple art.[25] However, the fact that the Church is also embracing artists such as Jorge Cocco and using his abstracted, postcubist imagery in the *Ensign* and in Church manuals, such as the 2019 *Come, Follow Me* manual for the New Testament,[26] is indicative that the modern Church is open to abstracted art and its potential benefits. To assist in helping members view art more symbolically and not literally, perhaps a footnote at the front of Church curriculum that includes art could say something like, "The art used herein is not to be interpreted as official doctrine nor historical reality. Art is symbolic and interpretive visual expression, not literal representation."

I mention abstraction and symbolism not only to inform the reader but also to contextualize my own depictions in this book. My paintings herein often lean much closer to realism than abstraction. However, I deliberately employ stylized abstraction in some of my paintings, such as *The First Visions*, *The Chamber of Father Whitmer*, or *Divers Angels*. I purposely use symbolism in color, composition, clothing, and characters to communicate concepts. There are halos and hanging scales and capes in *The Angel with a Drawn Sword*. These elements are not historically accurate, but they communicate necessary concepts and are thus "true" in the language of art. Also, although my images are often more representational than abstract, I don't want them to be photo-realistic. I purposely want to leave behind brushstrokes and gessoed texture and stain-colored underlayers. These are *paintings*, after all, not photographs. To paraphrase one of my professors at the University of Utah art school, "If you wanted it to look like a photo, just take a picture. It's a lot faster. If not, make it look like a *painting*."

Thus, you will see some variety in style and medium in the paintings in this book. Some are more realistic and others more abstracted or symbolic, depending on the purpose of the painting. A recognizable artist's style is good for marketing, but I don't want to confine myself to one particular approach. My style is to use whatever method

I feel is best to communicate the concepts and help people learn about the Restoration. Some mediums and styles lend themselves better than others in didactic artwork. Also, certain paintings herein are potential stand-alone pieces of fine art, and others are more illustrative scenes. Some took months to complete, others mere days. You may like some paintings or styles better than others. That's perfectly right and good. I do too! In fact, like a true artist, there are some images I will likely reapproach in the future with different compositions, styles, or mediums.

PAINTING DIFFICULT HISTORY

One last word on painting history. We are at a pivot point regarding how Church history is being approached by the institutional Church. Efforts like the Church's Gospel Topics Essays, the Joseph Smith Papers Project, new Church Educational System courses such as Foundations of the Restoration, and the new narrative Church history, *Saints*, are reflective of a more transparent, open, and nuanced approach to Church history that doesn't shy away from more difficult subjects. In fact, Church Educational System teachers were counseled by Elder M. Russell Ballard in 2016 to openly teach about Church topics that are "misunderstood," "less known," and even "controversial."[27] Some of the images you will see in this project fall into those categories, such as *The Ordination of Q. Walker Lewis*, *Relief Society Healing*, *Purgatory*, or *The Destruction of the "Nauvoo Expositor."* I feel that painting these images is needed at this time in our Church's history and is consistent with prophetic direction and the spirit of the Restoration. Indeed, in President Spencer W. Kimball's landmark talk, "The Gospel Vision of the Arts," he called for artists to paint "the story of the Restoration" and "the reestablishment of the kingdom of God on earth" but to also paint images that depict "the struggles and frustrations; the apostasies and inner revolutions and counter-revolutions of those first decades."[28] For whatever reason, we have largely overlooked the second part of President Kimball's prophetic call.

Latter-day Saints should live by this mantra in scripture: "Truth is knowledge of things *as they are*, and *as they were*" (Doctrine and Covenants 93:24; emphasis added), or as the Book of Mormon says, "The Spirit speaketh the truth. . . . Wherefore it speaketh of things as *they really are*" (Jacob 4:13; emphasis added). Truth is not a knowledge of things as we wished they are or hoped they were. When United States Founding Father John Adams learned that the famous painter John Trumbull was going to undertake a massive panorama of the Declaration of Independence, Adams wrote Trumbull a letter and asked some poignant questions, stating an important principle: "A few question[s] or two. Who, of your profession will undertake to paint a Debate or an Argument . . . in the Legislature? . . . Here the Revolution commensed. Then and there, the Child was born . . . Truth, Nature, Fact, should be your sole guide. Let not our Posterity be deluded by fictions under pretence of poetical or graphical Licenses."[29]

Trumbull didn't choose to depict any arguments or fights, instead he showed a group of forty-two men sitting or standing calmly with the document in hand, ready to approve. Generations later, we can mistakenly think that Congress was peaceful and all were united in declaring independence, when in reality there was abundant difficulty in the process. Lin-Manuel Miranda, in his smash-hit Broadway

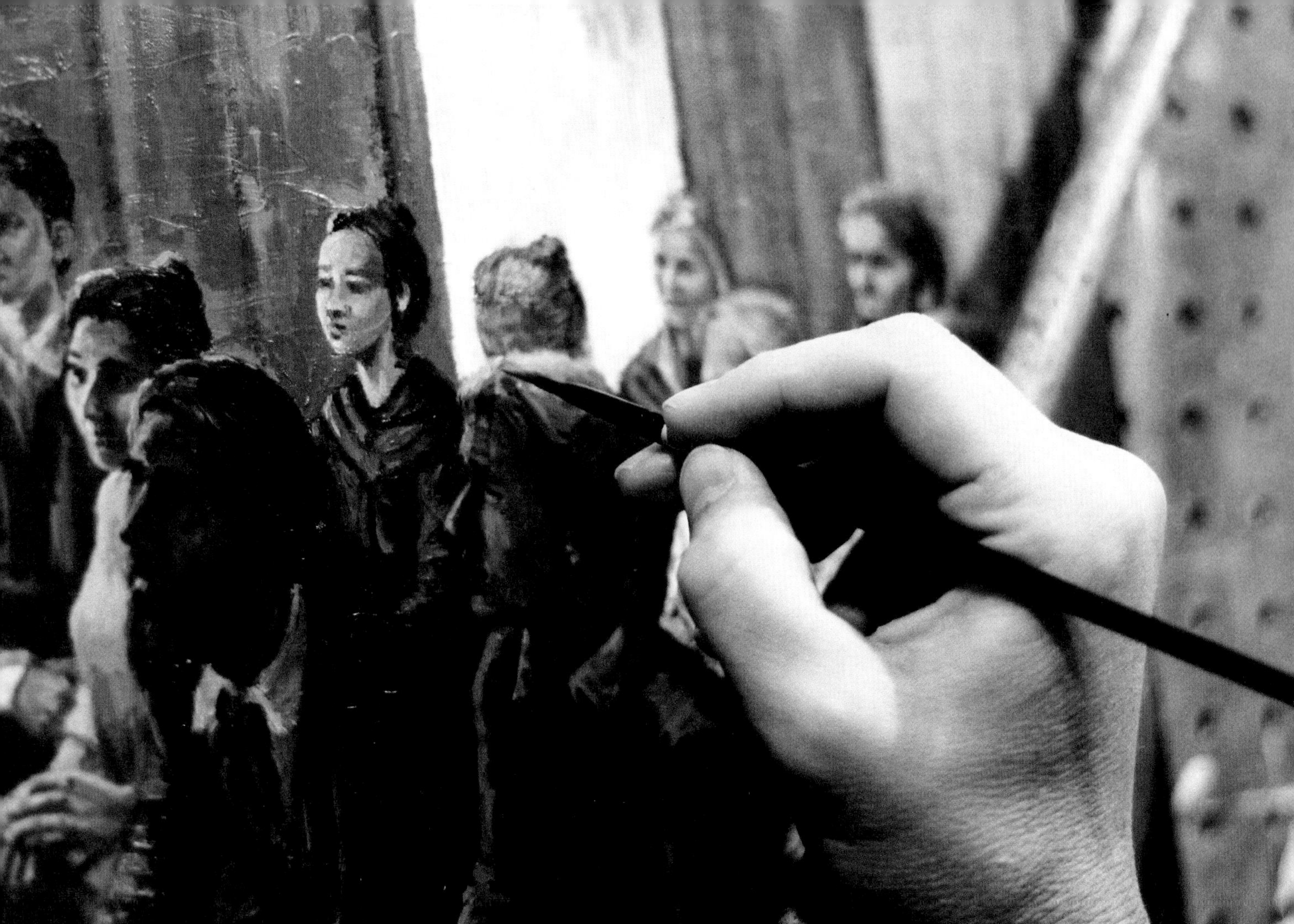

play *Hamilton*, originally proposed starting the play with a song called "No John Trumbull" to call attention to this conflicted reality:

You ever see a painting by John Trumbull?
Founding Fathers in a line, looking all humble
Patiently waiting to sign a declaration, to start a nation
No sign of disagreement, not one grumble
The reality is messier and richer, kids
The reality is not a pretty picture, kids
Every cabinet meeting is a full-on rumble
What you're 'bout to see is no John Trumbull[30]

Some paintings in this series are "no John Trumbull," both in artistic execution (Trumbull was a master) but also in depicting controversy. Remember, as Joseph Smith said, "Mormonism is truth."[31] Thus, I feel such paintings and discussions in this book are consistent with not just the history of the Latter-day Saints but the spirit of it as well. If you and I are seekers after truth, we never put our head in the sand; we never refuse to open the door of perplexity; we never give in to the urge to retreat to the ease of familiarity. This can be true in our religious art also. Scholar Terryl Givens has written, "Part of the challenge that today's Mormon artists face is . . . a strong church preference for noncontroversial art."[32] Another scholar, Karen Lynn, argued that Latter-day Saints will never really embrace art because of a culture of "the Disallowing of Perplexity."[33] I believe we must disallow this disallowance of controversy if we are interested in fostering the spirit of truth embodied in the Restoration.

I hope that in looking at and reading about some of these images in this book you find yourself a little perplexed at times, because discomfort can cause necessary reconsideration that leads us to further truth. As Latter-day Saint author Neylan McBaine wrote, "If it makes us uncomfortable, we could ask ourselves why are we uncomfortable. Is it because we have never seen it done that way?"[34] The same question can be asked for some of the images herein.

Repicturing the Restoration invites you to simultaneously be inspired, informed, confused, enriched, enlightened, and hopefully edified in the truth as you look at, learn about, analyze, apply, and discuss these new paintings and their write-ups. Whether or not these foster deeper belief in the restoration of the gospel of Jesus Christ through the Prophet Joseph Smith is up to you. Faith is a choice. In today's information age, however, ignorance is not. Because the spirit of the Restoration is synonymous with truth, then depicting such scenes from our history should be consistent with the values of all Latter-day Saints. As for me, the more I learn and teach Latter-day Saint history and doctrine—in its simultaneous simplicity and confounding complexity—the more deeply I believe. I hope these images facilitate further understanding and deeper belief for you as you repicture the Restoration.

NOTES

1. Leon Battista Alberti (1435), *On Painting*, rev. ed., trans. John R. Spencer (New Haven: Yale, 1966), 63.
2. Frank Milton Bristol, *The Ministry of Art* (New York: Eaton & Mains, 1897), 54–55.
3. Research by the author. With the help of my research assistant, Dylan Barton, we have compiled a list of every image published by the Church dealing with Church history or doctrine in *The Evening and the Morning Star*, *Messenger and Advocate*, *Elders' Journal*, *Times and Seasons*, *Millennial Star*, *Gospel Reflector*, *Nauvoo Neighbor*, *Gospel Light*, *The Prophet*, *New-York Messenger*, *People's Organ*, *Young Woman's Journal*, *Improvement Era*, *Mutual Improvement Messenger*, *Juvenile Instructor*, *Children's Friend*, *Relief Society Magazine*, and *Instructor*.
4. William A. Morton wrote and published a book for the Deseret Sunday School Union called *From Plowboy to Prophet: Being a Short History of Joseph Smith for Children* (Salt Lake City: Deseret Sunday School Union, 1912). The 130-page book was accompanied by eighteen illustrations by the artist Lewis A. Ramsey, such as Moroni visiting Joseph, Joseph and Oliver receiving the priesthood, the witnesses of the gold plates, and even lesser-known events such as Joseph stopping a runaway coach and his healing of Elijah Fordham. Opposite page 8 of the text, however, is the first known image of the First Vision published by the Church.
5. Herman Du Toit, "Preface," in *Art and Spirituality: The Visual Culture of Christian Faith*, ed. Herman du Toit and Doris R. Dant (Provo, UT: BYU Studies, 2008), xii.
6. BFA in painting and drawing, University of Utah, 1999 (studio art program). I was primarily trained in figure painting, with a heavy Postimpressionist emphasis.
7. Martha Howell and Walter Prevenier, *From Reliable Sources: An Introduction to Historical Methods* (Ithaca, NY: Cornell University Press, 2001), 1.
8. Dean C. Jessee, ed., *The Personal Writings of Joseph Smith* (Salt Lake City: Deseret Book, 1984), xiv.
9. See Anthony Sweat, "The Role of Art in Teaching Latter-day Saint History and Doctrine," *Religious Educator* 16, no. 3 (2015): 41–57.
10. Arnold Friberg, interview by Margot J. Butler, 3 June 1986, Salt Lake City, quoted in Vern Swanson, "The Book of Mormon Art of Arnold Friberg: Painter of Scripture," *Journal of Book of Mormon Studies* 10, no. 1 (2001): 30; emphasis in original.
11. Walter Rane, personal interview with the author, 7 February 2014.
12. J. Kirk Richards, personal interview with the author, 24 January 2014.

13. Richard Oman, "'Ye Shall See the Heavens Open': Portrayal of the Divine and the Angelic in Latter-day Saint Art," *BYU Studies* 35, no. 4 (1995): 119.
14. Jeffrey R. Holland, "Angels and Astonishment" (worldwide Church Educational System training broadcast, 12 June 2019).
15. See Gilbert Starling Jones, "Prayer of Valley Forge May Be Legend or Tradition or a Fact, Yet It Remains Symbol of Faith," *The Picket Post,* no. 9 (April 1945), in "Washington in Prayer," Historic Valley Forge (website).
16. Blake McGready, "Revisiting the Prayer at Valley Forge," *Journal of the American Revolution* (website), published 15 October 2018.
17. Shira Lurie, "Circular Letter to the States," George Washington's Mount Vernon (website).
18. "George Washington's Prayer for His Country," George Washington's Mount Vernon (website).
19. *The Man Who Shot Liberty Valance*, directed by John Ford (1962, Los Angeles: Paramount Pictures), as quoted by the character Maxwell Scott in "Quotes," *The Man Who Shot Liberty Valence* (1962), IMDb (website).
20. Jennifer Champoux, "Wise or Foolish: Women in Mormon Biblical Narrative Art," *BYU Studies Quarterly* 57, no. 2 (2018): 72.
21. Elise Petersen and Steven C. Harper, "Forming a Collective Memory of the First Vision," in *Eye of Faith: Essays in Honor of Richard O. Cowan*, ed. Kenneth L. Alford and Richard E. Bennett (Provo, UT: Religious Studies Center, Brigham Young University; Salt Lake City: Deseret Book, 2015), 15.
22. Scott Taylor, "New Missionary Handbook Is about More Than Following the Rules—It's about Becoming a Disciple," *Church News* (website), updated 15 November 2019. The art of the Savior used throughout the new *Missionary Handbook* is by artist J. Kirk Richards.
23. Richard Oman, "What Think Ye of Christ?," *BYU Studies* 39, no. 3 (2000): 85.
24. "Temple Art Seminary Summary," 12 June 2019 (a public meeting calling for more naturalistic, realistic images in the temples), 4.
25. "Even though abstract artwork can be beautiful and enlightening, it is best suited for venues outside the temple." "Temple Art Seminary Summary," 3.
26. See *Come, Follow Me—For Individuals and Families: New Testament 2019* (Salt Lake City: The Church of Jesus Christ of Latter-day Saints, 2019), 25, for a full-spread image of *The Call* by Jorge Cocco.
27. Elder Ballard gave a landmark talk in 2016 to CES religious educators in which he said, "Our curriculum [in the past], though well-meaning, did not prepare students for today. . . . More than at any time in our history, your students also need to be blessed by learning doctrinal or historical content and context by study and faith accompanied by pure testimony so they can experience a mature and lasting conversion to the gospel and a lifelong commitment to Jesus Christ. . . . [Provide] faithful, thoughtful, and accurate interpretation of gospel doctrine, the scriptures, our history, and those topics that are sometimes misunderstood . . . that are less known or controversial." M. Russell Ballard, "The Opportunities and Responsibilities of CES Teachers in the 21st Century" (worldwide Church Educational System training broadcast, 26 February 2016).
28. Spencer W. Kimball, "The Gospel Vision of the Arts," *Ensign*, July 1977.
29. John Adams to John Trumbull, 18 March 1817, in "Adams Papers," National Archive: Founders Online.
30. Lin-Manuel Miranda, "No John Trumbull," intro, track 1 on *The Hamilton Mixtape* (Hamilton Uptown Limited Liability Company, 2016).
31. "Letter to Isaac Galland, 22 March 1839," 51, The Joseph Smith Papers.
32. Terryl Givens, *People of Paradox* (New York: Oxford University Press, 2007), 335.
33. As cited in Givens, *People of Paradox*, 337.
34. Neylan McBaine, *Women at Church: Magnifying LDS Women's Local Impact* (Salt Lake City: Greg Kofford Books, 2014), 80.

PART ONE

NEW YORK AND PENNSYLVANIA

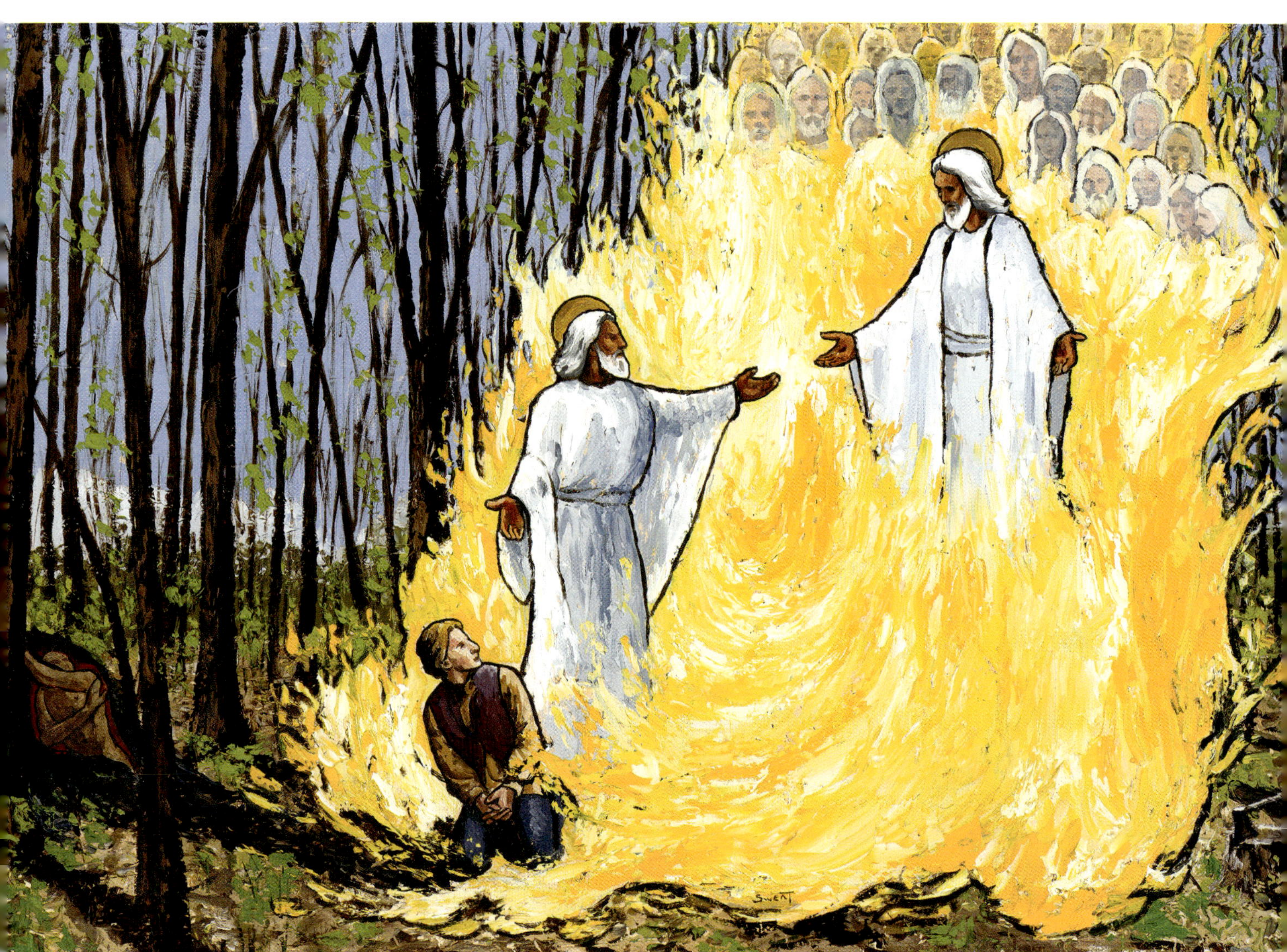

The First Visions (16" x 24", oil on board, 2018)

THE FIRST VISIONS

Timeline: Early Spring 1820

Related Verses: Joseph Smith—History 1:5–26

A BACKGROUND

When the teenage Joseph Smith entered the woods on his family farm to pray over his soul and inquire about which church he should join, the vision that burst forth from heaven changed his life and laid a pathway for the restoration of the gospel of Jesus Christ. The First Vision is among artists' most oft-depicted scenes of the Restoration. It was perhaps first visualized by an illustrator for former Church member T. B. H. Stenhouse's book *Rocky Mountain Saints* in 1873.[1] Danish convert C. C. A. Christensen was likely the first Latter-day Saint artist to paint the First Vision—a stained glass window six by ten feet mural for his Mormon Panorama scenes in 1878—but the painting has subsequently been lost. Joseph Young, the Salt Lake Temple architect, had Tiffany and Company create a stained glass window—twelve by four and a half feet—in 1892 for the Salt Lake Temple's Holy of Holies.[2] Since then, hundreds of artists have painted or sculpted the scene. Depictions of the First Vision have been published by the Church in the *Ensign* 167 times between 1971 and 2018, which—according to my research—is nearly double that of any Restoration theme other than depictions of pioneers.

If there are so many images, then why undertake a new image of the First Vision for this *Repicturing the Restoration* project? What does this painting add that others in the past have not? My image is a *harmony* of aspects from the nine contemporary historical accounts of the First Vision.[3] I have titled the painting *The First Visions* (plural) because it brings several unfolding events into one scene. It attempts to bring together into one image a cohesive picture, including some aspects not typically depicted in previous First Vision imagery.

For example, many accounts suggest that the Father and Son did not appear to Joseph at the same time. In his 1835 account of the vision,

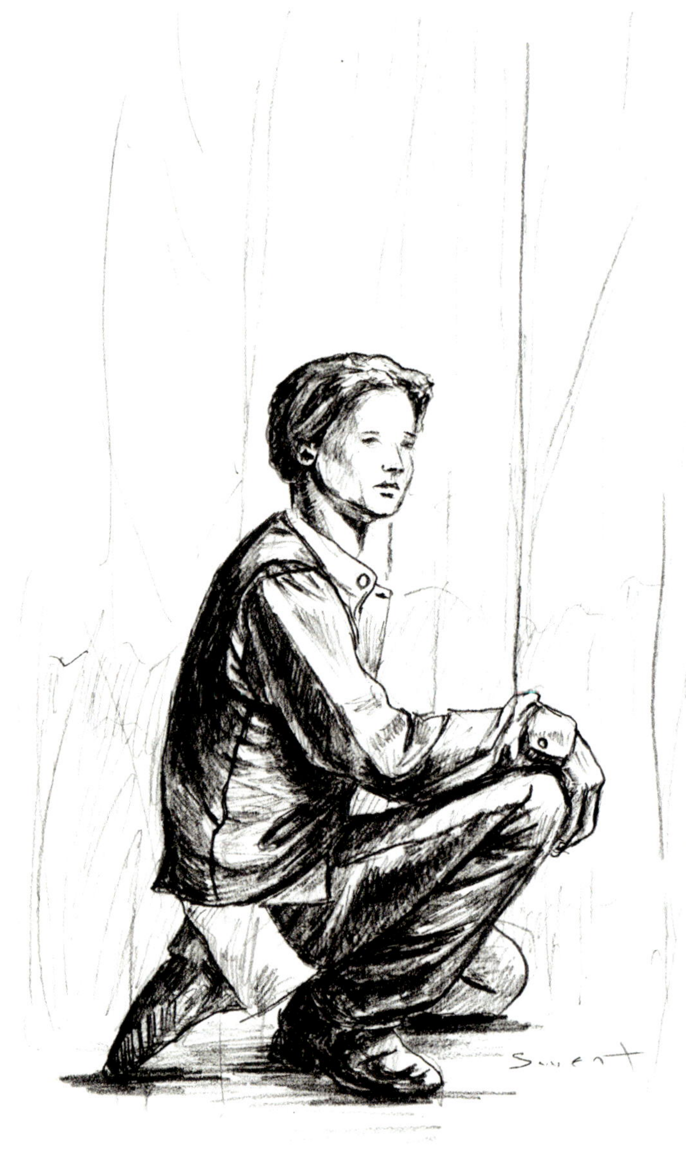

Joseph Smith said, "A personage appeard in the midst, of this pillar of flame which was spread all around, and yet nothing consumed, another personage soon appeard like unto the first, he said unto me thy sins are forgiven thee."[4] This idea is supported by two other accounts. One

was in an 1843 interview with newspaperman David Nye White: "Directly I saw a light, and then a glorious personage in the light, *and then another personage*, and the first personage said to the second, 'Behold my beloved Son, hear him.'"[5] German immigrant Alexander Neibaur's 1844 journal account says that Joseph reported he "saw a personage in the fire light . . . *after a w[h]ile a other person came to the side of the first*."[6] A simultaneous dual divine appearance, as often depicted, seems inaccurate.

Additionally, this image shows fire blazing out from heaven, wrapped around the figures in dramatic fashion. Most First Vision imagery uses softer, more gently diffused white light. The historical accounts, however, use the word "light" and "fire" almost interchangeably. Joseph's first writing in 1832 says he saw "a piller of ~~fire~~ light," as if searching for the right word.[7] Accounts in 1835, 1840, and 1844 all use the word "fire" in various places in their descriptions. Orson Pratt wrote in his 1840 account that Joseph feared the entire grove would be consumed in flames.[8]

In the 1835 account, Joseph makes an important statement that is not often visually depicted. At the close of it, he says, "And I saw many angels in this vision."[9] Depicted above the Father and Son in my image are a gathering of many types of heavenly angels—female and male—divinely assembled to witness and testify. In my estimation, the First Vision was probably much more expansive in heavenly scope than most assume or depict.

Included in this scene is also something not usually explicitly painted. Many of the First Vision accounts mention the adversary attempting to stop Joseph from praying, attacking him from "behind," rendering him speechless,[10] leading him to be "tempted by the powers of darkness,"[11] filling "his mind with doubts,"[12] and gathering "thick darkness"[13] around him. I know of only one other painting of the First Vision that shows the Father, Son, and Lucifer in the same grove scene (Paul Forester in 1980). In the bottom left corner of my image, Satan is painted fleeing, a flat pillar of darkness being pushed away from Joseph by the vertical pillar of flame.

Last, like paintings done by Walter Rane in the early 2000s, in my image the grove is depicted without much foliage instead of being full and leafy green. The official 1838 account says the vision was in the "early spring" (Joseph Smith—History 1:14), and in upstate New York, leaves often don't make their appearance until sometime in May. Although we don't know the month and day of the First Vision,[14] the browns of the branches and barely budding trees suggest an early spring grove getting ready to burst out of winter's dark slumber, a fitting metaphor for the fruits of the First Vision itself.

AN IMAGE

Central to my painting are the figures representing God the Father and his divine son, the Savior Jesus Christ. Some immediately wonder why I have Jesus on the left side of the Father, when typically Jesus is on his right in most paintings. That would have been an appropriate symbolic representation, although none of the accounts expressly says that's how they stood. The pose of the Father is meant to suggest that the Father has just finished speaking to Joseph and has now turned to the side, opening Joseph's view to the Savior, who is descending from heaven. You can see subtle crucifixion marks in the palms of Jesus's hands. The Father and Son appear in the midst

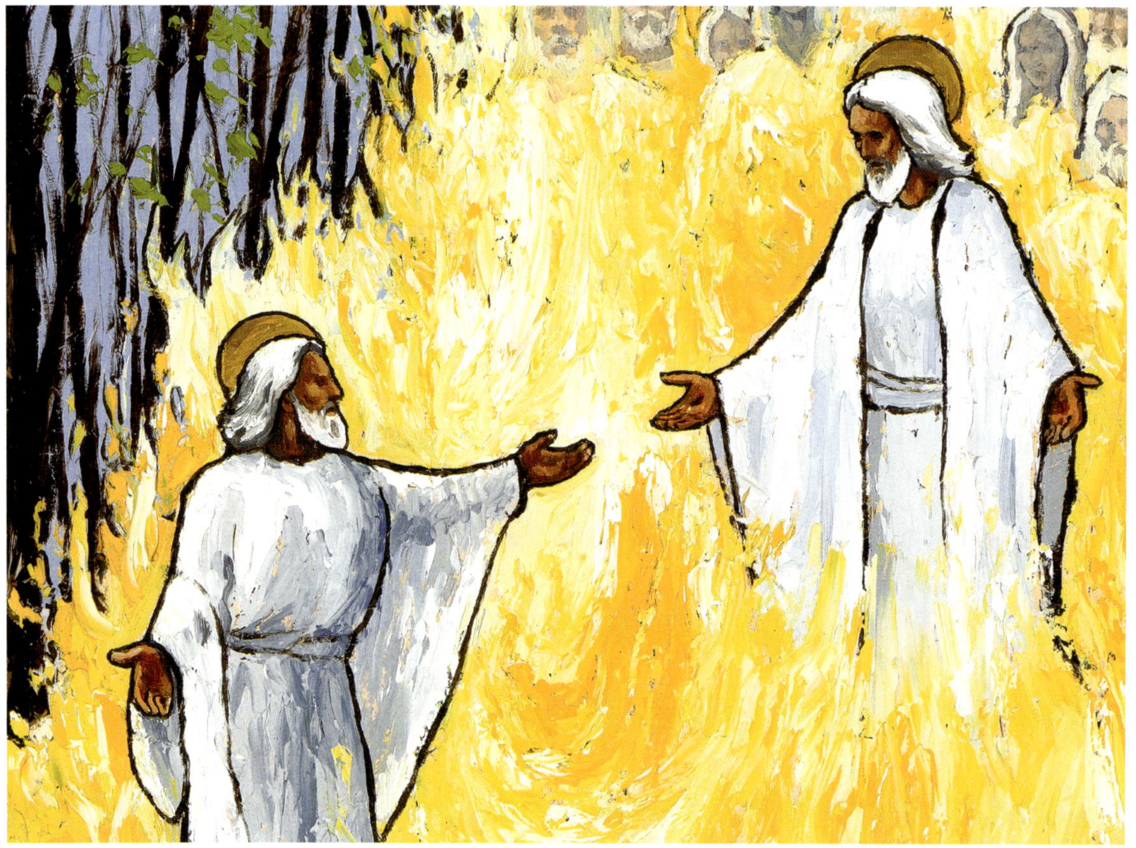

of this pillar of flame, resembling each other in likeness as the 1842 Wentworth letter account reports.[15] In a departure from one historical account (Alexander Neibaur says Joseph described Deity as having a "light complexion"[16]), I purposely painted the skin color of the Father and Son more bronzed, rather than the Euro white that we see in most Latter-day Saint or other Christian imagery. The Father and Son are a middle skin tone—as the Gods of humanity—to hearken more broadly to people of color across the world. You may have noticed the halos over God and Jesus, sometimes called a "nimbus."[17] Although merely a symbol, I chose to include those halos to suggest exaltation, as it typifies a crown of glory. In this way, the Father and Son are made distinct and exalted from the surrounding angels.

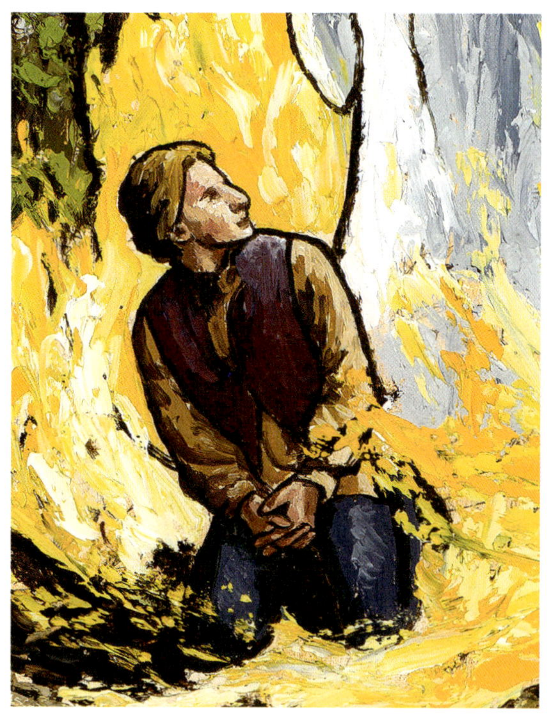

Joseph is kneeling on the ground, slightly leaning away, simultaneously joyful and fearful

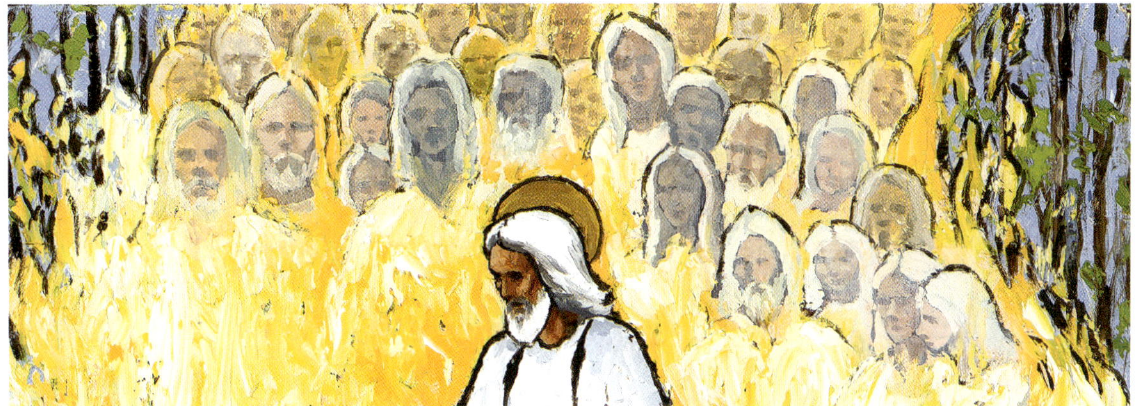

of what is happening (what would you think if a column of flame descended slowly out of heaven toward you?). In my painting, I depicted "this pillar of flame which was spread all around,"[18] as Joseph in 1835 reported, and Joseph is "enveloped in the midst of it,"[19] as Orson Pratt wrote in 1840. Joseph is not wearing the typically painted clothing of a white shirt and brown pants.[20] His thick, light brown overshirt, purple vest, and blue pants set him apart from the white clothing of the Father and Son and the brown earth tones of the foreground.

In a significant departure from previous First Vision imagery, herein I depicted a concourse of angels behind the Savior, based on the 1835 account's claim that Joseph saw many angels in the grove. I included both women and men as angels, of all races, to signify the global impact of the First Vision on humanity, past and present. This isn't noted anywhere in the documents but reflects an artistic license to suggest what I feel is a crucial, inclusive concept.

In the bottom left of the painting, fleeing from the fire (or light), the adversary is haloed in a symbolic scarlet red. I chose to depict Satan in a bodily shape. Is this correct? I don't know. I assume he has a spirit body because, doctrinally, all spirit is matter (see Doctrine and Covenants 131:7) and he is a spirit son of God. I painted him nude to suggest his lack of glory because often, the righteous are scripturally described as being "clothed with" or "clothed upon" as a symbol of purity, power, or faithfulness (see Revelation 7:9; 2 Nephi 9:14; Doctrine and Covenants 29:12). Satan's pose is an homage to Carl Bloch's classic painting *Jesus Casting Out Satan*.

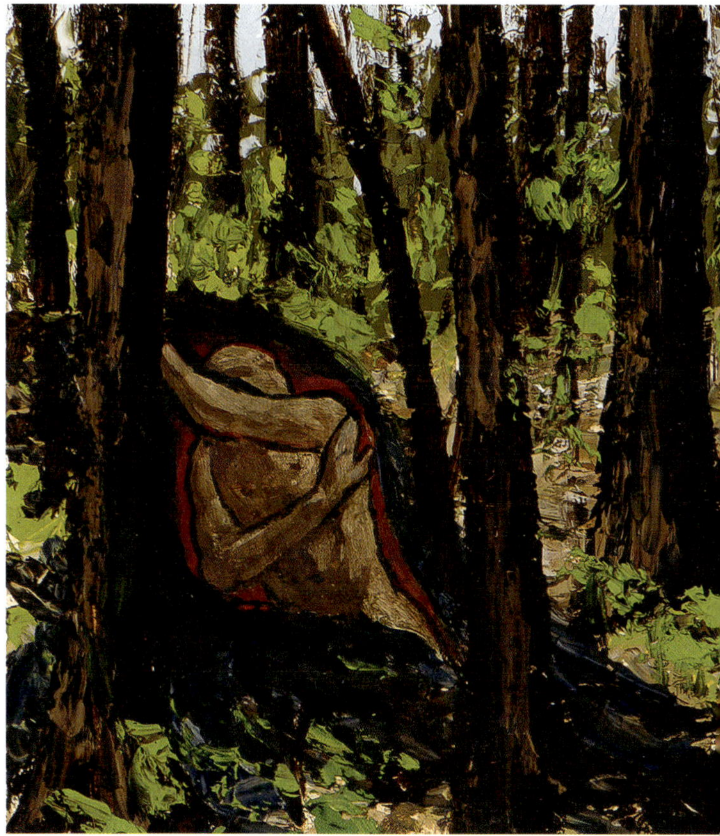

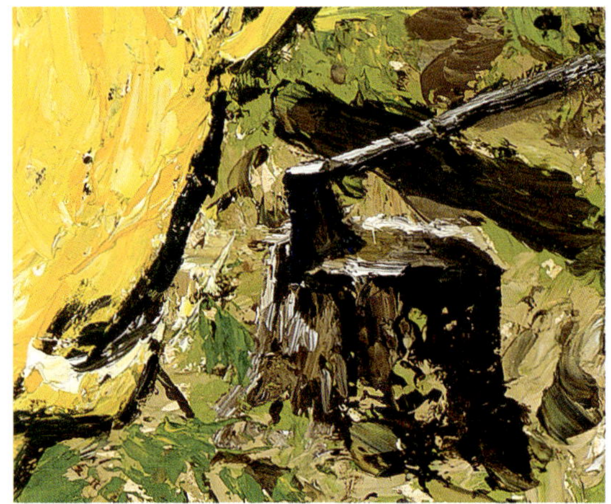

On the other side of the painting in the bottom right corner there's an axe in a stump, as Joseph reported in the 1843 newspaper account that he "went to the stump where I had stuck my axe when I had quit work"[21] to pray.

Last, the grove is just awakening from its winter hibernation, with leaves beginning to make their appearance, suggesting an early springtime and a preparatory springing forth of the Restoration.

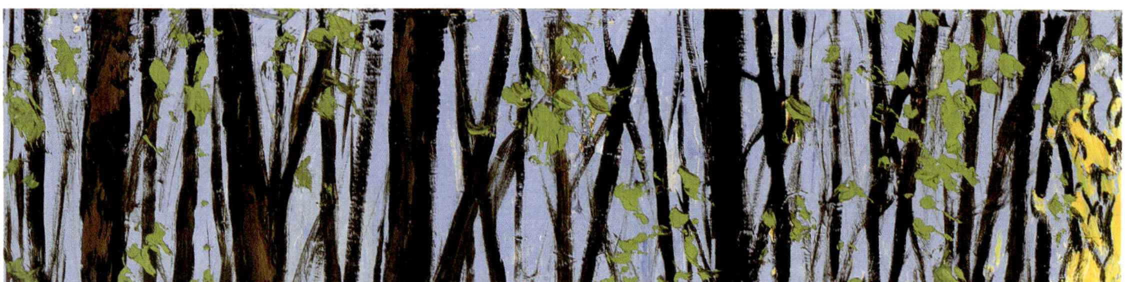

AN APPLICATION

Although it took a few decades for the First Vision to become well-known by the body of the Church, by the turn of the twentieth century it had become a defining doctrinal event and continues to be so today.[22] Why? Personal visions have happened to others. So why does Joseph's First Vision, in which his sins were forgiven, become the "hinge pin on which this whole cause" of the Restoration swings, according to President Gordon B. Hinckley, where "every truth that we offer concerning the validity of the work, all finds its root in the First Vision of the boy prophet"?[23] If we analyze the various First Vision accounts and look at what the Father and Son taught Joseph, what are the foundational *doctrinal* messages of the First Vision for Latter-day Saints?

One central message was that there was an apostasy in doctrinal truth, particularly through the Christian creeds, with "each [religion] pointing to his own particular creed as the summum bonum of perfection."[24] In the grove, God said to Joseph that "all their Creeds were an abomination in his sight,"[25] causing people to believe "in incorrect doctrines."[26] Notice how at issue were the *creeds* of Christianity. A creed is a formal statement of faith and doctrine. The word comes from the Latin *credo*, meaning "I believe."[27] The creeds that developed in the centuries after the death of Jesus's Apostles codified some of the doctrinal changes made during the Great Apostasy, particularly dealing with the nature of God and the concept of the trinity (God is one being, manifesting himself in three forms: the Father, the Son, and the Holy Ghost). Knowing the true nature of God is essential to faith[28] and to eternal life (see John 17:3). If we do not know

God's purposes, nor our relationship to him as his children, the plan of exaltation can become frustrated. Thus, Joseph Smith later wrote that the "creeds of the fathers" have caused children of God to have "inherited lies" and "filled the world with confusion" (Doctrine and Covenants 123:7). One of the reasons why the First Vision has become a defining doctrinal point of the Restoration is because it shattered trinitarian views of God espoused by some of the Christian creeds. President Hinckley said:

> We do not accept the Athanasian Creed. We do not accept the Nicene Creed, nor any other creed based on tradition and the conclusions of men.
>
> We do accept, as the basis of our doctrine, the statement of the Prophet Joseph Smith that when he prayed for wisdom in the woods, "the light rested upon me [and] I saw two Personages . . ." (Joseph Smith—History 1:17).
>
> Two beings of substance were before him. He saw them. They were in form like men, only much more glorious in their appearance. He spoke to them. They spoke to him. They were not amorphous spirits. Each was a distinct personality. They were beings of flesh and bone whose nature was reaffirmed in later revelations which came to the Prophet.[29]

A second major doctrinal message of the First Vision was its underlying emphasis on the need for the covenants and ordinances of the gospel. Levi Richards reported in 1843 that Joseph Smith said he was told "the Everlasting covena[n]t was broken"[30] or that "they have turned asside from the gospel," as the 1832 account says.[31] The *gospel* is clearly defined in the Book of Mormon and Doctrine and Covenants as faith in Jesus Christ, repentance, baptism by authority, reception of the Holy Ghost, and continuation in the faith (see 2 Nephi 31:2–16; 3 Nephi 27:13–21; Doctrine and Covenants 33:11–12). While it may seem apparent to many that living "the gospel" is essential to being saved in the kingdom of God, a post-Reformation emphasis on salvation by grace without works has led some Protestants to "reject baptism as being required for salvation" because "requiring anything in addition to faith in Jesus Christ for salvation is a works-based salvation."[32] Notice how the 1838 account reports the Lord saying the churches have "a form of godliness but they deny the power thereof."[33] The "power of godliness" is manifest in the ordinances and authority of the priesthood, for "without the ordinances thereof, and the authority of the priesthood, the power of godliness is not manifest unto men in the flesh" (Doctrine and Covenants 84:20–21). Putting these two ideas together, this message to young Joseph could be translated thus: *Joseph, the churches of your day teach some truth and do many good things, but they deny the essential need to receive the gospel by covenant baptism and lack the authority to perform the ordinances of exaltation.*

> Doctrinal messages of the First Vision center on (1) restoring the true nature of God and his plan and (2) the authority and covenants of exaltation.

These central messages of the First Vision—the true nature of God and his plan for his children and the restoration of the authority, ordinances, and covenants of exaltation—would become the focus of the prophetic mission of Joseph Smith over the next twenty-plus years. Indeed, it could be argued that the Restoration and its unique truth claims could mostly be summarized in those two points: restoring the true nature of God and his plan for his children and restoring the authority and covenants of exaltation. Both these foundational messages of the Restoration find their root in the messages of the First Vision of Joseph Smith.

AN ANALYSIS

1 Why are there differing accounts of the First Vision? Cohesively, all nine accounts tell a consistent general story of a young teenage boy, confused about religion, who goes to the woods to pray and has a vision of the divine. Details differ, however, depending on the account. One account mentions that Joseph simply saw "the Lord," while others are explicit about "two personages." One account mentions angels, others don't. One says Joseph was age fifteen (or "in the 16th year of his age"); others, fourteen years old. Some accounts mention details of the adversarial attack, others omit it. How does the audience change how an experience is related? How does the purpose of telling the story alter it? How does memory affect it or our interpretation of it? As Steven Harper has written, "The [First Vision] accounts reveal that he [Joseph Smith] consciously interpreted the experience and discovered meanings in it later that were not available to him when it occurred."[34] Think of personal experiences you have told to different groups over time and how you may have altered it in its retellings and why. If details differ, does that negate the experience? How might we compare First Vision accounts with the accounts of Jesus's resurrection in the Gospels? How do we reconcile differences in the retellings of foundational stories of faith?

2 How does the idea of "many angels," or the vision being more expansive in breadth of seeing into heaven, change your view of the First Vision? Was it the First *Vision*, or the First *Visitation*? Did God come to see Joseph, or was Joseph taken to see God? Joseph said, "My mind was taken away from the objects with which I was surrounded, and I was enwrapped in a heavenly vision"[35] and that afterward "when I came to myself again I found myself lying on <my> back looking up into Heaven."[36] If we had stumbled upon Joseph in the grove having the vision, what would we have seen? Does it change how we think of the event if we called it the First Visitation as compared to the First Vision?

3 Why are ordinances and authority central to Latter-day Saint theology? How does the need for authorized covenants make us a people of "the Church" who have a need for organized religion? Although today one may find God in the wilderness, as did the young Joseph Smith, how does a fundamental message of the First Vision, ironically, teach that personal encounters with the divine are insufficient for exaltation?

NOTES

1. T. B. H. Stenhouse, *The Rocky Mountain Saints: A Full and Complete History of the Mormons, from the First Vision of Joseph Smith to the Last Courtship of Brigham Young* (New York: D. Appleton, 1873), xxvi.
2. Richard Oman, "'Ye Shall See the Heavens Open': Portrayal of the Divine and Angelic in Latter-day Saint Art," *BYU Studies* 35, no. 4 (1995–96): 117–18.
3. For links to documents of all nine of the contemporary First Vision accounts, see "Primary Accounts of Joseph Smith's First Vision of Deity," The Joseph Smith Papers.
4. "Journal, 1835–1836, 24," The Joseph Smith Papers.
5. "Interview, 21 August 1843, extract," 3, The Joseph Smith Papers.
6. "Alexander Neibaur, Journal, 24 May 1844, extract," 23, The Joseph Smith Papers; emphasis added.
7. "History, circa Summer 1832," 3, The Joseph Smith Papers.
8. "He expected to have seen the leaves and boughs of the trees consumed." See "Appendix: Orson Pratt, *A[n] Interesting Account of Several Remarkable Visions*, 1840," 5, The Joseph Smith Papers.
9. "Journal, 1835–1836," 24, The Joseph Smith Papers.
10. "Journal, 1835–1836," 23.
11. "Appendix: Orson Pratt, *A[n] Interesting Account of Several Remarkable Visions*, 1840," 5.
12. "Orson Hyde, *Ein Ruf aus der Wüste (A Cry out of the Wilderness)*, 1842, extract, English translation," The Joseph Smith Papers.
13. "History, circa June 1839–circa 1841 [Draft 2]," 3, The Joseph Smith Papers.
14. Some have attempted to put the date at the end of March. See John C. Lefgren and John P. Pratt, "Oh, How Lovely Was the Morning: Sun 26 Mar 1820?," *Meridian Magazine*, 9 October 2002.
15. "'Church History,' 1 March 1842," 707, The Joseph Smith Papers.
16. "Alexander Neibaur, Journal, 24 May 1844, extract," 23.
17. "An indication (such as a circle) of radiant light or glory about the head of a drawn or sculptured divinity, saint, or sovereign." *Merriam-Webster*, s.v. "nimbus," accessed online.
18. "Journal, 1835–1836," 24.
19. "Appendix: Orson Pratt, *A[n] Interesting Account of Several Remarkable Visions*, 1840," 5.
20. However, in multiple academic settings, I have presented on the symbol of Joseph Smith being clothed in a recognizable costume of a white shirt and brown pants—a symbol used in nearly all paintings of him.
21. "Interview, 21 August 1843, extract," 3, The Joseph Smith Papers.
22. See James B. Allen, "Emergence of a Fundamental: The Expanding Role of Joseph Smith's First Vision of Mormon Religious Thought," in *Exploring the First Vision*, ed. Samuel Alonzo Dodge and Steven C. Harper (Provo, UT: Religious Studies Center, Brigham Young University, 2012), 227–60; see also Steven C. Harper, *First Vision: Memory and Mormon Origins* (New York: Oxford University Press, 2019).
23. *Teachings of Gordon B. Hinckley* (Salt Lake City: Deseret Book, 1997), 47.
24. "'Church History,' 1 March 1842," 706.
25. "History, circa June 1839–circa 1841 [Draft 2]," 3.
26. "Appendix: Orson Pratt, *A[n] Interesting Account of Several Remarkable Visions*, 1840," 5.
27. *Merriam-Webster*, s.v. "creed," accessed online.
28. "A *correct* idea of his character, perfections and attributes," emphasis in original. "Doctrine and Covenants, 1844," 41, The Joseph Smith Papers.
29. Gordon B. Hinckley, "What Are People Asking about Us?," *Ensign*, November 1998, 70–71.
30. "Levi Richards, Journal, 11 June 1843, extract," 16, The Joseph Smith Papers.
31. "History, circa Summer 1832," 3, The Joseph Smith Papers.
32. "Is Baptism Essential for Salvation?" *Got Questions* (website).
33. "History, circa June 1839–circa 1841 [Draft 2]," 3.
34. Steven C. Harper, "Remembering the First Vision," in *A Reason for Faith: Navigating LDS Doctrine and Church History* ed. Laura H. Hales (Provo, UT: Religious Studies Center, Brigham Young University; Salt Lake City: Deseret Book, 2016), 16.
35. "'Church History,' 1 March 1842," 706–7.
36. "History, circa June 1839–circa 1841 [Draft 2]," 3.

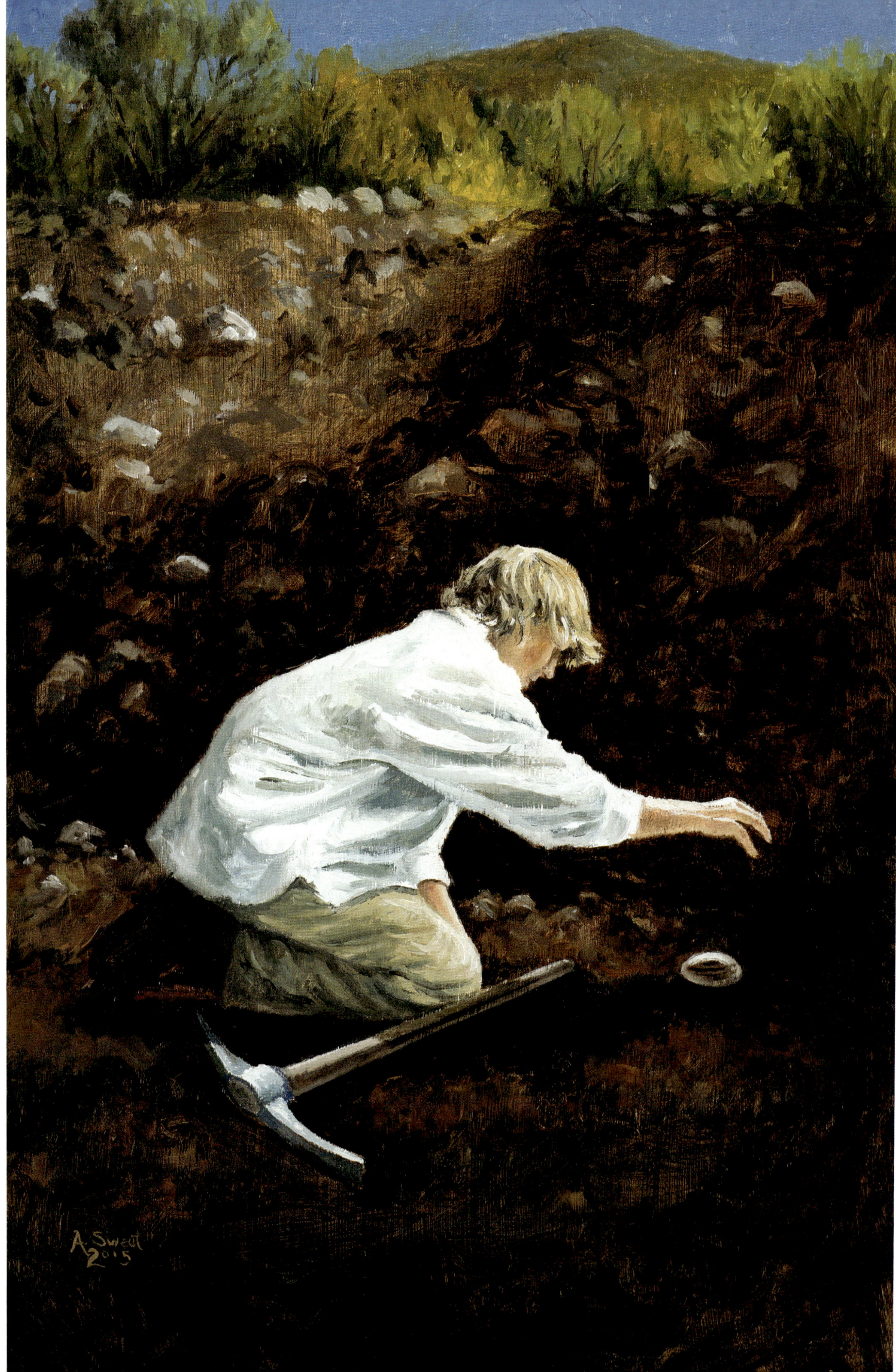

Gazelem, a Stone (11" x 17", oil on board, 2015)

GAZELEM, A STONE

Timeline: 1821–29
Related Verses: Joseph Smith—History 1:28–30, 42, 46, 53–54

A BACKGROUND

Mark Twain wrote in his 1876 novel *Tom Sawyer*, "There comes a time in every rightly-constructed boy's life when he has a raging desire to go somewhere and dig for hidden treasure."[1] Because Joseph Smith was a teenage farm boy who grew up in "indigent circumstances,"[2] digging the earth and struggling with poverty were part of his day-to-day reality. Like many of us today, there were those in Joseph's rural culture of western New York who believed God could intervene and help in their temporal plights. Rural citizens imagined the same earth they were plowing to produce wheat or corn might also yield ancient hidden valuables like gold or silver to relieve their poverty, if only they could locate them.

To help, some turned to religious folk practices, such as using divining rods and peep stones to try to locate lost and buried treasures.[3] Rural America was a spiritually awakened, protestant Christian land where biblical stories made familiar the use of tangible devices to mediate the divine, such as Jacob using "rods of green poplar, and of the hazel and chestnut tree" to increase his assets (see Genesis 30:37), Aaron using a rod to work wonders (see Numbers 17–18), or Joseph of Egypt using a silver divining cup (Genesis 44:5, 15). In 1825 the *Wayne Sentinel* in Palmyra reported that buried treasure had been found "by the help of a mineral stone . . . which becomes transparent when placed in a hat and the light excluded by the face of him who looks into it."[4] Scholars Michael MacKay and Nicholas Frederick wrote, "Joseph Smith likewise believed that the New York landscape was marked by an ancient world and with an abundance of ancient artifacts that could be accessed in the soil."[5] Historian Steven Harper said, "There is evidence that both Joseph and his father joined in some of the activities of a group of neighborhood treasure seekers who looked for buried riches in nocturnal rituals."[6]

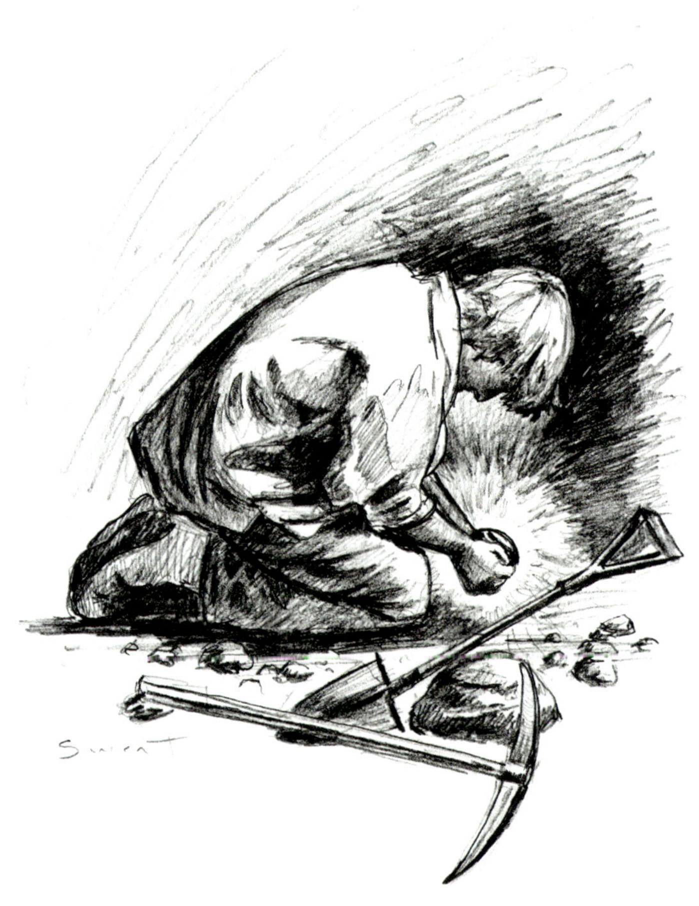

Although the historical record is somewhat unclear, it seems that sometime after the First Vision Joseph Smith found his own seer stone while digging a well on the Willard Chase property.[7] In an 1833 recollection published in *Mormonism Unvailed*, Willard Chase said that he was with Joseph Smith when they dug this well on Willard's family property and that after they had dug twenty feet deep, Willard found a curious stone. He showed it to Joseph, who, upon examining the stone, "placed it into his hat, and then his face into the top of his hat . . .

[and] began to publish abroad what wonders he could discover by looking into it."[8] More than one hundred years later, historian B. H. Roberts wrote in the Church's comprehensive history that this "Seer Stone" was a "chocolate-colored, somewhat egg-shaped stone which the Prophet found while digging a well in company with his brother Hyrum. . . . It possessed the qualities of Urim and Thummim, since by means of it—as described above—as well by means of the Interpreters found with the Nephite record, Joseph was able to translate the characters engraven on the plates."[9]

Some believe that Joseph Smith was led by God to find this brown seer stone. Jens Weibye, a late, thirdhand source, reports Eliza R. Snow to have stated: "The Prophet Joseph Smith had a Peepstone (called in the Book of Doc. & Covenants Gaslum) that he got by digging in a Ladies Garden 25 feet down in the Ground. The Lord Reviled to Joseph that such a stone was 25 feet down in the Ground but he (J. Smith) did not know how to get it; but he went to the Lady there owned the Garden and asked her if she did not wish to have a Well dug in her Garden, she said yes. . . . The Prophet found the Peepstone 25 feet down."[10]

The name "Gaslum" seems to come from Alma 37:23, where Alma tells Helaman about how the Lord will bring hidden things to light, promising, "I will prepare unto my servant Gazelem, a stone, which shall shine forth in darkness unto light." In early editions of the Doctrine and Covenants, the name "Gazelam" was sometimes used as a code name for Joseph Smith.[11]

As part of the Joseph Smith Papers Project, The Church of Jesus Christ of Latter-day Saints published photographs of Joseph Smith's brown seer stone in 2015.[12] Since that time, there has been increased interest in this aspect of Latter-day Saint history, yet no images had been painted showing young Joseph finding this stone. This painting, called *Gazelem, a Stone* (2015), was perhaps the first to do so.

AN IMAGE

I chose to show Joseph on his knees, reaching down to pick up the stone. I could have depicted him standing or stooping down, but being on his knees has the potential to connect his pose to prayer. He reaches forward, ready to pick up the stone but hasn't quite grasped it yet, much like his hold on his own gift as a seer.

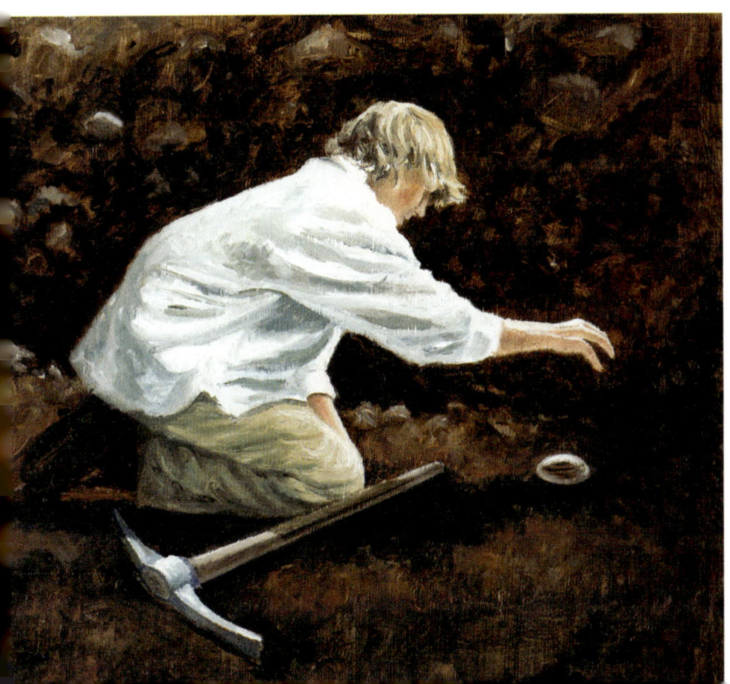

Compositionally, the stone sits in one of the darker parts of the painting, almost shining, calling out from "darkness unto light." I don't know any more than you do what differentiates a seer stone from any other rock, but the stone in my painting sits in higher light and more detail than the other stones that are roughly suggested as Joseph digs in the well.

The painting's composition is purposefully narrow, making it feel more like Joseph is placed down in a well. His pickax rests at his feet,

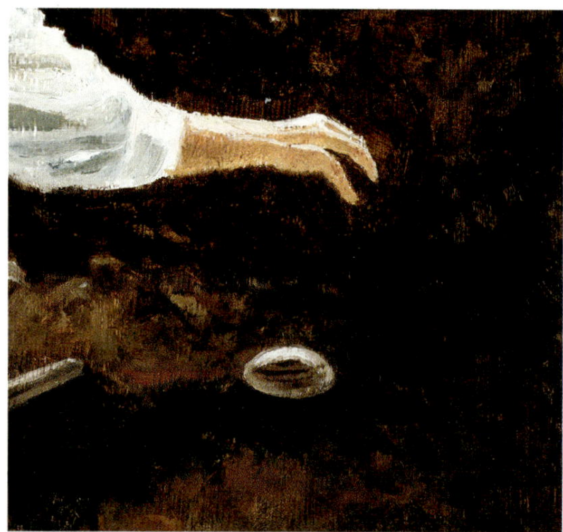

providing a visual narrative to the viewer that Joseph was digging when he found the stone. In the scene, I chose not to include others with Joseph to keep the story focused on young Joseph and avoid distracting the viewer, although Alvin Smith and Willard Chase were both likely there as well. The Chase farm is a little more than one mile from the Hill Cumorah, which is not viewable from their property, but I chose to place a large hill in the background as a reference to the hill where the Book of Mormon plates lay and where Joseph's gift as a seer would soon lead.

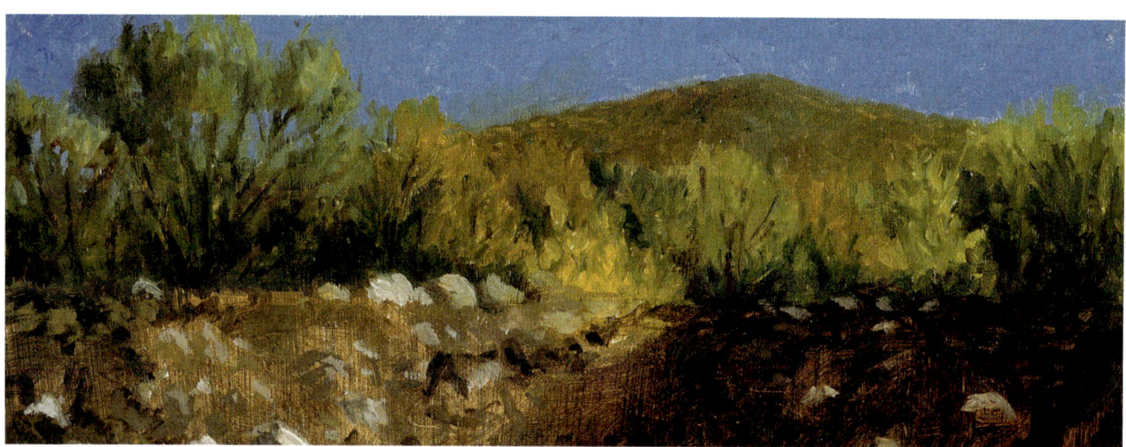

AN APPLICATION

It is not uncommon to hear that Joseph Smith was required to wait for four years before he could obtain the Book of Mormon plates as though it were some predetermined amount of time (see Joseph Smith—History 1:53). While that may be the case, it may also be that the plates could have been obtained earlier by Joseph Smith had he been prepared to receive them. As Steven Harper writes, "evidence indicates" that young Joseph Smith "was troubled by a nagging covetousness, complicated by his family's often being on the verge of, but never finally attaining, a comfortable living."[13] Richard Bushman says, "It may have taken four years for Joseph to purge himself of his treasure-seeking greed."[14] While his treasure hunting may have led him to acquiring his own seer stone and developing his gifts as a young seer, it is also possible that those very activities are what negatively tainted him from being immediately worthy to do the work of the Lord. The yearly meeting with Moroni on the hill where the Book of Mormon plates were located was a dual worthiness interview and divine schooling to help rectify the tainted but teachable young Joseph.

Joseph's mother remembers Moroni telling her young son, "You cannot get [the plates] untill you learn to keep the commandments of God <for it is not to get gain.>"[15] In Joseph's earliest 1832 journal history, he records that after arriving at the hill, he attempted to take the plates but was unable, so he "cried unto the Lord in the agony of my soul why can I not obtain them." Moroni appeared and told Joseph:

> You have not kept the commandments of the Lord which I gave unto you therefore you cannot now obtain them for the time is not yet fulfilled therefore thou wast left unto temptation that thou mightest be made acquainted ~~of~~ with the power of the advisary therefore repent and call on the Lord thou shalt be forgiven and in his own due time thou shalt obtain them for now I had been tempted of the advisary and saught the Plates to obtain riches and kept not the comandme[n]t that I should have an eye single to the Glory of God therefore I was chastened and saught diligently to obtain the plates and obtained them not untill I was twenty one years of age.[16]

Joseph's two stumbling blocks were apparently his desire for riches and self-glorification. Or, more simply put, *money* and *fame*—lusts that much of humanity can relate to and spiritually struggle with—past, present, and future. On learning of Joseph's obtainment and use of a seer stone, some modern-day people struggle with the *method* of Joseph's searching for riches but not the *motives*. They get hung up on the external—looking *into* stones—and fail to focus on the internal—looking *at* the heart. I am unaware of the Lord ever rebuking Joseph Smith for using seer stones. Indeed, some sources say that Joseph used this same brown stone he found at the Chase farm to translate portions of the Book of Mormon. I am aware, however, of the Lord rebuking what was in Joseph's heart. The object wasn't what mattered, but the objective did.

How many of us have let the cares of this world and the deceitfulness of riches choke out the word to make us spiritually unfruitful (see Matthew 13:22), obstruct our sense of divine mission and purpose, and taint our motives until we act inconsistently with what God desires? Money is not the problem, but the love of money

The object wasn't what mattered, but the objective did.

(see 1 Timothy 6:10) and listening to the shouts of the world over the whispering of the Spirit can be (see 1 Nephi 8:27–28). Like the stone itself, the external isn't the issue, it is what's happening internally that matters most.

Providentially, we can all repent if we have become sullied by the siren call of worldly "success" at the cost of spiritually seeking the kingdom of God. We, too, have a probationary period. We, too, like young Joseph, can learn how to "seek . . . first the kingdom of God and his righteousness" (Matthew 6:33) above all else. Whether or not we ever become wealthy and famous is irrelevant, but little may matter more than removing prideful desires for wealth and personal glory in order to fulfill our life's spiritual purpose and mission.

AN ANALYSIS

1 It is possible that Joseph Smith could have never obtained the Book of Mormon had he not purified his heart and motives. Joseph Knight Sr. remembers that during this 1826 meeting with Moroni, Joseph Smith learned that "if he would Do right according to the will of God he mite obtain [the plates] the 22nt Day of September Next and if not he never would have them."[17] What if Joseph hadn't qualified on the fourth year? Think how different *that* Restoration narrative would be! Nothing guaranteed Joseph's prophetic success or forbade him from failing (see Doctrine and Covenants 3:4). He had his agency. What does it say that at twenty-one years of age, Joseph Smith showed he was ready to obtain the plates?

2 While some in modern-day contexts understandably wonder about Joseph Smith's acquisition and use of a seer stone to seek for lost items and treasures in the earth, scholar Kerry Muhlestein has insightfully written, "Is there a real difference between Nephi being told where to hunt through a brass ball and God helping those who believe find lost cows through a rod, or lost pins through a seerstone? Will God direct those who honestly turn to him in whatever manner they expect, or must he always give revelation through a fleece laid on the ground (Judges 6:36–40)? . . . Should we expect God to refuse interaction with such a youth because he was seeking God in ways not familiar to us?"[18] Those are great questions. What do you think?

3 Historian Richard Bushman likened Joseph's early use of seer stones to a "preparatory gospel" for Joseph's later use of stones to receive revelation and translate the Book of Mormon.[19] Why would God use Joseph's cultural practice of seer stones to prepare him for his later work as a revelator, particularly if those methods negatively affected his motives? How does God use your modern cultural values and practices to aid you in your divine mission and work and to possibly purify your heart? If you were born in a different time and culture, would God use something else to work with in order to guide you to fulfill your mission? What about Joseph?

NOTES

1. Mark Twain, *The Adventures of Tom Sawyer* (Hartford, CT: American Publishing, 1876), chap. 25, Lit2Go (website).
2. "History, circa Summer 1832," 1, The Joseph Smith Papers.
3. See *Saints*, vol. 1: *The Standard of Truth, 1815–1846* (Salt Lake City: The Church of Jesus Christ of Latter-day Saints, 2018), 21.
4. "Wonderful Discovery," *Wayne Sentinel* (Palmyra, NY), 27 December 1825, 2, NYS Historic Newspapers.
5. Michael Hubbard MacKay and Nicholas J. Frederick, *Joseph Smith's Seer Stones* (Provo, UT: Religious Studies Center, Brigham Young University; Salt Lake City: Deseret Book, 2016), 6.
6. Steven C. Harper, "The Probation of a Teenage Seer: Joseph Smith's Early Experiences with Moroni," in *The Coming Forth of the Book of Mormon: A Marvelous Work and a Wonder*, ed. Dennis L. Largey, Andrew H. Hedges, John Hilton III, and Kerry Hull (Provo, UT: Religious Studies Center, Brigham Young University; Salt Lake City: Deseret Book, 2015), 24.
7. See *Saints*, 21.
8. E. D. Howe, *Mormonism Unvailed* (Paineville, OH: self-pub., 1834), 241.

9. B. H. Roberts, *Comprehensive History of The Church of Jesus Christ of Latter-day Saints* (Salt Lake City: The Church of Jesus Christ of Latter-day Saints, 1930), 1:129.
10. Jens Christian Anderson Weibye, Daybooks, no. 6, 22 September 1881, 143–44, as quoted in MacKay and Frederick, *Joseph Smith's Seer Stones*, 39.
11. See "Doctrine and Covenants, 1835," 243, The Joseph Smith Papers.
12. "Glossary," s.v. "Seer stone," The Joseph Smith Papers.
13. Harper, "The Probation of a Teenage Seer," 24.
14. Richard Lyman Bushman, *Joseph Smith: Rough Stone Rolling* (New York City: Alfred A. Knopf, 2005), 51.
15. "Lucy Mack Smith, History, 1844–1845," 11, bk. 3, The Joseph Smith Papers.
16. "History, circa Summer 1832," 4–5.
17. Dean C. Jessee, "Joseph Knight's Recollection of Early Mormon History," *BYU Studies* 17, no.1 (1976): 32.
18. Kerry M. Muhlestein, "Seeking Divine Interaction: Joseph Smith's Varying Searches for the Supernatural," in *No Weapon Shall Prosper: New Light on Sensitive Issues*, ed. Robert L. Millet (Provo, UT: Religious Studies Center, Brigham Young University; Salt Lake City: Deseret Book, 2011), 90.
19. Bushman, *Joseph Smith: Rough Stone Rolling*, 54.

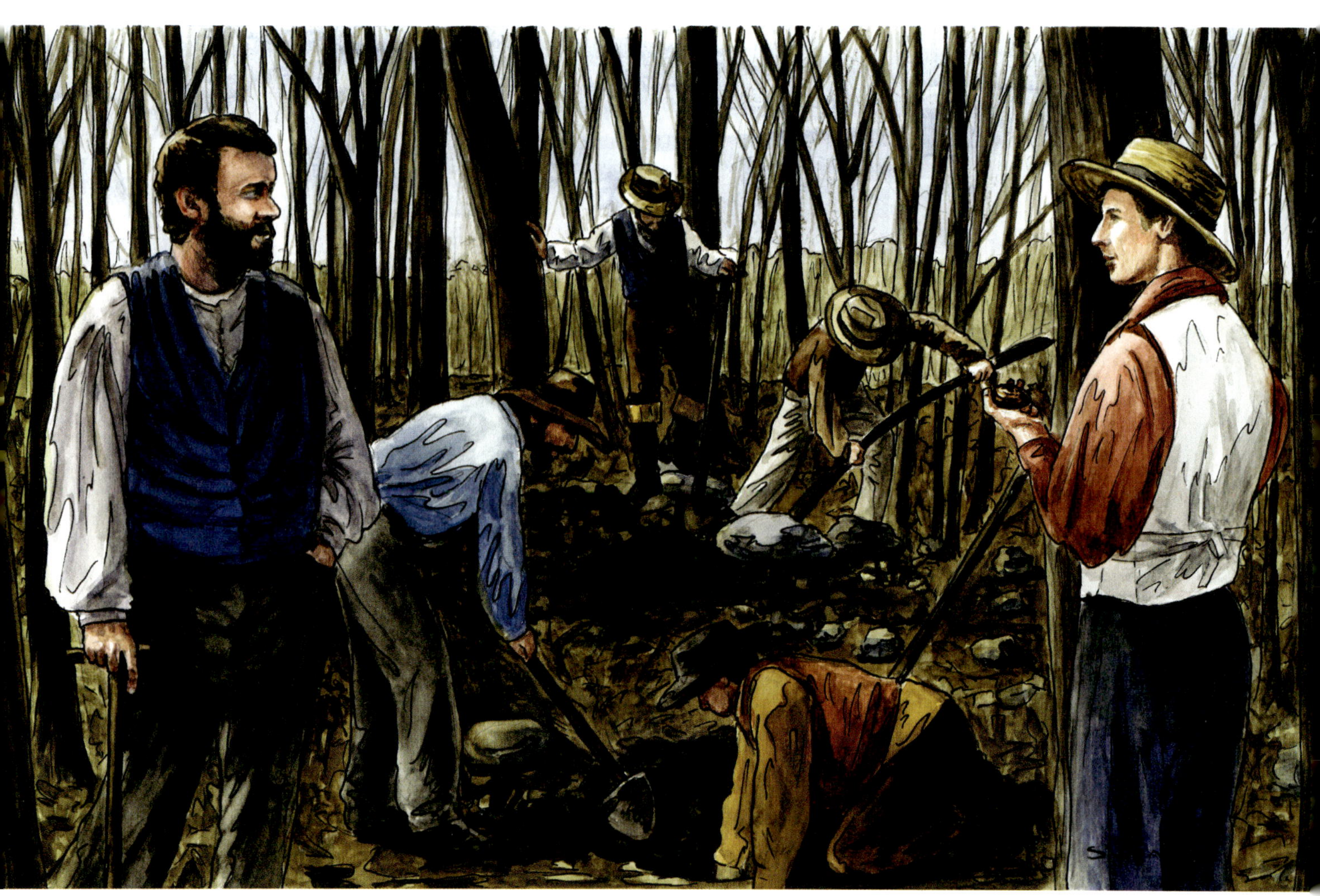

The Harmony Treasure Searcher (9" x 15", watercolor on illustration board, 2019)

THE HARMONY TREASURE SEARCHER

Timeline: November 1825–December 1827

Related Verses: Joseph Smith—History 1:55–58

A BACKGROUND

Stories of Joseph Smith's abilities as a local seer traveled past the confines of Palmyra and Manchester, New York. A few years after Joseph discovered his seer stone, Lucy Mack Smith remembered:

> A short time before the house was completed, a man by the name of Josiah Stoal came from Chenango County, New York, to get Joseph to assist him in digging for a silver mine. He came for Joseph from having heard, that he was in possession of certain means, by which he could discern things, ~~which~~ that could not be seen by the natural eye. Joseph endeavered to divert him from his vain project; but he was inflexible, and offered high wages to such as would dig for him; ~~in search of the mine~~; and was ~~*[2 words illegible]*~~ still very anxious ~~*[4 words illegible]*~~ to have Joseph work for him; consequently, he returned with the old gentleman; besides several others ~~that~~ who were picked up in the neighborhood, and commenced digging.[1]

The year was 1825, and the Smiths were desperately in need of money. The family had made the financial error of not paying their family mortgage when the rent collector failed to show months earlier, but now payment was due and foreclosure inevitable, lest money was secured.[2] Although by this time Joseph was reticent to use his gift for treasure searching,[3] the potential financial relief for the family proved too providential to pass up. Josiah Stowell, then fifty-five years old, hired both Joseph Sr. and Joseph Jr.—not quite twenty years old at the time—for the job. Their alleged[4] "Articles of Agreement" read:

We, the undersigned, do firmly agree, & by these presents bind ourselves, to fulfill and abide by the hereafter specified articles:

> First—That if anything of value should be obtained at a certain place in Pennsylvania near a Wm. Hale's, supposed to be a valuable mine of either Gold or Silver and also to contain coined money and bars or ingots of Gold or Silver, and at which several hands have been at work during a considerable part of the past summer, we do agree to have it divided in the following manner, viz.: Josiah Stowell, Calvin Stowell and Wm. Hale to take two-thirds, and Charles Newton, Wm. I. Wiley, and the Widow Harper to take the other third. And we further agree that Joseph Smith, Sen. and Joseph Smith Jr. shall be considered as having two shares, two elevenths of all the property that may be obtained, the shares to be taken equally from each third. . . .
>
> Township of Harmony, Pa., Nov. 1, 1825.[5]

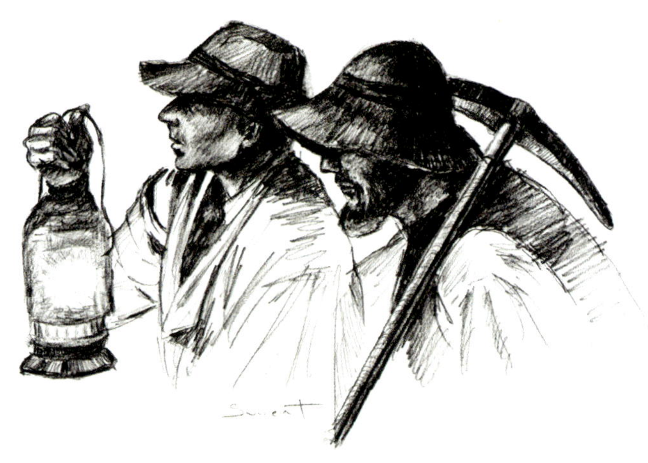

Joseph recalled in his later history that he traveled the 150 miles from Manchester to Harmony and that Josiah Stowell "took me among the rest of his hands to dig for the silver mine, at which I continued to work for nearly a month without success in our undertaking, and finally I prevailed with the old gentleman to cease digging after it. Hence arose the very prevalent story of my ~~have~~ <having> been a money digger."[6] At another time, in a self-imposed question-and-answer article in the Church's newspaper, the Prophet frankly admitted his money-digging adventures and the pay he received from Josiah Stowell, with a touch of indignant humor that the lowly job had taken on his public reputation:

> Question 10. Was not Jo Smith a money digger.
>
> Answer. Yes, but it was never a very profitable job to him, as he only got fourteen dollars a month for it.[7]

The search for treasure in Harmony was not without its finds. Joseph recalled, "During the time that I was thus employed I was put to board with a Mr Isaac Hale of that place, 'Twas there that I first saw my wife, (his daughter) Emma Hale."[8] At first Isaac Hale supported the Harmony treasure search, both by allowing the diggers to stay on a cabin on his property and also by acting as a witness to their articles of agreement. Before long, he grew suspicious not only of Joseph's role in the operation but also of Joseph's increased interest in his daughter and Emma's reciprocal feelings.[9] Joseph and Emma fell in love, and Joseph returned to Harmony the next year in late 1826 to continue courting Emma and to work for Josiah Stowell and another local, Joseph Knight Sr.[10] He would bring with him his fellow treasure-searching friend from Palmyra, Samuel Lawrence, both to continue looking for lost treasure and also to put in a good word for Joseph to Isaac Hale.[11]

Isaac Hale, understandably, was not supportive of Joseph's desire to marry his daughter. Joseph was, after all, an itinerant, poor, uneducated laborer from a faraway town who looked in seer stones for lost treasures. Isaac and his family were wealthy and respected, and his daughter, Emma (or "Emmy," as some called her), refined and educated.[12] Joseph recalled, with a hint of sadness, the familial opposition to their relationship: "So much was my wife's father excited, that he was greatly opposed to our being married, in so much that he would not suffer us to be married at his house, I was therefore under the necessity of taking her elsewhere."[13] Joseph and Emma would elope on 18 January 1827 and be married not far from the Stowell farm by a local squire.[14]

Joseph and Emma would go and live with Joseph's parents in Manchester for nearly a year but eventually return to Harmony in December 1827, bringing the golden plates Joseph had retrieved a few months earlier in September. The Hales offered Joseph and Emma a home and thirteen-acre lot across the street, which Joseph purchased a few years later for two hundred dollars.[15] Harmony did not yield earthly treasures, but it brought forth heavenly ones. Not only did Joseph meet and marry Emma, but in Harmony Joseph Smith would translate the majority of the Book of Mormon, receive the priesthood from John the Baptist and Peter, James, and John, be ministered to by Adam (see Doctrine and Covenants 128:20), and receive fifteen sections of the Doctrine and Covenants. The 1825 treasure-hunting expedition would forever alter the life of Joseph Smith and also the history of the Church he founded.

AN IMAGE

In this image, Josiah Stowell stands on the left of the viewer, and young nineteen-year-old Joseph Smith Jr. across the plane on the right. They are engaged in a conversation, and the composition invites the viewer to bounce back and forth between the two. In his left hand, Joseph Smith

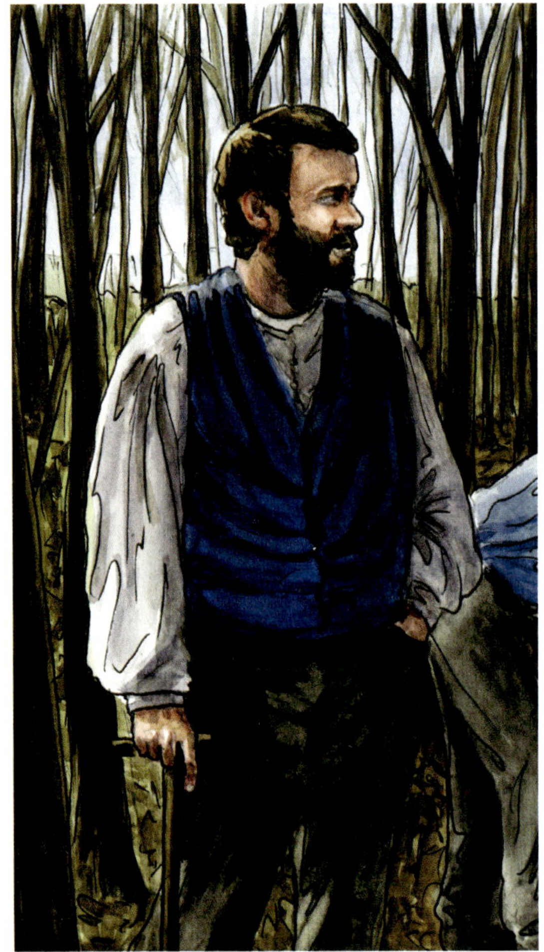

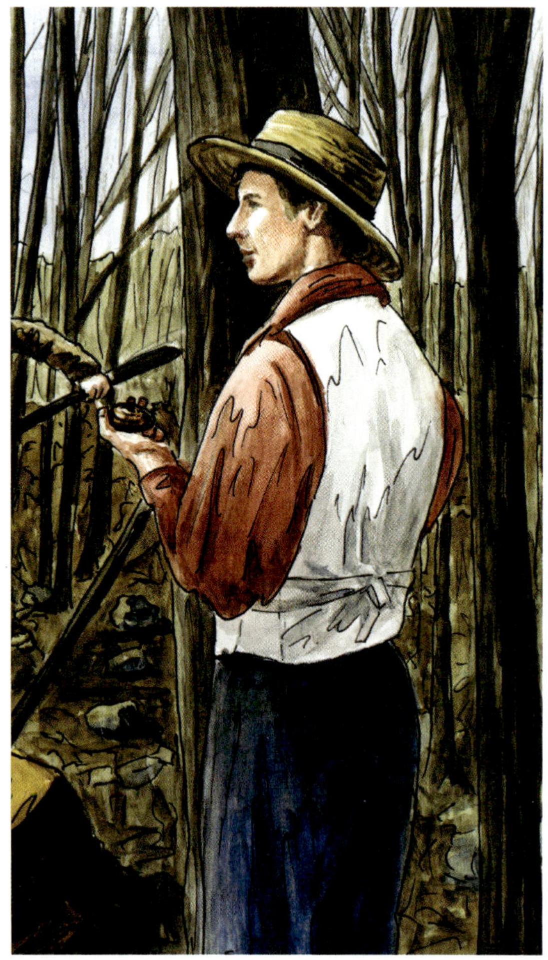

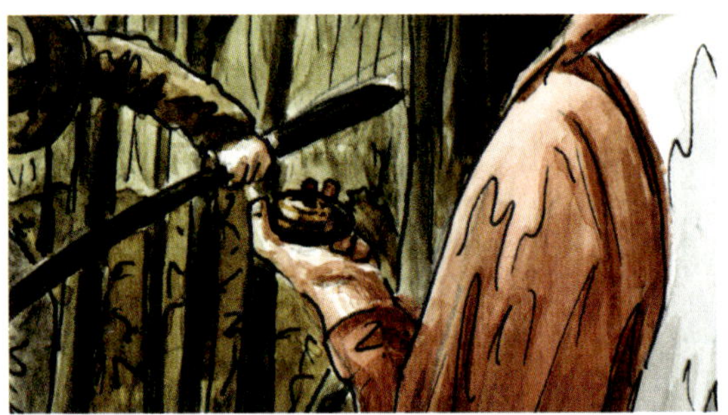

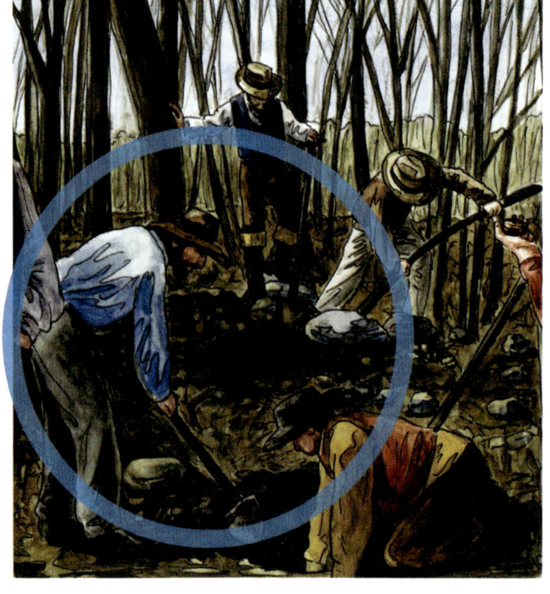

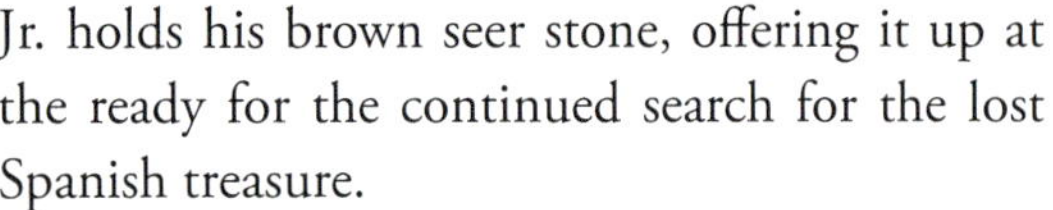

Jr. holds his brown seer stone, offering it up at the ready for the continued search for the lost Spanish treasure.

Four other men, representing those who also signed on to search for the treasure, dig and work in the background. They are positioned in the middle between the conversing Joseph Jr.

and Josiah Stowell. The working men are almost in a circle, suggesting a round-the-clock effort in digging. The woods are November bare and brown, as the days and weeks to find their hopeful treasures are few before the soil freezes over for a long winter.

AN APPLICATION

The first known instance of Joseph Smith being arrested stemmed from his 1825–26 treasure-hunting expedition on the Josiah Stowell property. Joseph was charged in March 1826 by Josiah Stowell's nephew for being a "disorderly person and an imposter" due to his claims as a seer.[16] Other than a few trial bills from the justice of the peace, no known contemporary documents exist detailing the events of the trial. Fifty years after the trial, in 1877, a man named William Purple wrote a reminiscence of the case in the *Chenango Union* paper.[17] While the secondhand and late reminiscent nature of the source cause responsible scholars to exercise some caution concerning its reliability, some of Purple's memories converge and agree with other sources on the arrest, and thus his comments can be potentially instructive.

Purple recalls that when Joseph Smith took the stand, Joseph showed the court his seer stone, and Purple described that when Joseph looked in his seer stone, "all intervening obstacles were removed, and that he possessed one of the attributes of Deity, an All-Seeing-Eye."[18] Josiah Stowell apparently was questioned in Joseph Smith's 1826 trial about whether he believed Joseph Smith could see hidden things with his stones. Stowell is said to have responded, "Do I believe it? no, it is not a matter of belief: I positively know it to be true."[19] Apparently, Joseph Smith Sr. also took the stand and testified that "he and his son were mortified that this wonderful power which God had so miraculously given him should be used only in search of filthy lucre, or its equivalent in earthly treasures." Purple remembers that Father Smith said that "his constant prayer to his Heavenly Father was to manifest His will concerning this marvelous power. He trusted that the Son of Righteousness would some day illumin[ate] the heart of the boy, and enable him to see His will concerning him."[20]

The idea that Father Smith desired God to show Joseph Jr. how to use his gift as a seer for something more than searching for treasure is poignant. It causes me to reflect on how many of us have been given gifts of time, talent, and means that are only used for base purposes rather than higher ones. Almost any gift from God can be turned into sin if selfish motives take over. The tongue that speaks words to bless and comfort can also blaspheme and curse. The hands that serve can become hands that steal. Procreative powers used to perpetuate families and express love in marriage can turn to sexual sin in the form of rape, adultery, and fornication. Every gift can be misused if we aren't watchful. Those that are musical can play to the wrong crowd. The business person can serve mammon but not God. The performer can please Babylon by

Almost any gift from God can be turned into sin if selfish motives take over.

mocking Zion. The scholar can bow to the academy but not the Almighty. The artist can paint incredible canvases of the wrong subjects. The wonders of the internet and social media that educate and connect can become traps that cause us to waste away our precious probationary period in a thoughtless stupor of swipes and clicks. Food used to properly feed our bodies can become undisciplined glutton that ruins our health.

We all are asked to work for Josiah Stowell in Harmony in 1825–26, aren't we? Like Joseph, only a constant prayer to Heavenly Father to manifest his will concerning our marvelous powers, abilities, and opportunities and trust that the Son of Righteousness will illuminate our hearts to enable us to see his will concerning the rightful use of these things.

AN ANALYSIS

1 In a later section of the Doctrine and Covenants when Joseph, Hyrum, Oliver Cowdery, and Sidney Rigdon traveled to Massachusetts to try to find some hidden treasure to relieve the Church's debts, the Lord called their efforts "follies." However, he said, "I . . . am not displeased with your coming [on] this journey" (Doctrine and Covenants 111:1) and promises them "much treasure" in terms of converts to bring to Zion in the city (Doctrine and Covenants 111:2). The Lord doesn't seem to condemn our ignorant efforts or our ineptitude laced with good intentions. He may, at times, even "wink" at them (see Acts 17:30). How have you seen that in your life?

2 Try and place yourself in Isaac and Elizabeth Hales' situation. What do you make of their reaction to Joseph Smith and his desire to court and marry their daughter, Emma? Although understandable, how do we not let someone else's hometown, upbringing, education, or financial status bias our beliefs and block our view of their positive character and potential?

3 Harmony would become the place for the restoration of the priesthood and the translation of the Book of Mormon. God foreordained both of those things, but did he intend for it to be done there? Perhaps so, but also, maybe not. How does God use our personal choices to fulfill our intended destinies? Reflect or discuss with someone how the Lord balances personal agency with foreordained mission. How has he done it in your life?

NOTES

1. "Lucy Mack Smith, History, 1845," 95, The Joseph Smith Papers.
2. See Richard Lyman Bushman, *Joseph Smith: Rough Stone Rolling* (New York City: Alfred Knopf, 2005), 42, 47.
3. See "Appendix: Reminiscence of William D. Purple, 28 April 1877 [*People v. JS*]," 3, The Joseph Smith Papers.
4. There is some question surrounding the validity of these "Articles of Agreement." Historians for the *Joseph Smith Papers* write, "No manuscript of the [Articles of Agreement] contract exists, and it is known only through its publication in Utah's then avowedly anti-Mormon *Salt Lake Daily Tribune*, fifty-five years after it was purportedly written and

two thousand miles distant. . . . Nevertheless, substantial corroborating evidence supports the plausibility of such an agreement." See the Historical Introduction to "Appendix 1: Agreement of Josiah Stowell and Others, 1 November 1825," 4, The Joseph Smith Papers.

5. "Appendix 1: Agreement of Josiah Stowell and Others, 1 November 1825," 4.
6. "History, 1838–1856, volume A-1 [23 December 1805–30 August 1834]," 8, The Joseph Smith Papers.
7. "*Elders' Journal*, July 1838," 43, The Joseph Smith Papers. See also "History, 1838–1856, volume B-1 [1 September 1834–2 November 1838]," 795, The Joseph Smith Papers.
8. "History, 1838–1856, volume A-1 [23 December 1805–30 August 1834]," 8.
9. See *Saints*, vol. 1: *Volume 1, The Standard of Truth, 1815–1846* (Salt Lake City: The Church of Jesus Christ of Latter-day Saints, 2018), 32; see also Bushman, *Joseph Smith: Rough Stone Rolling*, 51–53.
10. Dean C. Jessee, "Joseph Knight's Recollection of Early Mormon History," *BYU Studies* 17, no. 1 (1976): 4.
11. See Rich Troll, "Samuel Tyler Lawrence: A Significant Figure in Joseph Smith's Palmyra Past," *Journal of Mormon History* 32, no. 2 (2006): 64.
12. See Mark Staker, "Isaac and Elizabeth Hale in Their Endless Mountain Home," *Mormon Historical Studies* 15, no. 2 (2015): 7–8, 103.
13. "History, circa June 1839–circa 1841 [Draft 2]," 8, The Joseph Smith Papers.
14. See "Emma's Susquehanna: Growing Up in the Isaac and Elizabeth Hale Home," Church History, The Church of Jesus Christ of Latter-day Saints, posted 1 March 2019.
15. See "Agreement with Isaac Hale, 6 April 1829," 1, The Joseph Smith Papers.
16. "On 20 March 1826, JS appeared before Albert Neely, a justice of the peace in Bainbridge, Chenango County, New York, on charges of violating the state's disorderly persons statute. JS was most likely arrested and tried as a disorderly person because he was employed using a seer stone in the area in late 1825." See the Historical Introduction to "Introduction to *People v. JS*," The Joseph Smith Papers.
17. See "Appendix: Reminiscence of William D. Purple, 28 April 1877 [*People v. JS*]," 3.
18. "Appendix: Reminiscence of William D. Purple, 28 April 1877 [*People v. JS*]," 3.
19. "Appendix: Reminiscence of William D. Purple, 28 April 1877 [*People v. JS*]," 3.
20. "Appendix: Reminiscence of William D. Purple, 28 April 1877 [*People v. JS*]," 3.

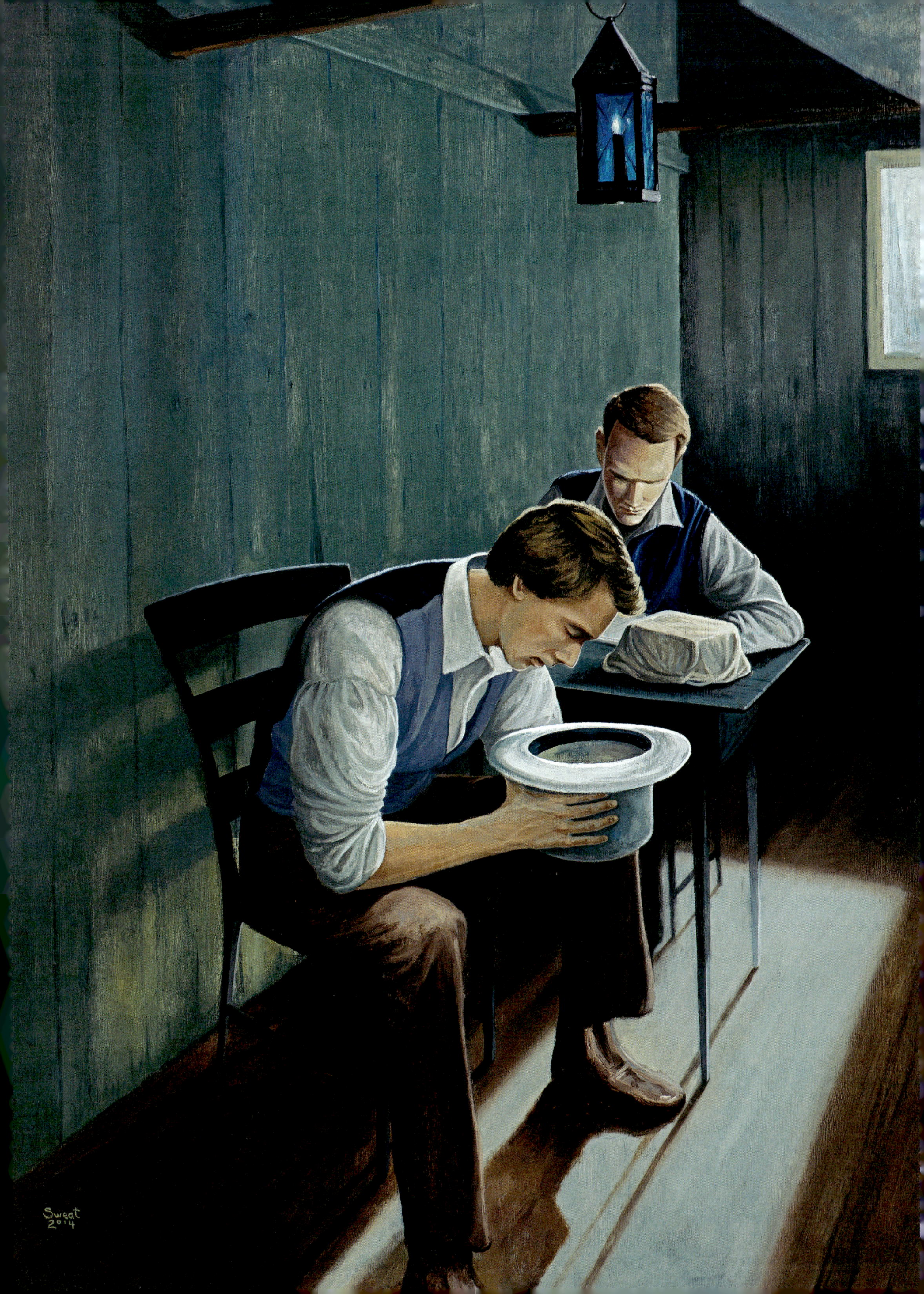
Sweat
2014

BY THE GIFT AND POWER OF GOD

Timeline: April 1828–June 1829

Related Doctrine and Covenants Sections: 3, 5, 10

A BACKGROUND

From the moment it burst on the public in March 1830, the production of the Book of Mormon mystified both critics and converts alike. How did an unlearned, twenty-four-year-old young man who had never written anything of substance in his life produce such a complicated, cohesive, and profound text? Particularly since, according to his wife, Emma, the newlywed Joseph Smith "could neither write nor dictate a coherent and well-worded letter; let alone dictating a book like the Book of Mormon."[1] Joseph Smith and his subsequent supporters believed the answer to this question is that the book is a divine translation of an ancient record given to Joseph by God. How did that happen?[2]

The Prophet Joseph Smith was relatively silent on the details of the Book of Mormon translation, once declining to tell "all the particulars of the coming forth of the book of Mormon" at an 1831 Church conference, saying it "was not expedient."[3] At other times, Joseph simply summarized the translation being done by the "gift and power of God,"[4] sometimes adding the line "by means of the Urim and Thummim" (Joseph Smith—History 1:64), or sacred stones that aided him in revelation. To understand the process of the Book of Mormon translation, we are left to rely on those who *saw* Joseph Smith translate, a type of primary source because they can relate what they personally observed of the translation process or what they heard him tell about it.[5] Let's take a look at some of them.

First, an early contemporary account (1829) of the translation by a skeptical source, Jonathan Hadley, a local printer who declined to print the Book of Mormon when he was approached with the offer by Joseph Smith. Hadley published the following in the *Palmyra Freeman* on 11 August 1829: "It was said that the leaves of the [gold] Bible were plates of gold, about eight inches long, six wide, and one eighth of an inch thick, on which were engraved characters or hieroglyphics. By placing the spectacles in a hat, and looking into it, Smith could (he said so, at least,)

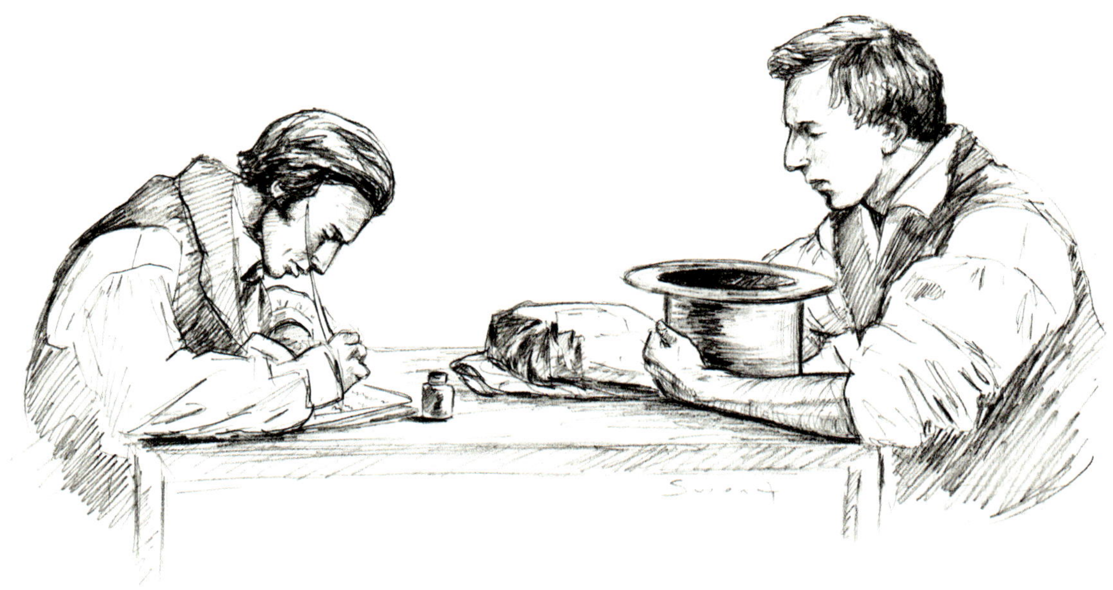

interpret these characters."[6] This is a secondhand account, as Hadley would have been told the details of the translation by someone else (assumedly Joseph Smith or Martin Harris, who had sought him out as a printer).[7] However, it is a strong contemporary account from 1829, the earliest on known record and before the Book of Mormon was published.

Here is another secondhand, contemporaneous account (1831), this time by a Shaker man who had heard Oliver Cowdery preach, saying that the Book of Mormon was translated by "two transparent stones in the form of spectacles" through which the translator "looked on the engraving & afterwards put his face into a hat & the interpretation then flowed into his mind."[8]

Some sources detailing the translation process are by individuals who believed in the Book of Mormon but did not remain with the body of the Church nor come westward to Utah. Near the end of her life, in an 1879 interview with her son Joseph III, Emma Smith recalled scribing for her husband while he translated, with Joseph "sitting with his face buried in his hat, with the stone in it, and dictating hour after hour with nothing between us. . . . The plates often lay on the table without any attempt at concealment, wrapped in a small linen table cloth."[9]

A late 1887 reminiscence by David Whitmer explained: "Joseph Smith would put the seer stone into a hat, and put his face in the hat, drawing it closely around his face. . . . A piece of something resembling parchment would appear, and on that appeared the writing. One character at a time would appear, and under it was the interpretation in English."[10]

There are also some translation sources by those who witnessed the translation and were part of the body of the Church when recounting the translation. Joseph Knight Sr. wrote: "Now the way he translated was he put the urim and thummim into his hat and Darkned his Eyes then he would take a sentance and it would apper in Brite Roman Letters. Then he would tell the writer and he would write it. Then that would go away the next sentance would Come and so on. But if it was not Spelt rite it would not go away till it was rite, so we see it was marvelous. Thus was the hol [whole] translated."[11]

In an 1881 interview with Edward Stevenson, Martin Harris said "that the Prophet possessed a seer stone, by which he was enabled to translate as well as from the Urim and Thummim, and for convenience he then used the seer stone." According to Stevenson, Martin explained the translating as follows: "By aid of the seer stone, sentences would appear and were read by the Prophet and written by Martin, and when finished he would say, 'Written.'"[12]

Herein I have given six sources that provide details about the Book of Mormon translation. All of them are tainted in various ways through a bias or as a secondhand nature or a late reminiscence. Independent of one another, however, what do they consistently and cohesively describe? Plates, seer stones whereupon words appeared, stones placed in a hat, and dictation to a scribe.

Although these are the general details of the Book of Mormon translation based on the known historical record, as of 2014 there were yet no paintings produced by Latter-day Saint artists or published in Church materials that depicted Joseph Smith translating the Book of Mormon using a seer stone or stones placed in a hat.[13] I decided to attempt to create this image because I felt it was important to have a visual that better matched the essence of the historical record.

AN IMAGE

This painting is the image that kicked off this entire project. When my Church history and doctrine colleagues Michael MacKay and Gerrit Dirkmaat told me about their book summarizing recent scholarship on the Book of Mormon, *From Darkness unto Light: Joseph Smith's Translation and Publication of the Book of Mormon*,[14] we agreed that I should produce a more historically accurate imagery of the translation to aid their publication. This painting was intended to be the feature image for that book, along with ten interior watercolor and ink illustrations.

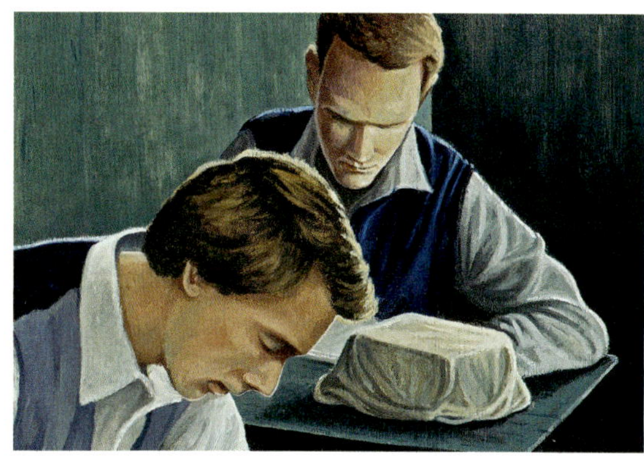

My image of the Book of Mormon translation is set from interior photographs taken in the replica Whitmer home on location in Fayette, New York, where Joseph and Oliver finished the translation of the Book of Mormon.[15] Here is one of the photos I took and used as reference:

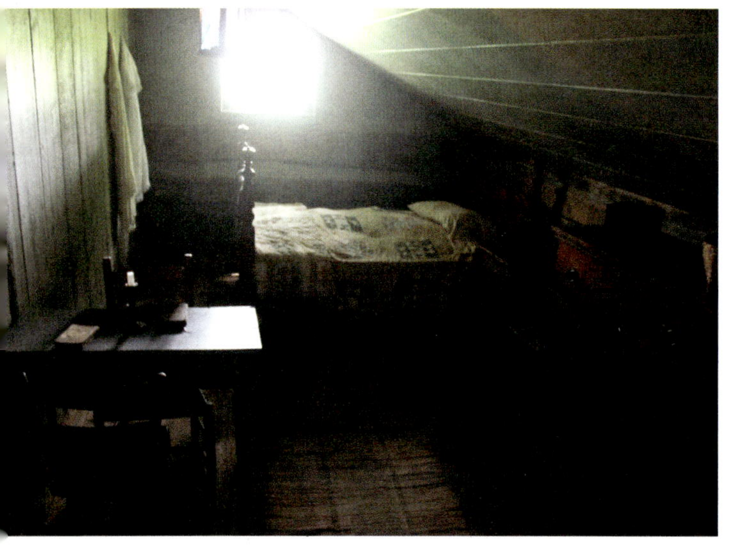

In the painting, I placed no sheet between Joseph and Oliver, unlike many other images, and the plates lie wrapped in a linen cloth, as Emma Smith explained. Both Joseph and Oliver were young at this time (twenty-three and twenty-two years old, respectively, in June 1829), and I wanted their youth reflected accurately in the image. The top hat is white, consistent with Martin Harris's description of the "old white hat"[16] that Joseph may have used.

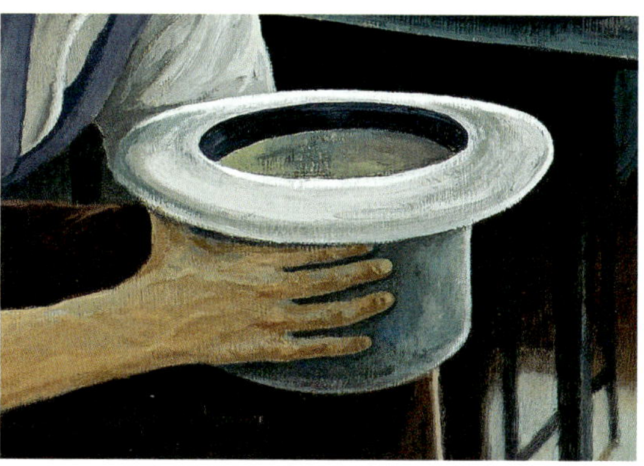

Although my image attempted to include basic historical accuracy, most notably Joseph's face is *not* "buried" in the hat, as some translation sources claimed. Why? There are three reasons I chose not to place his face fully in the hat: (1) Simply put, it didn't work visually for this composition. I wanted a viewer to immediately recognize Joseph Smith, and having his face in the hat was difficult for many to whom I showed preliminary sketches. (2) Using the language of art, I wanted to communicate the message of inspiration in this image. The human face carries a lot of subtle emotion, and burying Joseph's face made it difficult to portray concepts of prayer, study, focus, reverence, and revelation. A hat obscured those ideas visually. For example, here is one of the interior illustrations I created for the book *From Darkness unto Light*, with Joseph translating while Emma scribes. This painting just doesn't work as well visually. Compare that illustration to the following image, which I think works much better and shows revelatory concentration because Joseph's face is seen. (3) Joseph's face outside the hat still reflects historical reality. Logically, Joseph had to put his face into, and pull his face out of, the hat. In my painting, he almost looks like he is getting ready to tip forward, and the anticipation of that moment makes the viewer want to put his face into the hat, visually measuring Joseph's face and looking into the opening of the brim and fitting the two together. With this composition, your mind can imagine what Joseph is *about* to do. Having the face out of the hat helps to provide a more interactive and purposeful viewing experience.

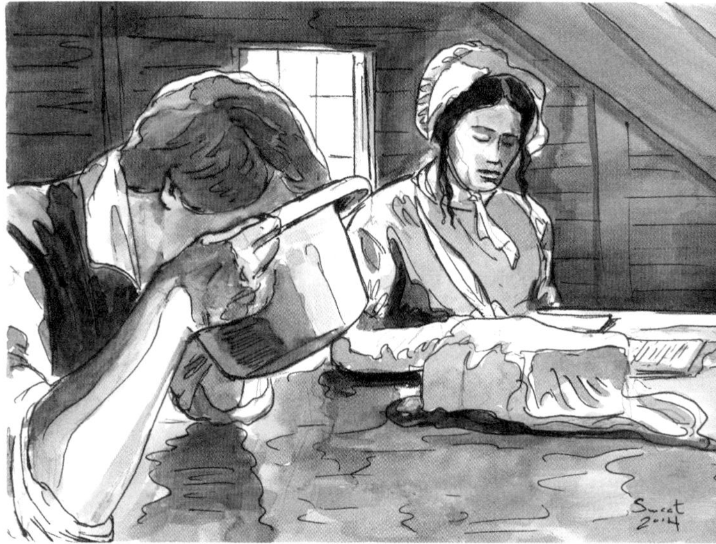

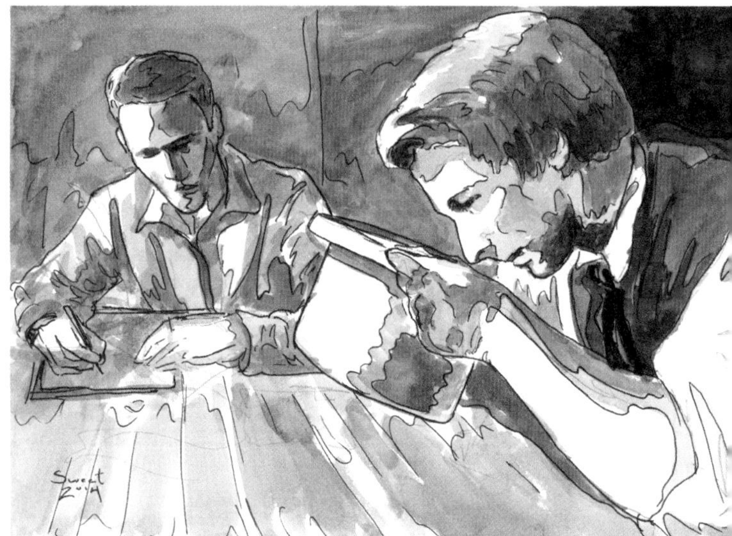

As the collective Church becomes more familiar and even comfortable with Joseph Smith's use of a hat while translating, we also need to be careful that we don't swing the pendulum too far by saying he *always* used a hat. While the hat is prevalent in many early sources, having Joseph's face buried in the hat could be a figure of speech, like saying that a girl who loves to read has her nose buried in a book. When I photographed images to use as I composed this painting, I acted and posed for Joseph. When I placed my face in a hat and tried to speak with the photographer, I couldn't because my voice was too muffled. I had to remove my face from the hat to speak clearly. It makes me wonder how Joseph would have clearly dictated a 500-plus-page book to a scribe articulately if his voice were continually muffled by his face literally being buried in his hat all the time. We should exercise caution, as some recent Church media has wisely done.[17]

That said, I placed the hat centrally in my painting and used the brightest white to pull the eye there, since that is what this painting provides that is most unique. I wanted the viewer to look at the hat first, to deal with it, think about it, examine it, and process it. Next, the eye then moves up to Joseph's face, seeing him move into

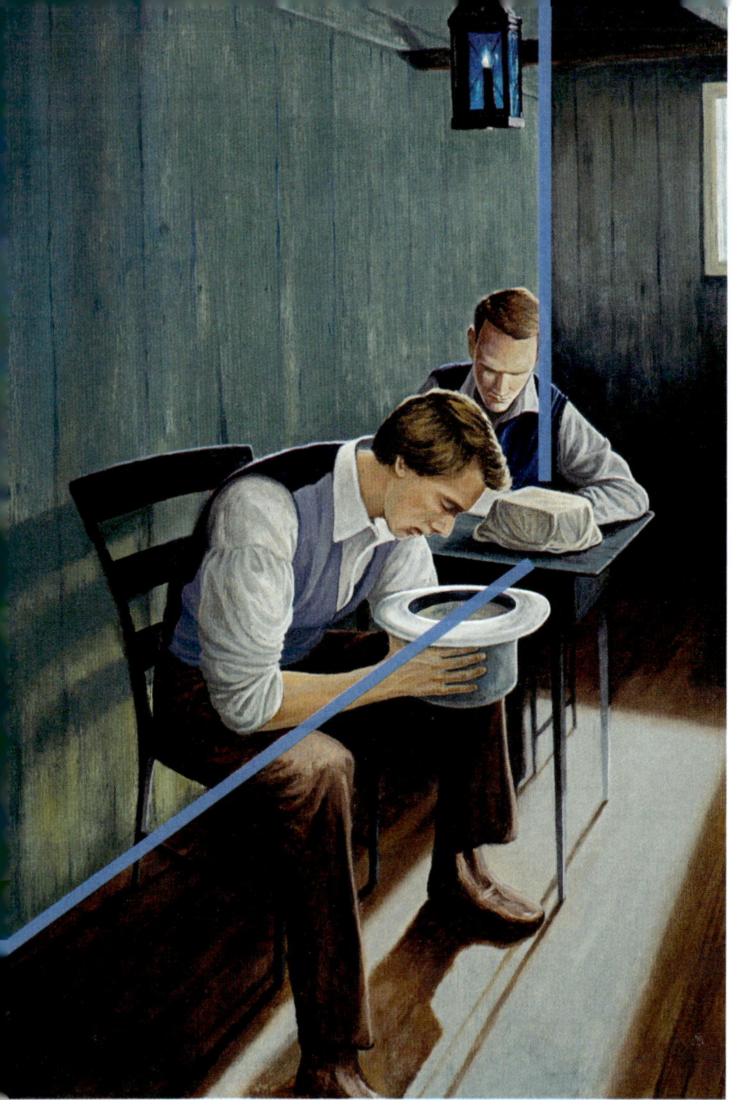

a revelatory mode and connecting it with the opening in the hat. The viewer then might naturally move to the covered plates on the table, differing from past visual representations of open plates and sheets. Next, the eye moves to Oliver Cowdery in the background as he sits and scribes "the sound of a voice dictated by the inspiration of heaven" (Joseph Smith—History 1:71, footnote). Deliberately, the diagonal line of the floor and wall joint coming in from the bottom left of the image and the vertical line made where the walls meet visually pass through Joseph and Oliver and lead the eye to the hat and the plates.

Finally, after the viewer examines the hat, Joseph, the plates, and Oliver, I hope his or her eye expands outward into the simplicity of the space. I intentionally included the window with sun streaming through, illuminating the ground and room to suggest ideas such as light, truth,

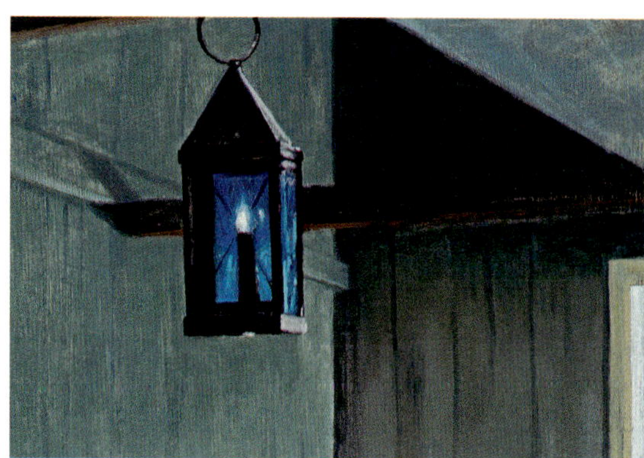

revelation, and inspiration shining on Joseph. After examining the central aspects of the painting, I hope the viewer's eye looks up and sees the black lantern above Joseph and Oliver. Without explaining, you can already deduce what that illuminated lantern might suggest and symbolize.

AN APPLICATION

The Book of Mormon and its production are, in the words of Emma Smith, "'a marvel and a wonder,' as much so as to anyone else."[18] Indeed, the Lord suggests many times in scripture that the Book of Mormon is a "marvelous work" (see Doctrine and Covenants 4:1; 6:1; 11:1; 12:1; 14:1). Synonyms of "marvelous" are many, and instructive. As you read the following synonym list, ask yourself, "What is so ______________ about the Book of Mormon?"

astonishing
awe-inspiring
awesome
awful
bewildering
breathtaking
confounding
difficult to believe
extraordinary
fabulous
improbable
incomprehensible
inconceivable
incredible
miraculous
phenomenal
remarkable
singular
spectacular
staggering
strange
stunning
supernatural
surprising
unbelievable
unimaginable
unlikely
unusual
wondrous

The Book of Mormon text is one of the best evidences for its authenticity. In Grant Hardy's groundbreaking work *Understanding the Book of Mormon*, he writes that, for instance, the phrase "'only Begotten of the Father, full of grace . . . and truth' . . . occurs only three times in the Book of Mormon, each time in the words of Alma. . . . Alma [also] uses the familiar phrase 'born again.' He is the only person in the Book of Mormon to do so. Similarly, the term 'born of God' appears nine times in the Book of Mormon, and eight of those quotations are from Alma."[19] This is but one small example of the complex, but obviously evident, internal consistency of the narrative voices of Book of Mormon authors. John Hilton III has demonstrated how the Book of Mormon prophet Jacob became a doctrinal, authoritative voice for the Nephites and that Nephi, King Benjamin, and Moroni deliberately cite Jacob's words as a foundational doctrinal teacher.[20] "The Book of Mormon," Elder Neal A. Maxwell said, "is like a vast mansion with gardens, towers, courtyards, and wings. There are rooms yet to be entered, with flaming fireplaces waiting to warm us. . . . Yet we as Church members sometimes behave like hurried tourists, scarcely venturing beyond the entry hall."[21]

The power of the Book of Mormon is in analyzing its text, not necessarily how that text was produced.

Although this image focuses on the process of the Book of Mormon translation, the power of the book is in analyzing its text, not necessarily how that text was produced. Regarding the *text* of the Book of Mormon translation, the Lord himself testified, "As your Lord and your God liveth it is true" (Doctrine and Covenants 17:6). For each of us, the spiritual quest of our lifetime is to better explore and be blessed by the marvelous mansion of the Book of Mormon text that Joseph Smith translated by the gift and power of God. This text is tangible evidence that "God does inspire men and call them to his holy work in this age and generation" (Doctrine and Covenants 20:11). The text of the "Book of Mormon will change your life. It will fortify you against the evils of our day. It will bring a spirituality into your life that no other book will," as President Ezra Taft Benson said.[22] Consistently studying the words of the Book of Mormon will bring "into your lives and into your homes an added measure of the Spirit of the Lord, a strengthened resolution to walk in obedience to His commandments, and a stronger testimony of the living reality of the Son of God," as President Gordon B. Hinckley taught.[23] The production of the Book of Mormon was indeed a marvelous miracle, but its divine wonder is in what it produces in the minds and hearts of the readers who earnestly explore its pages.

AN ANALYSIS

1 There are some who would prefer to think of the Book of Mormon translation as a purely as scholastic exercise rather than as a revelatory or miraculous one. While using the mind was a necessary part of the Book of Mormon translation (see Doctrine and Covenants 9:8), those who witnessed the translation called it miraculous. After all, nobody but God can make words appear and disappear on stones. That isn't very rational. Why do some want everything God does to be strictly logical? Is it always? Was the resurrection of Jesus Christ explainable or replicable by the scientific method? Why may God sometimes purposely work against human reasoning?

2 Why didn't God just give Joseph Smith an already translated text? Why make Joseph Smith go through all the effort to obtain the plates and then receive through divine stones an English translation of what the plates say? Could Moroni not have delivered it translated into English for Joseph? What may that tell us about the work of God and why he leaves work for us to do that he could have done for us? How have you seen that concept at play in your life? What is he trying to accomplish with us?

3 Some are bothered by the apparent inconsistencies in Church art related to the Book of Mormon translation.[24] How has previous Church-published art helped or hindered your understanding of the Book of Mormon translation? What responsibilities do you believe artists have to be historically accurate when it comes to Church history or scriptural scenes—and to what degree? Understanding the language of art, why may prior artists have chosen to depict the translation in the way they did? One prominent artist told me that the Church had approached him in the past about producing a painting of Joseph translating using the hat, but he hadn't done it because he felt that "it just looks odd. It probably won't communicate what the Church wants. . . . Some things just don't work visually."[25] Regardless of the art that is produced, how can we overcome source amnesia (as discussed in this book's introduction) and balance our learning of scriptural and Church history from historical sources—not merely artistic images?

NOTES

1. "Last Testimony of Sister Emma," *Saints' Herald*, 1 October 1879, 290.
2. Several paragraphs are adapted from my book *Seekers Wanted: The Skills You Need for the Faith You Want* (Salt Lake City: Deseret Book, 2019), 16–18.
3. "Minutes, 25–26 October 1831," 13, The Joseph

Smith Papers.

4. See the preface to the 1830 edition of the Book of Mormon. "Book of Mormon, 1830," iii, The Joseph Smith Papers.
5. For a good history and overview of the Book of Mormon translation, see "Book of Mormon Translation," Gospel Topics Essays, The Church of Jesus Christ of Latter-day Saints.
6. Jonathan Hadley, "Golden Bible," *Palmyra Freeman*, 11 August 1829, 2.
7. "Printer's Manuscript of the Book of Mormon" (introduction to Revelations and Translations: Volume 3), The Joseph Smith Papers.
8. Christian Goodwillie, "Shaker Richard McNemar: The Earliest Book of Mormon Reviewer," *Journal of Mormon History* 37, no. 2 (Spring 2011): 143.
9. "Last Testimony of Sister Emma," 289–90.
10. David Whitmer, *An Address to All Believers in Christ* (Richmond, MO: n.p., 1887), 12.
11. Dean C. Jessee, "Joseph Knight's Recollection of Early Mormon History," *BYU Studies* 17, no. 1 (Autumn, 1976): 35.
12. Edward Stevenson, "One of the Three Witnesses," *Deseret Evening News*, 13 December 1881, 4.
13. Since its inception in 1971 through 2014, the *Ensign* has depicted the translation of the Book of Mormon fifty-five times, repeatedly using seventeen different images. All the *Ensign* images are inconsistent with aspects of documented Church history regarding the translation process of the Book of Mormon. Only one painting shows Joseph Smith using the Urim and Thummim (see Gary Smith's painting, *Ensign*, November 1988, 46). None of the fifty-five images depict the translation process of the Book of Mormon as having occurred by placing a seer stone or the Nephite interpreters in a hat. The first image of Joseph translating the Book of Mormon using a hat appeared in LeGrand R. Curtis Jr., "The Translation of the Book of Mormon: A Marvel and a Wonder," *Ensign*, January 2020, 38–39. It appears to be a digitally altered screenshot from a recent Church film, *Days of Harmony*.
14. Michael Hubbard MacKay and Gerrit Dirkmaat, *From Darkness unto Light: Joseph Smith's Translation and Publication of the Book of Mormon* (Provo, UT: Religious Studies Center, Brigham Young University; Salt Lake City: Deseret Book, 2015).
15. Several paragraphs are an adapted summary of my appendix article "By the Gift and Power of Art," in MacKay and Dirkmaat, *From Darkness unto Light*, 238–41.
16. Joel Tiffany, *Tiffany's Monthly*, June 1859, 164.
17. The Church film shown at the priesthood restoration site, *Days of Harmony*, shows Joseph translating with Oliver, but artfully fades away from Joseph and pans to Oliver so nothing definitive is shown. Lee Groberg and Mark Goodman's 2017 remake of the documentary *Joseph Smith: American Prophet* shows Joseph translating with a hat, but his hand shields the rim of the hat as Joseph looks in without placing his face in it.
18. "Last Testimony of Sister Emma," 289–90.
19. Grant Hardy, *Understanding the Book of Mormon: A Reader's Guide* (New York: Oxford, 2010), 135–36.
20. See John Hilton III, "Jacob's Textual Legacy," *Journal of Book of Mormon and Restoration Scripture* 22, no. 2 (2013): 52–65.
21. Neal A. Maxwell, *Not My Will, But Thine* (Salt Lake City: Bookcraft, 1988), 33.
22. Ezra Taft Benson, "To the 'Youth of the Noble Birthright,'" *Ensign*, May 1986, 43.
23. Gordon B. Hinckley, "A Testimony Vibrant and True," *Ensign*, August 2005, 6.
24. See, for example, Bill McKeever and Eric Johnson, "A Seer Stone and a Hat—'Translating' the Book of Mormon," mrm.org; see also "What's Art Got to Do With It?," cesletter.org.
25. Walter Rane, personal interview with the author, 7 February 2014.

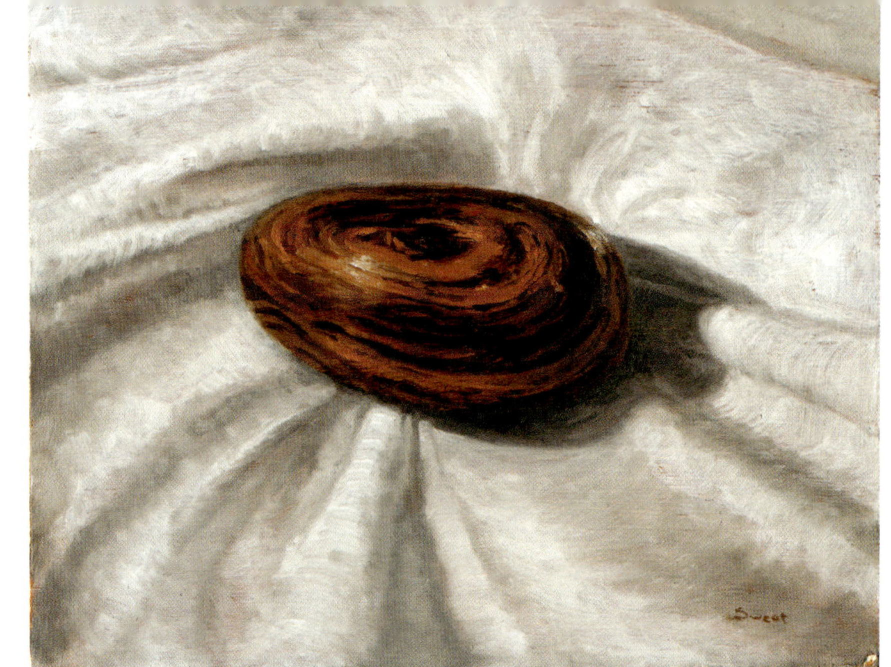

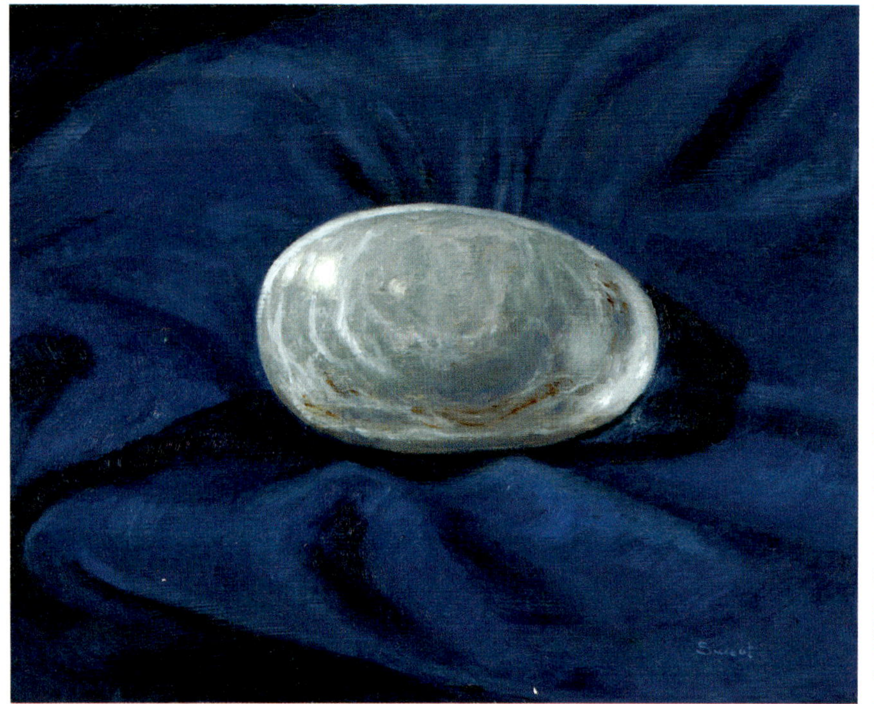

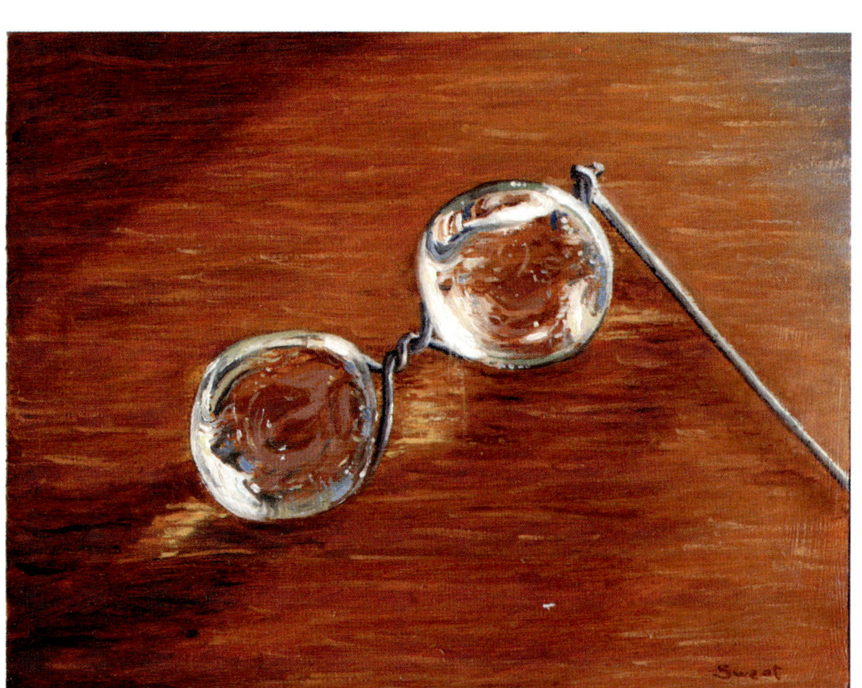

Urim and Thummim Triptych: The Brown Stone, the White Stone, and the Nephite Spectacles (8" x 10" each, oil on board, 2016)

URIM AND THUMMIM

Timeline: circa 1822–29

Related Doctrine and Covenants Sections: 3, 6, 7, 11, 14, 17, 130

A BACKGROUND

It is common to hear about the Urim and Thummim in Latter-day Saint teaching. Typically, this is in reference to the "two stones in silver bows" (Joseph Smith—History 1:35) that were found with the Book of Mormon plates and prepared to translate them. It is notable, however, that the Book of Mormon never refers to the translating devices that came with the plates by that name. Instead, they are often referred to as the "interpreters" (Mosiah 8:13, 19; Mosiah 28:20; Alma 37:21, 24; Ether 4:5). In the early restored Church, these interpreter stones[1] were sometimes referred to as the "spectacles." In Joseph's 1832 history, he mentions that "the Lord had prepared ~~specttickc~~ spectacles for to read the Book."[2]

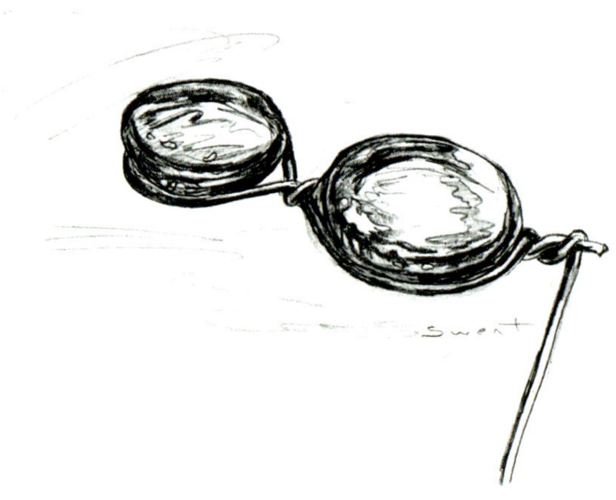

One of the best descriptions of the spectacles comes from Joseph Smith's mother, Lucy Mack Smith. She recalled that after Joseph retrieved the plates he handed her the spectacles: "~~Upon after~~ examing it <*> <(*with no covering but a silk handkerchief)> <found> that it consisted of 2 smooth <3 cornered diamonds set in glass and the glass was set in silver bows> ~~stones~~ con[n]ected with each other in the same way that old fashioned spectacles are made."[3]

Martin Harris, who likely saw the spectacles while Joseph translated, remembered, "The two stones set in a bow of silver were about two inches in diameter, perfectly round. . . . The stones were white, like polished marble, with a few gray streaks."[4]

So when did the Church begin calling the interpreters or spectacles the "Urim and Thummim"? Editors for the *Joseph Smith Papers* write that Joseph Smith "and other church members began referring to the instrument as the Urim and Thummim by 1832,"[5] likely as a way to connect the way God was working with the modern Church with how he worked with his children in dispensations past. W. W. Phelps wrote in the Church's newspaper *The Evening and the Morning Star* in January 1833 that Joseph translated the Book of Mormon "through the aid of a pair of Interpreters, or spectacles—(known, perhaps, in ancient days as Teraphim, or Urim and Thummim)."[6] Wouldn't it have been interesting if the Church had adopted the phrase "Teraphim"? Instead of "interpreters," "Urim and Thummim" became the common Church terminology, a biblical phrase found in the Old Testament (see Exodus 28:30; Leviticus 8:8; Numbers 27:21; Deuteronomy 33:8), associated with the high priest's office (see Exodus 28:30; Leviticus 8:8; Numbers 27:21; Ezra 2:63). Urim and Thummim were "tangible objects" where "God's purpose with men was made visible or audible to the priest," and they were "a medium of heavenly origin"[7] or "a means of revelation . . . by which God was pleased to speak to his people."[8] "Urim" translates as "lights" and "Thummim" as "perfections." The phrase implies "perfect light" or revelation.[9]

This definition is a good one to expand our understanding of the name. Urim and Thummim may be better thought of *as an umbrella term* that means "a device used to translate and receive revelation."[10] It is more than the spectacles, or interpreters. Indeed, one may see Joseph

Smith's brown stone as Urim and Thummim (see "Gazelem, a Stone"). Historian and Seventy B. H. Roberts wrote, "The Seer Stone referred to here was a chocolate-colored, somewhat egg-shaped stone. . . . It possessed the qualities of Urim and Thummim, since by means of it—as described above—as well by means of the Interpreters found with the Nephite record, Joseph was able to translate the characters engraven on the plates."[11] Emma Smith recollected that Joseph Smith used the brown stone to translate portions of the Book of Mormon. Emma said, "Now the first that my husband translated, was translated by the use of the Urim, and Thummim [i.e., the spectacles or interpreters], and that was the part that Martin Harris lost, after that he used a small stone, not exactly, black, but was rather a dark color."[12] Martin recalled that Joseph "possessed a seer stone, by which he was enabled to translate as well as from the Urim and Thummim, and for convenience he then used the seer stone,"[13] but he did not specify the color of the stone.

Thus, a Gospel Topics Essay reads: "These two instruments—the interpreters and the seer stone—were apparently interchangeable and worked in much the same way such that, in the course of time, Joseph Smith and his associates often used the term 'Urim and Thummim' to refer to the single stone as well as the interpreters."[14] Therefore, when Joseph Smith says he translated the Book of Mormon by means of "Urim and Thummim," it is hard to determine if he is speaking strictly about the spectacles, or

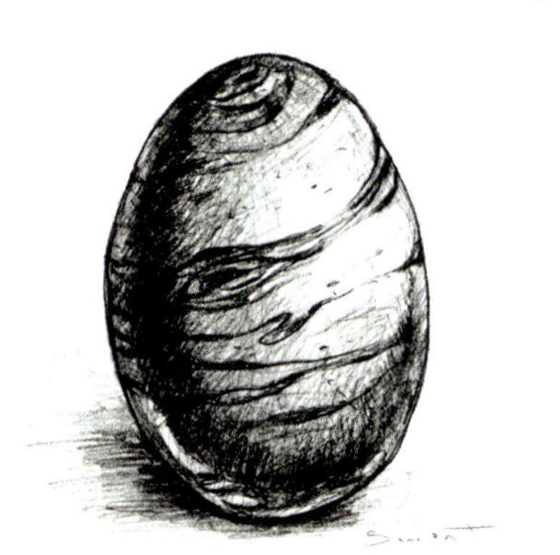

also including the brown stone in this summary. He may be saying, *I translated the Book of Mormon by using sacred stones that revealed the text.*[15]

Joseph Smith apparently possessed another Urim and Thummim, a white seer stone he likely discovered by 1826 that he may have kept with him throughout his life.[16] Some, including Wilford Woodruff, saw this seer stone in Joseph's possession in Nauvoo.[17] Lorenzo Snow showed Joseph Robinson the white seer stone, and Robinson left this description: "[The] Seer stone was the shape of an egg though not quite so large, of a gray cast something like granite but with white stripes running round it. It was transparent."[18] Another person who saw it described it as having a "whitish, glassy appearance, though opaque, resembling quartz."[19] Michael MacKay and Nicholas Frederick write that "there is evidence that the Book of Mormon translation . . . could have been done with the white stone rather than the brown stone."[20]

AN IMAGE

These three paintings are meant as a series, or a triptych as it is sometimes called, using the broader definition of "a set of three associated artistic, literary, or musical works."[21] Placing them side by side by side helps tell the story of a broader umbrella definition for "Urim and Thummim." These paintings were used for and published in the book *Joseph Smith's Seer Stones*, the white stone being the cover art.

The *Brown Stone* is painted based on photographs of Joseph's stone published by the Church through the Joseph Smith Papers Project.[22] This stone is roughly 5.5 inches long and 3.5 inches wide and shaped like a long egg.[23] I used a sample replica stone, provided to me by my colleague Alex Baugh, to photograph (see photo below) and then modified it to fit the shape, colors, and striping as shown in the Joseph Smith Papers Project photographs (see painting below).

The striping in my painting isn't exact but closely follows the same patterns as the actual brown stone photographs from the Joseph Smith Papers Project. For visual interest, I placed the stone resting in a linen cloth, like it had just been unwrapped or set down in the cloth that covered the plates. The swirls and lines in the folds provide visual movement, almost wrapping into the striping of the stone, and the shadows provide depth and dimensionality.

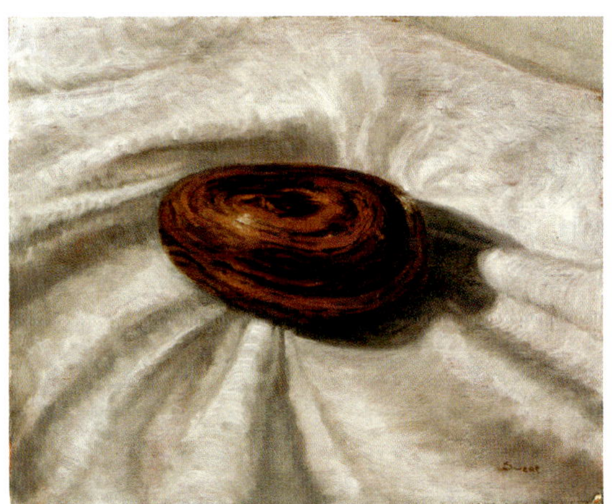

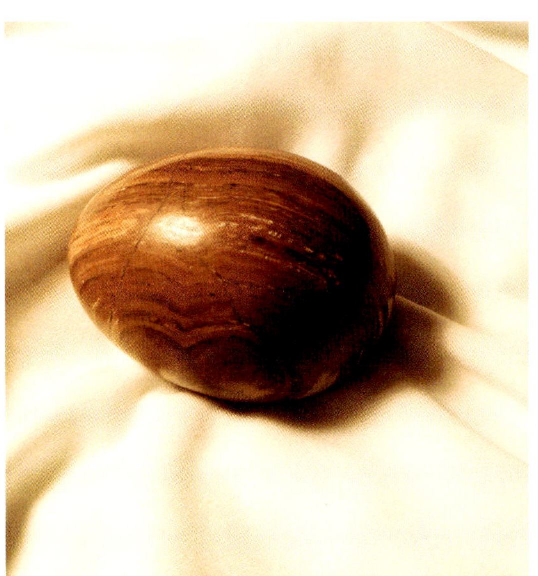

The *White Stone* is placed in a dark blue folded cloth. This was done to provide high contrast to the white stone and also because blue is a rich, royal color—like the stone is resting in a regal space, which it seemed to do spiritually for Joseph throughout his lifetime. The blue also balances and brings out the gray blues in the stone itself. In a painting, color in one area draws out and emphasizes similar colors in another. As there is no known photograph of the white stone, I had to rely upon descriptions, cited earlier, that say it was a gray cast of a stone like granite and had white stripes around it. It was also described as being transparent yet opaque (or unable to see through), like quartz. That's an interesting combo to try to visually depict.

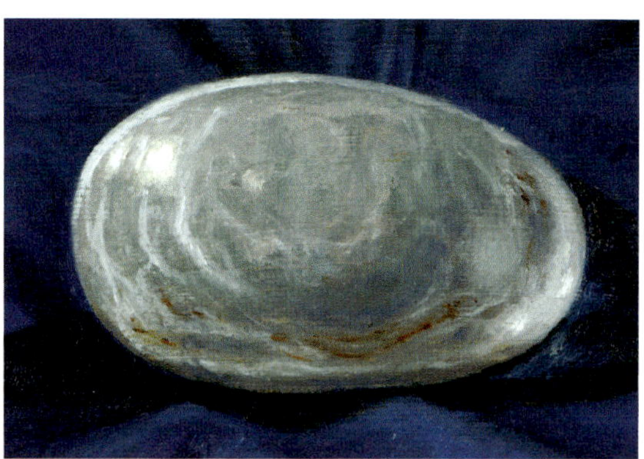

Thus, my image shows a stone that is grayish with white stripes and not transparent, but the bottom right has some light almost shining

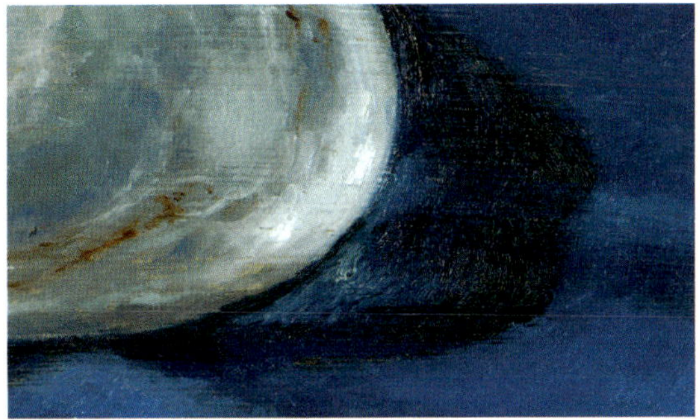

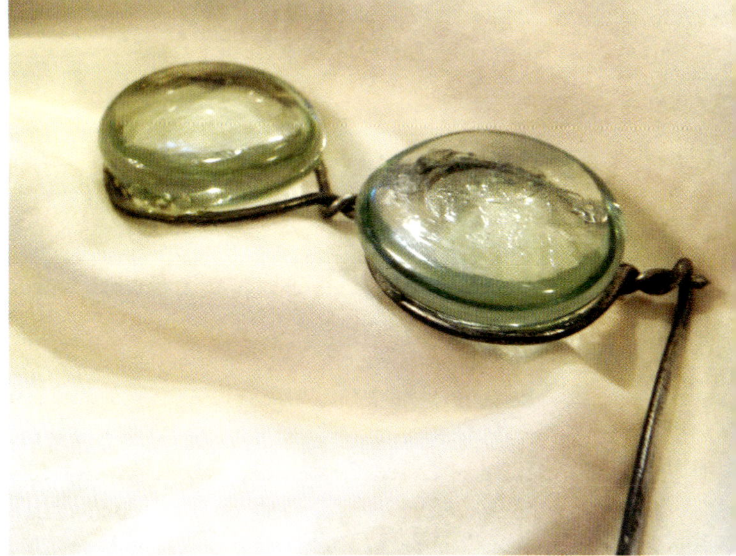

through it and refracting on the blue cloth, making the stone appear somewhat translucent.

The Nephite Spectacles was a harder image to produce. I created my own prototype out of wire and round, whitish glassy stones that have some streaks in them (like Martin Harris's description earlier) to photograph. The image (upper right) shows my protype (modeled after a replica in the Joseph Smith Building at Brigham Young University) and is one of the photographs I considered using for the final painting.

Frankly, I didn't know what to make of Lucy Smith's description that the spectacles' stones were "3 cornered diamonds set in glass." Does that mean they are stones within stones? Some have represented them as one triangle and another inverted triangle, which can form a star of David when put together.[24] There are no sources

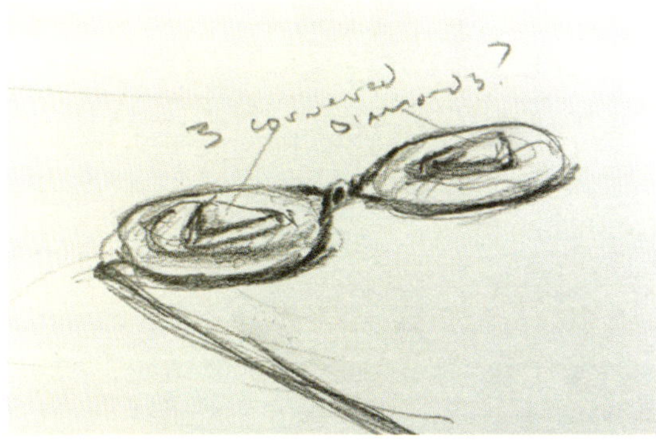

of which I am aware that say they were triangles that could be folded or inverted together to form a star of David. It seems to be conjectural. I toyed with representing the spectacles as the three-corner triangles in a compositional study:

Ultimately, I was uncertain. I chose not to speculate and kept the spectacles as round, glassy stones set in silver bows (see paintings below, left

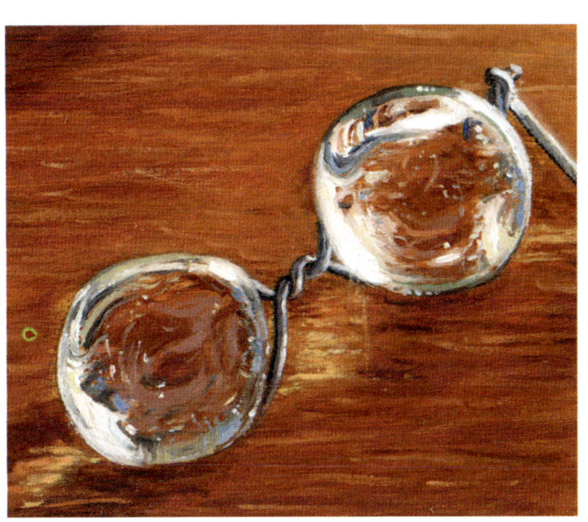

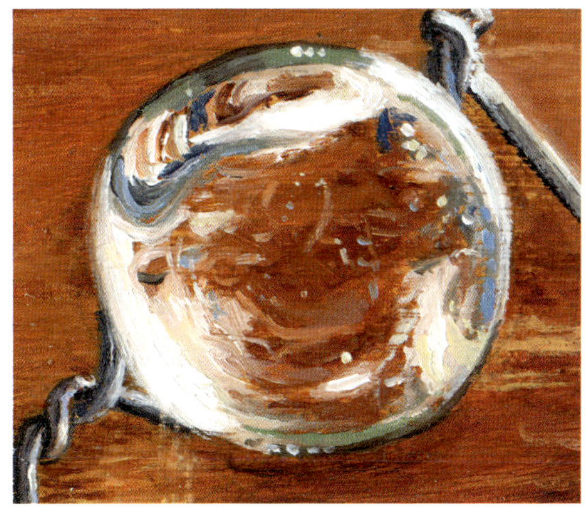

and right). The stones are purposely not completely transparent, like reading glasses. Words needed to appear on them to give the translation. Light shines through them onto the brown, desk-like background, suggesting revelation coming through them.

The swirls and blues and light in them were purposeful, suggesting an earth "like a sea of glass" (Doctrine and Covenants 130:7), Urim and Thummim revealing heavenly words to Joseph Smith as he translated the Book of Mormon.

AN APPLICATION

"Urim and Thummim" is not a relic of Old Testament or Church history past. Indeed, it seems part of our heavenly future. The Doctrine and Covenants teaches that those who enter the celestial kingdom will have access to two Urim and Thummim. The first will be "this earth, in its sanctified and immortal state" that "will be a Urim and Thummim to the inhabitants who dwell thereon, whereby all things pertaining to an inferior kingdom . . . will be manifest" (Doctrine and Covenants 130:9). The second will be a "white stone" that "will become a Urim and Thummim to each individual who receives one, whereby things of a higher order of kingdoms will be made known." This "white stone is given to each of those who come into the celestial kingdom" (Doctrine and Covenants 130:10–11). The earth will reveal lower orders of things, and a personal white stone, higher ones. Indeed, this sacred white stone that each receives in the celestial kingdom is connected to a sacred "new name" that "no man knoweth save he that receiveth it. The new name is the key word" (Doctrine and Covenants 130:11). "Urim and Thummim" is a broader term than we may assume (so broad it includes the earth!), and using Urim and Thummim seems to be something that will be part of celestial activities for those who inherit eternal life in the kingdom of God.

> "Urim and Thummim" is not a relic of Old Testament or Church History past. Indeed, it seems part of our heavenly future.

President Dieter F. Uchtdorf even likened using our telestial smartphones to celestial seer stones:

> In reality, most of us use a kind of "seer stone" every day. My mobile phone is like a "seer stone." I can get the collected knowledge of the world through a few little inputs. I can take a photo or a video with my phone and share it with family on the other side of our planet. I can even translate anything into or from many different languages! . . .
>
> If it is possible for me to access the knowledge of the world through my phone, who can question that seer stones are impossible for God?[25]

AN ANALYSIS

1 In his 1838–39 history, Joseph Smith says that God prepared the spectacles or interpreters "for the purpose of translating the book [of Mormon]" (Joseph Smith—History 1:35). Indeed, he often speaks of "*the* Urim and Thummim" in the singular (Joseph Smith—History 1:52, 59, 62; emphasis added). According to Joseph Knight Sr., Joseph Smith said the "glasses" were powerful and that with them, "I can see any thing; they are Marvelus."[26] If the "interpreters" were prepared to translate the Book of Mormon and these spectacles were so powerful, why did Joseph Smith also seem to use other seer stones he had obtained to translate the Book of Mormon? In using these stones to translate, was Joseph looking at the plates *through* the stones or looking *on* the stones at the words that appeared? Do you think the spectacles were like modern eyeglasses, completely transparent? If Joseph looked *through* the stones onto the plates, how did he see the English words that appeared to give the translation? Where did those words appear and how?

2 Why are we sometimes hesitant to embrace the idea that Joseph Smith used Urim and Thummims throughout his life and that they will apparently be part of celestial life? What role may enlightenment culture have in the tendency for some to relegate seer stones to a mythical past but not to an intelligent future?

3 What differentiates a regular stone from a seer stone? Is it the item or the individual that makes it work as a revelatory device? If revelation is a gift from God, does the stone matter? If not, then why prepare certain stones for Joseph and other prophets to find and use? Is it a combination of the right gift plus the right device?

NOTES

1. The stones that came with the plates were likely the ones given to the brother of Jared (see Ether 3:23; Doctrine and Covenants 17:1).
2. "History, circa Summer 1832," 5, The Joseph Smith Papers.
3. "Lucy Mack Smith, History, 1844–1845," 7–8, bk. 5, The Joseph Smith Papers.
4. "Mormonism," *Tiffany's Monthly* 5 (May 1859): 46–51; (July 1859): 119–21; (Aug. 1859): 163–70.
5. "Glossary," s.v. "Urim and Thummim," The Joseph Smith Papers.
6. "The Book of Mormon," *Evening and the Morning Star*, January 1833, 58.
7. C. Houtman, "The Urim and Thummim: A New Suggestion," *Vetus Testamentum* 40, fasc. 2 (April 1990): 229–30.
8. Cornelis Van Dam, *The Urim and Thummim: A Means of Revelation in Ancient Israel* (Warsaw, IN: Eisenbrauns: 1997), xi.
9. *Baker's Evangelical Dictionary of Biblical Theology*, ed. Walter A. Elwell (Grand Rapids, MI: Baker Books, 1996), s.v. "Urim and Thummim." See Paul Y. Hoskisson, "Urim and Thummim," in *Encyclopedia of Mormonism*, ed. Daniel H. Ludlow (New York: Macmillan, 1992), 4:1499–1500.
10. "Glossary," s.v. "Urim and Thummim."
11. B. H. Roberts, *Comprehensive History of the Church of Jesus Christ of Latter-day Saints* (Salt Lake City: The Church of Jesus Christ of Latter-day Saints, 1930), 1:129.
12. Emma Smith Bidamon, Nauvoo, to Emma Pilgrim, 27 March 1870, in *Early Mormon Documents*, ed. Dan Vogel (Salt Lake City: Signature Books, 1996), 1:532–33.

13. Edward Stevenson, "One of the Three Witnesses," *Deseret Evening News*, 13 December 1881, 4.
14. "Book of Mormon Translation," Gospel Topics Essays, The Church of Jesus Christ of Latter-day Saints.
15. See "Joseph Smith Documents Dating through June 1831," introduction to *Documents, Volume 1: July 1828–June 1831*, The Joseph Smith Papers.
16. "By 1826, JS had at least two seer stones." "Glossary," s.v. "Seer stone," The Joseph Smith Papers. MacKay and Frederick write, "Joseph Smith was known to have kept his white stone with him throughout his life," in Michael Hubbard MacKay and Nicholas J. Frederick, *Joseph Smith's Seer Stones* (Provo, UT: Religious Studies Center, Brigham Young University; Salt Lake City: Deseret Book, 2016), 127. See also Wilford Woodruff, Journal, 18 May 1888, Church History Library.
17. Wilford Woodruff, Journal, 27 December 1841, Church History Library.
18. Richard Marcellus Robinson, "The History of a Nephite Coin," 30 December 1934, Church History Library, as cited in MacKay and Frederick, *Joseph Smith's Seer Stones*, 83–84.
19. Pomeroy Tucker, *Origin, Rise, and Progress of Mormonism*, 129–30, as cited in MacKay and Frederick, *Joseph Smith's Seer Stones*, 77–78.
20. MacKay and Frederick, *Joseph Smith's Seer Stones*, 84.
21. *Pocket Oxford English Dictionary*, ed. Maurice Waite (New York: Oxford University Press, 2002), s.v. "Triptych."
22. For photographs of the brown stone, see "Glossary," s.v. "Seer stone," The Joseph Smith Papers.
23. See "Note on Seer Stone Images," The Joseph Smith Papers.
24. See, for example, the picture in Miguel Barker-Valdez, "urim-and-thummim-joseph-smith," *Rational Faiths* (blog), 8 December 2012.
25. Dieter F. Uchtdorf, Facebook, 21 June 2016.
26. Dean C. Jessee, "Joseph Knight's Recollection of Early Mormon History," *BYU Studies* 17, no. 1 (1976): 6.

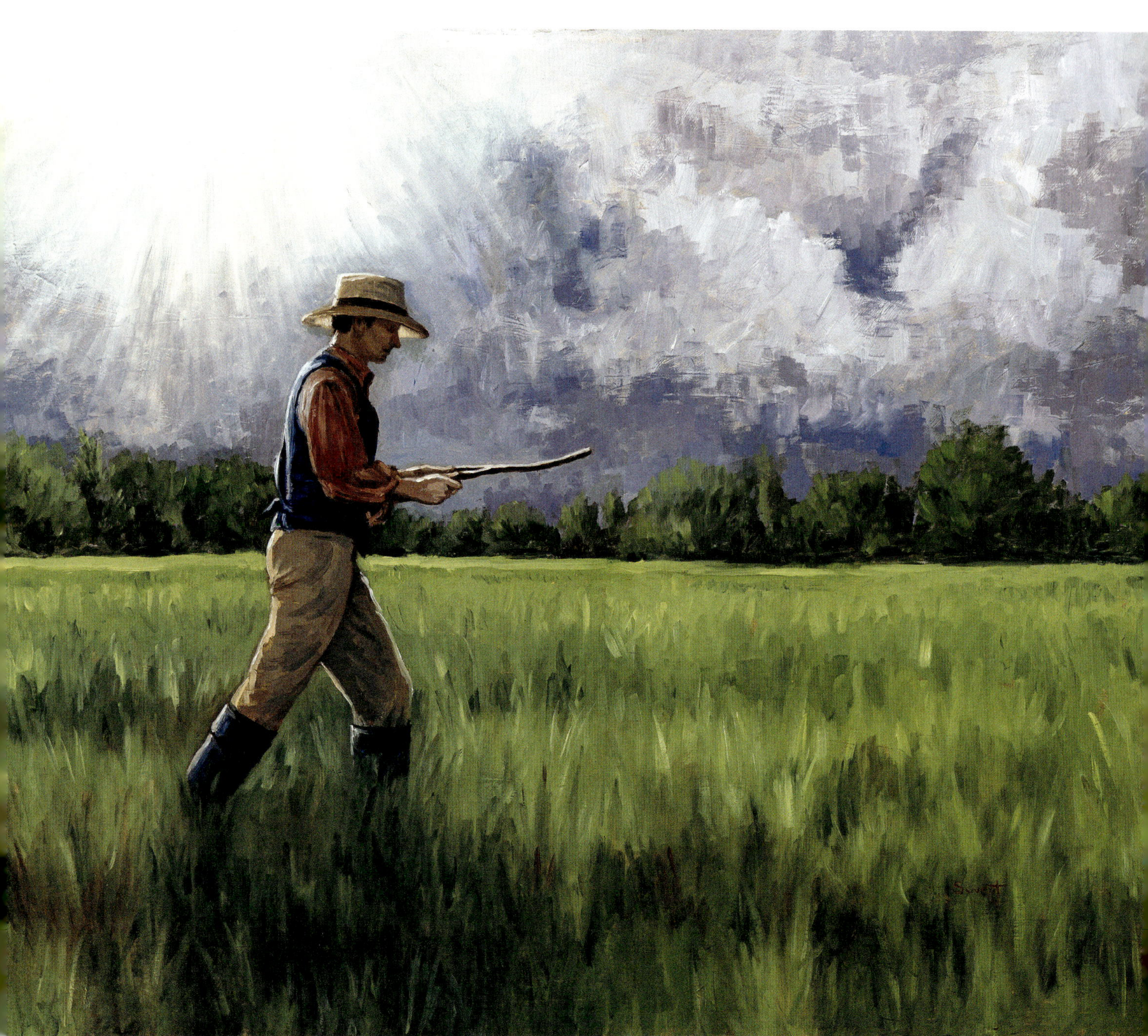

Oliver Cowdery's Gift of the Rod (16" x 20", oil on board, 2018)

OLIVER COWDERY'S GIFT OF THE ROD

Timeline: Spring 1829

Related Doctrine and Covenants Sections: 6, 8, 9

A BACKGROUND

In March 1829, Joseph Smith was told in a revelation to "stop [translating the Book of Mormon] for a season, even until I command thee again; then thou mayest translate again. . . . Stand still until I command thee, and I will provide means whereby thou mayest accomplish the thing which I have commanded thee" (Doctrine and Covenants 5:30, 34). The Prophet lacked a scribe after Martin Harris lost 116 pages of the Book of Mormon manuscript. Where could Joseph get a new full-time scribe? Joseph's mother Lucy recalled in her history that Joseph said, "[I] have commenced translating again, and Emma writes for me; but the angel said that the Lord would send me a scribe, and <I> trust his promise will be verified."[1]

On 5 April 1829 a teacher named Oliver Cowdery arrived at Joseph's home in Harmony, Pennsylvania, a man whom Joseph had never met until that time (see Joseph Smith—History 1:66). Oliver had heard of Joseph's work in translating the Book of Mormon when he took a teaching position in Manchester, New York, where he boarded with Joseph Smith's parents.[2] Oliver prayed about the matter and was given a witness by God that the work was true. It "seems working in my very bones, and I cannot for a moment get it out of my mind,"[3] Joseph's mother remembers him telling her. It was "impressed upon his mind, that he should yet have the privilege of writing for Joseph."[4] Joseph Smith wrote in his 1832 history that the "Lord appeared unto a young man by the name of Oliver Cowd[e]ry and shewed unto him the plates in a vision and also the truth of the work and what the Lord was about to do through me his unworthy Servant therefore he was desiorous to come and write for me ~~and~~ to translate."[5]

Following the end of the school term, Oliver Cowdery traveled to Harmony with Joseph's brother Samuel and arrived on a Sunday. Joseph and Oliver talked about his experiences late into the evening. On Monday they attended to some business, and on Tuesday, 7 April 1829, after knowing him for only two days, Oliver Cowdery began scribing when Joseph resumed translating the Book of Mormon.

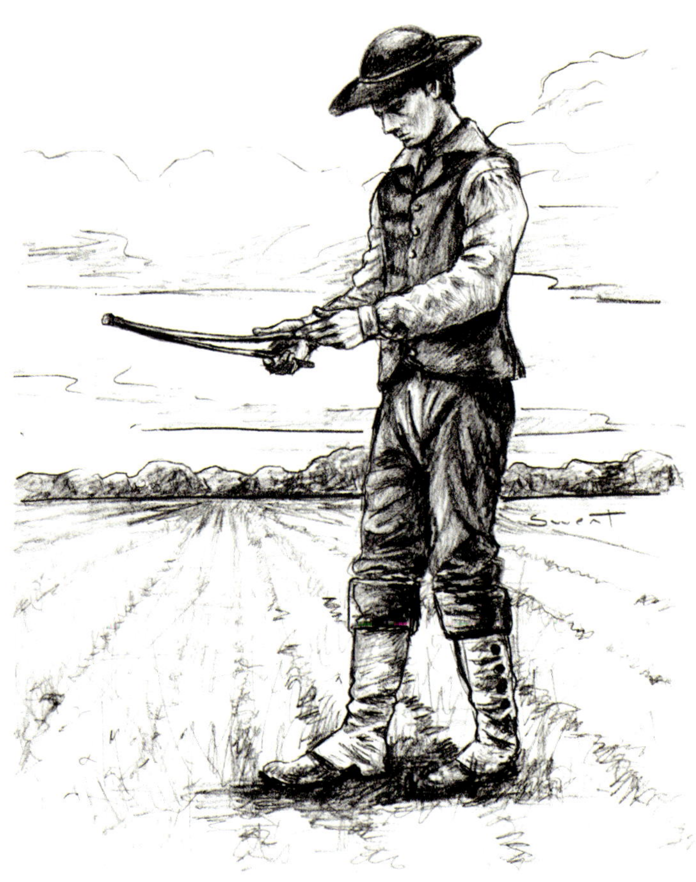

As Oliver watched Joseph translate, he desired to do the same. The Lord told Oliver he had a gift and if he would "inquire," he would "know mysteries which are great and marvelous" (Doctrine and Covenants 6:11). The Lord told Oliver in the same revelation, "I grant unto you a gift, if you desire of me, to translate, even as my servant Joseph" (Doctrine and Covenants 6:25). As Joseph continued to translate and Oliver wrote, the Lord reaffirmed Oliver's gifts in another revelation, found today in Doctrine and Covenants 8. In it the Lord trains Oliver about the process of revelation and "the manifestation of my Spirit" (8:1), telling him that the Holy Ghost will work "in your mind and in your heart" (8:2) and that "this is the spirit of revelation" (8:3). The Lord then likened this gift of revelation and translation to yet *another* third gift Oliver had that had "told you many things" before, even "the gift of Aaron" (8:6). The earliest written version of Doctrine and Covenants 8, however, was not that Oliver Cowdery had the "gift of Aaron" but "the gift of working with the sprout." God caused "this thing of Nature rod to work in your hands" the Lord told Oliver, and it was "the work of God."[6]

Below is Doctrine and Covenants 8 in Manuscript Revelation Book 1, copied circa March 1831 by John Whitmer.[7]

This "rod" or "sprout" or "thing of nature" that Oliver held in his hands is likely a reference to the practice of using divining rods, or a Y-shaped branch to locate water or broken earth in a field, still common in some agricultural areas today.[8] The Church history manual *Revelations in Context* says, regarding Doctrine and Covenants 8, "Many Christians in Joseph Smith and Oliver Cowdery's day similarly believed in divining rods as instruments for revelation. Oliver was among those who believed in and used a divining rod."[9]

It seems that in section 8 the Lord was trying to teach Oliver Cowdery about the gift of revelation and translation—how you have to pay attention to the mind and heart and be in tune—and likened it to Oliver's use of divining rods to make a connection with which he could relate. In the 1835 Doctrine and Covenants, the phrase was changed from "gift of the rod" to "the gift of Aaron,"[10] likely as a way to connect the present way God worked with Oliver to the miraculous past, like the miracles Moses and Aaron performed with rods (see Exodus 4:17; Numbers 17).

AN IMAGE

This painting shows Oliver Cowdery working in an open field and holding a Y-shaped branch gently in his hands as he pays attention to its subtle guiding movements. The clouds are stormy, suggesting both water (for which Oliver may be searching) and also light and darkness

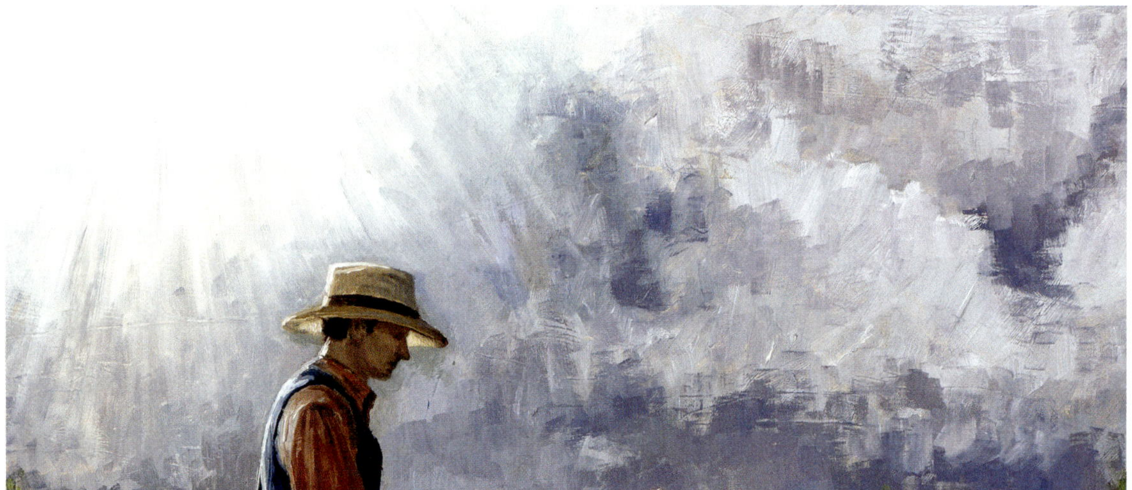

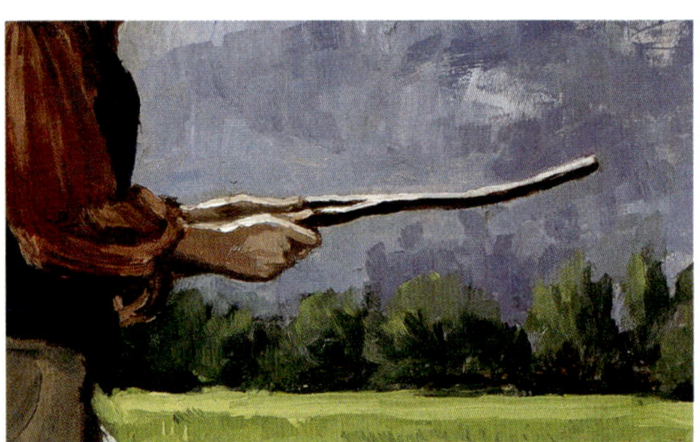

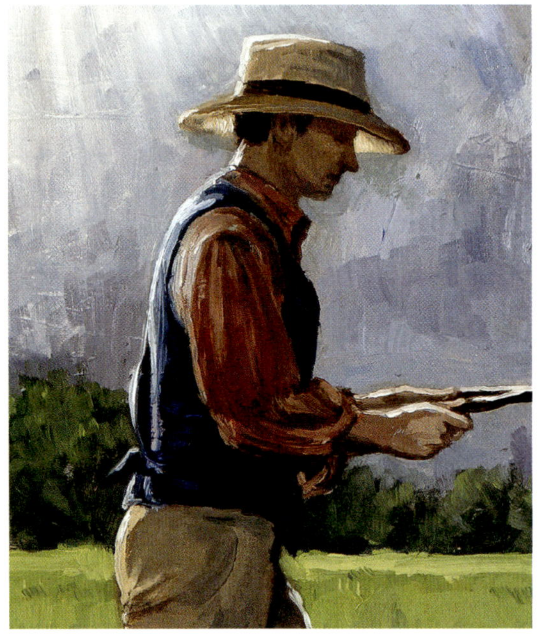

(which Oliver must learn to discern). In the top image, the sun shines through, referencing the Lord's teachings to Oliver on revelation and inspiration to guide him.

Artistically and symbolically, I love the sun poking through the bottom of Oliver's hat as if it is illuminating his mind.

Compositionally, Oliver's red shirt draws the viewer to that warm, strong color in contrast to the cooler earth tones in the rest of the painting.

Notice also how in the composition Oliver is situated on the left side of the panel. This is deliberate, because I could have placed him squarely in the middle. There are two reasons I chose not to. First, there is a *rule of thirds* in composition that suggests that things which are divided into thirds are more pleasing to the eye than things broken in half (see facing page).

Secondly, placing Oliver walking on the left third of the viewing panel leaves a large space in front of him open. Visually, the open space causes the viewer to walk him forward, creating a sense of motion and allowing one to visually imagine him, with his slight lean and bent legs, walking forward. Notice how all of this works better than my alternate compositional sketch, which placed Oliver in the center, standing statically with his head bowed.

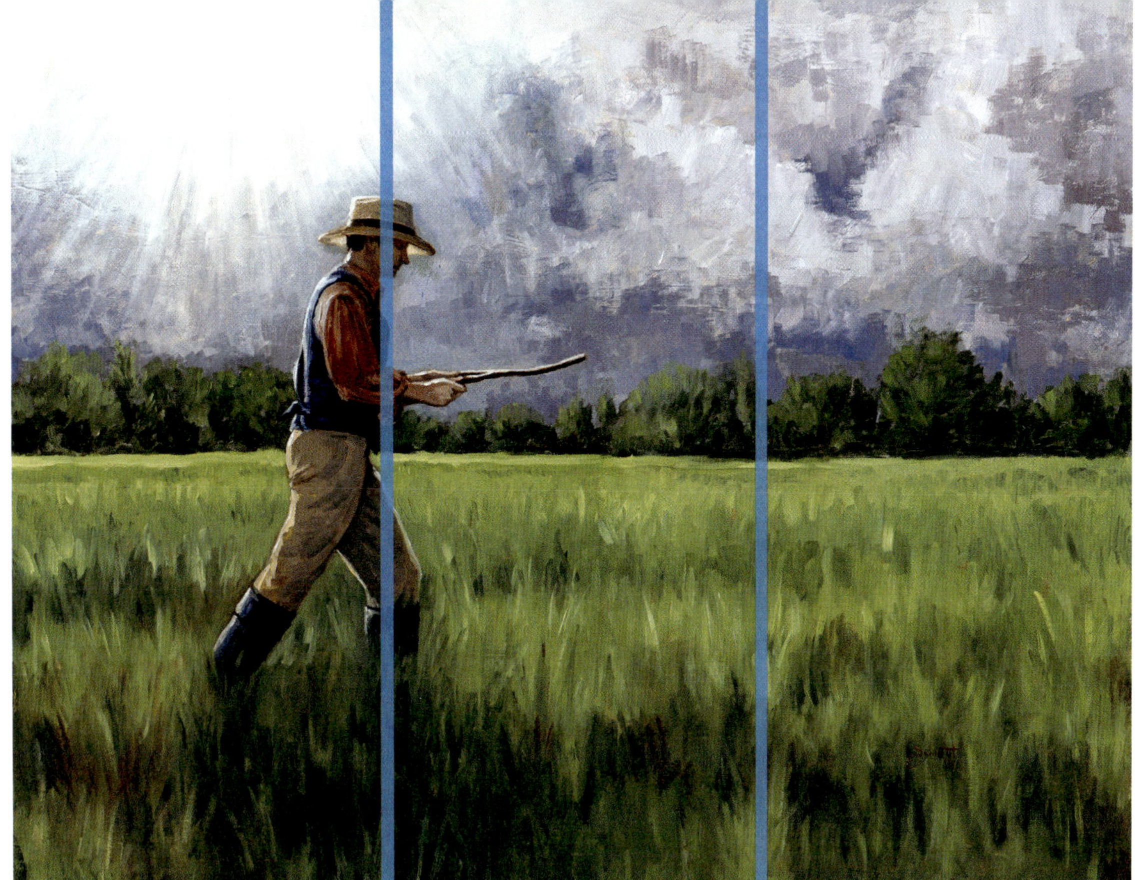

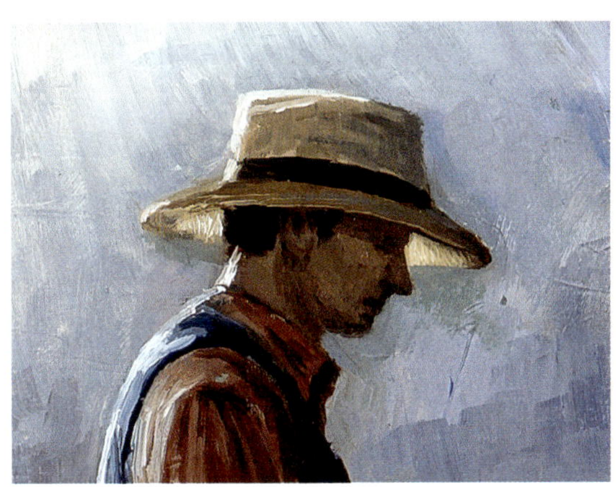

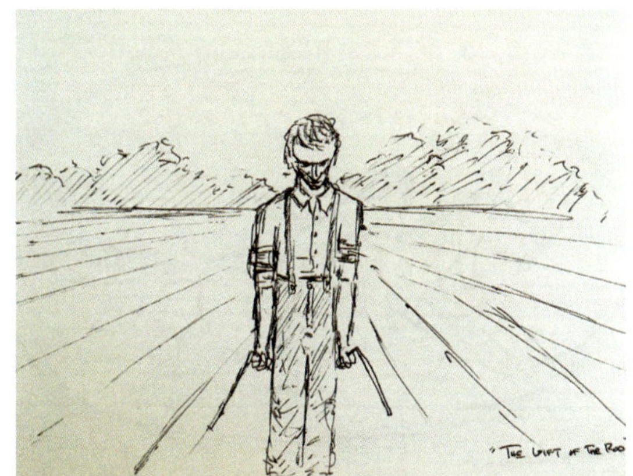

AN APPLICATION

Apparently, Oliver attempted to translate a portion of the Book of Mormon, putting into practice some of the principles of revelation and translation he had learned through his past use of divining rods and the new revelations given him through Joseph Smith. The revelatory words he hoped to receive, however, "did not come easily," and Oliver "grew frustrated and confused."[11] A follow-up revelation came, saying, "Behold, it is because that you did not continue as you commenced, when you began to translate, that I have taken away this privilege from you" (Doctrine and Covenants 9:5). Oliver had thought God would just give him the translation, "when you took no thought save it was to ask me" (9:7). The Lord then reminded Oliver, and by extension us, that when we seek to cultivate the gift of revelation, "you must study it out in your mind; then you must ask me if it be right" (9:8). The Lord closed the window on Oliver's Book of Mormon translation attempts, saying, "It was expedient when you commenced; but you feared, and the time is past, and it is not expedient now" (9:11), leaving the translation task to Joseph alone.

You did not continue as you commenced. You feared. You didn't work hard enough at it. You froze. You missed it. Ouch. When I was contemplating a PhD, it was a busy time in my life. I had recently finished my master's degree. I was teaching seminary full-time for the Church Educational System. My wife and I had just had our fourth child, and our oldest was eight. We had just moved into a new house and were still trying to finish basement rooms. It just wasn't the best time, I reasoned, to pursue a PhD. I wanted to wait until things were slower and easier (everyone who is middle-aged and just read that sentence has my permission to laugh out loud). I felt, however, this incessant pull to pursue my doctorate degree. The idea of getting a PhD "occup[ied] my mind, and press[ed] itself upon my feelings the strongest" (Doctrine and Covenants 128:1). I knew it was the Spirit working in my mind and heart, trying to move me forward in faith. But I resisted. I feared the work, the study, the effort, the sacrifice it would entail, but I could also taste the opportunities it would create. I was conflicted.

One day, while searching for direction, I read Doctrine and Covenants 9, and the Lord's words to Oliver hit me hard. I knew there was a window of opportunity for me and that if I didn't act now that window would close and likely latch permanently shut. The Lord was saying to me that I must continue as I had commenced with my master's degree. I couldn't fear the work, because things wouldn't come easily. I couldn't sit back and wait. I couldn't freeze. Otherwise, I would miss it, and the Lord would say, "It was right at the time, but it isn't right anymore." I didn't want that to happen. I learned from Oliver and Doctrine and Covenants 9, thanked the Lord, and acted. I am forever grateful I did.

We can't fear the work, or things that don't come easily. We can't sit back and wait. We can't freeze. Otherwise, we will miss our opportunities.

AN ANALYSIS

1 While divining rods may seem foreign and a bit strange to many modern sensibilities, how many of us pray to God to bless our hands in our daily work (writers, artists, musicians, medical doctors, mechanics, students, etc.)? Or have you ever practiced "bibliomancy,"[12] the act of randomly opening scriptures and reading wherever the pages fell, reading the verses as a sign from God of a divinely intended message? How many stories have you heard about people being spiritually directed to know which way to turn the wheel of a car to avoid trouble or to be led down a fortuitous path? Pay attention the next time you hear a missionary talk about being urged by the Spirit to know which specific door they should knock on or person they should speak with. What is the

difference between Oliver seeking for his hands to be led through divining rods by God to bless his farm and your seeking of God to bless your hands to be led and inspired by God in your work, to the pages of scripture you providentially turn to, at the wheel of your car, or at the knock of a door?

2 Elder Dallin H. Oaks reminded us, "It should be recognized that such tools as the Urim and Thummim, the Liahona, seerstones, and other articles have been used appropriately in biblical, Book of Mormon, and modern times."[13] How do we know how to use physical objects to aid in revelation "appropriately" in modern times? If someone used divining rods today, is that wrong? Why or why not? To manifest God's will, how can the scriptures help to appropriately guide us through questions about using physical objects such as rods, stones, metals, oils, or other oracles? Where do we cross the line between honest seeking of truth through our cultural understanding and occultic error and mystical mischief? Think of examples in the scriptures where God used earthly objects to tap into divine power. What matters more, the method or the motive?

3 Remember, Doctrine and Covenants 9 (an oft-cited section relating to personal revelation) was given in the historical context of the Book of Mormon translation. What did it mean that Oliver Cowdery had to "study it out" and "feel" that the translation was right? How much latitude did the translator have to express the concepts and characters on the plates? Would the words read exactly the same, say King Benjamin's discourse, if Oliver Cowdery had translated them as opposed to Joseph Smith? Do you think the Book of Mormon is a "tight" translation in its English expressions, or a "loose" translation altered by the vocabulary and idioms of its translator?

NOTES

1. "Lucy Mack Smith, History, 1845," 138, The Joseph Smith Papers.
2. "Lucy Mack Smith, History, 1845," 140.
3. "Lucy Mack Smith, History, 1845," 141.
4. "Lucy Mack Smith, History, 1845," 141.
5. "History, circa Summer 1832," 6, The Joseph Smith Papers.
6. "Revelation, April 1829–B [D&C 8]," 13, The Joseph Smith Papers.
7. See source note to and the scanned text of "Revelation, April 1829–B [D&C 8]," 13.
8. For a modern example of a person using divining rods, see, for example, Riana Mondavi, "Water Witching 101," The Divining Rod, 5 June 2012, YouTube video, 3:41; and Tom Roznowski, "The Divining Rod," Journey Indiana, 26 September 2013, YouTube video, 3:45.
9. Jeffrey G. Cannon, "Oliver Cowdery's Gift: D&C 6, 7, 8, 9, 13," in *Revelations in Context: The Stories behind the Sections of the Doctrine and Covenants*, ed. Matthew McBride and James Goldberg (Salt Lake City: The Church of Jesus Christ of Latter-day Saint, 2016), 17. Editors for *The Joseph Smith Papers* write, "Like many of his contemporaries, Cowdery probably used divining rods to find water or minerals," in the Historical Introduction to "Revelation, April 1829–B [D&C 8]"; see also Richard Lyman Bushman, *Joseph Smith and the Beginnings of Mormonism* (Urbana: University of Illinois Press, 1984), 98.
10. "Doctrine and Covenants, 1835," 161, The Joseph Smith Papers.
11. *Saints*, vol. 1, *The Standard of Truth, 1815–1846* (Salt Lake City: The Church of Jesus Christ of Latter-day Saints, 2018), 63.
12. Dictionary.com, s.v. "Bibliomancy."
13. Dallin H. Oaks, "Recent Events Involving Church History and Forged Documents," *Ensign*, October 1987, 65.

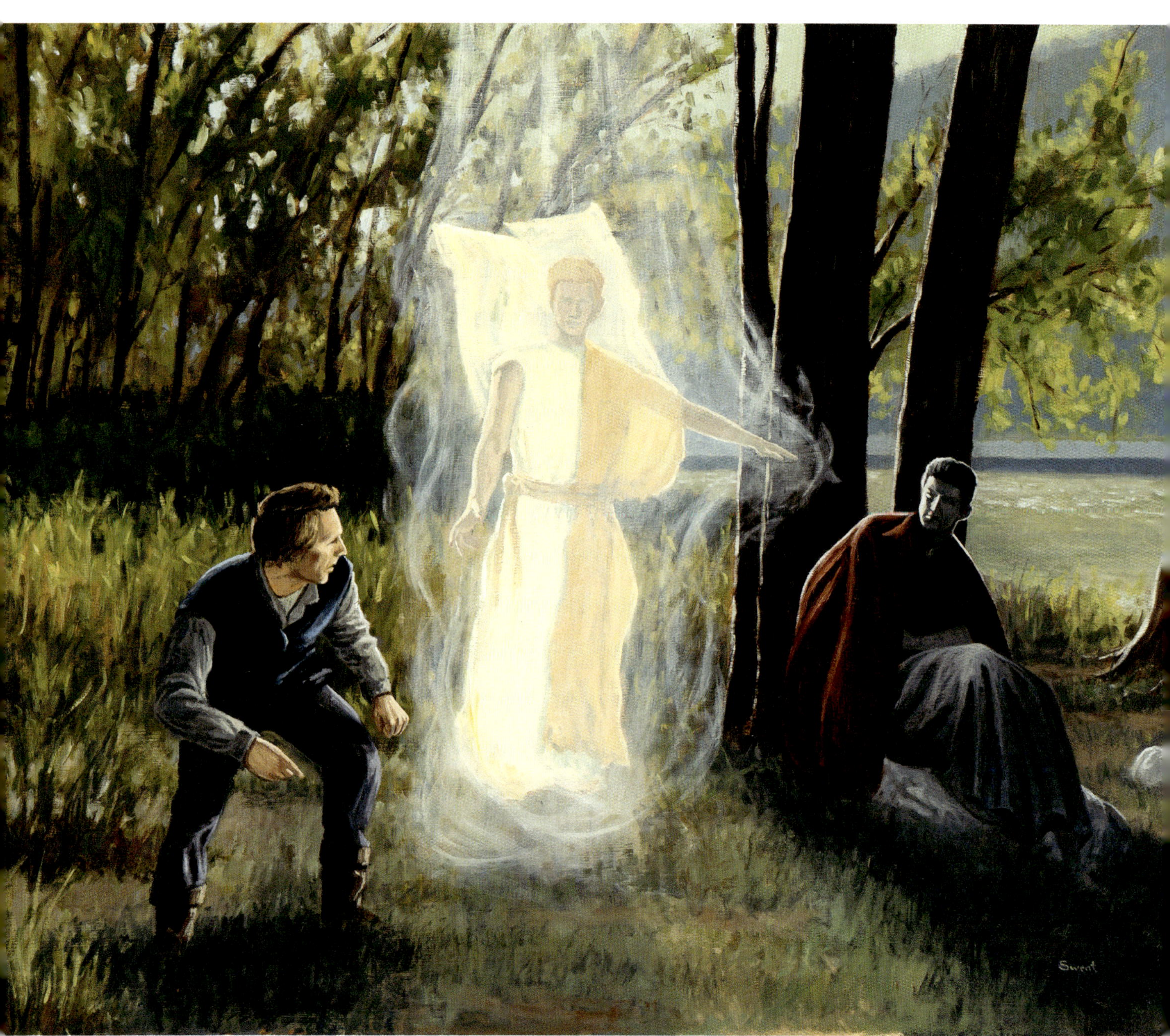

Michael Detecting the Devil (22" x 28", oil on board, 2016)

MICHAEL DETECTING THE DEVIL

Timeline: circa December 1827–January 1831

Related Doctrine and Covenants Sections: 128–29

A BACKGROUND

At some point when Joseph Smith lived in Harmony (December 1827–January 1831), a foundational but sometimes overlooked event took place near the Susquehanna River. Satan appeared to the Prophet, disguised as an angel of light, apparently trying to deceive Joseph. Another angel, Michael (or Adam), appeared to aid Joseph Smith by exposing the devil disguised as a false messenger of truth. Joseph Smith gives a small summary of this event in Doctrine and Covenants 128:20 when he wrote of angels who had ministered to him and mentions, "Michael on the banks of the Susquehanna, detect[ed] the devil when he appeared as an angel of light!"

Later sermons by Joseph Smith give deeper potential insight into this obscure scriptural summary. It seems Adam may somehow have given Joseph keys to detect true messengers of God from false ones. In 1839 Wilford Woodruff recorded in his journal a sermon that Joseph gave, drawing two small keys facing each other and writing:

> Joseph presented the following [key] to the Twelve. . . . In order to detect the devel when he transforms himself nigh unto an angel of light. When an angel of God appears unto man face to face in personage & reaches out his hand unto the man <& he> takes hold of the angels hand & feels a substance the same as one man would in Shaking hands with another he may then know that it is an angel of God. . . . But if a personage appears unto man & offers him his hand & the man takes hold of it & he feels nothing or does not sens any substance he may know it is the devel. . . . In keeping in mind these things we may detec[t] the devil that he decieved us not.[1]

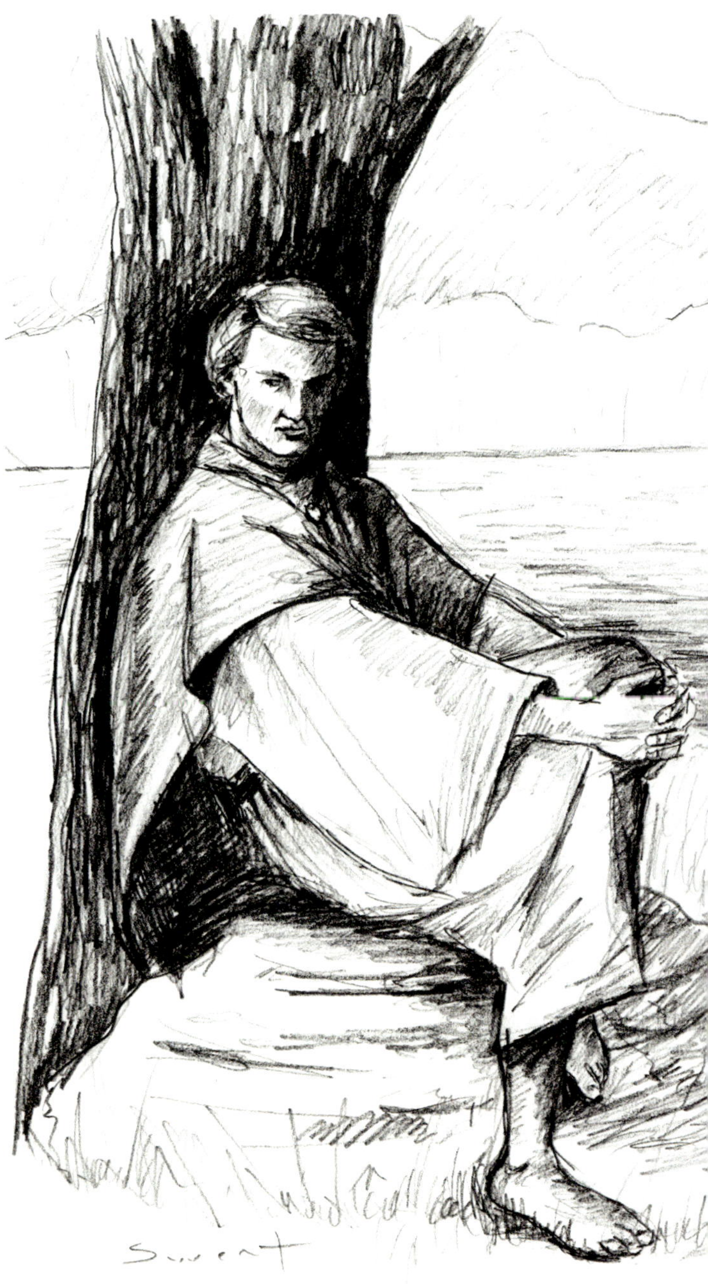

Related to this, in May 1842, Joseph Smith taught that there "are certain signs & words by which false spirits & personages may be detected from true.— which cannot be revealed to the Elders till the Temple is completed."[2] In his journal for 9 February 1843, Joseph recorded that he gave some instruction to Parley P. Pratt and others, saying, "An angel appears to you how will you prove him. ask him to shake hands. if he has flesh & bones—he is an Angel. . . . if David Patten [a recently martyred apostle] or the Devil came. how would you determi[n]e should you take hold of his hand you would not feel it. if it were a false administrtin he would not do it. true spirit will not give his hand the Devil will. 3 Keys."[3]

These teachings to Parley Pratt and others became the primary source material for Doctrine and Covenants 129 about "three grand keys by which the correct nature of ministering angels and spirits may be distinguished" (section heading). These "grand keys" (129:9) on distinguishing the devil and unrighteous spirits from angels and righteous spirits seem to relate back to Michael (Adam) on the banks of the Susquehanna and became part of the temple instructions Joseph gave in Nauvoo.

This dramatic, historically and theologically rich event simply had to be painted.

AN IMAGE

I envision this painting as the moment Satan is detected by Michael. The adversary sits over in a darkened area of the scene, shadowed by some trees, his pale color suggesting his lack of glory and eternal life. He sits, acquiescing to the glorified Michael, who points out the deception.

I painted Joseph hunched over—a little shocked and surprised at what has just transpired. I don't know to what extent Joseph believed Satan to be an angel of light or truth. I imagine the experience startled him, and I wanted his pose to suggest conflicted, deceived, and hesitant emotion.

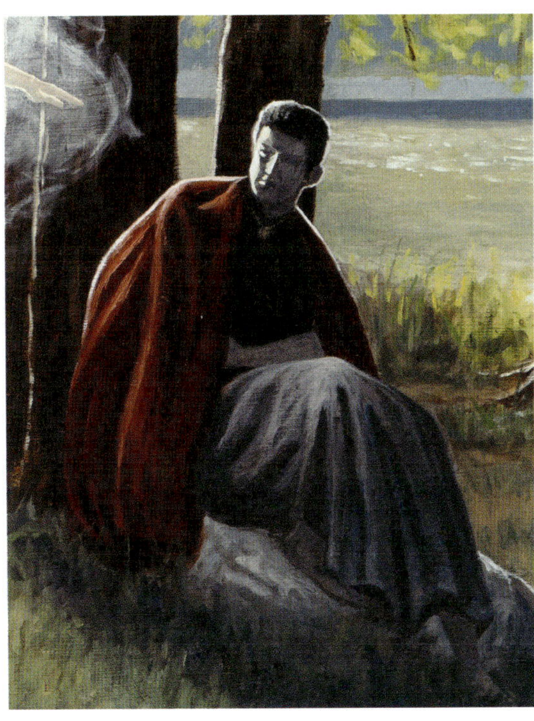

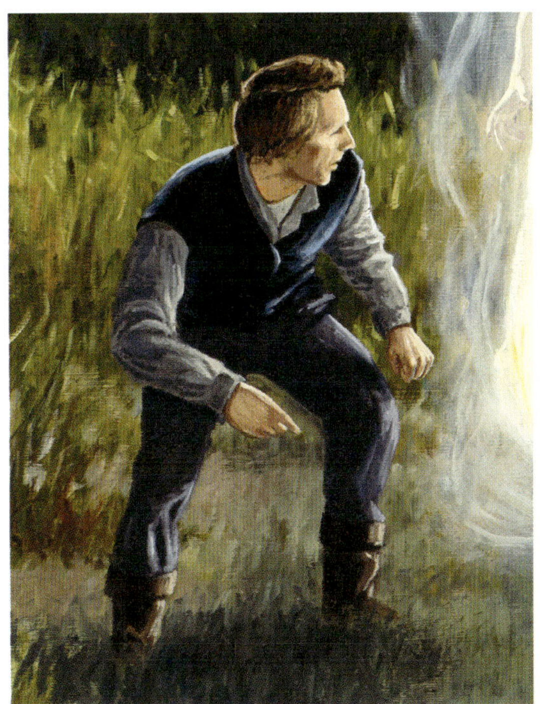

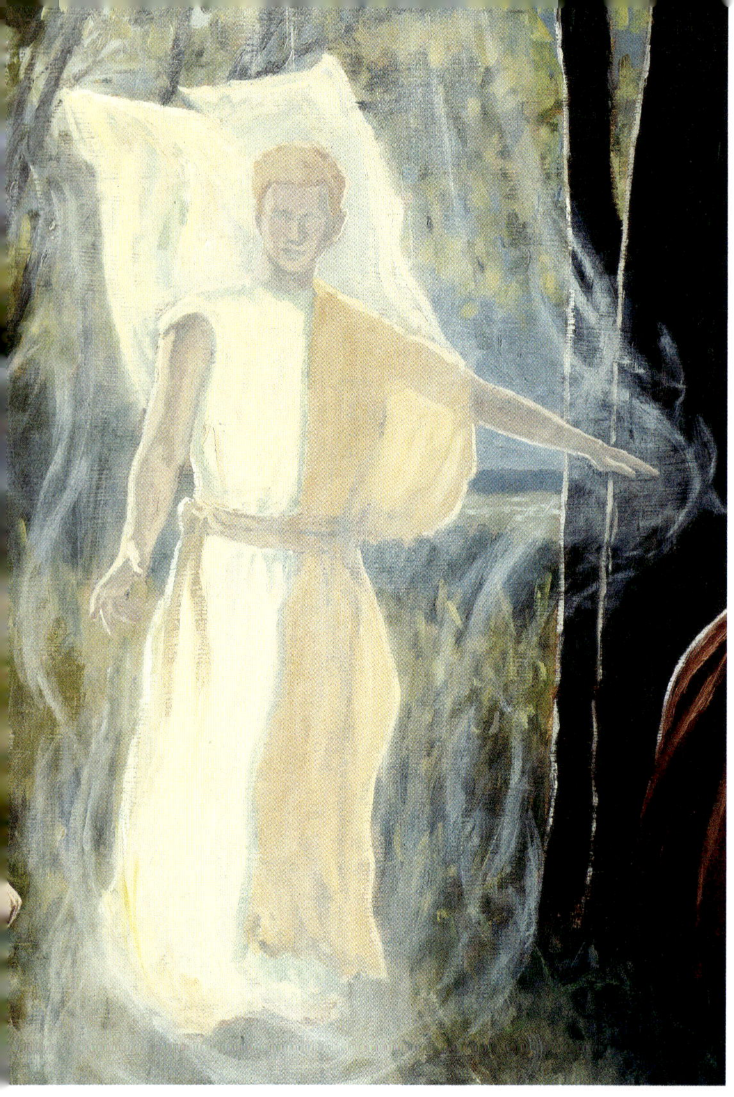

The painting deliberately places Michael in between Joseph and Satan, acting as a protector and delineator of truth. Michael's left hand outstretches in a manner to both accuse and cast Satan aside. Michael is surrounded with light and glory, his cape floating upward as though he has just descended from heaven. His right hand is extended to Joseph, the moment before he likely gives grand keys about shaking hands with angels and spirits in order to discern true messengers of God from false ones.

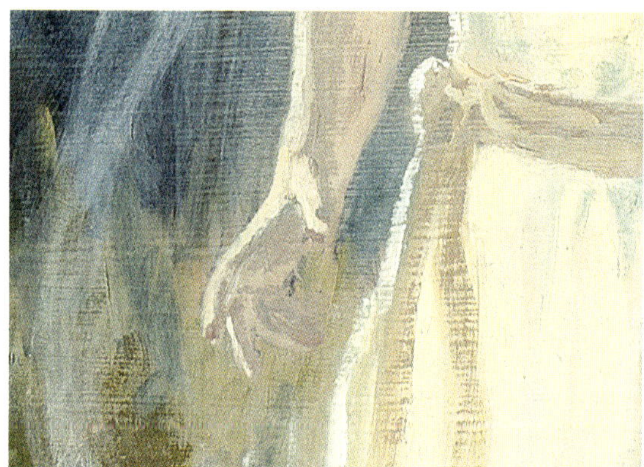

AN APPLICATION

These teachings from Michael (or Adam) to Joseph Smith can sometimes be hard to practically process and apply. Most of us do not have literal encounters with deceptive angels or actual heavenly ones from God. So, what do we make of these teachings, in practical terms? At minimum, it seems Joseph would expect us to at least seek interactions with celestial beings. While that may never happen, it isn't unrealistic. After all, the Aaronic Priesthood "holds the keys of the ministering of angels" (Doctrine and Covenants 13:1), and their ministering may not be as uncommon as we think. Elder Jeffrey R. Holland taught:

> Time in this setting does not allow even a cursory examination of the scriptures or our own latter-day history, which are so filled with accounts of angels ministering to those on earth, but it is rich doctrine and rich history indeed.
>
> Usually such beings are *not* seen. Sometimes they are. But seen or unseen they are *always* near.[4]

Indeed, angels are "round about you, to bear you up" (Doctrine and Covenants 84:88). One of the listed spiritual gifts that we can seek to expediently obtain in faith is "the beholding of angels and ministering spirits" (Moroni 10:14).

Second, if angels minister, then devils deceive. In one way or another, the adversary has sought and will seek to lead astray (Moses 4:4), even through supposed spiritual experiences (see Doctrine and Covenants 28:11; 50:3). Elder Gary E. Stevenson said, "In the same way that the adversary tried to deceive Moses [or Joseph Smith], he seeks to trick you. He has always pretended to be something that he is not. He always attempts to hide who he truly is."[5] Thus another spiritual gift that each of us must seek for and acquire is the gift of "the discerning of spirits" (46:23), or to be able to judge that which is of God and is not (see 50:17–25). Part of becoming endowed with the power of God in our everyday lives is to be able to clearly discern truth from error, right from wrong, and true servants of God from false ones. It is a test for every generation, not just for young Joseph Smith on the banks of the Susquehanna.

Part of becoming endowed with the power of God in our everyday lives is to be able to clearly discern truth from error, right from wrong, and true servants of God from false ones.

AN ANALYSIS

1 Certainly, the adversary is aware of the teachings in Doctrine and Covenants 129. What causes him to feel compelled to reach for someone's hand? Why can he not hold his ground like a true messenger? Is this a literal teaching of Joseph Smith or a symbolic one? Did Joseph always adhere to this rule, such as when an angel with a drawn sword appeared to him (see "An Angel with a Drawn Sword" in this book). How can we ensure we aren't deceived today and led astray from truth by devils disguised as angels of light?

2 What do you make of the line in Doctrine and Covenants 129: it is "contrary to the order of heaven for a just man to deceive" (129:7)? How do we balance deception and discretion? Why does deception sometimes cause more harm than blatant dishonesty? How can we better strive to be honest and avoid deception as we seek to become true servants of God?

3 Two of the listed spiritual gifts in scriptures are related to receiving the ministering of angels and the discerning of spirits. How can we be more open to and even seek for the ministering of angels, in appropriate ways? Why might it seem that angels ministered more to Saints of the past, yet not as often or as dramatically today? Is that true? Why or why not?

NOTES

1. "Discourse, 27 June 1839, as Reported by Wilford Woodruff-B," 85, The Joseph Smith Papers.
2. "Discourse, 1 May 1842, as Reported by Willard Richards," 94, The Joseph Smith Papers.
3. "Journal, December 1842–June 1844; Book 1, 21 December 1842–10 March 1843," 173–74, The Joseph Smith Papers.
4. Jeffrey R. Holland, "The Ministry of Angels," *Ensign*, November 2008, 29.
5. Gary E. Stevenson, "Deceive Me Not," *Ensign*, November 2019, 95.

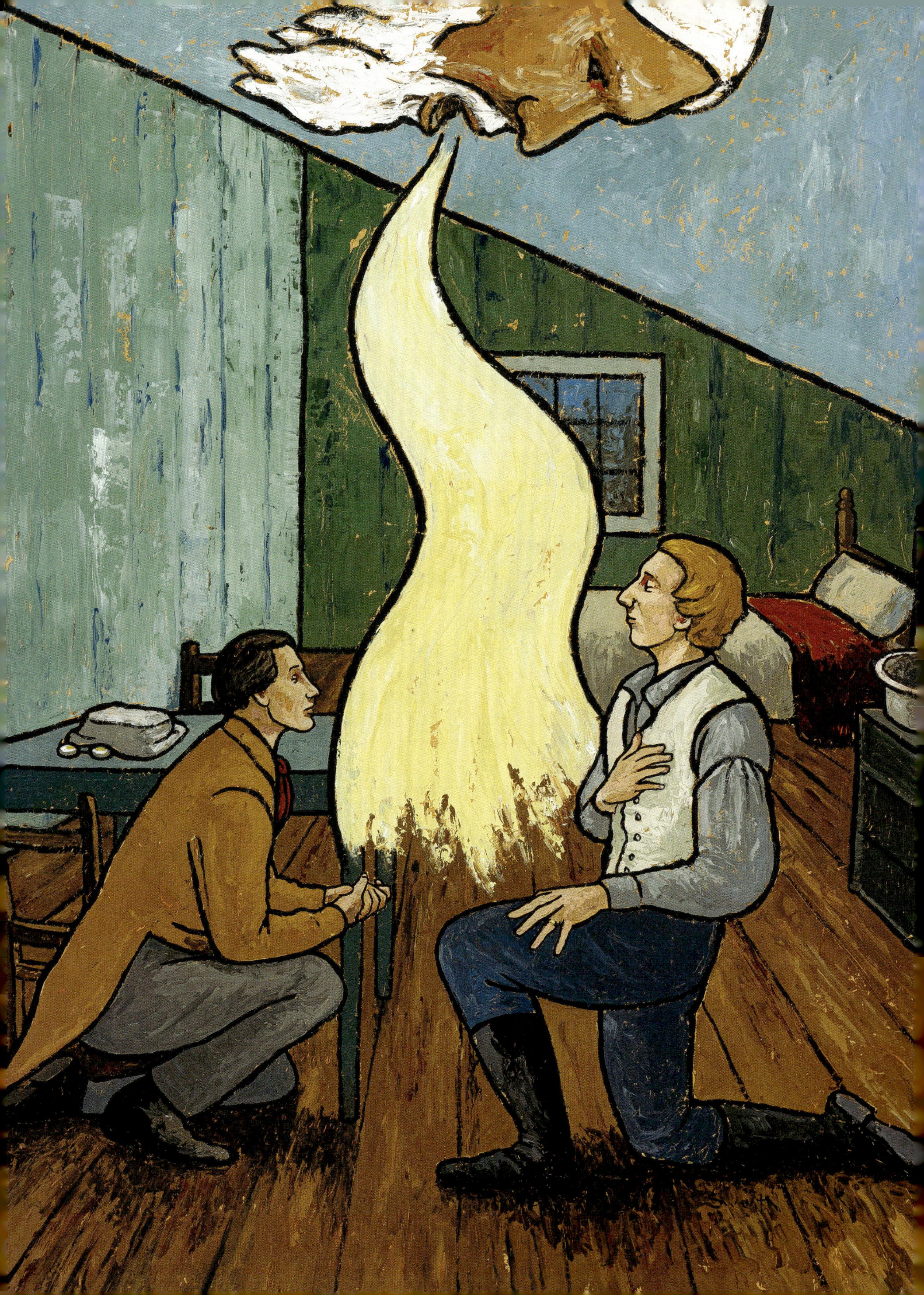

THE CHAMBER OF FATHER WHITMER

Timeline: Summer 1829

Related Doctrine and Covenants Section: 128

A BACKGROUND

Sometime in June 1829, Joseph Smith and Oliver Cowdery were wrapping up the translation of the Book of Mormon at the Peter and Mary Whitmer farm home in Fayette, New York. A month earlier in May 1829, back in Harmony, Pennsylvania, they had been visited by the angel John the Baptist, and a short time later (circa late May)[1] by the angels Peter, James, and John, who also gave Joseph and Oliver priesthood authority. John the Baptist conferred upon Joseph and Oliver "the keys of the ministering of angels, and of the gospel of repentance, and of baptism by immersion" (Doctrine and Covenants 13:1), and Peter, James, and John had given them the authority of the apostleship and to be "especial witnesses of my name, and bear the keys of your ministry" (27:12) and with it "the keys of [Christ's] kingdom, and a dispensation of the gospel for the last times" (27:13). After Joseph and Oliver were visited on 15 May 1829 by John the Baptist, they went to the Susquehanna River and baptized one another (see Joseph Smith—History 1:71). After Peter, James, and John visited them shortly thereafter, however, there is no record that Joseph Smith and Oliver Cowdery gave each other the gift of the Holy Ghost. When did they take this important step, and why? According to Joseph, it has to do with the voice of God speaking to them in the chamber of Peter Whitmer Sr.

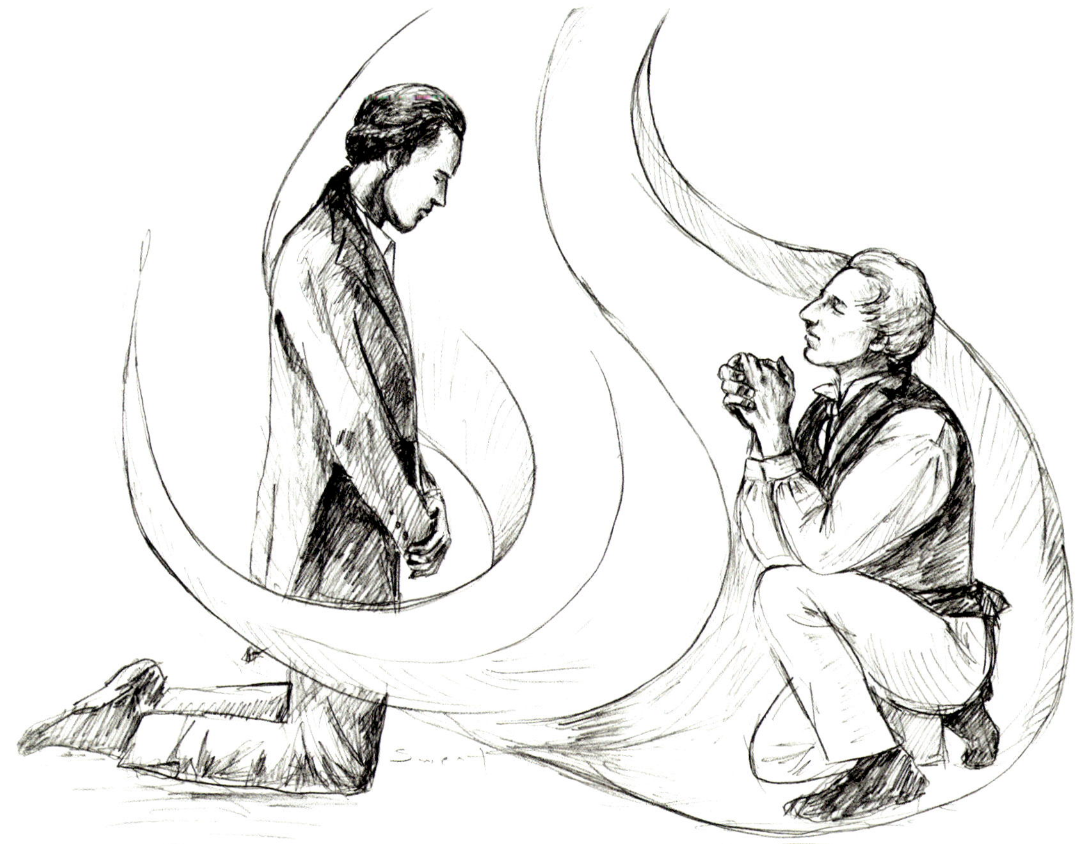

Joseph records that one day while they were in a bedroom at the Whitmer home as they continued to translate the Book of Mormon, they "became anxious to have that promise realized to [them], which the Angel that conferred upon [them] the Aaronick Priesthood had given [them], viz: that provided [they] continued faithful; [they] should also have the Melchesidec Priesthood, which holds the authority of the laying on of hands for the gift of the Holy Ghost." Although they had been baptized and received keys from Peter, James, and John, according to Joseph they had yet to receive the gift of the Holy Ghost. They decided to pray about it, and the Prophet said, "We had not long been engaged in solemn and fervent prayer, when the word of the Lord, came unto us in the Chamber, commanding us; that I should ordain Oliver Cowdery to be an Elder in the Church of Jesus Christ, and that he also should ordain me to the same office." Although they were confirmed as apostles, they apparently had not been set apart to the office of elder nor had they been authorized to lay on of hands to confer the Holy Ghost. Did they do it then, in the chamber, after the Lord spoke to them? No. Joseph's 1838–39 history says, "We were however commanded to defer this our ordination untill, such times, as it should be practicable to have our brethren, who had been and who should be baptized, assembled together, when we must have their sanction to our thus proceeding to ordain each other . . . and then attend to the laying on of hands for the gift of the Holy Ghost, upon all those whom we had previously baptized."[2] Accordingly, the Prophet and Oliver Cowdery were sustained as the first and second elders of the Church at its organization on 6 April 1830 and proceeded to ordain one another elders and then "laid [their] hands on each individual member of the Church present that they might receive the gift of the Holy Ghost, and be confirmed members of the Church of Christ."[3]

Although largely forgotten today, Joseph Smith considered his sacred experience in a bedroom of Peter Whitmer Sr.'s home an important part of the restoration of Latter-day Saint authority to confer the gift of the Holy Ghost. Joseph mentioned the experience in his official history, and in a now canonized letter, Doctrine and Covenants 128:21. Just after listing Peter, James, and John (128:20) Joseph writes of "the voice of God in the chamber of old Father Whitmer" (128:21), along with angels who gave Joseph authority.

Historical narratives are constructed by both official communications and informal conversations. Over time, certain aspects are emphasized and promoted while others become deemphasized and forgotten. I created this painting to give a visual representation to help us remember this sacred event that has hitherto been undepicted and often overlooked.[4]

AN IMAGE

As with many of the heavenly images in this series, I stylized and abstracted this event in my visual depiction. Abstraction has its benefits. It allows for the artist to be more interpretive, and the viewer usually embraces those interpretations better because it isn't depicted in a hyperrealistic painting that is often confused with historical reality. Abstracting this image works well because historians, theologians, scholars, and ecclesiastical Church leaders disagree about the meaning of what happened in the chamber of Father Whitmer, or they simply don't know. I felt a stylized, abstracted painting best fit this somewhat nebulous Church history event.

Looking at the painting, one notices the large, oversized head of God at the top of the composition. I made him proportionately huge to speak to his greatness and grandeur in comparison to the smaller, weaker mortals.

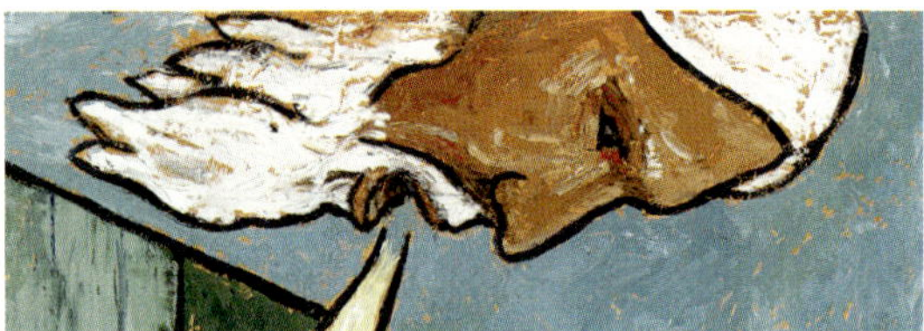

One aspect of this history that is unclear is what is meant by the "voice of the Lord." Does that mean this was a revelatory experience, a visionary one, or a physical visitation in the room? I don't know. Joseph also speaks of "the *voice* of Peter, James, and John" (Doctrine and Covenants 128:20; emphasis added) just before he mentions "the *voice* of God in the chamber of old Father Whitmer" (128:21; emphasis added). We know that Peter, James, and John physically visited Joseph Smith. Was this experience with God in the chamber the same? Perhaps, but maybe not. Thus a strong black line delineates the head of God in the blue (symbolizing heaven) with the paneled green walls of the bedroom.

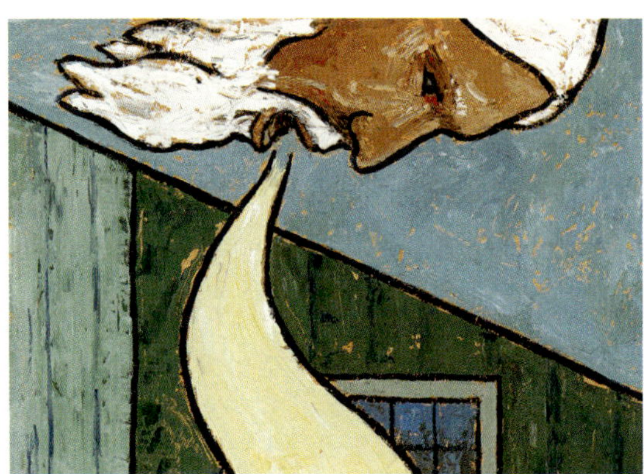

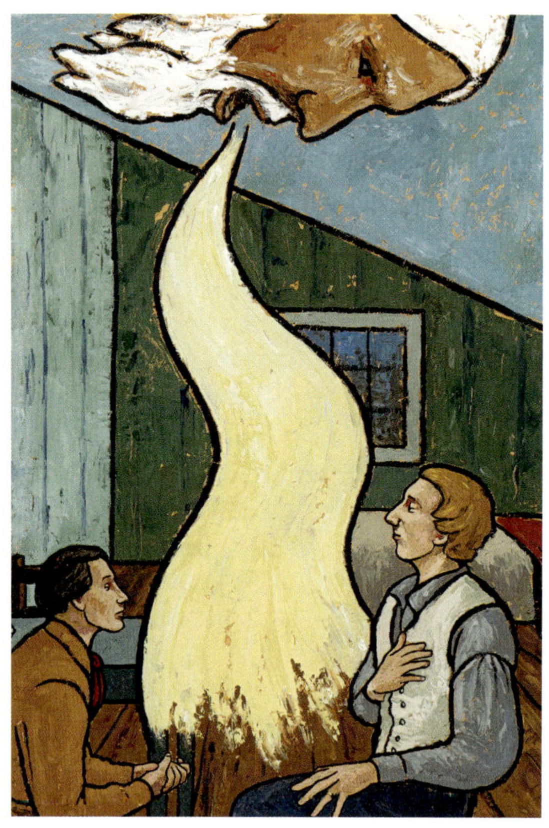

I chose to depict the "voice" as a flowing yellow shape coming down out of heaven. It creates a swirling motion as it enters the hearts of both Joseph and Oliver. They kneel, eyes closed, in the act of prayer. Oliver's clasped hands and Joseph's hand on his heart suggest their earnestness and heartfelt desire to obtain the gift of the Holy Ghost.

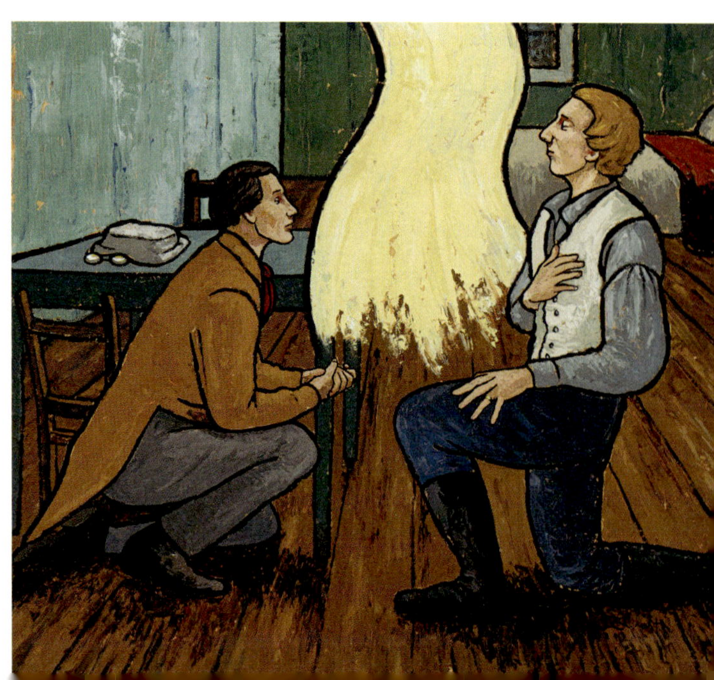

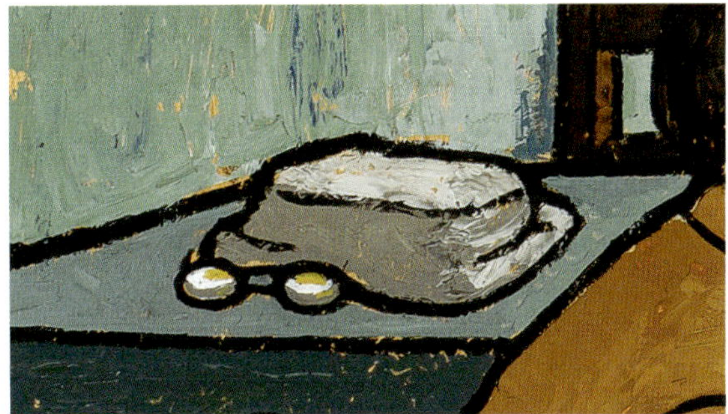

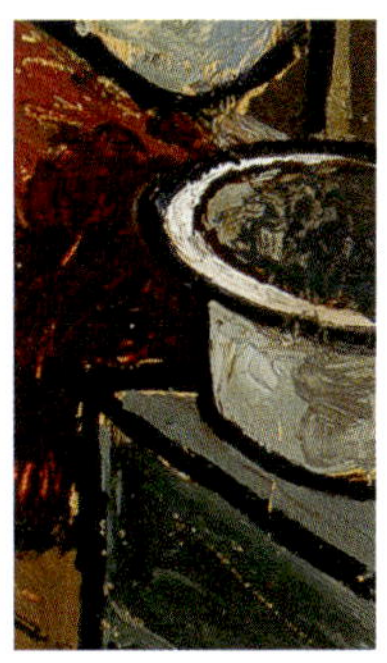

Because they are finishing the translation of the Book of Mormon, the plates lie on the table wrapped in a cloth, with the spectacles—or Urim and Thummim—on the table. On the opposite side sits Joseph's white top hat that he sometimes used in translating.

The compositional feel of this painting was inspired by Vincent Van Gogh's classic *Bedroom* paintings,[5] with the perspective lines of the floorboards, the bed, and hard-outlined dark paint around the main elements. Most the entirety of this painting is done with my palette knife. This forces me to stay a bit more abstract and painterly and less realistic, as Van Gogh often painted, which helps to create a mystical feel.

In my image I hope you connect with the idea of God speaking through the veil, his voice coming down like fire—representing the Holy Ghost—leading to Joseph and Oliver's prayerful hands, with the compositional lines leading the viewer upward to heaven and outward toward others.

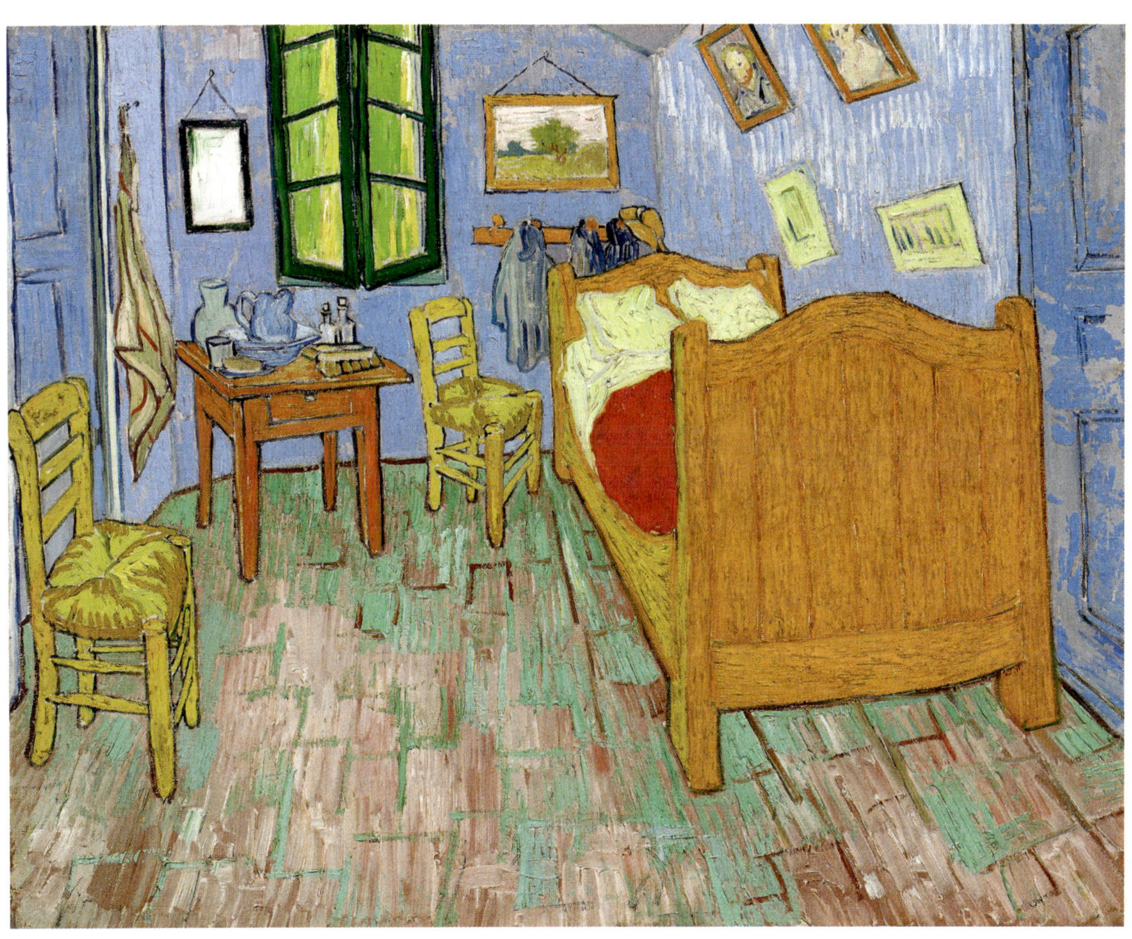

AN APPLICATION

In the Church we are accustomed to summarizing the restoration of the Melchizedek Priesthood by the visit of Peter, James, and John. The restoration of the Melchizedek Priesthood, however, is broader than this one single event. In an 1841 discourse, Joseph Smith taught, "All priesthood is Melchizedeck; but there are different portions or degrees of it."[6] *All priesthood is Melchizedek.* If we remember that all priesthood is Melchizedek, or part of the "Order of the Son of God" (Doctrine and Covenants 107:3), this helps us when we read seemingly contradictory statements, such as these by Joseph Smith:

- May 1829: "**Peter, James, and John, who held the keys of the priesthood of Melchisedeck.**"[7]
- June 1829: Chamber of Father Whitmer, "We now became anxious to have that promise realized to us, which the Angel that conferred upon us the Aaronick Priesthood had given us, viz: that provided we continued faithful; **we should also have the Melchesidec Priesthood**, which holds the authority of the laying on of hands for the gift of the Holy Ghost."[8]
- June 1831: Joseph wrote, "**~~The authority of the melechisedec~~ <priesthood> ~~was manifested and~~ <I> conferred, <the high priesthood> for the first time**, upon several of the elders."[9]

Each of these different events was part of the restoration of the Melchizedek Priesthood, or restoring the Order of the Son of God. Mark L. Staker and Curtis Ashton summarized, "While the Melchizedek Priesthood was restored at the time Peter, James and John laid their hands on Joseph and Oliver, a process of further understanding and even committal of priesthood keys unfolded at more distant places over a longer period of time. . . . Historical documents make clear that after Peter, James, and John restored the Melchizedek Priesthood near Harmony, additional understanding and keys were revealed and committed to Joseph."[10] The restoration of the Melchizedek Priesthood also includes Moses, Elijah, and Elias (see Doctrine and Covenants 110) as well as Gabriel, Rafael, and Michael, along with "divers angels, from Michael or Adam down to the present time, all declaring their dispensation, their rights, their keys, their honors, their majesty and glory, and the power of their priesthood" (128:21).

It may be more accurate to say that Peter, James, and John restored the keys of the kingdom of God or that they restored the Melchizedek Priesthood, rather than inferring that the Melchizedek Priesthood was completely restored by them. The restoration of the Order of the Son of God was a gradual process over time involving several events. Throughout his entire life, Joseph Smith continued to grow in his understanding of the priesthood, and he continued to receive and restore priesthood power and authority, culminating in the ordinances found in the holy temple. From the reception of the Holy Ghost through the sealing in the holy temple, each of us is being restored line upon line to the holy Order of the Son of God, or Melchizedek's priesthood.

"All priesthood is Melchizedeck; but there are different portions or degrees of it."

AN ANALYSIS

1 Why don't we discuss the chamber of Father Whitmer as part of our standard priesthood narrative in the Church? Why does the discussion center only on John the Baptist; Peter, James, and John; and the Lord, Moses, Elias, and Elijah? If Joseph Smith included it, why and when did this event get left out? Should it be reintroduced? What does this event say about how historical narratives are constructed? How can this concept help us become more comfortable with some shifting narratives about our own Church history? How is this very book and painting project attempting to do that? Should it?

2 When we trace a typical priesthood line of authority for a man to be an elder, in the Church we commonly tie that authority back to the keys of authority given by Peter, James, and John. If that is true, how do we square the typical Peter, James, and John narrative with what may have happened in the chamber of Father Whitmer? What does it mean that Peter, James, and John conferred the "keys of the kingdom" (Doctrine and Covenants 128:20) upon Joseph and Oliver? Is it possible that Joseph and Oliver held all the keys of authority from Peter, James, and John but had to be authorized by subsequent revelations and heavenly visitations to exercise all these keys (such as by the Lord in the chamber of Father Whitmer and later by the Lord, Moses, Elias, and Elijah)? Is that how Joseph Smith explained it? How would you explain it?

3 Were Joseph and Oliver ordained as apostles before they were ordained as elders? If so, why did they need to wait to become elders by vote of the Church at its organization but not to become apostles? If they were already apostles, couldn't they have conferred the Holy Ghost? If they weren't ordained apostles by Peter, James, and John, when were they ordained as such?

NOTES

1. See Larry C. Porter, "Dating the Melchizedek Priesthood," *Ensign*, June 1979, 5–10.
2. "History, circa June 1839–circa 1841 [Draft 2]," 26–27, The Joseph Smith Papers.
3. "History, 1838–1856, volume A-1 [23 December 1805–30 August 1834]," 37, The Joseph Smith Papers.
4. Credit to my colleague Michael Hubbard MacKay for his insights related to this subject. See his forthcoming article "The Chamber of Father Whitmer: Exploring the Restoration of the Melchizedek Priesthood as a Process in Joseph Smith's History," slated for publication in *BYU Studies Quarterly* 59, no. 4 (2020).
5. For a good summary and view of Van Gogh's *Bedroom* paintings, see "Van Gogh's Bedrooms," About the Paintings, Art Institute of Chicago (online).
6. "Account of Meeting and Discourse, 5 January 1841, as Reported by William Clayton," 5, The Joseph Smith Papers.
7. "History, 1838–1856, volume A-1 [23 December 1805–30 August 1834]," 18; emphasis added.
8. "History, 1838–1856, volume A-1 [23 December 1805–30 August 1834]," 26–27; emphasis added.
9. "History, 1838–1856, volume A-1 [23 December 1805–30 August 1834]," 118; emphasis added.
10. Mark L. Staker and Curtis Ashton, "Where Was the Priesthood Restored?," history.churchofjesuschrist.org, updated 25 February 2019.

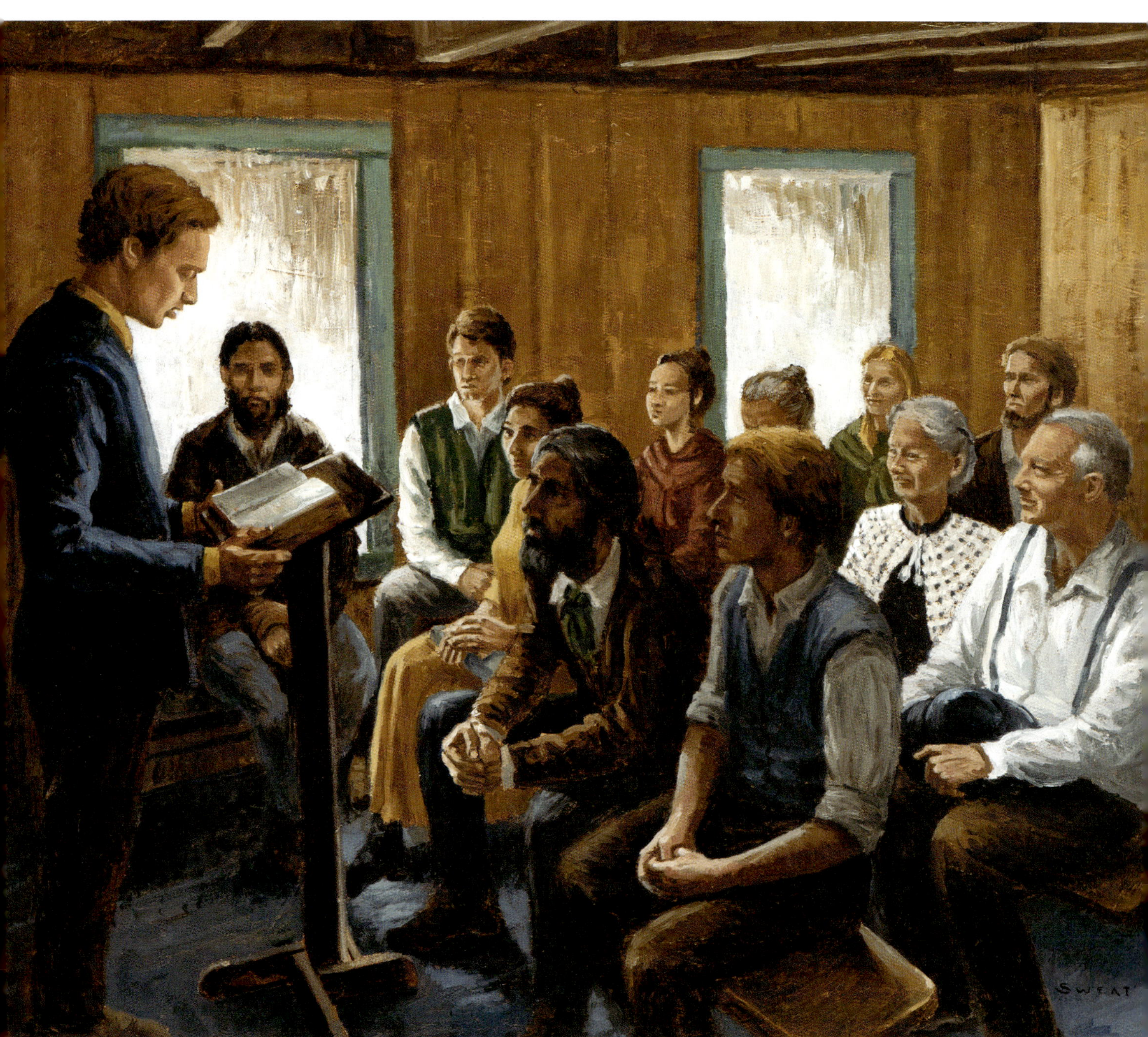

First to Be Faithful: The Colesville Branch (16" x 20", oil on board, 2019)

FIRST TO BE FAITHFUL: THE COLESVILLE BRANCH

Timeline: Summer 1829–Summer 1831

Related Doctrine and Covenants Sections: 24, 26, 37, 38

A BACKGROUND

If you head north from Joseph Smith's home in Harmony, Pennsylvania, and follow the Susquehanna River, in about twenty-two miles you arrive in Colesville (modern Nineveh), New York. Near Colesville lived two early supporters of Joseph Smith: Josiah Stowell and Joseph Knight Sr. Joseph Smith had become acquainted with these families when he was employed by Josiah Stowell and came to Harmony to search for a purported lost silver mine (see "The Harmony Treasure Searcher"). Intermittently staying and working with both families, Joseph Smith formed close friendships with them and some of their children, such as Joseph Knight's sons Joseph Jr. and Newel Knight.[1] The Stowells and Knights became some of the earliest supporters of Joseph's prophetic mission and the translation of the Book of Mormon. Both Joseph Knight and Josiah Stowell traveled up to Manchester, New York, and were in the Smith home on the night that Joseph received the Book of Mormon plates from the angel Moroni.[2] When Joseph began translating in Harmony, Joseph Knight Sr. provided temporal assistance. He recalled, "I Bought

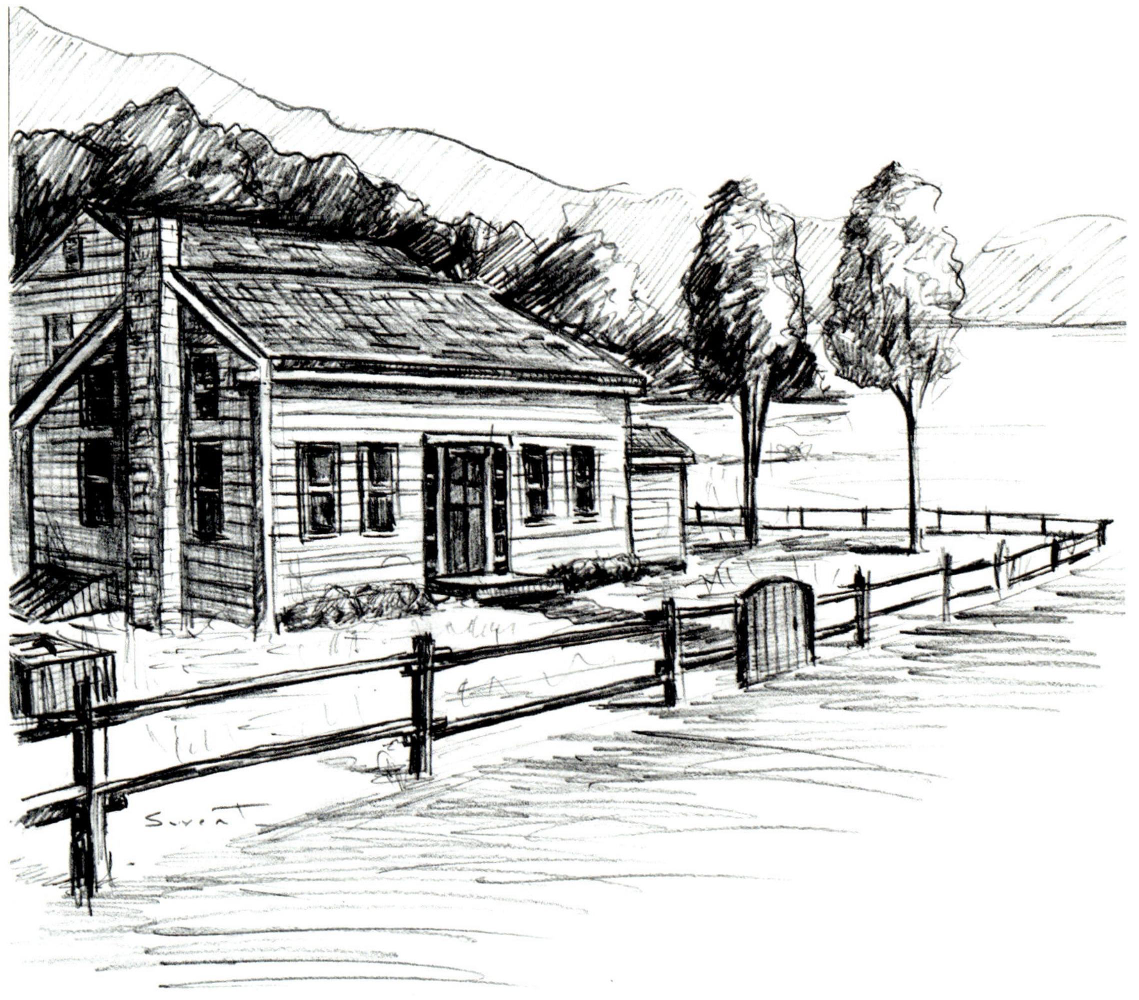

a Barral of Mackrel and some lined paper for writing. And when I Came home I Bought some nine or ten Bushels of grain and five or six Bushels taters [potatoes] and a pound of tea, and I went Down to see him and they ware in want. . . . Then they went to work and had provisions enough to Last till the translation was Done."[3]

Perhaps the first miracle ever performed in the Church was the healing of Newel Knight. One day Newel was possessed by some sort of evil spirit and "acted upon in a very strange manner. . . . He was caught up off the floor of the apartment and tossed about most fearfully." Joseph "rebuked the devil, and commanded him in the name of Jesus Christ to depart from [Newel Knight]." Newel immediately had a vision and said that the Spirit of the Lord "caught me up off the floor, and that my shoulder and head were pressing against the beams." Joseph said, "As may be expected, such a scene as this contributed much to make believers of those who witnessed it, and finally, the greater part of them became members of the Church."[4]

In June 1830 the "Knight family members and some of their neighbors were among the first to join the Church in 1830. Later that year they became the nucleus of one of the first (if not the first) branches organized in the Church," including the "Pecks, DeMilles, Stringhams, Culvers, Slades, Badgers, Hineses, and Carters."[5] The Colesville Saints are likely the first recognized unit of the Church in its history, with around sixty members (roughly half the Church membership at that time). Hyrum Smith came and lived with Newel Knight and presided over the Colesville branch for a few months in the fall of 1830.[6] After he left, Newel Knight presided over the branch.[7] These faithful Saints' time in Colesville, however, was about to come to an end.

Joseph wrote a letter to the Colesville branch on 2 December 1830. In it, he told them of "perilous times" in the world and prophesied that "the time is soon at hand that we shall have to flee whithersoever the Lord will, for safety. . . . And all those who obey his commandments are his elect, and he will soon gather them from the four winds of heaven, from one quarter of the earth to the other, to a place whithersoever he will."[8]

That same month, in December 1830, Joseph Smith received a revelation near Fayette, New York, telling the church to "assemble together at the Ohio" (Doctrine and Covenants 37:3), where a large number of converts had been baptized in the vicinity of Kirtland, Ohio. The revelation told Joseph not to leave to Ohio until he had "strengthened up the church whithersoever it is found, and more especially in Colesville; for, behold, they pray unto me in much faith" (37:2).

Joseph called for a conference to be held in Fayette to discuss the gathering. Newel Knight wrote on 1 January 1831, "A new year is now opening upon us. Who can tell the results of the present year. Tomorrow commences the third ~~year~~ Conference held by the Church of Jesus Christ in this dispensation." At this conference on 2 January, Joseph Smith received Doctrine and Covenants 38, giving the Church in New York and Pennsylvania the "commandment that ye should go to the Ohio" (38:32). Newel wrote in his journal, "Having returned from Conference, in obedience to the commandment which had been given, I togather with the Coalesville branch began to make preparations to go to Ohio. . . . As might be expected we wer obliged to make great sacrifices of our property. The most of my time was occupied visiting the Brethren and helping to arrange our affairs so that we might be ready to go in one Company and journey to gether from here to Ohio."[9]

Freeborn DeMill sold sixty-one acres, Aaron Culver sold one hundred acres, and Newel Knight sold sixty.[10] Joseph Knight Sr. put up his

Colesville farm for sale and left it with a lawyer-agent to dispose of after he vacated. A notice in the *Broome Republican* says: "The farm lately occupied by Joseph Knight, situate in the town of Colesville, near the Colesville Bridge—bounded on one side by the Susquehanna River, and containing about one hundred and forty two acres. On said Farm are two Dwelling Houses, a good Barn, and a fine Orchard. *The terms of sale will be liberal.*"[11]

Newel recorded, "Ha[v]eing made the best arrangements we could for the Journey, we bade adieu to all we had [h]eld dear on this earth, except the few who had embraced the gospel of the new and everlasting gospel as covenant as revealed through Joseph Smith Jr, together with the little of our earthly substance which we could take with us."[12]

By mid-April 1831, about sixty members from Colesville were on their way to Ohio to gather there with the Saints.[13] Historian Larry Porter wrote, "From the very inception of 'Mormonism,' the Saints comprising the Colesville Branch linked their lives inexorably with the Restored Gospel. . . . They relinquished family, friends, homes and material comforts in pursuit of their testimonies."[14] This little branch, likely the church's first organized "unit," are models of being first to be faithful. I wanted to paint an image to commemorate their place and example in Latter-day Saint history, which has hitherto been underdepicted visually.

AN IMAGE

This image represents members of the Colesville branch gathering for a meeting. The photograph I used for this image is from a picture I took in the restored Joseph Knight Sr. home in Colesville (Nineveh), New York while on a travel study with Brigham Young University students.

I see the person at the pulpit as Newel Knight, the Prophet's faithful friend who would preside over the branch after Hyrum Smith's departure and lead the group to gather to Ohio.

The book on the lectern is the Book of Mormon. I imagine Newel reading from its pages, perhaps about Lehi and his family leaving behind their precious belongings and home to gather where the Lord called them, something the Colesville Saints could readily relate to. I like to think of this scene as happening *after* they have received the call to gather to Ohio, and they are fortifying each other's faith in the difficult decision to go. A father and son, maybe Hezekiah Peck and his son, Reed Peck, sit in the foreground on benches. Hezekiah leans forward, contemplating the effects this decision will have.

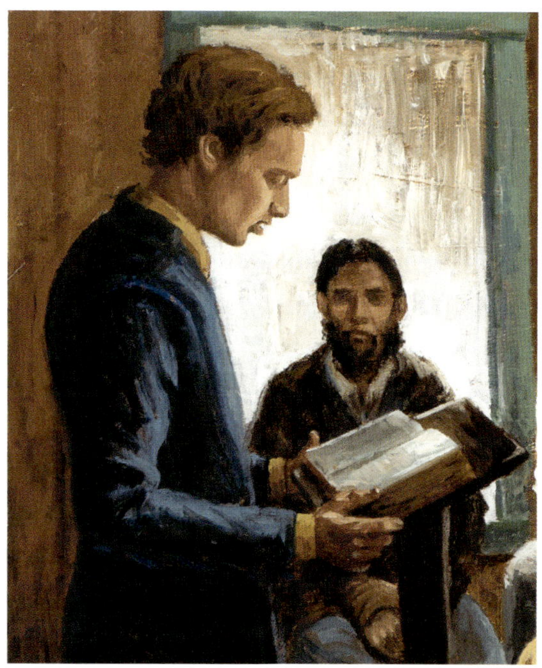

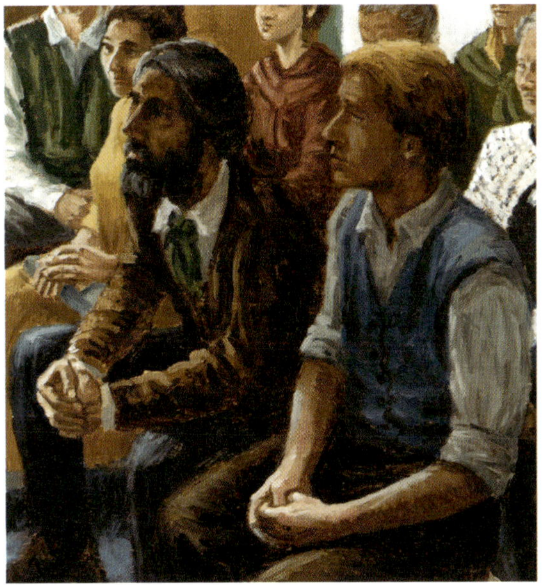

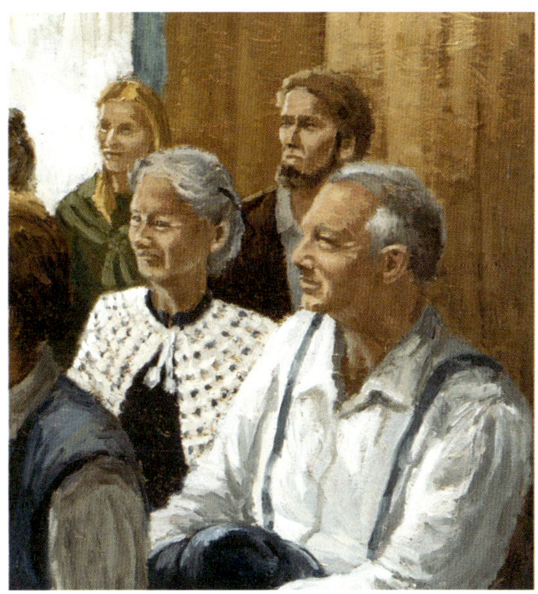

Young Reed Peck, who would have been about sixteen years old,[15] listens, understandably concerned and hesitant.

Joseph and Polly Knight sit toward the back of the scene and watch their son preside, firm in the light of their testimonies that will take them in their mature age from their comfortable home to unknown and faraway places, where they will eventually die. What faith!

Others from the Colesville branch, representing the DeMilles, Stringhams, Culvers, Slades, Badgers, Hineses, and Carters, listen on, ready and willing to follow the will of the Lord.

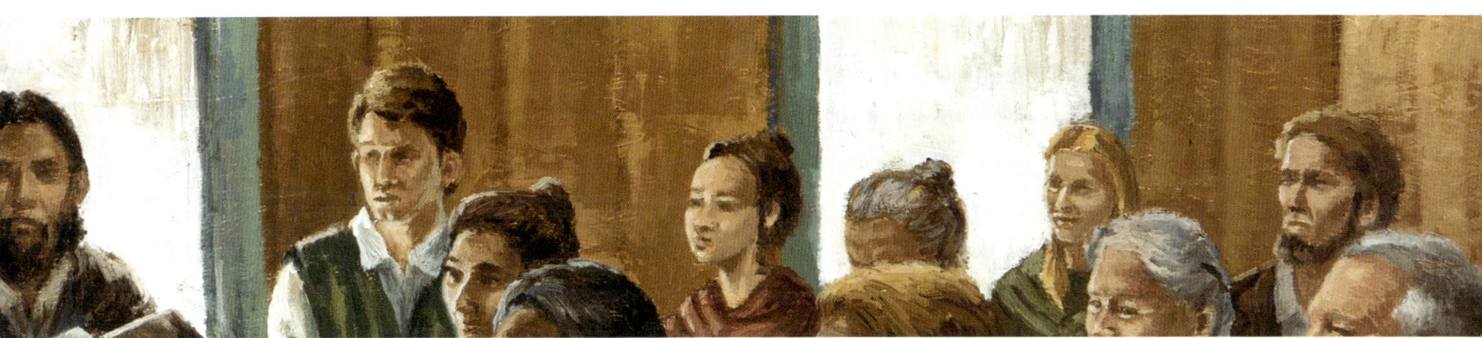

AN APPLICATION

I marvel at the faith of those, past and present, who are willing to leave all to follow the Lord. Peter, James, John, and Andrew. Lehi and Sariah and Ishmael with their families. I have also wondered at those of us who seem unable to do so. Why are we sometimes so possessive of possessions? The rich young ruler in the New Testament, who was so obedient, seemingly lacked the ability to give away his goods to the poor and follow Jesus, so "he went away sad, because he had great wealth" (Mark 10:22 New International Version). Although we often care too much about our earthly belongings, at times the Lord seems almost unconcerned about them. To the Colesville and other New York Saints who were called to gather to Ohio, the Lord somewhat tersely said, "And they that have farms that cannot be sold, *let them be left* or rented as seemeth them good" (Doctrine and Covenants 38:37; emphasis added). *Let them be left*, like they don't matter. At another time when the Saints were called together and some people were struggling to let go of their goods, the Lord asked, "What is property unto me?" (117:4), and then he asked why we "covet that which is but the drop, and neglect the more weighty matters?" (117:8).

I remember feeling monetarily conflicted when I felt directed by the Lord to become a full-time religious educator for the Church Educational System instead of pursuing a career in art or business. I was grateful and honored to be offered a full-time teaching position, but I was also worried about our family finances. Although the Church Educational System provides well enough for a modest middle-income lifestyle, you don't become a seminary teacher to be wealthy. After signing my contract, I remember talking with a coworker at my business job (which paid me nearly twice as much as the church contract I had just signed). I still remember where I was standing when I told him what I was going to do, and he said to me, "You are a fool." I wondered if he was right. Maybe I was a fool. I wasn't completely sure I was making the right decision. At that very moment, however, the Spirit brought a scripture to my mind with clarity and power. It whispered, "Beware of covetousness: for a man's life consisteth not in the abundance of the things which he possesseth" (Luke 12:15). It was almost like God was saying to me, "Are you willing to let go of the material to follow the spiritual?"

The issue is not about what we have. The issue is about what we are willing to let go of.

Don't misunderstand me. The Lord needs some wealthy Saints. The issue is not about what we have. The issue is about what we are willing to let go of. He needs all Saints to live the law of sacrifice and consecration. God needs all Saints to place him above possessions, to love the Lord more than we love our land. He desires us all to first follow prophets and not merely chase profits. "For what is a man profited, if he shall gain the whole world, and lose his own soul?" the Lord asks insightfully (Matthew 16:26). The Colesville Saints, rich and poor, understood and lived these priority principles about property and faithfully gave theirs up. May we each be willing to do the same today.

AN ANALYSIS

1 We are told to pray over our material and temporal concerns (see Alma 34:20), but we are also told to do things such as give possessions away, leave them behind, sell them off, and, as the

First Presidency has taught, to "pay [tithing] first, even when you think you do not have enough money to meet your other needs," promising us that "doing so will help you develop greater faith, overcome selfishness, and be more receptive to the Spirit."[16] Receiving temporal things can be a spiritual blessing, but being willing to give them away may be even more so. How have you been blessed by temporal sacrifice?

2 When calling them to gather to Ohio, the Lord reminded some of the New York Saints to "let every man esteem his brother as himself," and he repeated it for emphasis (Doctrine and Covenants 38:24–25). How can unconsciously equating money with success, wealth with capacity, and possessions with happiness negatively affect our ability to see each other as equals, be generous with our resources, and let go of material possessions? How do we refrain from buying into the "lie of the meritocracy"[17] so we can better build Zion?

3 Why is there strength in numbers and security in community? How can we, like the Colesville branch, help strengthen our local branches and wards, especially during difficulty? In our self-actualization age, how do we avoid retreating into individualism and effectively use the family and our Church congregations to help combat its cultural emphasis?

NOTES

1. See Dean C. Jessee, "Joseph Knight Sr.'s Recollection of Early Mormon History," *BYU Studies* 17, no. 1 (1976): 4. See also Larry C. Porter, "The Colesville Branch and the Coming Forth of the Book of Mormon," *BYU Studies* 10, no. 3 (1970): 3.
2. See Jessee, "Joseph Knight Sr.'s Recollection," 6.
3. Jessee, "Joseph Knight Sr.'s Recollection," 10.
4. "History, 1838–1856, volume A-1 [23 December 1805–30 August 1834]," 41, The Joseph Smith Papers.
5. Joseph F. Darowski, "The Journey of the Colesville Branch: D&C 26, 51, 54, 56, 59," in *Revelations in Context: The Stories behind Sections of the Doctrine and Covenants*, ed. Matthew McBride and James Goldberg (Salt Lake City: The Church of Jesus Christ of Latter-day Saints, 2016), 41.
6. See Michael Hubbard MacKay and William G. Hartley, *The Rise of the Latter-day Saints: The Journals and Histories of Newel Knight* (Provo, UT: Religious Studies Center, Brigham Young University; Salt Lake City: Deseret Book, 2019), 23–24.
7. See "Knight, Newel," People, The Joseph Smith Papers.
8. MacKay and Hartley, *Rise of the Latter-day Saints*, 27–28.
9. MacKay and Hartley, *Rise of the Latter-day Saints*, 32.
10. See Porter, "Colesville Branch," 10.
11. *Broome Republican*, 5 May 1831, as quoted in Larry C. Porter, "A Study of the Origins of The Church of Jesus Christ of Latter-day Saints in the States of New York and Pennsylvania, 1816–1831" (PhD diss., Brigham Young University, 1971), 298–99; emphasis added.
12. MacKay and Hartley, *Rise of the Latter-day Saints*, 32.
13. See *Our Heritage: A Brief History of The Church of Jesus Christ of Latter-day Saints* (Salt Lake City: The Church of Jesus Christ of Latter-day Saints, 1996), 18, which puts the number at sixty-eight. See also "John Whitmer, History, 1831–circa 1847," 31, The Joseph Smith Papers, which puts it around sixty: "Br Joseph Smith Jr. and Sidney Rigdon, in company with eight other elders, with the church from Colesville New York, consisting of about sixty souls, arivd in the month of July."
14. Porter, "Colesville Branch," 13.
15. Reed Peck was born circa 1814. See "Peck, Reed," People, The Joseph Smith Papers.
16. "Tithes and Offerings," in *For the Strength of Youth* (Salt Lake City: The Church of Jesus Christ of Latter-day Saints, 2011), 38.
17. David Brooks, "Finding the Road to Character" (Brigham Young University forum address on 22 October 2019), BYU Speeches.

PART TWO

OHIO AND MISSOURI

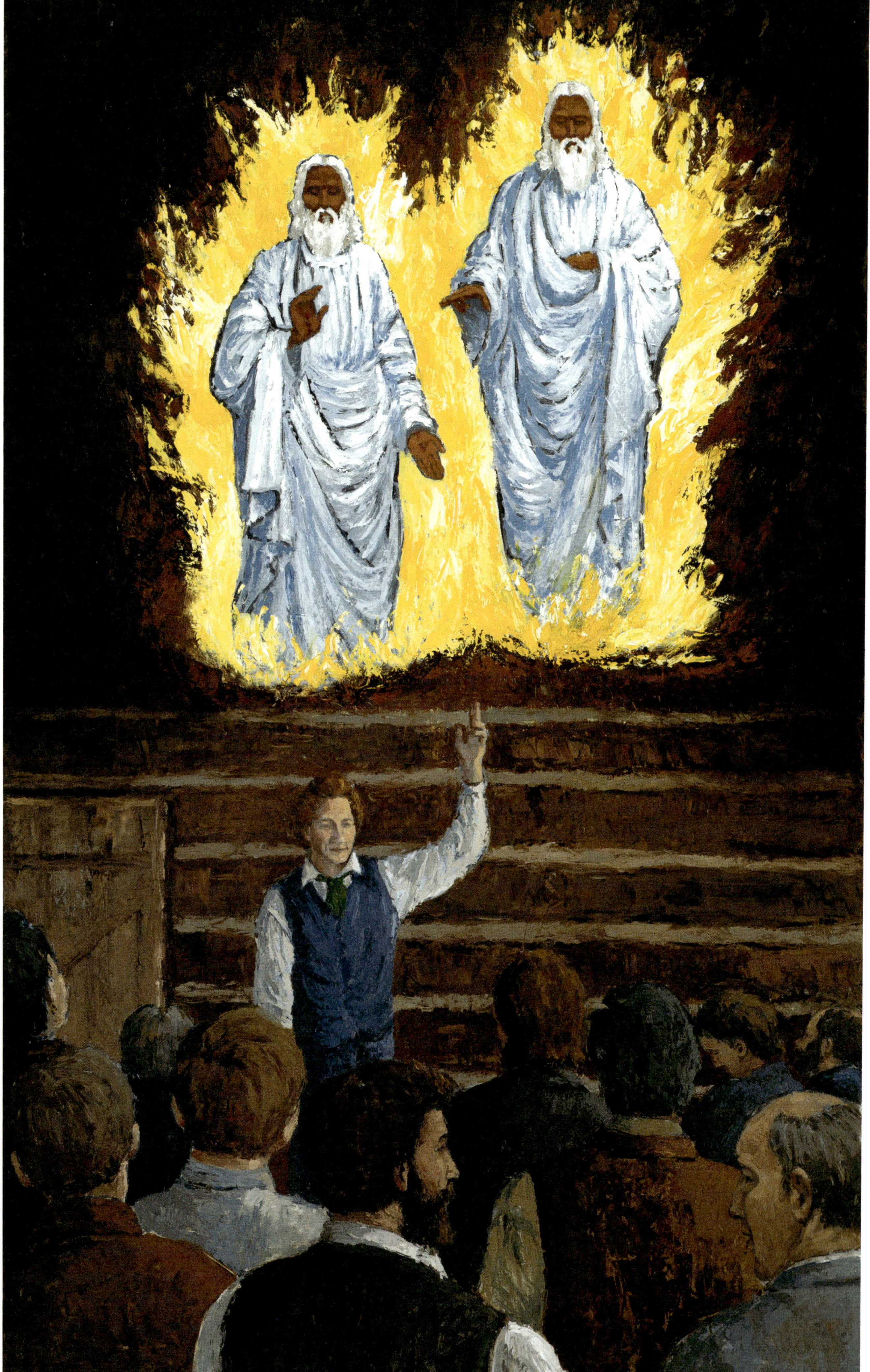

Endowment at the June 1831 Conference (48" x 30", oil on board, 2019)

ENDOWMENT AT THE JUNE 1831 CONFERENCE

Timeline: January–November 1831

Related Doctrine and Covenants Sections: 38, 44, 67

A BACKGROUND

The first "endowment" of this dispensation did not take place in the Red Brick Store in Nauvoo, nor the Kirtland Temple, nor the Newel K. Whitney Store with the School of the Prophets. Joseph Smith gave the first endowment of this dispensation in June 1831 at a little log schoolhouse on the Isaac Morley farm near Kirtland. Heeding the revealed call for the Church to gather to Ohio (see Doctrine and Covenants 37) and "that the elders of my church should be called together" (44:1), about sixty men[1] gathered for the June 1831 conference to receive an endowment of promised power. The Lord had commanded, "Ye should go to the Ohio; and there I will give unto you my law; and there you shall be endowed with power from on high" (38:32). John Corrill remembered in his history, "There was a revelation received, requiring the prophet to call the elders together, *that they might receive an endowment*. This was done, and the meeting took place some time in June."[2]

The word *endowment* is commonly defined today in the Church as a "gift,"[3] but importantly, the word *endowment* also means to receive a "capacity, power or ability."[4] At this June 1831 conference, the Lord was to give these faithful Saints some divine capacity, power, and ability, and to "pour out my Spirit upon them in the day that they assemble themselves together" (Doctrine and Covenants 44:2). Here Joseph ordained the first men in this dispensation to be high priests after the order of Melchizedek.[5] He promised them power with this high priestly ordination—power to perform miracles,[6] power to seal people up to eternal life,[7] power like Enoch or Melchizedek of old to "break mountains" and "divide the seas" and "put at defiance the armies of nations" (Joseph Smith Translation,

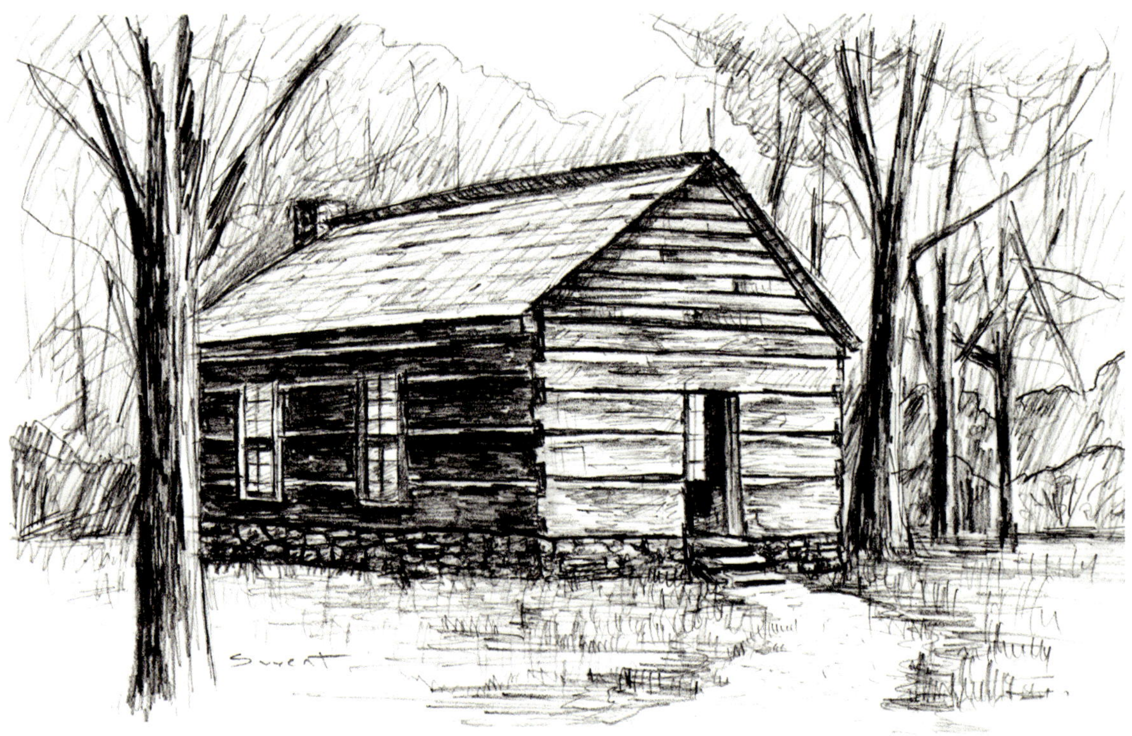

Genesis 14:30–31). John Corrill's later history connected this high priesthood power with the order of Melchizedek, recalling, "The Malchisedec [Melchizedek] priesthood was then for the first time introduced, and conferred on several of the elders. In this chiefly consisted the endowment—it being a new order—and bestowed authority."[8] This order of Melchizedek's priesthood was being "an high priest after the order of the covenant which God made with Enoch" (JST, Genesis 14:27), or "after the Order of the Son of God" (Doctrine and Covenants 107:3).

In addition, Joseph had learned through his translation of the Bible that high priests have the power "to stand in the presence of God" (JST, Genesis 14:31). If these new high priests could purify and sanctify themselves they—like the brother of Jared, Moses, Isaiah, Nephi, or Jacob—could have the power and ability to rend the veil and see God face-to-face (see Ether 3:6–15; Exodus 33:9–11; Isaiah 6:1–5; 2 Nephi 11:2–3). At the meeting, the Prophet Joseph was unusually moved upon by the Holy Ghost[9] and, experiencing a heavenly vision, said, "I now see God, and Jesus Christ on his right hand."[10] The Prophet turned to the men with him and prophesied boldly that "not three days should pass away, before some should see the Savior face to face."[11] Or, as Levi Hancock recollected, Joseph promised at this conference, "You shall see the Lord."[12] The men strove to realize this blessing, and some miraculously did. Lyman Wight, following his ordination to the high priesthood by Joseph Smith, prophesied and "saw the hevans opened, and the Son of man sitting on the right hand of the Father."[13] Harvey Whitlock reportedly "saw the heavens open and Jesus standing at the right hand of God the Father. This was the beginning in our day of ordinations to the office of a High Priest."[14]

But many of these frontier elders were not yet ready to be endowed with high priestly power nor to rend the veil and know the Lord. John Corrill recalled, "Some doubting took place among the elders, and considerable conversation was held on the subject. The elders not fairly understanding the nature of the endowments, it took some time to reconcile all their feelings."[15]

At the conference, an evil influence even overtook some. John Whitmer recalled, "While the Lord poured out his spirit, upon his servants, the Devil took occation, to make known his power, he bound Harvy Whitlock <and John Murdock> so that he could not speak and others were affected but the Lord showed to Joseph the Seer, the design of this thing, he commanded the devil in the name of Christ and he departed to our Joy and comfort."[16] Joseph related this exposing of the adversary at the June 1831 conference as revealing "~~the man of sin~~"[17] (see 2 Thessalonians 2:3)—the devil trying to thwart the potential endowment of high priestly power.

Joseph later summarized the entire June 1831 conference this way: "<I> conferred, <the high priesthood> for the first time, upon several of the elders. It was clearly evidint that the Lord gave us power. . . . Great harmony prevailed. Several were ordained; Faith was strengthened; and humility, so necessary for the blessing of God to follow prayer, characterized the saints."[18]

Although the conference was successful from Joseph and some others' perspectives, these newly ordained high priests yet had work to do to become more fully endowed with power. The Lord chastised some of them a few months later saying, "Ye should receive the blessing which was offered unto you," but "there were fears in your hearts," and "this is the reason that ye did not receive" (Doctrine and Covenants 67:3). He was likely referring to high priestly endowments of power. The Lord promised them anew that if they would strip themselves of their jealousies and fears, and humble themselves, "the veil shall be rent and you shall see me and know that I am" (67:10), and they would be able to "see and know that which was conferred upon you by the hands of my servant Joseph Smith" (67:14). Wanting them to receive these high priestly powers and blessings, Joseph asserted that "could we all come together with one heart and one mind in perfect faith the vail might as well be rent to day as next week or any other time." There was, however, still a need to first "cleanse ourselves and covenant before God, to serve him."[19] Joseph's efforts to endow the Saints with power would soon lead him to organize the School of the Prophets and build a holy temple.

AN IMAGE

Because the June 1831 conference was the first attempt to endow Saints with high priestly power, I wanted to paint an image to convey in one scene the experiences and ideas from this seminal moment in Church history. The interior is set in the log cabin on the Morley farm. The general composition of the painting is thin and vertical, trying to draw the viewer to look upward. Joseph stands in the center of the frame, his countenance a visionary white and almost transparent, smiling, directing the men in the room—and simultaneously the viewer—to look up to behold the Father and Son.

Above Joseph stand the Father and Son in radiant fire and glory. Notice how some of the flames almost create crowns above them.

The figures of the Father and Son are an homage to the way they were depicted in some early Latter-day Saint stained glass, in particular from the 1913 First Vision window in the Los Angeles Adams Ward building.

Notice the dark tones that are behind the

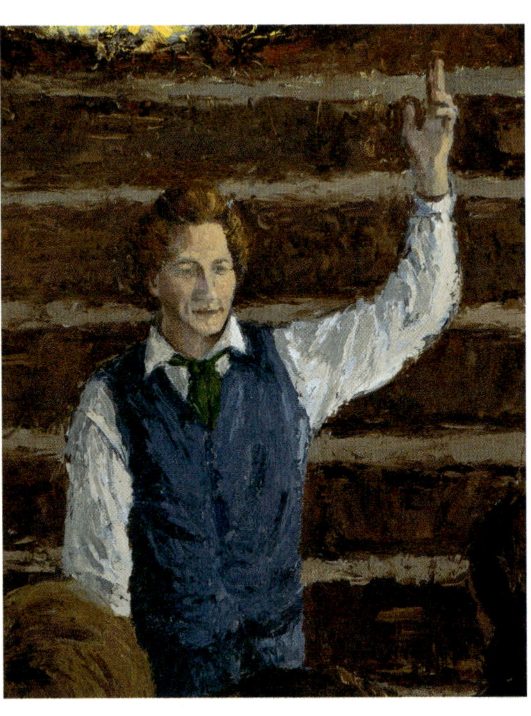

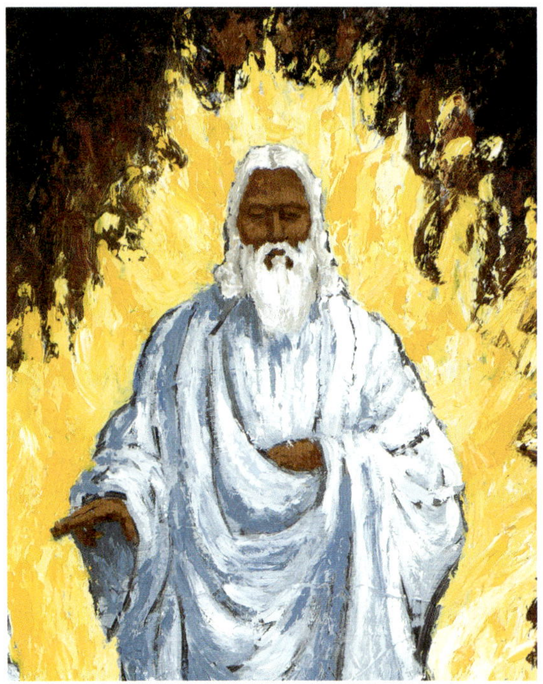

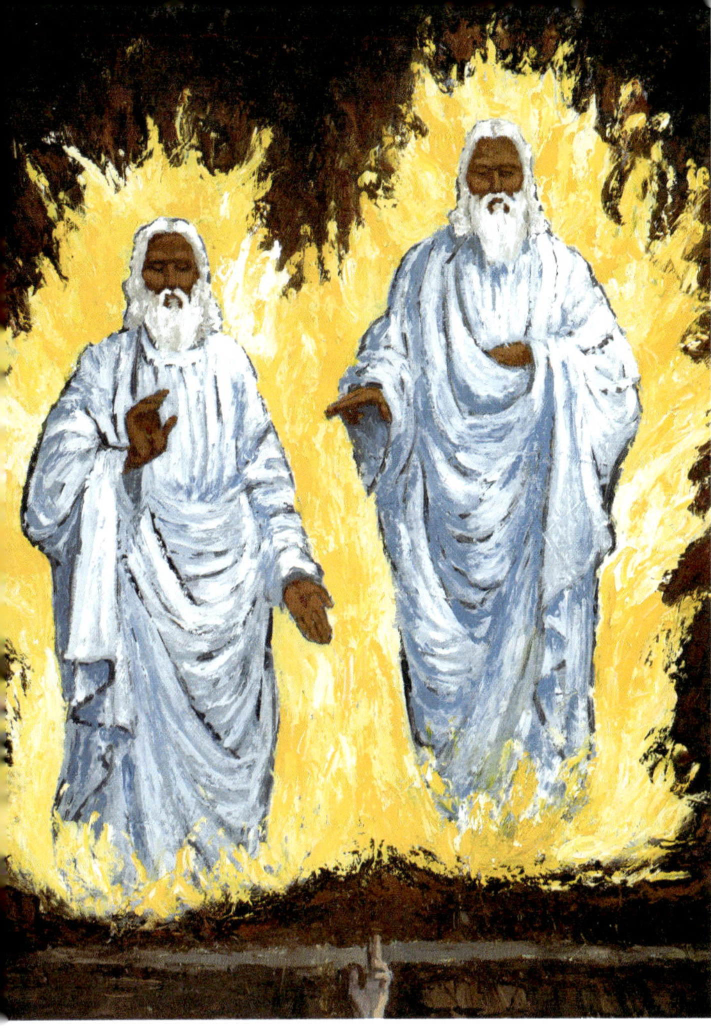

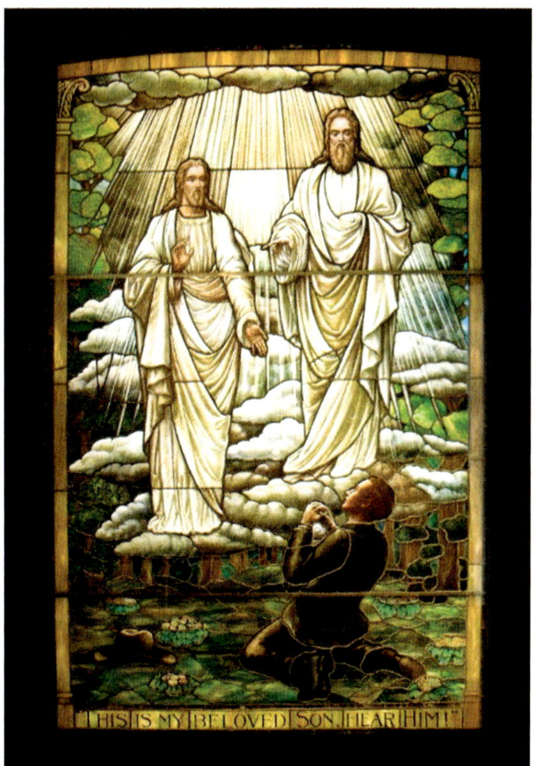

flames of the Father and Son. These symbolize how the dark, adversarial influence tries to thwart endowment and how the light and glory of God overpowers them.

Turning our attention to the men in the room, they represent the varied reactions to Joseph's teachings and promises of heavenly power. Some look upward and seem to see and experience, while others look downward and even slumber, failing to grasp what could be theirs. Yet others look at each other, doubting, reasoning, questioning, fearfully unable to reconcile their pride with divine promises.

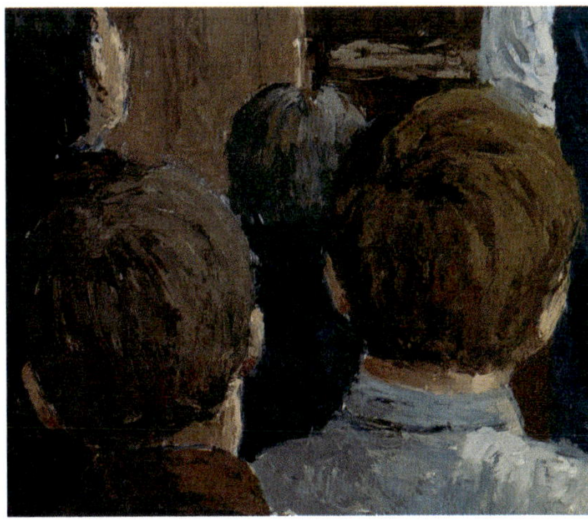

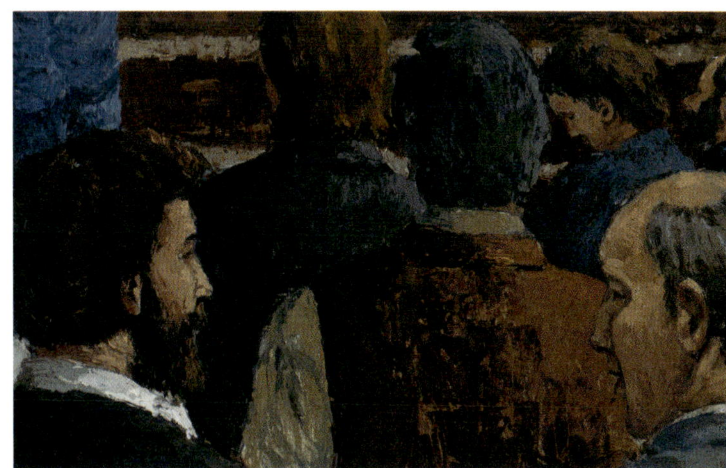

AN APPLICATION

Today in the Church when we think of "high priest," we often associate the term only with an ecclesiastical office. We think of stake presidency members and high councilmen and bishoprics. After the June 1831 conference Joseph began to make use of high priests to govern ecclesiastically (see Doctrine and Covenants 68:15, 19; 107:17). But let us also remember that the origins of high priesthood are theological, associated with investing and endowing people with power and authority of ancient high priests like Melchizedek and Enoch. It is an order of how one lives and communes with God and is related to "administering spiritual things," even "to have the privilege of receiving the mysteries of the kingdom of heaven, to have the heavens opened unto them, to commune with the general assembly and church of the Firstborn, and to enjoy the communion and presence of God the Father, and Jesus" (107:10, 19). Thus the June 1831 conference has two resulting divisions when we think of high priests—one an ecclesiastical, and the other a theological line.

Today, the administrative or ecclesiastical finds its fruition in Church government with General and local authorities being presiding high priests. The theological results of the June 1831 conference and the promised endowment of spiritual power see its fruition in the sacred temple endowment. Through sacred symbols and ceremonies, men and women are taught how to harness the power of God, learn his mysteries, part the veil and commune with him, and become high priests and priestesses.

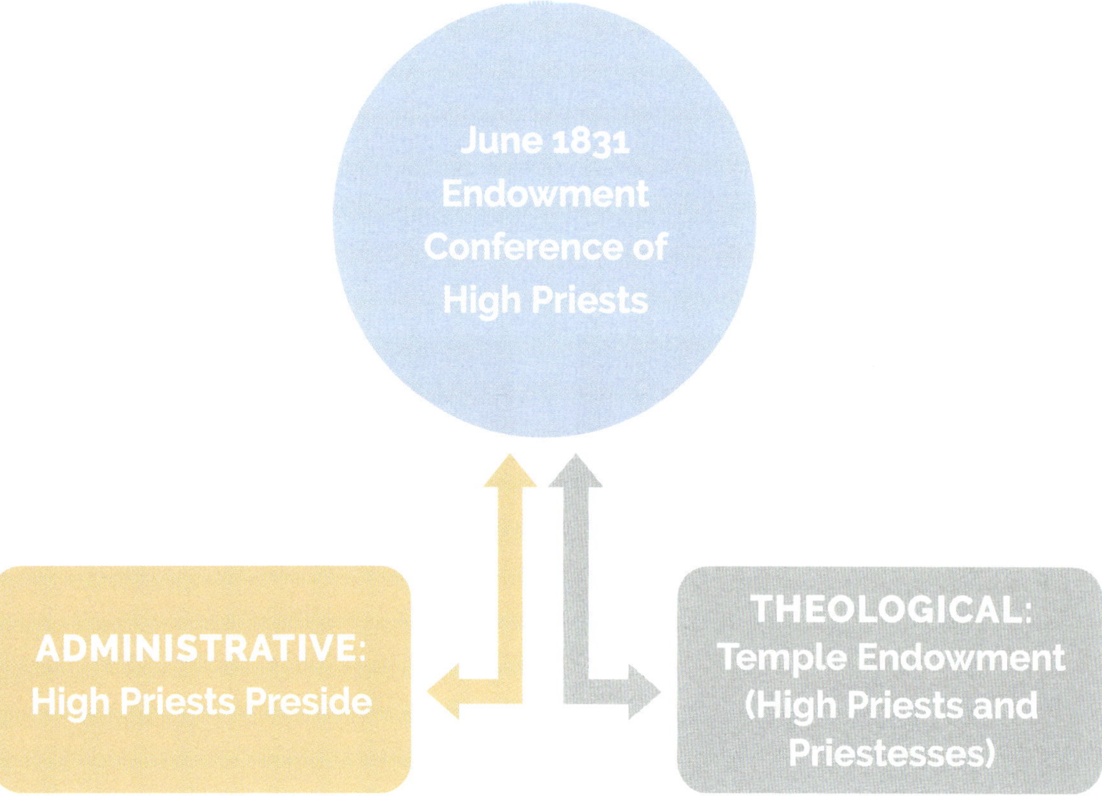

Great harmony prevailed. Several were ordained. Faith was strengthened.

Thus, in a way, today we are all part of the June 1831 conference. The same endowment of high priestly power is extended to you and me. Do we believe it? Do we grasp it? Do we experience it? Or do we doubt it, fear it, experience darkness because of it, slumber through it, or ignore it? This scene of the June 1831 conference could summarize the entire prophetic mission of Joseph Smith in microcosm: striving to endow a people to experience heavenly power and experiencing varied results from those who hear this invitation.

AN ANALYSIS

1 Read Alma 13 through the lens of the theological idea of being a high priest or priestess instead of viewing it only as a Church administrative or ecclesiastical function. What do you learn?

2 There are some today who push back against Joseph's 1831 promise for people to have the heavens opened to them and see God and commune with heaven. Although this promise to see God is repeated in scripture to the early Saints (see Doctrine and Covenants 67:10–13; 88:68; 93:1), some today feel that it doesn't apply or is overly zealous. Visions of Deity are too lofty, too grand, too much for nominal Saints—it's a purview and privilege reserved for prophets, not common people. In the August 1999 *Ensign*, however, President James E. Faust wrote a message called "Lost Horizons," saying: "I would surmise that all who are members of this great Church have a desire to see the face of the Savior. This is an available blessing [cites Doctrine and Covenants 93:1]. Too few of us catch sight of this horizon as we fail to avail ourselves of God's promises."[20] What do you think? Does it set us up for failure to strive for this promise? Is it realistically attainable? Is it a dangerous idea that plants a seedbed for deception and spiritual excess? Or are we losing horizons and living far beneath our privileges as potential high priests and priestesses?

3 How does our understanding that there is an order of priesthood patterned after Jesus—and later named after Melchizedek—potentially change or add to our view of what we think the "Melchizedek Priesthood" means? In 1831 Joseph Smith seems to associate the Melchizedek Priesthood with powerful experiences and manifestations, saying that at the June 1831 conference, "The authority of the Melechisedec priesthood was manifested and conferred, for the first time, upon several of the elders."[21] How do we become part of the Order of the Son of God and Melchizedek? How might this view inform discussions related to how women have priesthood, and become part of this order through the temple?

NOTES

1. The conference minutes list sixty-two attendees. See "Minutes, circa 3–4 June 1831," 3–4, The Joseph Smith Papers. John Corrill remembered it being "about fifty elders." See "John Corrill, *A Brief History of the Church of Christ of Latter Day Saints*, 1839," 18, The Joseph Smith Papers.
2. "John Corrill, *A Brief History of the Church of Christ of Latter Day Saints*, 1839," 18; emphasis added.
3. See "Temples," in *True to the Faith* (Salt Lake City: The Church of Jesus Christ of Latter-day Saints, 2004), 171.
4. *Merriam-Webster*, s.v. "endowment," accessed online defines it as a "natural capacity, power, or ability." TheFreeDictionary.com, s.v. "endowment," defines it as "a natural gift, ability, or quality."
5. Joseph's history says that at the June 1831 conference, "the authority of the melechisedec priesthood was manifested and <I> conferred, <the high priesthood> for the first time, upon several of the elders." See "History, 1838–1856, volume A-1, [23 December 1805–30 August 1834]," 118, The Joseph Smith Papers.
6. Editors for *The Joseph Smith Papers* write, "Jared Carter, for instance, associated the ability to perform miraculous healings with those ordained to the high priesthood," in the Historical Introduction of "Minutes, circa 3–4 June 1831," 4.
7. Speaking to some newly called high priests, the Lord says, "You shall be given power to seal them up unto eternal life. Amen" (Doctrine and Covenants 68:12). In October 1831, the Prophet Joseph Smith taught that "the order of the High priesthood is that they have power given them to seal up the Saints unto eternal life." "Minute Book 2," 11, The Joseph Smith Papers.
8. "John Corrill, *A Brief History of the Church of Christ of Latter Day Saints*, 1839," 18.
9. Jared Carter wrote in his journal of Joseph at the June 1831 conference that "not with standing he [Joseph] is not naturaly talanted for a speaker yet he was filled with the power of the holy ghost so that he s[p]oke as I never heard man speak for god by the power of the holy Ghost spoke in him." "Jared Carter Journal, 1831 January-1833 January 20," 17, Church History Catalog, The Church of Jesus Christ of Latter-day Saints, MS 1441.
10. *The Life of Levi W. Hancock*, typescript BYU-S, BYU Special Collections, 32.
11. Michael Hubbard MacKay, Gerrit J. Dirkmaat, Robert J. Woodford, and William G. Hartley, eds., *Documents, Volume 1: July 1828–June 1831*, vol. 1 of the Documents series of *The Joseph Smith Papers*, ed. Dean C. Jessee, Ronald K. Esplin, Richard Lyman Bushman, and Matthew J. Grow (Salt Lake City: Church Historian's Press, 2013), 322. It should be noted that this reference to Joseph's promise of seeing Jesus's face was made by Ezra Booth in November of 1831 as he was writing an antagonistic article in the newspaper *Ohio Star*. Ezra had apostatized shortly after his ordination to the high priesthood and attendance at the June 1831 conference. Joseph Smith's promise to these men to see God is corroborated by Levi Hancock's recollection of the event that Joseph promised some men that "You shall see the Lord." *JSP*, D1:323.
12. *JSP*, D1:323.
13. "John Whitmer, History, 1831–circa 1847," 28, The Joseph Smith Papers. Or, he "stepted out on the floor and said I now see God and Jesus Christ at his right hand." *JSP*, D1:323.
14. "The Papers of Zebedee Coltrin," in E. Cecil McGavin, *The Record of the Spanish Fork Branch* (29 April 1866 to 1 December 1898), 250–51, Church History Library, Salt Lake City.
15. "John Corrill, *A Brief History of the Church of Christ of Latter Day Saints*, 1839," 18.
16. "John Whitmer, History, 1831–circa 1847," 29.
17. "History, 1838–1856, volume A-1 [23 December 1805–30 August 1834]," 118.
18. "History, 1838–1856, volume A-1 [23 December 1805–30 August 1834]," 118.
19. "Minute Book 2," 11.
20. James E. Faust, "Lost Horizons," *Ensign*, August 1999, 4–5.
21. "History, 1838–1856, volume A-1 [23 December 1805–30 August 1834]," 118.

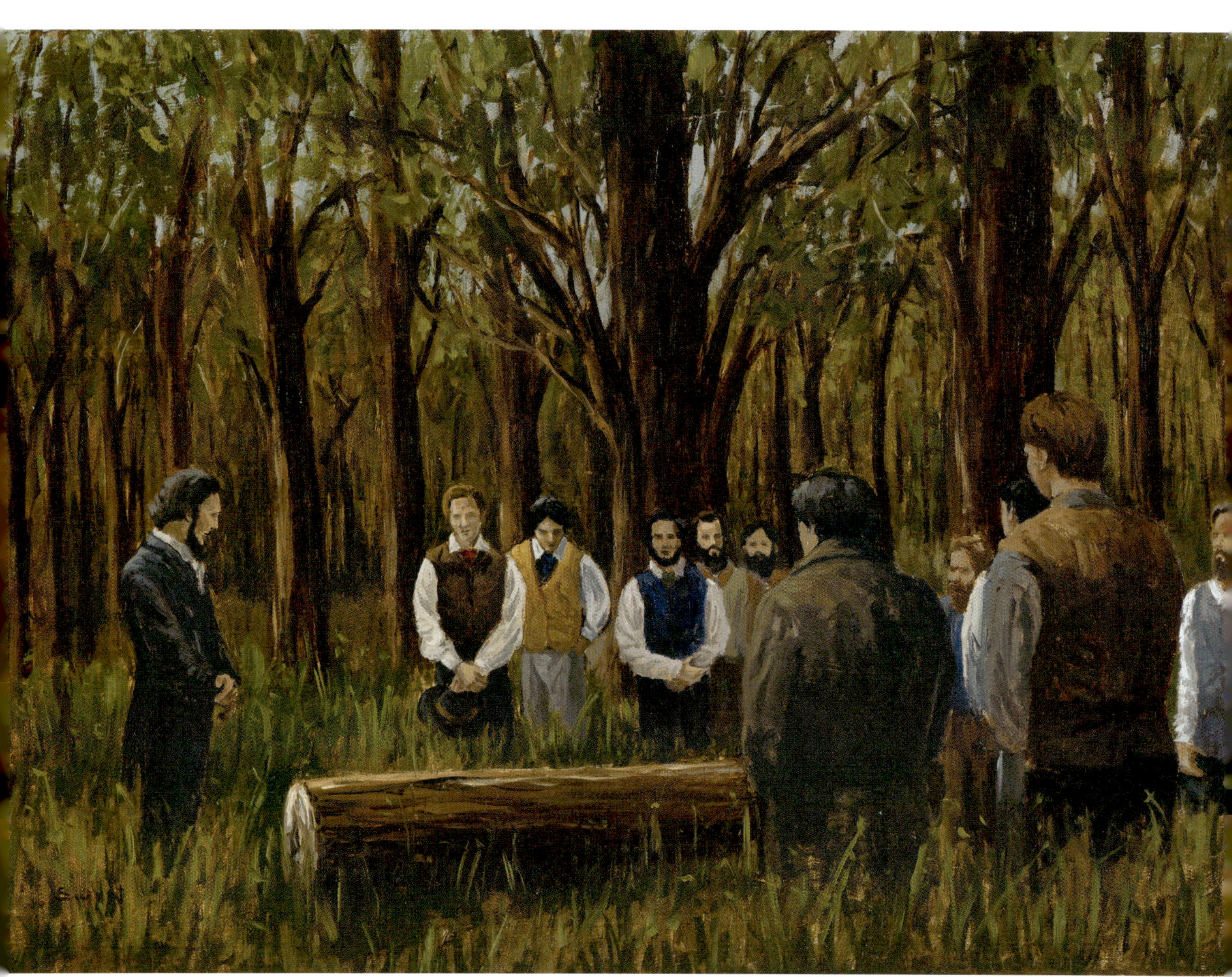

Dedicating the Land of Zion (14" x 20", oil on board, 2019)

DEDICATING THE LAND OF ZION

Timeline: June–August 1831

Related Doctrine and Covenants Sections: 54, 56, 57, 58, 59, 60, 98, 101

A BACKGROUND

While translating the Book of Mormon in the summer of 1829, the Prophet Joseph learned about God's promise of a holy city to be built called Zion, or the "New Jerusalem" (see 3 Nephi 21:23–24; Ether 13:3–6). Although the New Jerusalem was to be established in the Americas, the Prophet did not initially know where the city of Zion would be established. In September 1830, Joseph received a revelation in which the Lord gave the first hint: "Zion shall be built . . . on the borders by the Lamanites," with a future promise that the exact location "shall be given hereafter" (Doctrine and Covenants 28:9). At that time, the states of Missouri and Arkansas formed the western boundary of the United States. Land west was unorganized and sometimes known as the Indian Territory.

In the fall of 1830, Oliver Cowdery and three other missionaries were called by the Lord to leave New York to "go unto the Lamanites" (Doctrine and Covenants 28:8) and preach the gospel. Before they left, the missionaries signed a solemn covenant before God showing their twofold intention to (1) "go forth unto the Lamanites, to proclaim glad tidings of great joy unto them, by presenting unto them the fulness of the Gospel," and (2) "also, to rear up a pillar as a witness where the Temple of God shall be built, in the glorious New-Jerusalem."[1]

The missionaries to the Lamanites would travel over a thousand miles westward, following Lake Erie and eventually the Missouri River until they arrived at a small new settlement with a few dozen buildings on the westward edge of America. This new settlement was named Independence, Missouri.

Back in Ohio at the June 1831 conference, Joseph Smith received a revelation from the

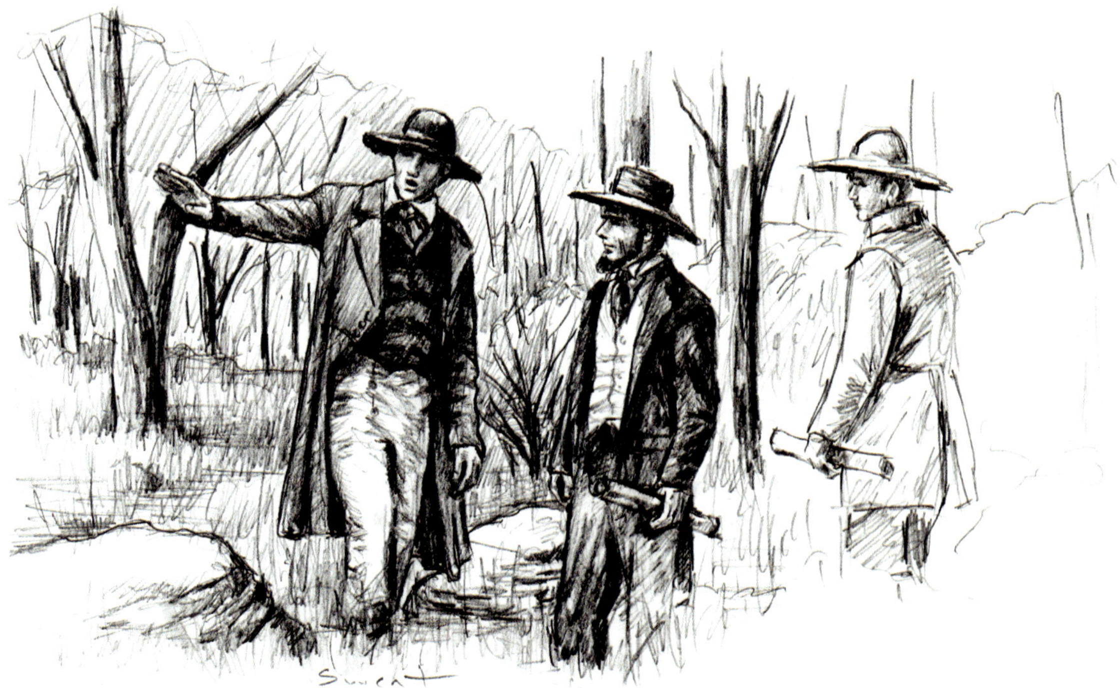

Lord directing him to personally travel to Missouri to hold the next Church conference there, calling many to go there and preach the gospel along the way. The Lord revealed that Missouri would be the "land which I will consecrate unto my people" (Doctrine and Covenants 52:2) for Zion, the New Jerusalem.

Before journeying to Missouri, Joseph learned by revelation that the Colesville Branch of the Church should be among the first to begin settling the land of Zion. Earlier, the Colesville branch faithfully left New York to follow the Lord's call to gather to Ohio (see "First to Be Faithful: The Colesville Branch"). They had gathered to Ohio and settled on Leman Copley's large farm in the summer of 1831 but shortly afterward were evicted from the property after Leman Copley faltered in his faith and broke his consecration covenant (see the section heading for Doctrine and Covenants 54). Without anywhere to live, the Lord called the Colesville Saints to go farther west to be among the first Saints to settle in western Missouri, warning them to be prepared to "seek ye a living like unto men, until I prepare a place for you" (see 54:8–9). Newel Knight, the leader of the Colesville branch, recalled, "On receiving the above, we who had Constituted the Coles-[ville Saints] set immediately to prepare for the journey. And on the third day of July [1831] Took passage with the Coalsville Company . . . for Independence."[2]

Joseph F. Darowski writes, "Leaving Thompson in early June 1831, sixty members of the [Colesville] branch reached Kaw Township in Jackson County, Missouri, on July 26 after a journey of about a thousand miles. Though Joseph Smith had arrived shortly before the Colesville Saints, they had the distinction of being the first branch of the Church to settle the land that had been [promised] as Zion."[3]

Shortly after the Colesville Saints left Ohio, Joseph Smith, Sidney Rigdon, and Bishop Edward Partridge set out for Missouri with several elders. Along the way, they preached the gospel:

> [While] talking about their hopes for Zion.
>
> Joseph spoke optimistically about the church in Independence. . . .
>
> As they neared Jackson County, the men admired the gently rolling prairie around them. With plenty of land for the Saints to spread out, Missouri seemed like the ideal location for Zion.[4]

When they reached Independence, Missouri, however, "the elders were unimpressed by what they saw."[5] Independence was an untamed, "vast wilderness."[6] A newly ordained high priest named Ezra Booth thought "the prospect appeared somewhat gloomy" and said Joseph and Sidney were "disappointed" with what they found.[7] The Prophet commented that western Missouri seemed degraded and "a century behind the times," asking God, "When will the wilderness blossom as the rose; when will Zion be built up in her glory, and where will thy Temple stand, unto which all nations shall come in the last days?"[8]

Despite these reservations, the Lord confirmed in a revelation, "The land of Missouri . . . is the land which I have appointed and consecrated for the gathering of the saints. Wherefore, this is the land of promise, and the place for the city of Zion." The Lord then indicated exactly where the city should be built: "The place which is now called Independence is the center place; and a spot for the temple is lying westward, upon a lot which is not far from the courthouse" (Doctrine and Covenants 57:1–3).

A few weeks later, on 2 August 1831, Joseph Smith, Sidney Rigdon, Oliver Cowdery, and other elders stood with members of the recently arrived Colesville branch to dedicate the land for building the New Jerusalem—the city of Zion. Twelve men, representing the twelve tribes of Israel, carried and symbolically laid a log to commemorate the building of Zion.[9]

Oliver Cowdery selected a small, rough stone and laid it down for a cornerstone.[10] Sidney Rigdon spoke, and pointedly asked the attendees several questions: "Do you receive this land for the land of your inheritanc[e] with thankful hearts from the Lord? answer from all we do, Do you pledge yourselves to keep the laws of God on this land, which you have never have kept in your own land? we do. Do you pledge yourselves to see that others of your brethren, who shall come hither do keep the laws of God? We do." Sidney then offered the dedicatory prayer for the land of Zion and "after prayer he arose and said, I now pronounce this land consecrated and dedicated to the Lord for a possession and inheritanc for the Saints, (in the name of Jesus Christ having authority from him.) And for all the faithful Servants of the Lord to the remotest ages of time. Aamen."[11]

The place to establish the city of Zion was now dedicated, and the inhabitants had promised to obey the Lord as consecrated, covenant Saints of one mind and heart to dwell in righteousness, like Enoch's people of old.

AN IMAGE

This painting shows Sidney Rigdon on the left, head bowed and arms folded, ready to dedicate the land of Zion in prayer.

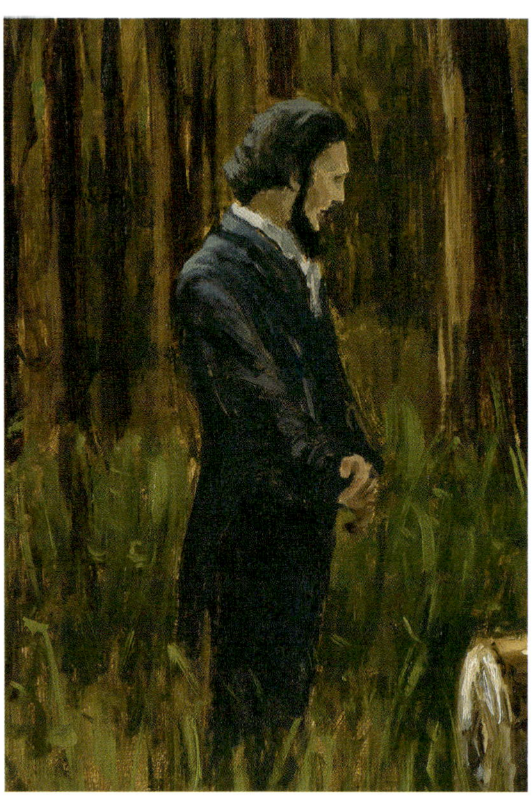

Joseph Smith and Oliver Cowdery stand to the viewer's right, observing the ceremonial process.

Counting Sidney, Oliver, and Joseph, there are twelve men—representing the twelve tribes of Israel—who carried the log. The other men present would be Ohio Saints such as Isaac

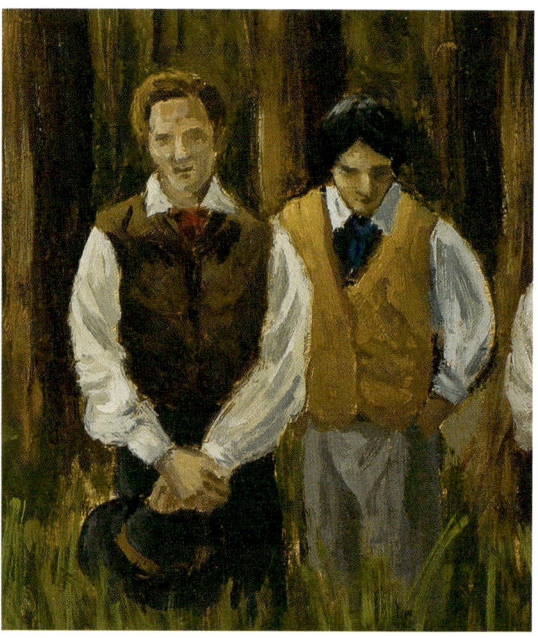

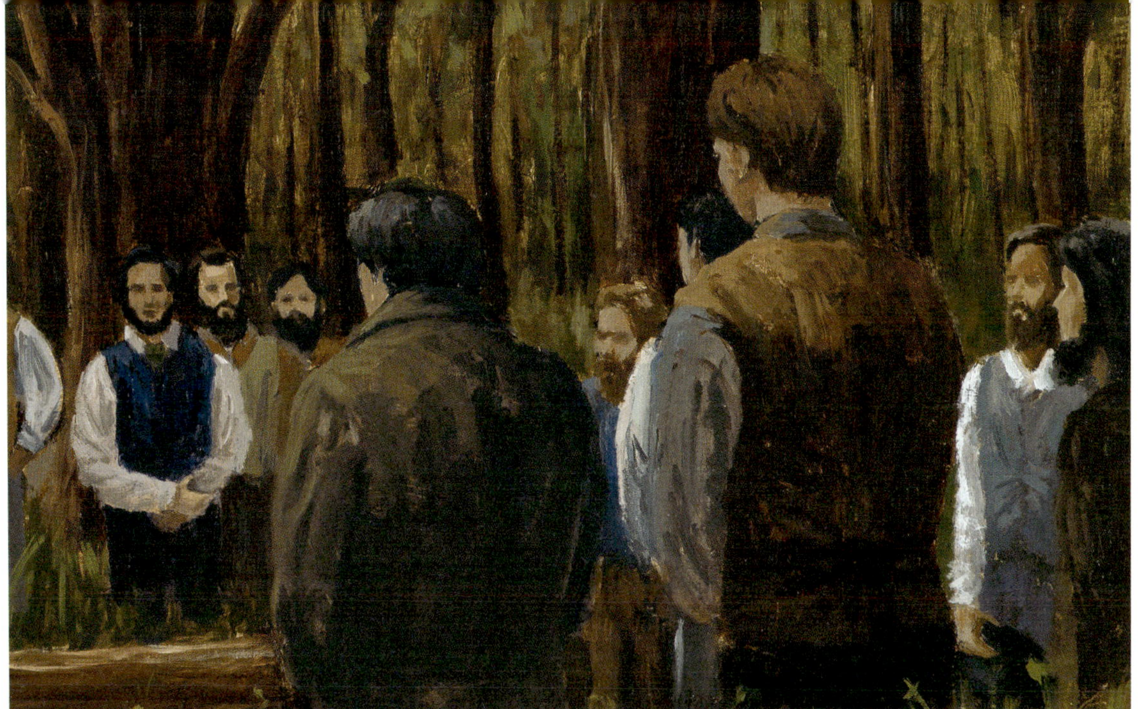

Morley and Ezra Booth, and Colesville Saints such as Joseph and Newel Knight, and Hezekiah and Ezekiel Peck.[12]

The men have just placed this symbolic log on the ground of this untamed wilderness that they hope to transform into a beautiful, holy city of Zion.

Although Kaw Township (twelve miles west of Independence) and the area where the dedication took place likely would have had more evidence of settlement, I chose to depict this moment in unsettled woods. The tall grass and unencumbered trees suggest the audacity of the task at hand to cause the wilderness to blossom as a rose and rise into a city of New Jerusalem.

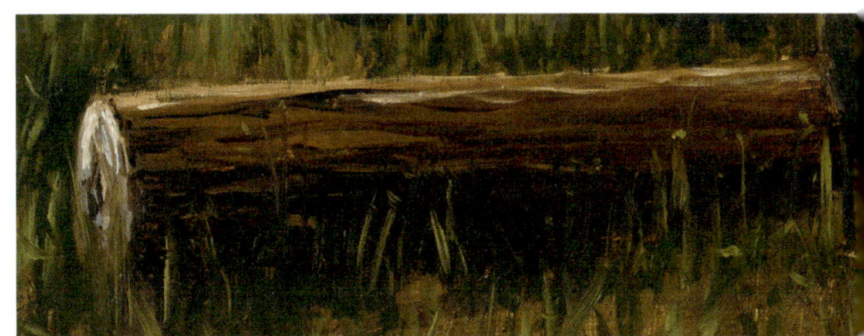

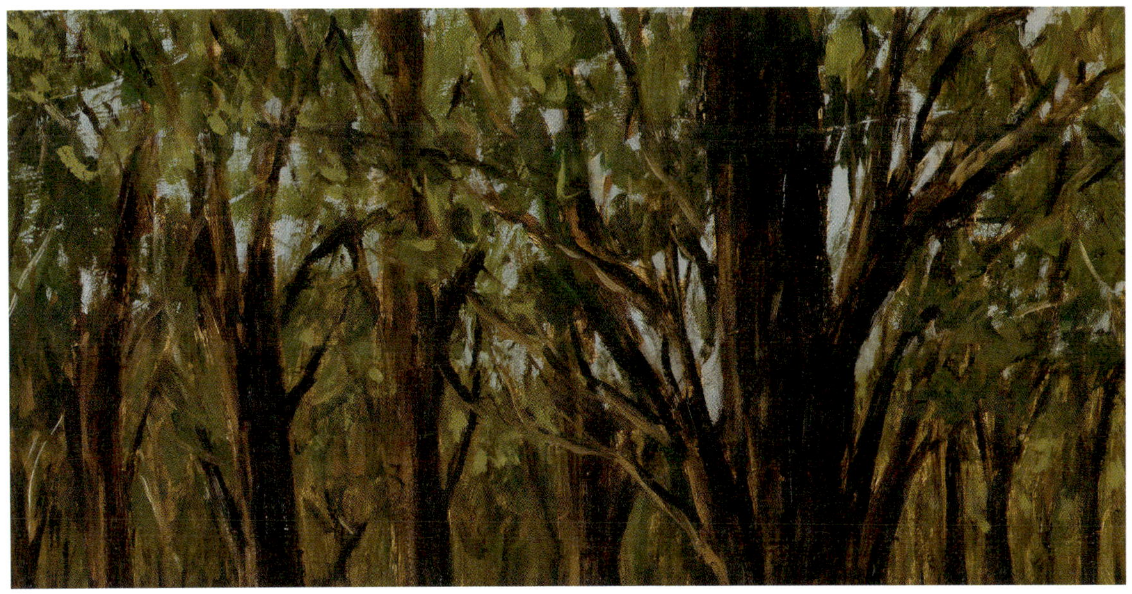

AN APPLICATION

Joseph Smith's vision of Zion, as expressed in his own history, would be a city where "the gathering of the elect of the Lord, out of every nation on earth" would take place, centered around a temple, where each man and woman would be "filled with sacred knowledge, as the waters cover the great deep"; where the people would be "of one heart and one mind" and would "walk with God like Enoch" because they would be "free from Sin." Zion would be a place where "honest men" build up "a city of righteousness" so holy that "even ~~the~~ <upon the> bells ~~on the horses, shall be~~ <of the Horses shall be written> Holiness to the Lord."[13] It was to be a holy city to gather the faithful in preparation for the impending destruction before the Second Coming[14] (see Doctrine and Covenants 45:66–71).

Joseph was specific about planning the layout of this city, and he drew up two maps, one in 1831 and another in 1833. These one-mile-square maps became the prototype for Latter-day Saint cities: A uniform grid pattern laid out in a north-south orientation, with straight streets crossing at right angles, centered on a temple. In fact, for the city of Zion, Joseph inserted twenty-four "temples" (or dedicated Church buildings) in the center of this city. When the city plot reached the population limit, the instructions on it said to "lay off another [one-mile-square plot] in the same way and so fill up the world in these last days and let every man live in the City for this is the City of Zion."[15]

Before this grand vision could be realized, however, the Saints were driven out of Independence by local residents who clashed with the Saints over politics, religion, economics, and culture (see section heading for Doctrine and Covenants 98). Before their eviction from Independence, Joseph Smith warned the Saints in Independence in January: "Repent, repent, is the voice of God, to Zion, & yet strange as it may appear, yet it is true mankind will persist in self Justification until all their eniquity is exposed & their character past being redeemed, & that which is treasured up in their hearts be exposed to the gaze of mankind, I say to you — (& what I say to you, I say to all) hear the <warning.> voice of God lest Zion fall, & the Lord ~~swore~~ swear in his wrath the inhabiteints of Zion shall not enter into [his] rest."[16]

The Lord seemed to place the Saints' disobedience at the center of the expulsion from Independence. In a revelation on the causes for the conflict, the Lord said it was "in consequence of their [the Saints'] transgressions" (Doctrine and Covenants 101:2). He indicated that there "were jarrings, and contentions, and envyings, and strifes, and lustful and covetous desires among them; therefore by these things they polluted their inheritances. They were slow to hearken unto the voice of the Lord their God" (101:6–7).

> The tenth article of faith states "that Zion (the New Jerusalem) will be built upon the American continent" (Articles of Faith 1:10). Do we have faith in that article of faith?

The Church has never yet again attempted to build the city of Zion. Today, the Independence temple lot is divided between the Community of

Christ, The Church of Jesus Christ of Latter-day Saints, and the Church of Christ (Temple Lot).

The Lord did promise, however, that "Zion shall be redeemed, although she is chastened for a little season" (Doctrine and Covenants 100:13). Speaking of the city of Zion's redemption, the Lord gave a parable and when asked, "When shall these things be?" the Lord responded, "When I will" (101:59–60). An article of faith states, "We believe in the literal gathering of Israel and in the restoration of the Ten Tribes; that Zion (the New Jerusalem) will be built upon the American continent" (Articles of Faith 1:10). Do we have faith in that article of faith?

Reflecting many years later on the failure to build the city of Zion, President Brigham Young said, "We look forward to the day when the Lord will prepare for the building of the New Jerusalem, preparatory to the City of Enoch's going to be joined with it when it is built upon this earth. We are anticipating to enjoy that day, whether we sleep in death previous to that, or not."[17]

AN ANALYSIS

1 Why did the Lord direct Joseph and the early Saints to build the city of New Jerusalem if God knew they would fail? Why doesn't the Lord tell us that things won't work out before we ever start them? If they would have better heeded his counsel, do you think they would they have accomplished it?

2 Why do you think we have not yet built the city of Zion? It is money? Land? The People? Timing? What might stop us? The Lord said that "this is Zion—THE PURE IN HEART" (Doctrine and Covenants 97:21). Speaking of Enoch's Zion of old, Moses explains, "And the Lord called his people Zion, because they were of one heart and one mind, and dwelt in righteousness; and there was no poor among them" (Moses 7:18). Some reasons why the Lord said Zion was not yet redeemed was that his people needed to be "taught more perfectly, and have experience, and know more perfectly concerning their duty" and that they were not yet "endowed with power from on high" (Doctrine and Covenants 105:10–11). Is this still the reason? Do we lack purity, unity, consecration, understanding, experience, knowledge, or power, or all of the above? Or are we ready and able as a people, but the Lord isn't asking us to build it for some reason? In the past thirty years (since 1990) of general conference, there has been only one talk that has referenced the "New Jerusalem."[18] What are your thoughts on why the city of New Jerusalem seems to not be a central focus of the modern Church as it was in Joseph's day?

3 Some say that section 45 of the Doctrine and Covenants suggests that people will physically gather to Zion from all nations (see 45:69–71). Section 29 says, "they shall be gathered in unto one place upon the face of this land" (29:8). Our tenth article of faith calls it a "literal gathering of Israel" (Articles of Faith 1:10). Do you think the gathering will be a collective, global, literal gathering to prepare the Saints for the Second Coming? If so, why? If not, why not? Relatedly, does building the New Jerusalem still need to be in Independence, Missouri? The Lord promised that "Zion shall not be moved out of her place" (Doctrine and Covenants 101:17; see also 97:19). But can it move? At another time, however, the Lord said to the early Saints that as they were "hindered by their enemies" from building "up a city and a house unto my name, in Jackson county, Missouri"

that "it behooveth me to require that work no more at the hands of those sons of men, but to accept of their offerings" (124:51, 49). Could the Lord designate and dedicate another, more convenient center place for the New Jerusalem or excuse the Church from ever building the city of New Jerusalem altogether?

NOTES

1. "Covenant of Oliver Cowdery and Others, 17 October 1830," 1, The Joseph Smith Papers.
2. Michael Hubbard MacKay and William G. Hartley, *The Rise of the Latter-day Saints: The Journals and Histories of Newel Knight* (Provo, UT: Religious Studies Center, Brigham Young University; Salt Lake City: Deseret Book, 2019), 36.
3. Joseph F. Darowski, "The Journey of the Colesville Branch: D&C 26, 51, 54, 56, 59," in *Revelations in Context: The Stories behind Sections of the Doctrine and Covenants*, ed. Matthew McBride and James Goldberg (Salt Lake City: The Church of Jesus Christ of Latter-day Saints, 2016), 43.
4. *Saints*, vol. 1, *The Standard of Truth, 1815–1846* (Salt Lake City: The Church of Jesus Christ of Latter-day Saints, 2018), 129.
5. *Saints*, 129.
6. "History, 1838–1856, volume A-1 [23 December 1805–30 August 1834]," 127, The Joseph Smith Papers.
7. Ezra Booth, in E. D. Howe, *Mormonism Unvailed* (Painesville, OH: self-pub., 1834), 199.
8. "History, 1838–1856, volume A-1 [23 December 1805–30 August 1834]," 127.
9. "History, 1838–1856, volume A-1 [23 December 1805–30 August 1834]," 137.
10. Booth, in Howe, *Mormonism Unvailed*, 198.
11. "John Whitmer, History, 1831–circa 1847," 32, The Joseph Smith Papers.
12. See "John Whitmer, History, 1831–circa 1847," 32, note 95.
13. "History, 1838–1856, volume B-1 [1 September 1834–2 November 1838]," 680.
14. Editors for the *Joseph Smith Papers* write, "One distinctive element of early Mormon millenarianism was the belief that the righteous must be physically gathered in preparation for the advent of the Christ." Dean C. Jessee, Mark Ashurst-McGee, and Richard L. Jensen, eds., *Journals, Volume 1: 1832–1839*, vol. 1 of the Journals series of *The Joseph Smith Papers*, ed. Dean C. Jessee, Ronald K. Esplin, and Richard Lyman Bushman (Salt Lake City: Church Historian's Press, 2008), xxxiv.
15. "Plat of the City of Zion, circa Early June–25 June 1833," 1, The Joseph Smith Papers.
16. "Letter to William W. Phelps, 11 January 1833," 19, The Joseph Smith Papers.
17. John A. Widtsoe, comp., *Discourses of Brigham Young* (Salt Lake City: Deseret Book, 1925), 184.
18. D. Todd Christofferson, "Come to Zion," *Ensign*, November 2008, 37, 40. A search of "New Jerusalem" on Mark Davies's "LDS General Conference Corpus" yielded the result of only Elder Christofferson's talk having referenced the "New Jerusalem" in the past thirty years of general conferences.

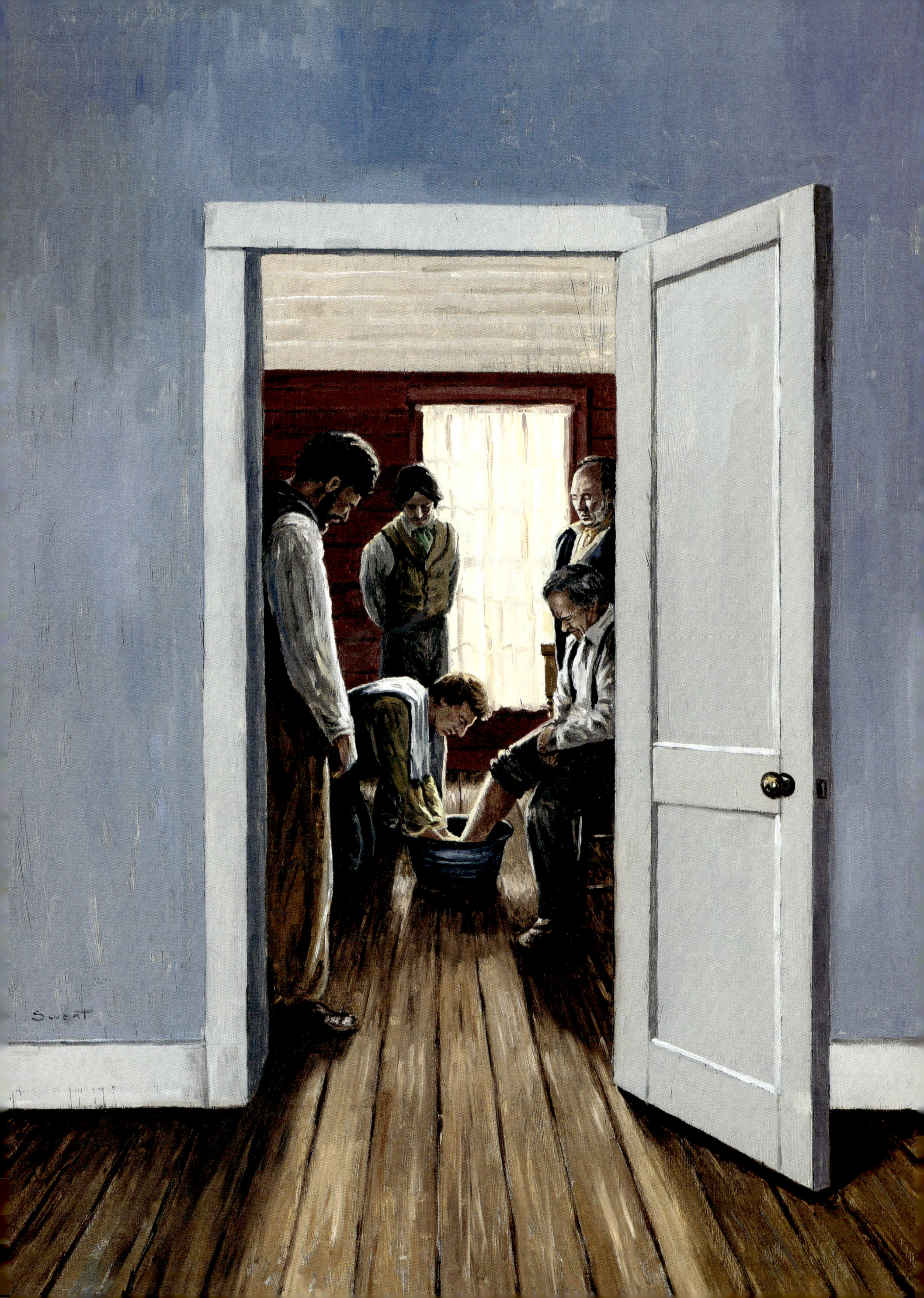
Sweat

INITIATION TO THE SCHOOL OF THE PROPHETS

Timeline: December 1832–April 1833

Related Doctrine and Covenants Sections: 84, 88, 89, 97

A BACKGROUND

In Doctrine and Covenants 67, some leading Latter-day Saints were told that they were "not able to abide the presence of God now, neither the ministering of angels" and that they needed to "continue in patience until ye are perfected" (Doctrine and Covenants 67:13). How could the Lord better prepare them to become endowed with power and part the veil to commune with God (see "Endowment at the June 1831 Conference")? The answer was this: build a temple and form a School of the Prophets.[1]

You've likely heard about the School of the Prophets. We generally talk about the school as a place where elders were prepared to go on missions, or learn the doctrines of the Church and various academic subjects of the world (see Doctrine and Covenants 88:78–80)[2] or where they learned they should quit chewing tobacco and drinking alcohol (see section 89). All of this is true, but there was also a deep, sacred purpose to the school: to prepare them to abide the presence of God and commune with him. The Lord told school members: "Therefore, sanctify yourselves that your minds become single to God, and *the days will come that you shall see him; for he will unveil his face unto you*" (88:68; emphasis added).

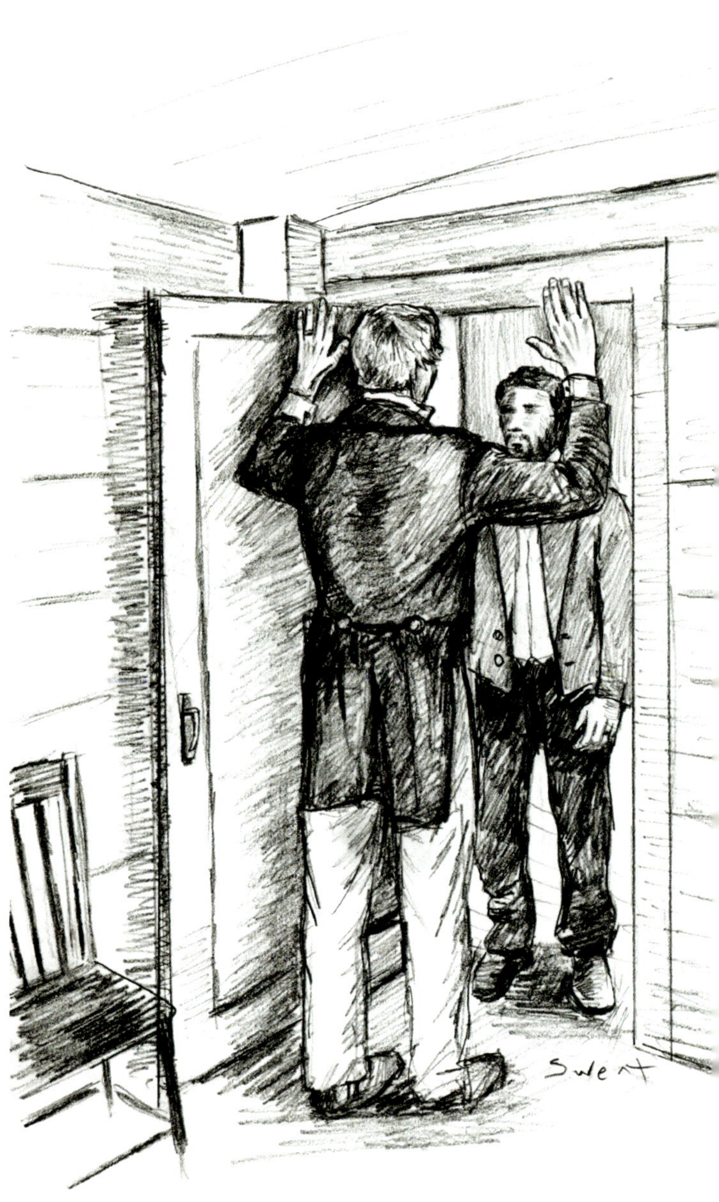

To help realize this blessing, the Lord laid out some specific requirements to sanctify these men. "Cease from all your light speeches," they were told, and from inappropriate "laughter, from all your lustful desires, from all your pride and light-mindedness, and from all your wicked doings" (Doctrine and Covenants 88:121). To qualify for God's presence, they must "love one another" and "learn to impart one to another as the gospel requires" (88:123)—a reference to obey the revealed law of consecration (see 42:30). These men were to commit to living these things "with uplifted hands toward heaven" by making a covenant "to walk in all the commandments of God blameless" (88:132–33). The Lord also introduced "the ordinance of the washing of feet" (88:139). This ordinance would induct them into the school and make them "clean from the blood of this generation" (88:138) and purify them for the presence of God. A pattern to approach the Lord was starting to be revealed: be cleansed from your sins by a ritual washing, commit to be holy, obedient, and chaste, and consecrate your life to serving God and man by covenant.

Joseph and his associates didn't waste time, and within a month of receiving the revelation to start the school, they began to meet in a small upper room in the Newel K. Whitney store in Kirtland, Ohio. Notes for the opening day read as follows:

> Wednesday Jan^{ry} 23^{d} Meet agreeable to adjournment. Conference opened with Prayer by the President and after much speaking praying and singing, all done in Tongues proceded to washing hands faces & feet in the name of the Lord as commanded ~~by~~ of God each one washing his own after which the president guirded himself with a towel and again washed the feet of all the Elders wiping them with the towel . . . at the close of which scene Br F G Williams being moved upon by the Holy Ghost washed the feet of the President. . . . The President said after he had washed the feet of the Elders, as I have done so do ye wash ye therefee [therefore] one anothers feet pronouncing at the same time through the power of the Holy Ghost that the Elders were all clean from the blood of this generation. . . . Having continued all day in fasting & prayer before the Lord at the close they partook of the Lords supper.[3]

Speaking about this initiation into the school through the washing of feet, Joseph preached a few years later in 1835: "We must attend to the ordinance of washing of feet; it was never intended for any but official members, it is calculated to unite our hearts, that we may be one in feeling and sentiment and that our faith may be strong, so that satan cannot over throw us, nor have any power over us."[4]

Wonderful things happened at the organization meeting. After the washing of feet and in a spirit of fasting and prayer, they prophesied and spoke in tongues "as on the day of pentecost" and experienced "the most Glorious outporings of the spirit of God that had ever been witnessed in the church at that time."[5] Some women showed up to the original meeting, such as Lucy Mack Smith, who rushed over to the Newel K. Whitney upper room to witness and participate in the spiritual outpouring along with her husband and sons. Because the brethren met consistently during the months of January through April 1833 and sanctified themselves, God fulfilled his veil-parting promise to some. Zebedee Coltrin related one such sacred experience where he and other school members remarkably saw Jesus Christ *and* Heavenly Father:

> At one of these meetings after the organization of the school, . . . while engaged in silent prayer, kneeling, with our hands uplifted, . . . a personage walked through the room from east to west, and Joseph asked if we saw him. *I saw him* and suppose the others did and Joseph answered that is Jesus, the Son of God, our elder brother. Afterward Joseph told us to resume our former position in prayer, which we did. Another person came through; he was surrounded as with a flame of fire. . . .The Prophet Joseph said this was the Father of our Lord Jesus Christ. *I saw Him.*[6]

Truly, these men were learning how to approach God and gaining the power and capacity to be blessed with his presence in order to commune with him. This was indeed a "School of the Prophets" (Doctrine and Covenants 88:127), or a "company of the prophets" (1 Samuel 19:20), a modern school of Melchizedeks and Moseses whose instructions and actions would form the foundation for later temple-centric teachings revealed through Joseph Smith and found in the holy temple today.

AN IMAGE

This image depicts the organization of the School of the Prophets in the upper room of the Newel K. Whitney store as Joseph Smith washes the feet of an initiate. This is a hitherto undepicted, important scene from the Restoration. While it is a sacred scene and would lay the foundation for more elaborate washing and anointing later in the temple, Joseph Smith related this January 1833 washing to the Savior washing the feet of his disciples—a sacred scene between Jesus and his disciples that has been artistically depicted hundreds of times in historical Christianity and repeatedly published by The Church of Jesus Christ of Latter-day Saints.[7]

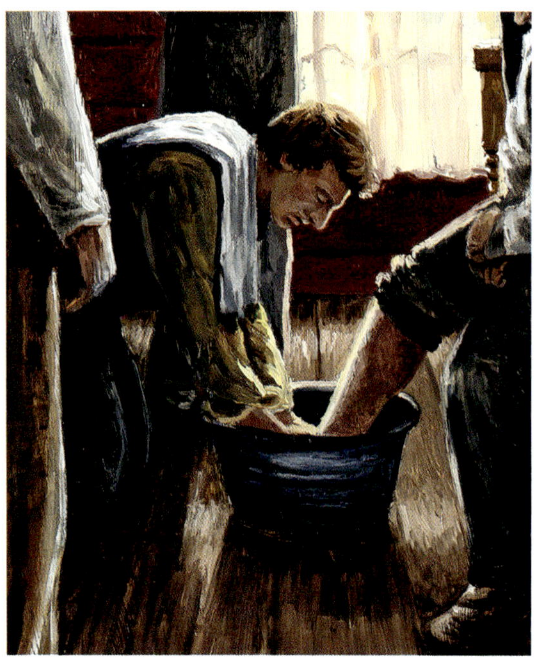

Joseph's father, Joseph Smith Sr., stands at the top right, and Frederick G. Williams watches near the window. I imagine the man standing closest to the door, acting almost like a guardian, as someone like Joseph's brother William Smith, who was present. Joseph has a towel over his shoulder, although perhaps he had the towel "girded" about his waist.

An important part of the composition of this scene is the decision to place the viewer *outside* the room, looking in. I could have composed and created the entire painting like this (bottom right image).

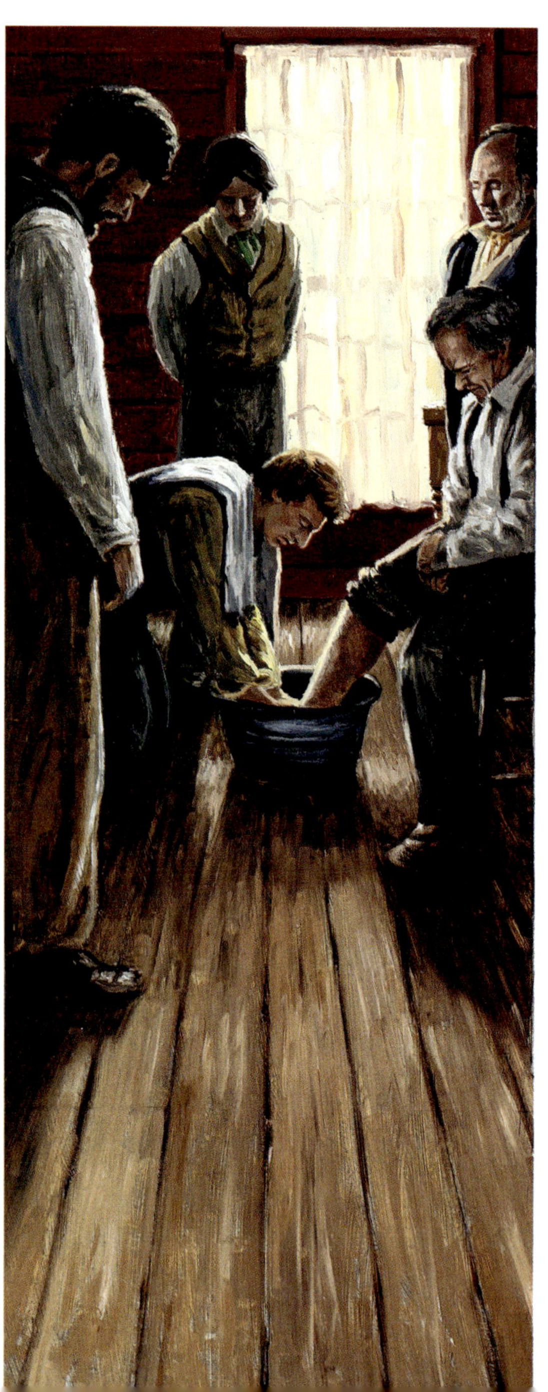

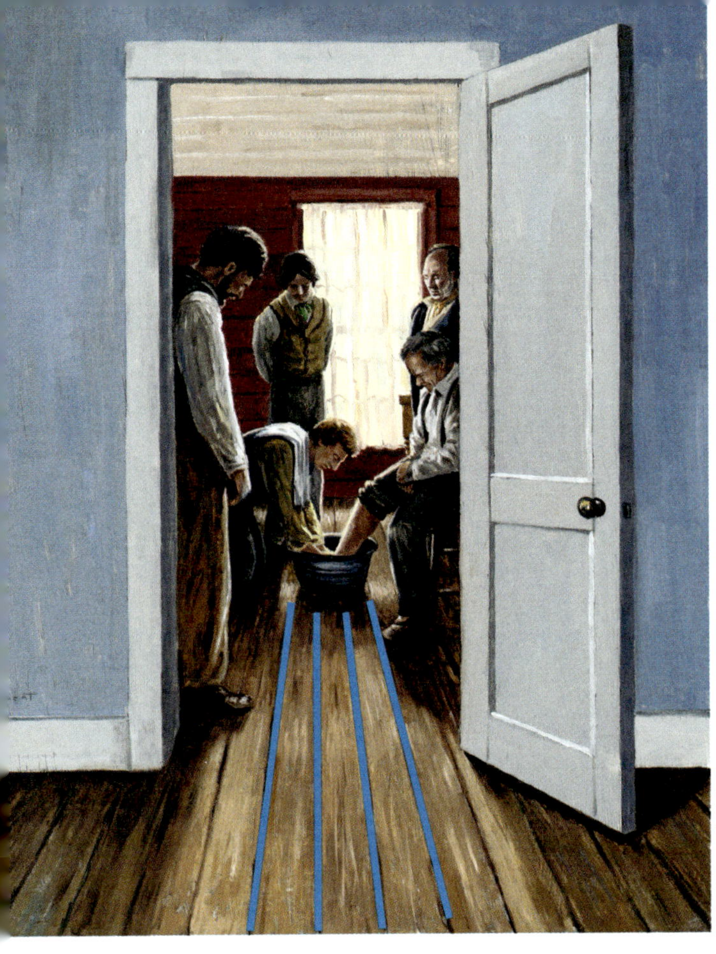

Adding a second room a layer back into the composition does a few things. It allows me to use the perspective lines on the floor to direct a viewer through a door into the room and to the Prophet.

More importantly, this composition sends a purposeful message that this initiation to the School of the Prophets was limited at first (as the viewer stands outside of it in another room) but eventually its purposes would be made open to all through the later ordinances of the temple. The open door acts as a symbol of this invitation to all.

The photograph for this painting from which I worked was taken in the upper room of the Newel K. Whitney store, the rich red of the room familiar to anyone who has visited, its warm tones balancing and contrasting against the blue walls of the outer room.

AN APPLICATION

In a major 2019 study of 1,156 Latter-day Saints across the United States (The Next Mormons Survey), a list of nine things was given about the respondents' favorite part of being a member of the Church. The data was divided and analyzed by generation (Boomer/Silent, GenX, Millennials).

All three generations listed the same three aspects as their favorite (eternal families, the focus on the Savior, and faith). However, "both Millennials and GenXers ordered temple worship dead last out of nine possible favorite aspects of being Mormon. . . . Something about the temple is not 'clicking' with Millennials and GenXers," wrote the author, Jana Reiss.[8] One reason why some in the younger generations don't rank the temple as a favorite aspect of being a Latter-day Saint may have to do with the lack of preparation or instruction they receive. President Ezra Taft Benson taught, "As a consequence, many [younger people] do not develop a real desire to go to the temple, or when they go there, they do so without much background to prepare them for the obligations and covenants they enter into. I believe a proper understanding or background will immeasurably help prepare our youth for the temple."[9]

One great way to prepare for the temple endowment is to study the revelations of the Doctrine and Covenants. In particular, sections 67, 84, 88, 89, 93, 95, 97, 107, 109, 110, 124, 128, 129, 130, 131, and 132. Within the pages of the Doctrine and Covenants, we see the Lord reveal to Joseph Smith the central themes found in the holy temple today bit by bit, concept by concept, covenant by covenant. The teachings given for the School of the Prophets in Doctrine and Covenants 88 contain many of those. The instructions for the School seek to sanctify Saints so they can be prepared for their priestly ministry and commune with God. It teaches them to abstain from inappropriate laughter and light-mindedness, to be obedient and chaste, to live the law of consecration, to be clean, to make covenants, and to participate in ordinances like ritual washings. These teachings lay the foundation for some temple instruction today. Sister Bonnie D. Parkin, former Relief Society General President, taught, "In the temple, we further covenant to be obedient, to sacrifice, to keep ourselves worthily pure, to contribute to the spreading of truth, to be chaste, to pray, to live the gospel, and to be forever faithful."[10] Elder David A. Bednar reminded the Saints that "the doctrinal purposes of temple ordinances and covenants have been taught extensively by Church leaders" such as those related to "the law of obedience, the law of sacrifice, the law of the gospel, the law of chastity, and the law of consecration."[11]

When we fail to appropriately discuss and learn about the doctrinal and historical background of the temple and its covenants and ordinances, we fail to prepare ourselves and others sufficiently to truly understand the endowment and gain its potential priesthood power. The temple itself specifically teaches what not to disclose, which includes what "we specifically promise in the temple not to reveal" and "the special symbols associated with the covenants."[12] The Church has great resources available to help individuals prepare for temple attendance at churchofjesuschrist.org/temples.

The power and capacity to come into the presence of God and commune with him to learn his ways and gain a fullness of his blessings is synonymous with "endowment" and has been promised to God's people from the beginning. The temple is the place that symbolizes and provides the rituals (ordinances) and actions (covenants) needed to bring this to pass. Remember, there is a difference between the "endowment" (the power and capacity to enter the presence of God and receive of his fullness) and the "presentation of the endowment" (a teaching tool). One is a power, the other a pedagogy. The pedagogy has and will yet change to communicate the power. The first pedagogy to communicate the power of endowment began with Joseph Smith and the School of the Prophets in 1833 and continues today in the modern-day School of the Prophets—the holy temple.

> Within the pages of the Doctrine and Covenants we can see the Lord reveal to Joseph Smith bit by bit, concept by concept, covenant by covenant, the central themes found in the holy temple today.

AN ANALYSIS

1 Why are we sometimes so reticent to talk about the temple, even in Church settings or with private family when aspects of it can be discussed with appropriate reverence? Baptism and sacrament and other ordinances are also sacred and holy, yet we often clearly and openly discuss

the purposes and doctrines surrounding these ordinances. Is it because we should not talk about certain aspects of the temple outside its walls, so we err on the side of caution to not really discuss it at all? Is it because we ourselves do not truly understand the endowment so we struggle to explain it? How can we more clearly and appropriately teach, talk, and testify about the temple to others so they can have a proper foundation in order to gain their own understanding of its covenants, ordinances, and purposes?

2 Joseph Smith received the Word of Wisdom roughly one month after the School of the Prophets was organized. How can learning about the purposes of the School of the Prophets help you better understand the purposes of the Word of Wisdom? How can we shift the narrative from those who explain it as only a *health* code to also explain its larger purpose as a *holiness* code connected to the endowment?

3 Is it appropriate to depict gospel ordinances in art and film? If so, which ones and how? Is it a public versus private delineation (for example, baptism is public, so we can paint baptisms; but temple ordinances are private, so we shouldn't depict those)? If so, should we not depict private rituals like images of fathers' blessings or healings of the sick or patriarchal blessings? What about temple-centric images such as Moses ordaining Aaron in his priestly clothing or Samuel anointing David? What about sacred things like visions or angels? What about images of God? Knowing the power of visuals, should we depict *more* temple-centric themes, not *fewer*? Or should it be vice versa?

NOTES

1. This history section is modified from parts of Anthony Sweat, *The Holy Invitation* (Salt Lake City: Deseret Book, 2017), 17–20.
2. The entry for the "School of the Prophets" in the Joseph Smith Papers glossary summarizes it as "a school to prepare elders of the church for their ministry," where their "instruction was to include both sacred and secular topics." "Glossary," s.v. "School of the Prophets," The Joseph Smith Papers. The Church's *Guide to the Scriptures* calls it "a school for the purpose of training the brethren in all things pertaining to the gospel and the kingdom of God."
3. "Minutes, 22–23 January 1833," 7–8, The Joseph Smith Papers.
4. "Discourse, 12 November 1835," 33, The Joseph Smith Papers.
5. "Lucy Mack Smith, History, 1844–1845," 9, bk. 13, The Joseph Smith Papers.
6. Minutes, Salt Lake City School of the Prophets, 11 October 1883, as quoted in "House of Revelation," *Ensign*, January 1993, 31–43; emphasis added.
7. See Del Parson's *Jesus Washing the Apostles' Feet (Jesus Washing the Feet of the Apostles)*, in Gospel Media, churchofjesuschrist.org; or Laurie Olson Lisonbee's *Jesus Washes an Apostle's Feet*, history.churchofjesuschrist.org; or *The Last Supper* Bible Video, which depicts the washing of feet, churchofjesuschrist.org.
8. Jana Reiss, *The Next Mormons* (New York: Oxford, 2019), 55.
9. *Teachings of Presidents of the Church: Ezra Taft Benson* (Salt Lake City: The Church of Jesus Christ of Latter-day Saints, 2014), 174.
10. Bonnie D. Parkin, "Celebrating Covenants," *Ensign*, May 1995, 78.
11. David A. Bednar, "Prepared to Obtain Every Needful Thing," *Ensign*, May 2019, 103.
12. Bednar, "Prepared to Obtain Every Needful Thing," 103.

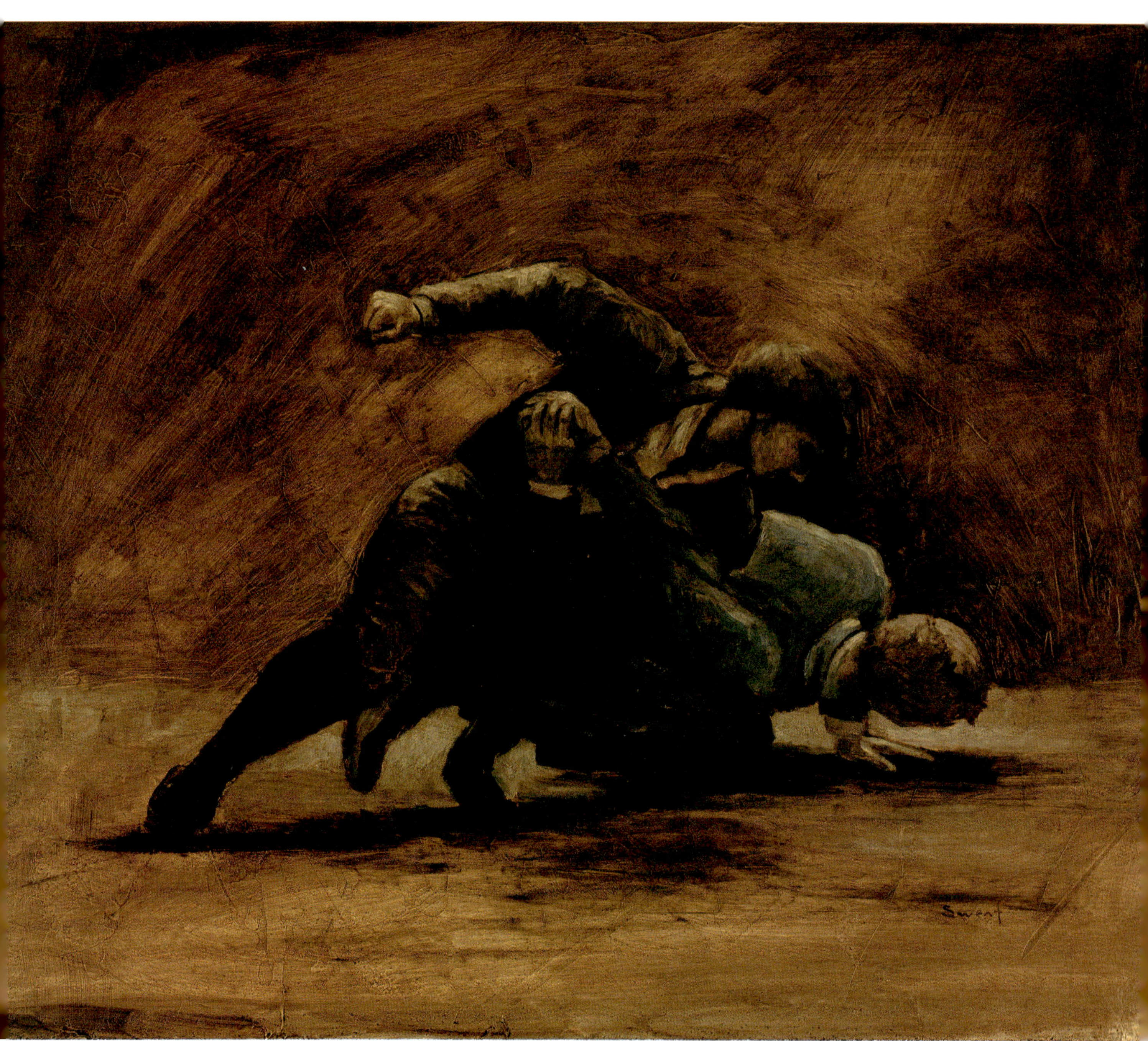

The Fierce Lions: Joseph and William Fight and Forgive (16" x 20", oil on board, 2019)

JOSEPH AND WILLIAM FIGHT AND FORGIVE

Timeline: December 1835–January 1836

Related Doctrine and Covenants Sections: 64, 98

A BACKGROUND

In Church history, we often hear narratives about Joseph Smith's brother Hyrum and sometimes about his brothers Alvin or Samuel. Joseph's little brother William Smith was one of the original members of the Quorum of the Twelve Apostles,[1] but he usually receives much less attention. In December 1833, Joseph wrote a blessing about his brother that explains some potential reasons why: "Bro William [Smith] is as the firce Lion who divideth not the spoil because of his strength and in the pride of his heart he will neglect the more ~~weightier~~ weighty matters until his soul is bowed down in sorrow and then he shall return and call on th[e] name of his God and shall find forgivness and shall wax valient therefor he shall be saved unto the utter most. . . . The blessings of the God of Jacob shall be in the midst of his house notwithstanding his rebelious heart."[2]

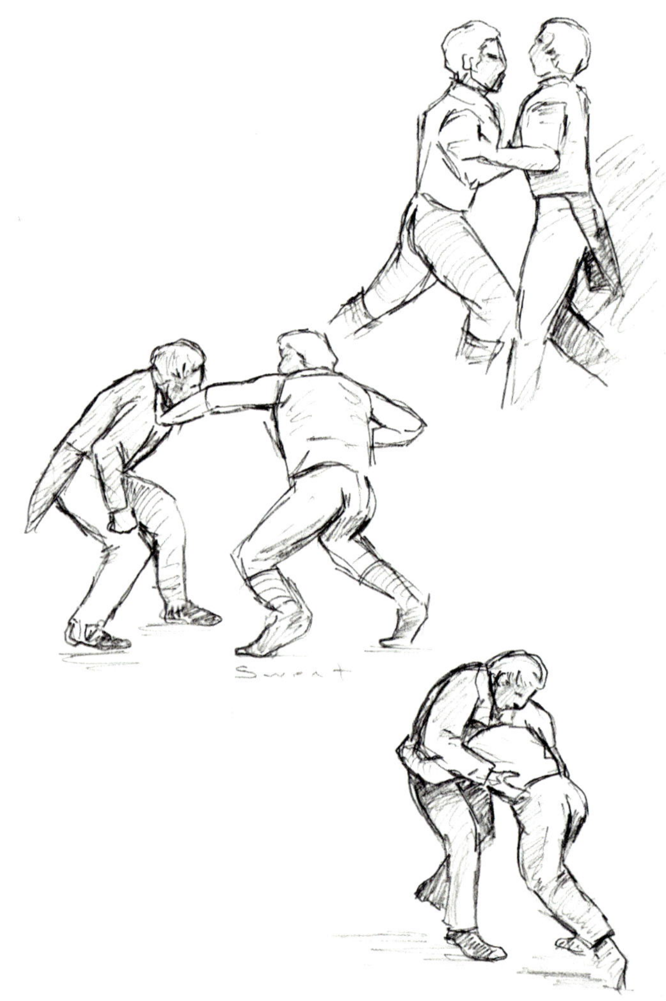

An event occurred on Wednesday, 16 December 1835, that gives potential insight into this blessing and William's nature. At William's home a debate was taking place, and he "bec[a]me much enraged" and lost his temper and "used violence upon my person."[3] That person was his older brother, Joseph Smith.

Joseph had rebuked William for the way he acted at the debate, interrupting people and telling others (including Hyrum) that they couldn't speak. Joseph told William he "manifisted, an inconciderate and stubourn spirit" that "was as ugly as the Devil."[4] Father Smith was there because he lived in the same home with William and, acting in the role of a dad trying to keep the peace, told everyone to be quiet. Joseph was about to leave the house and obey his father's directive to be silent, but his pride got the better of him. Joseph reflected on "finishing [William's] house and providin flour for your family &c and also father had possession in the house, as well, as your self," and thus he reasoned he had "the privilege of speaking in my fathers house. . . . Therefore [he] said I will speak, for I built the house, and it is as much mine as yours."[5] In hindsight, Joseph should have walked away.

Joseph's critical rebuke toward William enraged his younger brother, and William physically attacked. Joseph would later write to William, describing the fight from his perspective:

> I saw that your indignation was kindled against me, and you made towards me, I was not then to be moved, and I thought, to pull off my loose coat, least it should tangle me, and you be left to hurt me, but not with the intention, of hurting You, but you was to[o] soon for me, and having once fallen into the hands of a mob, and ~~now~~ been wounded in my side, and now into the hands of a brother, my side gave way, and after having been rescued, from your grasp, I left your house, with, feelings that were indiscribale, the scenery had changed, and all those expectations, that I had cherished, when going to your house, of brotherly kindness, charity forbearance and natural, affection, that in duty binds us not to make eachothers offenders for a word. ~~but~~
>
> But alass! abuse, anger, malice, hatred, and rage <with a lame side> with marks, of violence <heaped> upon ~~my body~~ me by a brother, were the reflections of my disapointment, and with these I returned home, not able to sit down, or rise up, without help.[6]

In other words, William violently seized on the Prophet before Joseph could remove his coat to fight back, and William beat up Joseph badly enough that afterward, Joseph struggled to move. These are two strong, grown brothers in a physical altercation; two Church leaders—a prophet and an apostle—beating up one another. Unless repentance and forgiveness were offered, the injured body of Joseph had the potential to fracture the Smith family and even the Quorum of the Twelve or the Church.

William wrote a letter to Joseph two days later, on 18 December 1835, humbly extending an olive branch of confession:

> Brother Joseph— Though I do not know but I have forfeited all right and title to the word brother, in concequence of what I have done. . . .
>
> When I reflect upon the ingury I have done you, I must confess that I do not know what I have been ~~doing~~ about. I feel sorry for what I have done and humbly ask your forgiveness. I have not confidence as yet to come and see you for I feel ashamed of what I have done, and as I feel now I feel as though all the confessions that I could make verbally or by writing, would not be sufficient to atone for the transgressions. Be this as it may, I am willing to make all the restitution you shall require. If I can stay in the church as a member— I will try to make all the satisfaction possible.
>
> Yours with respect
> Wm. Smith[7]

Joseph wrote in return, "In your letter you asked my forgivness, which I readily grant, but it seems to me, that you still retain an idea, that I have given you reasons to be angry or disaffected with me. . . . I brought salvation to my fathers house, as an instrument in the hand of God, when they were in a miserable situation, You know that it is my duty to admonish you when you do wrong this liberty I shall always take, and you shall have the same privelege."[8]

Although Joseph begins by quickly granting forgiveness, it is not hard to see some lingering difficult feelings in Joseph's reply and a desire to put William in check. Joseph writes, however, "I desire brother William that you will humble yourself, I freely forgive you. . . . And now may God have mercy upon my fathers house, may God take away enmity, from betwe[e]n me and thee, and may all blessings be restored, and the past be forgotten forever, may humble repentance bring us both to thee <O God> and to thy power and protection."[9]

Despite the well-intended words, there were still unresolved feelings. The next day, 19 December, Joseph wrote in his journal: "I have had many solemn feelings this day Concerning my Brothe[r] William."[10] The following day the internal family turmoil continued, "Sunday the 20th At home all day and took solled [solid] Comfort with my Family had many serious reflections."[11]

On New Year's Day, 1836, a type of family

intervention occurred to help heal the breach. Joseph and William met in person along with his brother Hyrum, their uncle John Smith, their father Joseph Smith Sr., and family friend Martin Harris. Joseph Smith Sr. spoke up:

> [Father Smith] expressed his feelings on the ocasion in a verry feeling and pathetic manner even with all the sympathy of a father whose feelings were wounded deeply on the account of the difficulty that was existing in the family, and while he addressed us the spirit of God rested down upon us in mighty power, and our hearts were melted Br. William made an humble confession and asked ~~our~~ my forgiveness for the abuse he had offered me and wherein I had been out of the way I asked his forgivness, and the spirit of confission and forgiveness, was mutual among us all, and we covenanted with each other in the Sight of God and the holy angels and the brethren, to strive from henceforward to build each other up in righteousness, in all things. . . . And while gratitude swelled our bosoms, [and] tears flowed from our eys.— I was then requested to close our interview which I did with prayer, and it was truly a jubilee and time of rejoiceing.[12]

AN IMAGE

In this painting, William Smith attacks Joseph in a fury, his right hand clenched and ready to inflict abuse upon his brother.

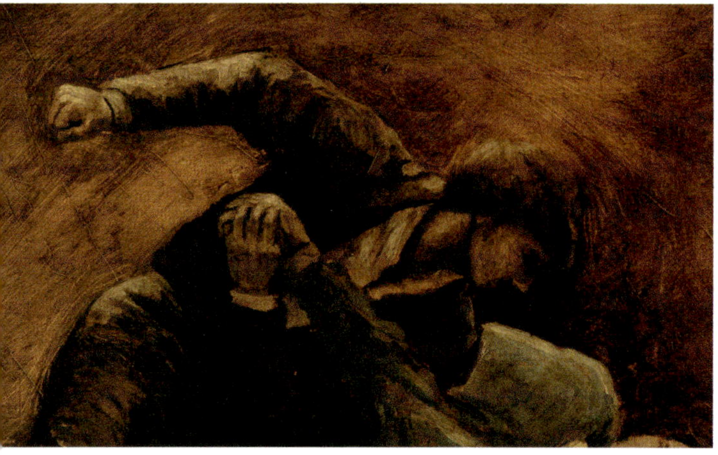

Joseph is bent to the floor, his arm and side twisted (which side he claimed was lame from the injury from the mob that attacked him, likely when he was tarred outside the John Johnson home in Hiram, Ohio, in March 1832).

I painted the scene with the brothers alone, in an undefined dark, monochromatic space, as the fight produced similar dreary and lonely results for the two of them. I also left the painting

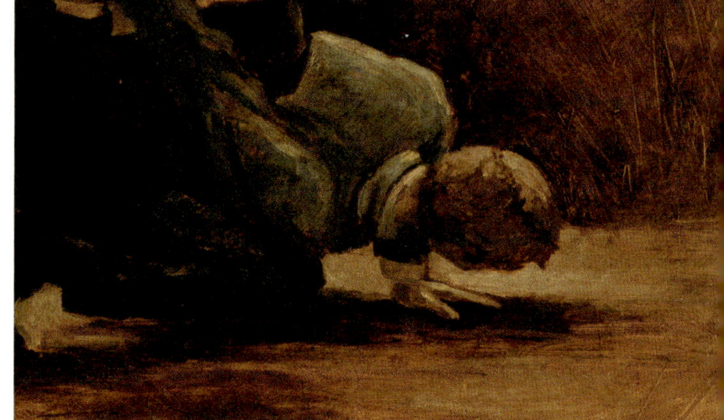

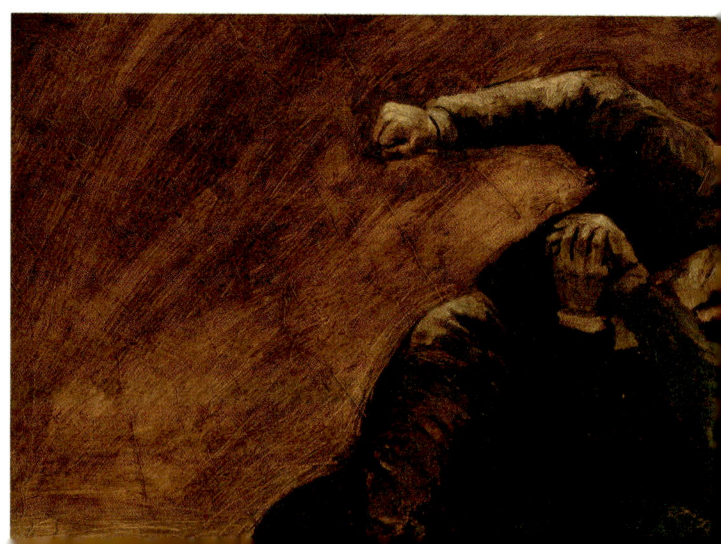

somewhat rough and unfinished, with scratches and purposefully rough patches in the gesso—the roughness and marks of the panel matching the roughness and marks from the moment.

AN APPLICATION

It is evident from reading Joseph Smith's journals that he deeply loved his family members. Time and time again, his journal entries are filled with concerns and prayers and visits with them—which is likely why this fight troubled Joseph even more and weighed down his soul. We all can relate to hurtful words or actions hurled toward loved ones during heated moments of anger and pride. We often wish we could pull them back, but—like email or internet rants—once they are out, there is no retraction mechanism. Spiritually, however, there is.

The only recourse to ours and others' failings is the divine law of forgiveness. Although this story between Joseph and William is painful, it is also insightful. I love this story because William's fierceness of a lion that came through in his fists of fury also comes through in the nobleness of his confession. Joseph is a prophet but also an older brother. His elderly pride and self-justification drip off the pages of these letters, but the greatness of his heart and brotherly desire to love and forgive and forget also saturate the sheets. Indeed, this story between Joseph and William contains pride, power, violence, justification, abuse, and malice, but those are balanced out and ultimately outweighed by confession, forgiveness, love, repentance, and humility. And isn't that what Christianity is all about? Although this story may seem negative toward Joseph the Prophet or William the Apostle in that it exposes some weakness, it actually strengthens my faith in their callings because it shows how, being human, they also lived the gospel of love, the gospel of forgiveness, and the gospel of family.

Just a few years earlier, Joseph translated Jesus's words in the Book of Mormon: "Forgive us our debts, as we forgive our debtors" (3 Nephi 13:11). Joseph had received a revelation in 1831, teaching, "Wherefore, I say unto you, that ye ought to forgive one another; for he that forgiveth not his brother his trespasses standeth condemned before the Lord. . . . Of you it is required to forgive all men" (Doctrine and Covenants 64:9–10). He had taught the Independence Saints who had been driven from the promised land that forgiving many times, even up to "seventy times seven," was required to be justified (see Doctrine and Covenants 98:39–45). This story shows Joseph and William living these divine teachings of forgiveness. The question that remains today is, Will we?

This story contains pride, power, violence, justification, abuse, and malice, but those are balanced out and ultimately outweighed by confession, forgiveness, love, repentance, and humility. And isn't that what Christianity is all about?

AN ANALYSIS

1 For a time, there was an emphasis by some in the Church to not share stories of moments of prophetic weakness, such as this one, that are true but may not be considered faith promoting.[13] What do you think? What is the balance between being transparent and open about history and Church leaders, while not focusing unduly on negative elements of human weakness? What is helpful about only focusing on the positive, and what may be hurtful? Similarly, what is helpful about being transparent and open, and what may be hurtful?

2 What is the balance of forgiving yet not forgetting? Are we under an obligation when we forgive others to allow them to fully be part of our lives again, like Joseph did with William? Or for self-protection, can we forgive from our heart but not forget out of our mind nor allow others to reenter our lives depending on the severity of the offense?

3 When we trespass against others, how can we muster the courage to own up to our errors? William Smith mentioned he couldn't bring himself to face Joseph, and it took a few weeks for them to meet face-to-face to reconcile. What helps you bring the requisite humility to ask for forgiveness? Why is asking for forgiveness face-to-face sometimes better than in written words? When may it not be?

NOTES

1. "Minutes, Discourse, and Blessings, 14–15 February 1835," 149, The Joseph Smith Papers.
2. "Journal, 1832–1834," 38–41, The Joseph Smith Papers.
3. "Journal, 1835–1836," 69–70, The Joseph Smith Papers.
4. "Journal, 1835–1836," 82.
5. "Journal, 1835–1836," 82–83.
6. "Journal, 1835–1836," 83.
7. "Journal, 1835–1836," 77–79.
8. "Journal, 1835–1836," 84, 86.
9. "Journal, 1835–1836," 84, 86–87.
10. "Journal, 1835–1836," 87.
11. "Journal, 1835–1836," 87.
12. "Journal, 1835–1836," 95–96.
13. See, for example, Boyd K. Packer, "The Mantle Is Far, Far Greater Than the Intellect" (address to religious educators, Brigham Young University, 22 August 1981), churchofjesuschrist.org.

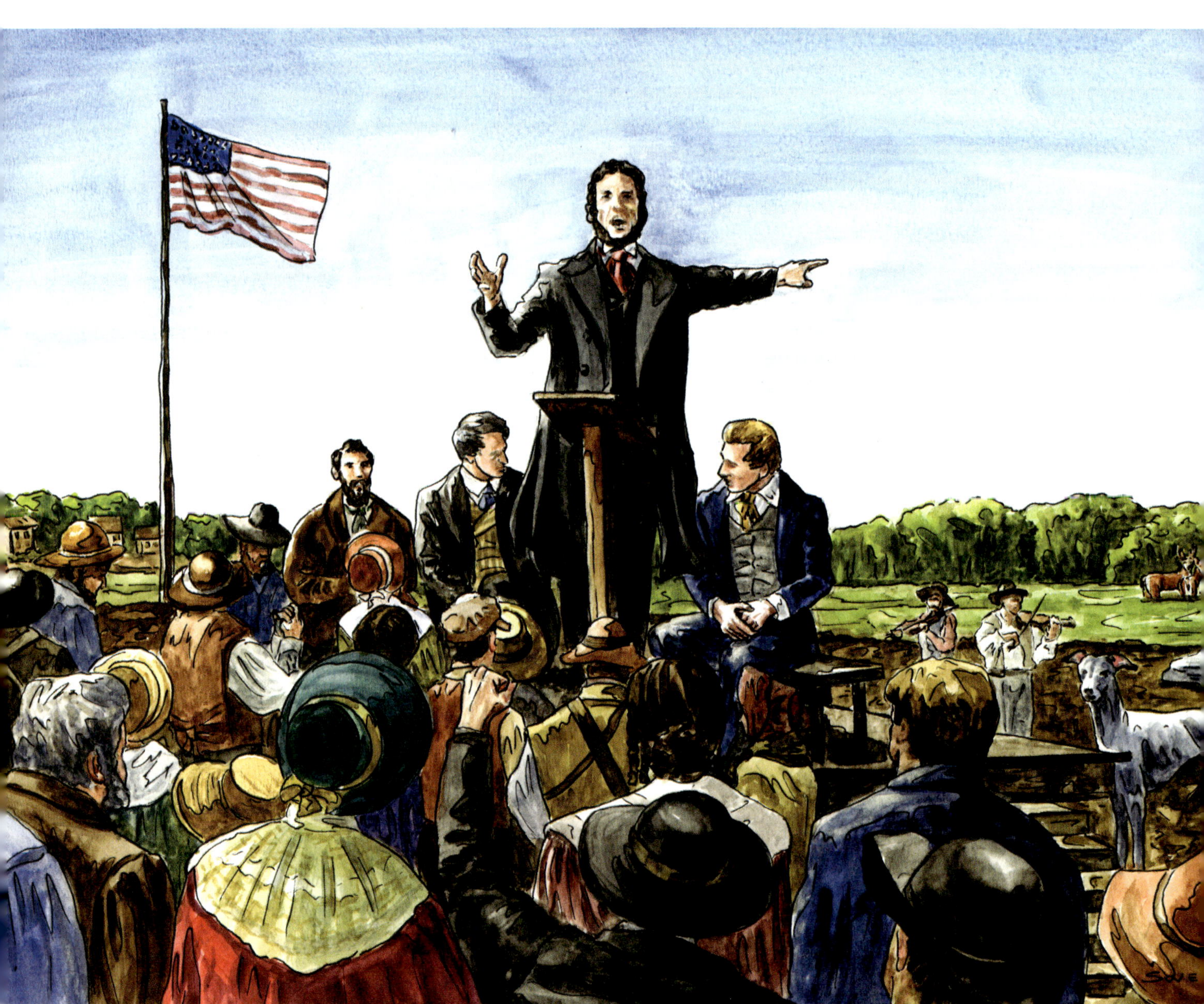

Sidney's Sermons (12" x 16", watercolor and ink on illustration board, 2019)

SIDNEY'S SERMONS

Timeline: June 1838–October 1838

Related Doctrine and Covenants Sections: 98, 115–16, 121–23

A BACKGROUND

The Church suffered two monumental setbacks in the 1830s. The first was the 1833 expulsion from their land of Zion in Independence, Missouri, at the hands of *external* vigilante mobs. The second was in 1838 in Kirtland, Ohio, when the Church fled their temple and city due in large part to threats by *internal* dissenters of the Church.[1] In an uncanonized revelation, the Lord commanded the First Presidency and "all your faithfull friends" to "get out of this place and gather themselves together unto Zion."[2] Joseph Smith and Sidney Rigdon left the same day the revelation came, and they directed faithful Church members in Ohio to also flee and gather with other Saints in northern Missouri. In April the Lord designated a city called Far West as the new headquarters of the growing Church, calling it "a holy and consecrated land" (Doctrine and Covenants 115:7).

As Joseph and Sidney settled in Far West, they saw that the Church there faced continued external tensions from Missouri locals in surrounding counties, as well as similar internal dissent by apostates. In March and April 1838, four prominent Church leaders were excommunicated in Far West on various charges.[3] What should Joseph and the First Presidency do? In Independence, the Church didn't fight back against mobs, and they lost their New Jerusalem. In Kirtland, Church members allowed threats from dissenters to drive them away from their homes and temple. "Aware of the realities" in Far West, wrote historian Richard Bushman, "Joseph decided that the Saints could not back down again."[4]

At the height of these difficulties in Missouri in the summer of 1838, Sidney Rigdon, the first counselor in the First Presidency, gave two influential speeches. One speech primarily targeted internal apostates, the other was aimed largely at external mobs. On 17 June 1838 Rigdon gave

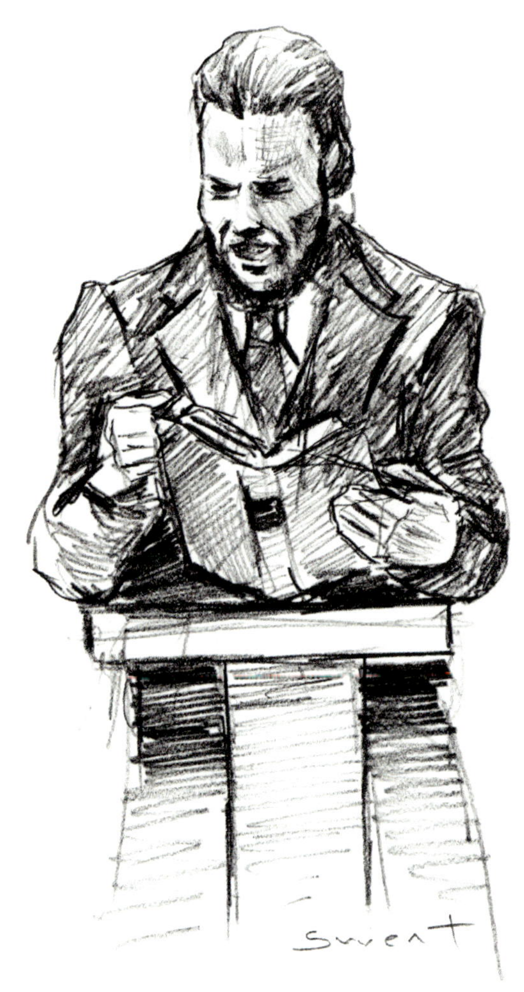

what was later termed the "Salt Sermon." A few weeks later at an Independence Day public celebration of the temple cornerstones, Rigdon gave his 4 July "oration."

John Corrill remembered the Salt Sermon this way:

> The dissenters kept up a kind of secret opposition to the presidency and church. They would occasionly speak against them, influence the minds of the members against them and occasionally correspond with their enemies

> abroad; and the church it was said would never become pure unless these dissenters were routed from among them. Moreover if they were suffered to remain they would destroy the church. . . . President Rigden delivered from the pulpit, what I call the salt Sermon. "If the salt have lost its saviour [savor] it is ~~of~~ thenceforth good for nothing but ~~but~~ to be cast out and trod[d]en under the feet of men," was his text, and although he did not call names in his sermon, yet it was plainly understood that he meant that dissenters or those who had denied the faith, ought to be cast out and literally troden underfoot. . . .
>
> This sermon had the desired effect. Excitement was produced in the church, and, suffice it to say, that in three or four days several of the dissenters became much alarmed ~~from the~~ and fled from the place in a gr[e]at fright, and their families soon followed.[5]

John Whitmer, who was one of the recently excommunicated Church leaders, recalls, "They preached a sermon called it the Salt sermon in which these gideonites understood that they should drive the disenters as they termed those who believed ~~that~~ not. . . . Their band of gadeantons kept up a guard and watched our houses and abused our families and threatened them if they were not gone by morning they would be drove out & threttened our lives if they ever saw us in Far West."[6]

Who were these "Gideonites" that helped drive out dissenters? They are more commonly known as the "Danites," or originally the "members of the society of the Daughter of Zion."[7] Named Danites (perhaps by Joseph Smith)[8] after the biblical warring tribe of Dan (see Judges 18), the Danites were an "an oath-bound military society organized among the Latter-day Saints in Missouri in summer 1838 to defend the Church of Jesus Christ of Latter-day Saints from internal and external opposition."[9] Like other antebellum frontier communities who organized safety committees to warn out undesirable people and activities in their towns,[10] the Danites desired to intimidate Church dissenters from Far West and cleanse the Church of apostates. According to early Church member John Corrill, "[The Danites] entered into a covenant, that the word of the presidency should be obeyed, and none should be suffered to raise his hand or voice against it. . . . The first presidency did not seem to have much to do with [the Danites] at first: they would, however, go into their meetings occasionally, and sanction their doings."[11]

Reed Peck testified against Church leaders at a 29 November 1838 hearing about "Mr. Rigdons 'Salt Sermon'" and claimed that "Mr Rigdon said in the same Sermon that he would assist to erect a gallows on the Square and hang them all [the dissenters], Jos Smith Jr was present and followed Mr Rigdon after he had made the above declaration and said he did not wish to do any thing unlawful . . . [but] said that he approved of Mr Rigdons sermon & called it a good sermon."[12] The day of the Salt Sermon, the Danites delivered a warning to five prominent excommunicated Church leaders to leave Far West within three days or "vengeance would overtake you sooner or later."[13] The dissenters fled in a fright.

A few weeks after the Salt Sermon, President Rigdon delivered yet another public sermon, this one aimed at warning external mobs threatening the Church in surrounding communities. This sermon was delivered on 4 July 1838, America's Independence Day. A grand processional parade led by the First Presidency was held to lay the cornerstones of the Far West Temple. Under an American flag on a tall liberty pole, President Rigdon climbed a platform and delivered a fiery sermon to the Saints, full of defiant rhetoric. Referencing the directives to deal with aggressors in Doctrine and Covenants 98, Rigdon thundered:

> We take God and all the holy angels to witness this day, that we warn all men in the name of Jesus Christ, to come on us no more forever, for from this hour, we will bear it no more, our rights shall no more be trampled

> on with impunity. The man or the set of men, who attempts it, does it at the expense of their lives. And that mob that comes on us to disturb us; it shall be between us and them a war of extermination, for we will follow them, till the last drop of their blood is spilled, or else they will have to exterminate us: for we will carry the seat of war to their own houses, and their own families, and one party or the other shall be utterly destroyed.—Remember it then all MEN."[14]

He reminded the saints, "We will never be the agressors," but "the persecutions which we have had to endure, for the l[a]st nine years" had caused the Saints to "proclaim ourselves free" from oppressors.[15] When Sidney finished his oration, the crowd of Saints thundered their support with "a shout of hosanna.[16]

The stage was set for war, which would come within a matter of months.

AN IMAGE

This painting contains elements from both of Sidney Rigdon's influential sermons in the summer of 1838, but primarily depicts the 4 July oration. The flag frames the composition, standing above the rest, an important visual symbol for the subject of the sermon, its twenty-six stars including the recently admitted state to the Union: Missouri.

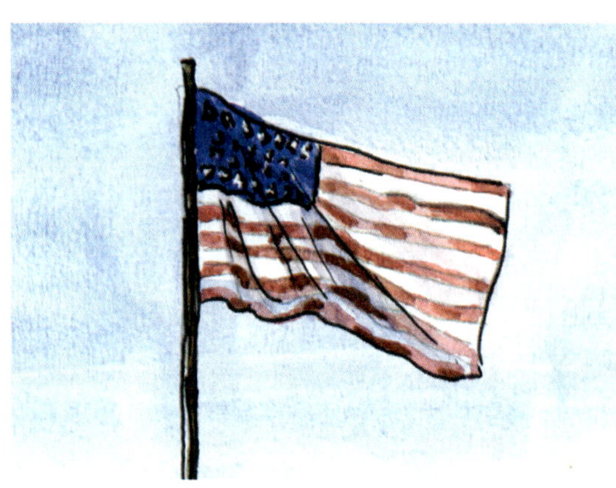

Sidney stands in the center of the composition, viewers looking slightly up to him as though they are part of the crowd. Rigdon points with his left hand over the horizon, as though he is simultaneously casting out dissenters and challenging potential outlying attackers—his right hand raising up as if to whip the crowd into a frenzy. Behind him on the stand sit Joseph and Hyrum, who, with Sidney, compose the First Presidency. They pass each other somewhat hesitant looks about the nature and potential ramifications of President Rigdon's directives, a course they seemingly approve though they seem

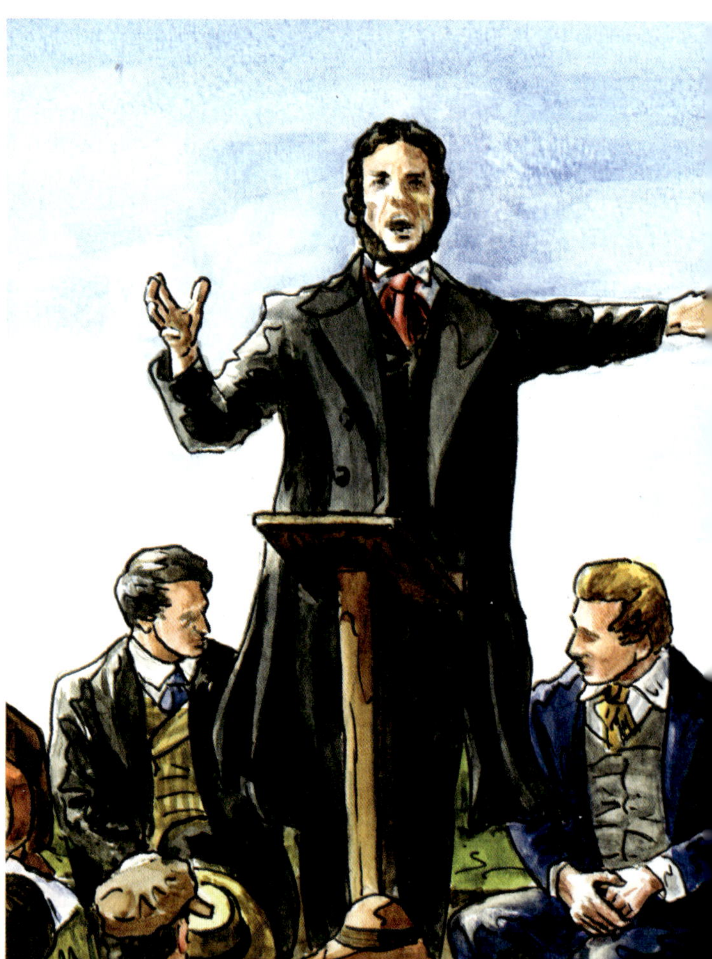

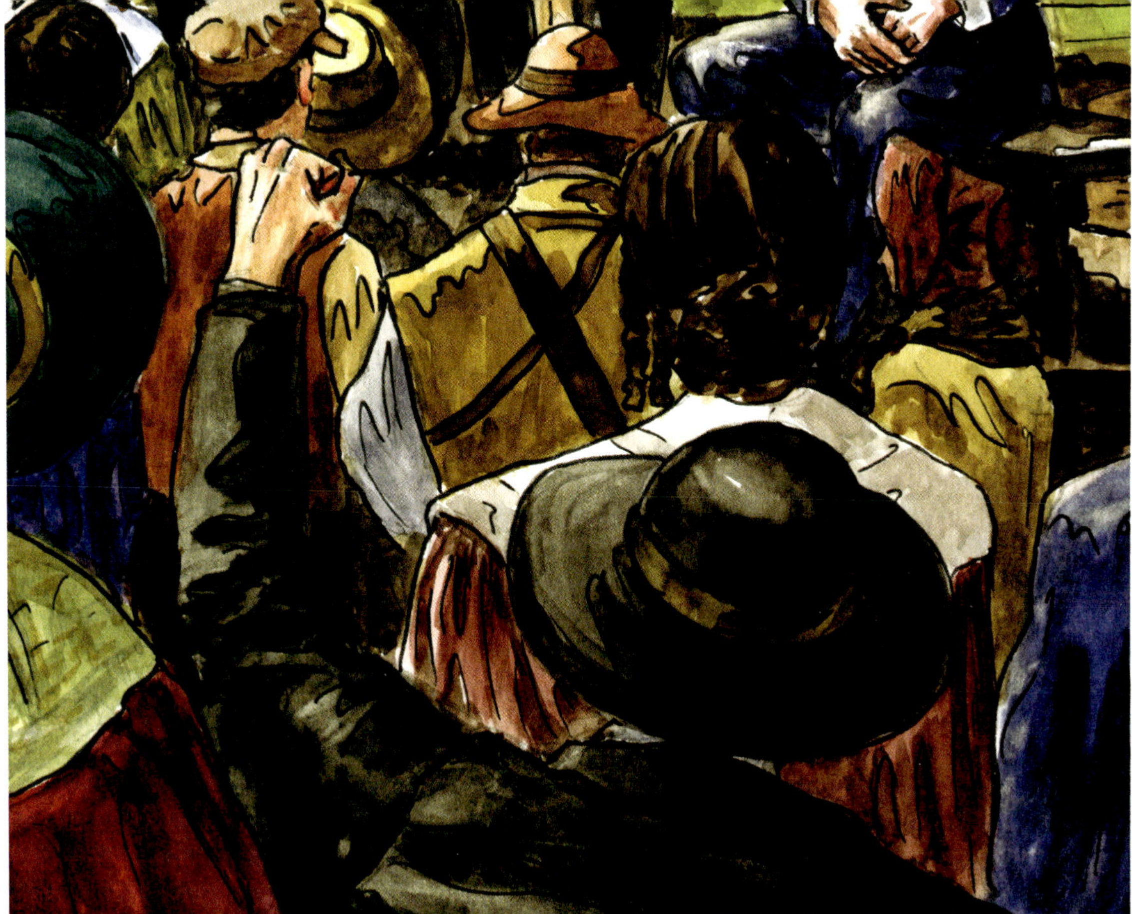

unsure about the results it may produce.

In the crowd stand members of the Church, women and men ready to shout "Hosanna!" to President Rigdon's remarks. A man symbolizing a Danite raises his clenched left fist, showing vigilante approval.

Two fiddlers stand in the back, representing the processional parade band and being ready to play a song composed by Levi Hancock for the occasion (to be sung by Solomon Hancock).[17]

On the right of the image, just below a temple cornerstone, stands a greyhound dog ready to pursue two deer that stand on the horizon. This represents an analogy Joseph gave of the apostates bounding over the prairies as they fled from Far West after the Salt Sermon like a deer running away from a hound.[18]

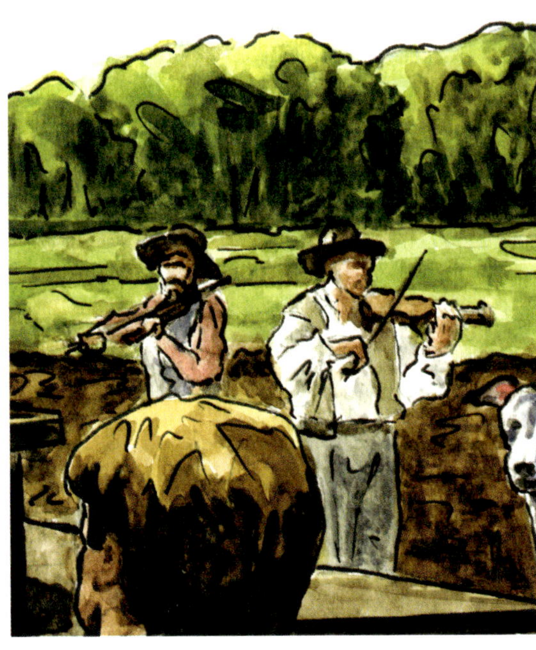

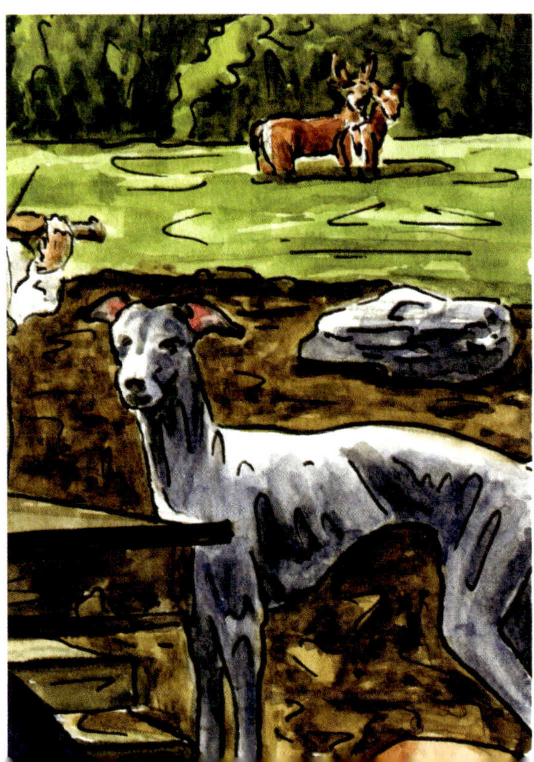

AN APPLICATION

War broke out in the fall of 1838 between the Saints and the state of Missouri, and Joseph Smith with other Church leaders were arrested on charges of treason. When Joseph Smith languished in Liberty Jail during the winter of 1839, he had much time to reflect on what went wrong in Missouri. Joseph wrote a letter to the Church from Liberty Jail around 22 March 1839. Parts of that letter have been canonized in Doctrine and Covenants 121, 122, and 123. In his letter are classic verses on principles of proper priesthood leadership, cited over and over in Church settings and applied to being a good parent or spouse or ecclesiastical leader. It is interesting, however, to read and learn from these famous verses in their historical context regarding Sidney's summer 1838 sermons, Church dissenters, and the Danites.

It is easy to be bothered by the harsh, forceful, and intimidating approach some took in the summer of 1838. Joseph writes, "We have learned by sad experiance that it is the nature and disposition of almost all men as soon as they get a little authority as they suppose they will imediately begin to [e]xercise unritious dominion."[19] Whom did he have in mind? Just a few pages later in the letter, Joseph writes, "And again I would further suggest the impropriety of the organization of bands or companies by covenant or oaths by penalties <or ~~secrecy~~ secrecies> but let the time past of our experiance and sufferings by the wickedness of Doctor [Sampson] Avard suffise,"[20] referring to Sampson Avard, one of the generals of the Missouri Danites and a primary leader of the group. It is evident that by the winter of 1839, Joseph regretted the approach of the summer of 1838. It is possible that Joseph even regretted his own actions, or lack thereof, regarding the Danites and his sanctioning of some of their initial actions (although he was "ignorant as well as innocent"—in his words—of the full measure of their "pernicious" doings).[21] We aren't accustomed to reading Doctrine and Covenants 121's condemnation of unrighteous dominion through the lens of potential mistakes made by the First Presidency, or even Joseph himself, but such an application is not without possibility. Joseph writes his resolve in the letter, "Your humble servant or servants intend from henceforth to disapprobate every thing that is not in accordance with the fulness of the gospel of Jesus Christ and is not of a bold and frank and an upright nature."[22]

We aren't accustomed to reading Doctrine and Covenants 121's condemnation of unrighteous dominion through the lens of potential mistakes made by the First Presidency, or even Joseph himself, but such an application is not without possibility.

The Lord through Joseph reminds us that no power or influence "can or ought to be maintained by <[vi]rt[ue]> of the Priesthood only by persuasion by long suffering by gentleness and meekness and by love unfaigned by kindness by pure knowledge which shall greatly enlarge the soul without hypocrisy and without guile"[23] (see Doctrine and Covenants 121:41–42). The Danite influence in the summer and fall of 1838 was negative[24] and short lived. Sidney's inflammatory rhetoric in the Salt Sermon and 4 July oration had similar damaging influence. Unless you and I learn how to lead by love, persuade by principles of the priesthood, and resolve conflict through righteousness, our personal influence will be equally short lived and negative.

AN ANALYSIS

1 This history about Sidney's sermons in the summer of 1838 highlights what seems to be a doctrinal dilemma laid out in the New Testament and the Book of Mormon: When do we turn the other cheek if someone attacks (see Matthew 5:39–40), and when do we, as Captain Moroni taught, defend our religion and our freedom "even unto bloodshed" (Alma 43:47)? What do you make of examples in scripture where intimidation, coercion, or violence is used to accomplish righteous purposes (see, for example, 1 Nephi 4, Alma 60, or Joshua 6)? Is violence ever appropriate for Saints? When and why or why not?

2 The Saints in northern Missouri in 1838 seemed to have taken the position of self-defense when they perceived the civil authorities would not protect their constitutional freedoms. How would you react if your peace and family were threatened and civil authorities could not or would not defend your rights?

3 What do we learn from this history about proper and improper ways to react toward and deal with members in our families or our local congregations who choose to distance themselves from the Church, apostatize from or leave it, or even fight against the Church or its leaders?

NOTES

1. Editors for the *Joseph Smith Papers* write, "The [excommunicated Ohio] dissenters claimed that J[oseph] S[mith] was a fallen prophet who had led the church astray and that his followers were heretics. Their fervor led to threats of violence." Historical introduction to "Revelation, 12 January 1838–C," The Joseph Smith Papers.
2. "Revelation, 12 January 1838–C," 1.
3. John Whitmer, W. W. Phelps, David Whitmer, and the Assistant President of the Church, Oliver Cowdery. See Jacob W. Olmstead, "Far West and Adam-ondi-Ahman: D&C 115, 116, 117," in *Revelations in Context: The Stories behind Sections of the Doctrine and Covenants*, ed. Matthew McBride and James Goldberg (Salt Lake City: The Church of Jesus Christ of Latter-day Saint, 2016), 236.
4. Richard Lyman Bushman, *Joseph Smith: Rough Stone Rolling* (New York: Alfred A. Knopf, 2005), 354–55.
5. "John Corrill, 'Brief History,' Manuscript, circa 1838–1839," 52–54, The Joseph Smith Papers.
6. "John Whitmer, History, 1831–circa 1847," 86–87, The Joseph Smith Papers.
7. See "Glossary," s.v. "Danites," The Joseph Smith Papers.
8. Joseph Smith would claim he named the group "Danites" at a meeting years later in Nauvoo. Joseph said, "The Danite system never had any existence,

the term grew out of a term I made an off when the brethren prepared to defend themselves from the mob in Far West,—the in reference to the stealing of Macaiahs images—if the enemiy comes the Danites will be after them, meaning the brethren in self defince." "Nauvoo City Council Rough Minute Book, November 1842–January 1844," 36, The Joseph Smith Papers.

9. "Glossary," s.v. "Danites."
10. See Alexander L. Baugh, "'We Have a Company of Danites in These Times': The Danites, Joseph Smith, and the 1838 Missouri-Mormon Conflict," *Journal of Mormon History* 45, no. 3 (2019): 5.
11. "John Corrill, *A Brief History of the Church of Jesus Christ of Latter day Saints*, 1839," 31, The Joseph Smith Papers.
12. "Minutes and Testimonies, 12–29 November 1838, Copy [*State of Missouri v. Gates et al. for Treason*]," 44–45, The Joseph Smith Papers.
13. "Appendix 1: Letter to Oliver Cowdery and Others, circa 17 June 1838," 1, The Joseph Smith Papers.
14. "Appendix 3: Discourse, circa 4 July 1838," 12, The Joseph Smith Papers.
15. "Appendix 3: Discourse, circa 4 July 1838," 12.
16. "*Elders' Journal*, August 1838," 60, The Joseph Smith Papers.
17. "History, 1838–1856, volume B-1 [1 September 1834–2 November 1838]," 800, The Joseph Smith Papers.
18. See "Journal, March–September 1838," 46–47, The Joseph Smith Papers. See also "John Whitmer, History, 1831–circa 1847," 86–87.
19. "Letter to Edward Partridge and the Church, circa 22 March 1839," 3, The Joseph Smith Papers.
20. "Letter to Edward Partridge and the Church, circa 22 March 1839," 7.
21. "Letter to the Church in Caldwell County, Missouri, 16 December 1838," 5, The Joseph Smith Papers. Alex Baugh writes that Joseph Smith "was fully aware of the Danite organization and its leaders, and even sanctioned some of their early activities," although "it was not until after the surrender of the Mormons to Missouri authorities that he was made more completely aware of the subversive teachings and instructions perpetrated by the society's leaders. Baugh, "'We Have a Company of Danites,'" 1–2. Editors for *The Joseph Smith Papers* write, "JS attended at least one of the society's meetings and reportedly expressed approval of its aims, but the precise nature of his involvement with the organization is unclear." "Glossary," s.v. "Danites."
22. "Letter to Edward Partridge and the Church, circa 22 March 1839," 7.
23. "Letter to Edward Partridge and the Church, circa 22 March 1839," 3.
24. Alex Baugh writes, "The activities and operations of the Caldwell County militia and the formation of the Mormon paramilitary organization known as the Danites, proved to be negative and led to the civil disturbances in late 1838 during what became known as the Missouri-Mormon War." "'We Have a Company of Danites,'" 1.

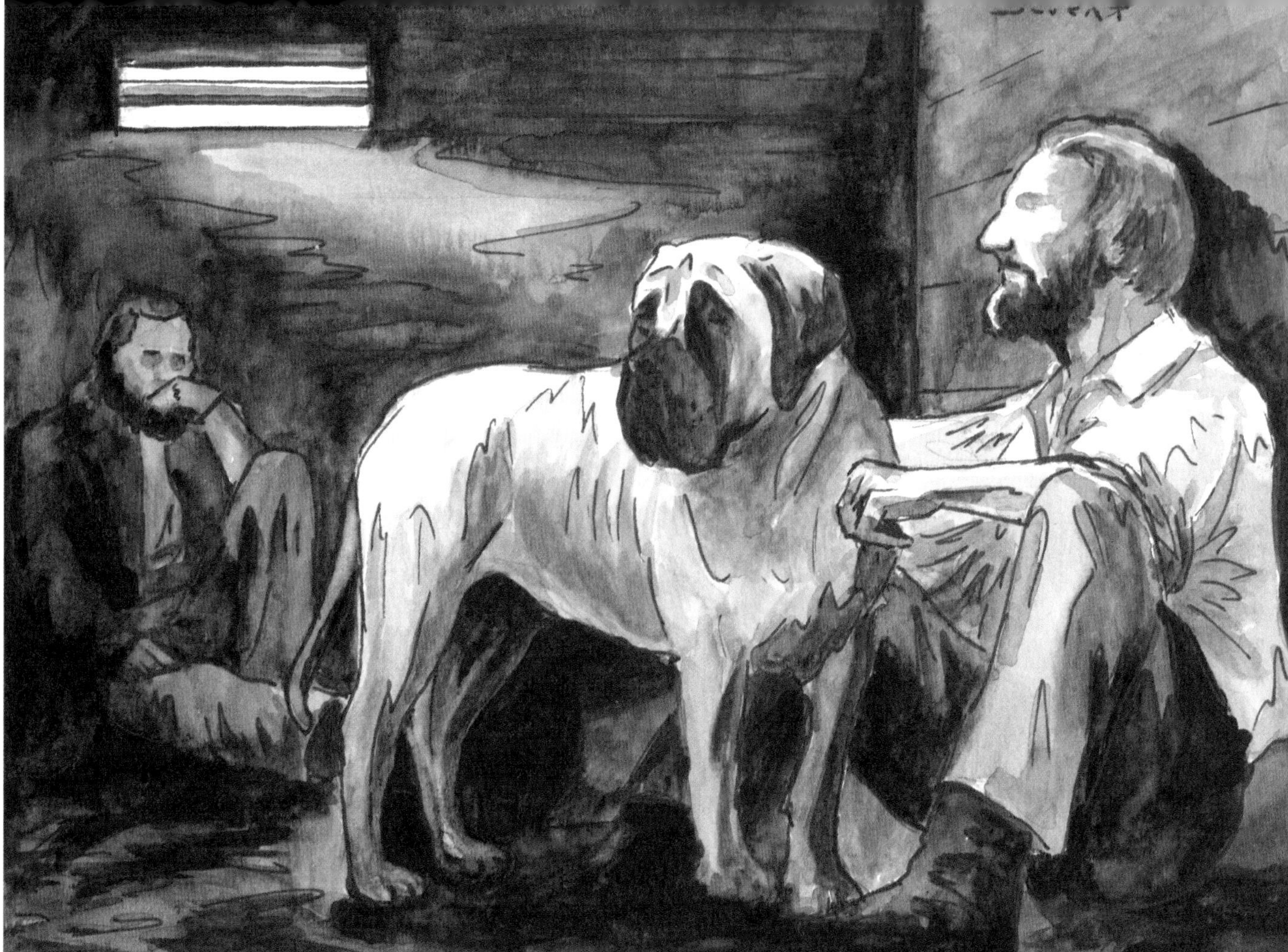

Old Major in Liberty Jail (6.25" x 8.25", watercolor and ink on illustration board, 2010)

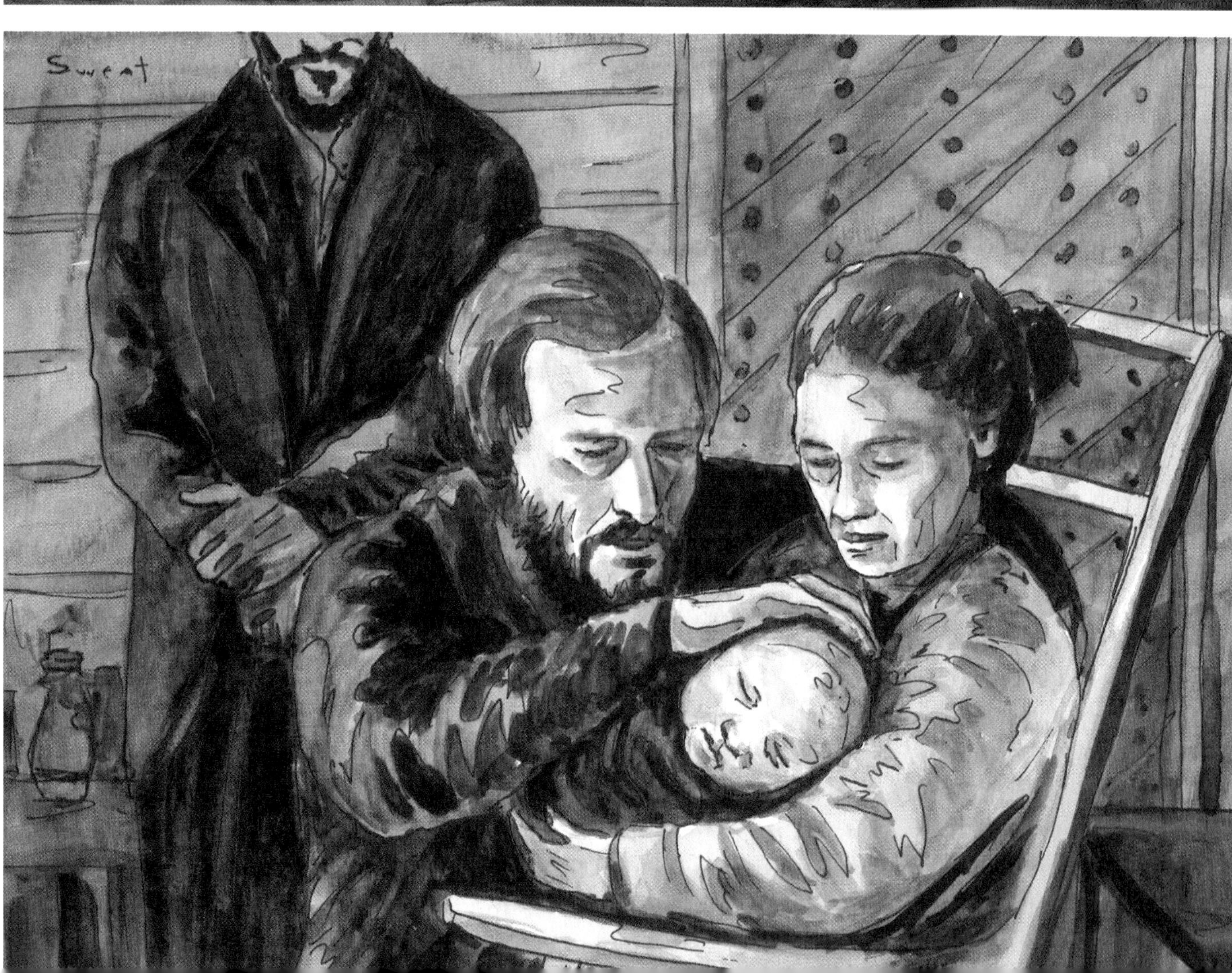

Hyrum Blessing Joseph F. Smith (6.25" x 8.25", watercolor and ink on illustration board, 2010)

IMAGES OF COMFORT AT LIBERTY JAIL

Timeline: December 1838–April 1839

Related Doctrine and Covenants Sections: 121–23

A BACKGROUND

Most Latter-day Saints are aware of the imprisonment of Joseph Smith and a half dozen other Church leaders in the Clay County Jail in Liberty, Missouri, awaiting charges of treason from December 1838 to April 1839. The miserable conditions, the food, the height of the ceiling, the cold, the hunger, the sickness, the suffering, the entire experience is well covered in traditional Church teaching. For example, the term "Liberty Jail" has been mentioned in general conference 152 times.[1] There are also well-known paintings of Liberty Jail, such as Liz Lemon Swindle's painting of Joseph praying and Greg Olsen's painting with Joseph writing letters to the Saints from prison, along with other portrayals in Church films. The re-creation of Liberty Jail at the Church history site in Liberty and another cut-out replica at the Church History Museum in Salt Lake City have also contributed to common awareness of the difficulties Joseph and other Church leaders experienced in Liberty Jail.

As opposed to the suffering endured inside its cold walls, the two images herein represent lesser-known events in Liberty Jail that offered a few warm comforts from home. One is based on research detailing that Joseph Smith may have had his large dog, Old Major, with him for a time in Liberty Jail.[2] Humans' best friend in Liberty Jail? Perhaps so! In a late reminiscence a man named Aaron Harlan wrote, "I visited with Joseph Smith at Nauvoo several different times . . . and played with his dog. . . . [Joseph] added that when he was a prisoner in Missouri, that dog could not be separated from him, and for months when he slept, that dog always remained asleep by his side."[3]

Joseph's dog was a white or light tan English mastiff, likely given to the Prophet in 1834 on the march from Ohio to Missouri known as Zion's Camp. At the camp, "this dog was greatly attached to Joseph and was generally by his side," said George A. Smith.[4] Missouri historian Alex Baugh, who first authored the publication on

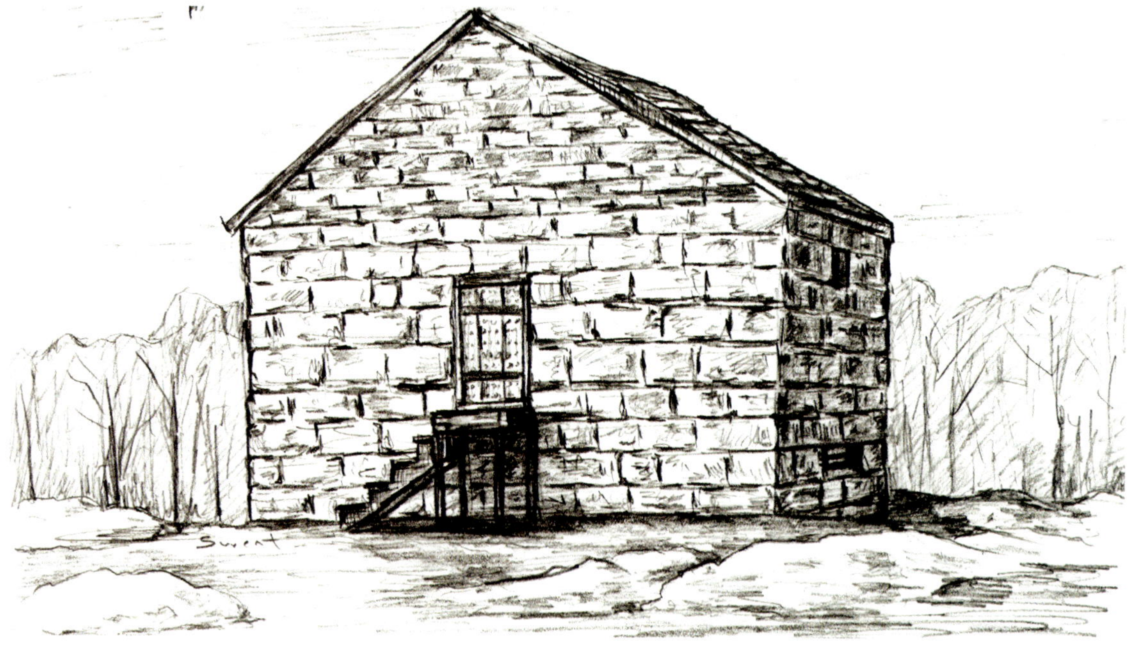

Joseph's dog in Liberty, writes, "Joseph Smith may have been allowed to have Major with him during part of the time he was incarcerated in Missouri, and if so, this was perhaps the most significant role this pet played in Joseph's life. . . . If Joseph Smith was allowed to have his dog with him during his Missouri imprisonment, it is not known exactly when Major was actually with him, but there are some clues."[5]

Baugh details that Emma Smith visited her husband in Liberty Jail on three occasions. On the first occasion, it is possible she brought the dog with her for protection and left him there with Joseph and the other prisoners. Baugh writes that, based on the timing of Emma's visits, "Major spent at least a month (December 20, 1838 to January 21, 1839) but possibly up to six weeks (December 8, 1838 to January 21, 1839), with Joseph Smith in the jail."[6] Emma likely took Old Major back with her after a visit to Liberty Jail on 21 January 1839 as she prepared to flee Missouri and go east to Illinois.

After Emma's departure, Joseph wrote her a letter on 21 March 1839, suggesting that he missed Old Major, "Try to gain time and write to me a long letter and tell me all you can and even if old major is alive yet."[7] Joseph wrote Emma again on 4 April 1839, saying, "I want <to> see little Frederick, Joseph, Julia, and Alexander, Joana, and old major.[8]

Aaron W. Harlan's letters to the *Keokuk Daily Post* in Keokuk, Iowa, in 1888, give his late recollection that Joseph told him Old Major was with him during his imprisonment in Missouri. Harlan recited how much the dog meant to Joseph Smith when Harlan recalled: "I have ate with [Joseph Smith] at his table and played with his dog, and on noticing the dog was getting old, I said to Mr. Smith, 'Your dog is unusually fat.' 'Yes,' said Mr. Smith, 'he lives as I do and shall as long as we both live."[9]

Some may wonder why Joseph would be allowed to keep an animal with him in prison. Baugh writes, "It is important to note that during this era, regulations regarding the incarceration of inmates were not like they are today. Prisoners were not only allowed to have visitors, but family members and friends were permitted to take up lodging for a day or two or even for weeks at a time. . . . It may not have been out of place for the Mormon prisoners to have had other privileges, including the keeping of a dog."[10]

This idea of the relative privileges of nineteenth-century American frontier prisoners, including family staying overnight, provides a transition to discuss the second image of comforts of home at Liberty Jail. The writers of *Saints* assert, "In February 1839, Hyrum's wife, Mary, and her sister Mercy visited the prisoners [in Liberty Jail] with Hyrum's newborn son, Joseph F. Smith. Mary had not seen Hyrum since before she gave birth in November. The delivery and a severe cold had left her almost too weak to travel to Liberty. But Hyrum had asked her to come, and she did not know if she would have another chance to see him."[11]

Mercy Fielding Smith later recorded, "About the first of February [late January] 1839, by the request of her husband, my sister (Mary) was placed on a bed in a wagon and taken on a journey of about 40 miles to visit him [Hyrum] in prison, her infant son Joseph F. then being about eleven weeks old. . . . We arrived at the prison in the evening. We were admitted and the doors closed upon us, a night never to be forgotten. A sleepless night."[12] The sisters only stayed one night and left for home the next day. Mercy does not record what happened that night or the next day, but Edward Stevenson, who "looked upon the jail in 1838" and was a contemporary of Hyrum's, recalled in a later reminiscence a sweet blessing that was given to the future sixth President of the Church: "Joseph F. Smith, with his mother, visited his father in this same jail, and although but an infant, received a blessing under his hands."[13] Although Stevenson recalls this blessing, in known documents neither Hyrum Smith nor his wife, Mary Smith, mentions the blessing, nor do any of the prisoners or jailers. Baugh concludes, however, "Given the circumstances—this being the first time Hyrum had seen his new son and the fact that Mary was making preparations to leave Missouri (suggesting that it might be some time before Hyrum would be reunited with her and the children)—it seems likely that Hyrum would use the occasion to give a blessing."[14]

Although Liberty Jail was a time of intense suffering and difficulty for Joseph and his fellow prisoners, there were also moments of comfort, moments of home, moments of love, and moments of revelation. While both these events in Liberty Jail—Old Major's presence and Joseph F. Smith's blessing—are based on some later reminiscences and some logical deduction by Baugh (and therefore subject to some necessary questions related to reliability), I wanted to illustrate these scenes to provide some alternate images of comfort that may have helped the prisoners endure the suffering that transpired in Liberty Jail. There is something tender to the idea that Joseph Smith had the company of a beloved dog in the hardships of Liberty Jail. When I completed this painting, I first shared it on social media, and people were touched by it more than I had anticipated. One person wrote, "How comforting!" and another, "This warms my heart!"

AN IMAGE

In the illustration of Joseph with Old Major, I wanted Joseph sitting and petting his dog in a pose with which any dog owner is familiar. Major stands close but looks outward, almost protective—as mastiffs are known to be.

There's a hint of a smile on Joseph's bearded face, suggesting a moment of solace in the presence of his pet.

I placed Old Major in the bottom portion of the jail, the dungeon area. I don't know if that is right or not, as it would have required lowering down and lifting up a dog that could weigh around 150 pounds. Likely Major would have stayed outside or in the upper, main floor. This is where artistic needs bend the unknowns of history to communicate to viewers—placing Joseph and his dog in the dungeon portion with the cell window and bar creates a more recognizable

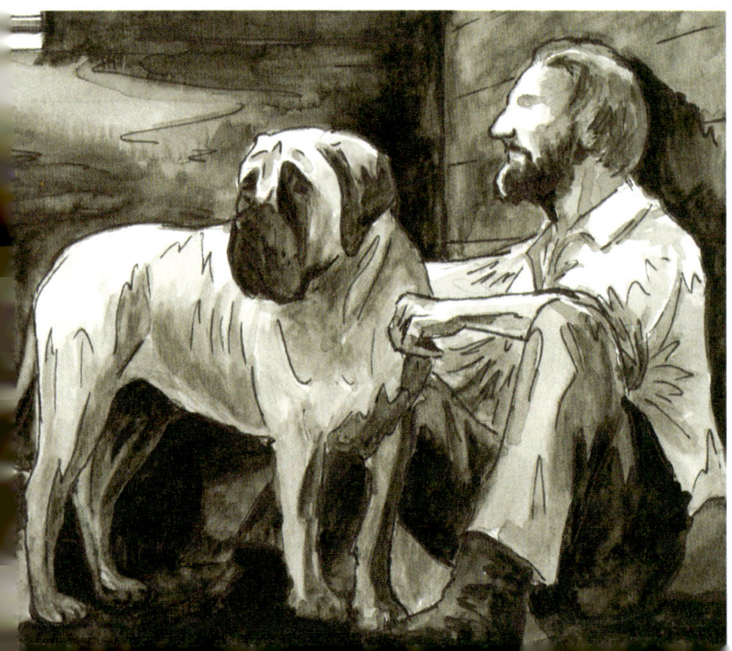

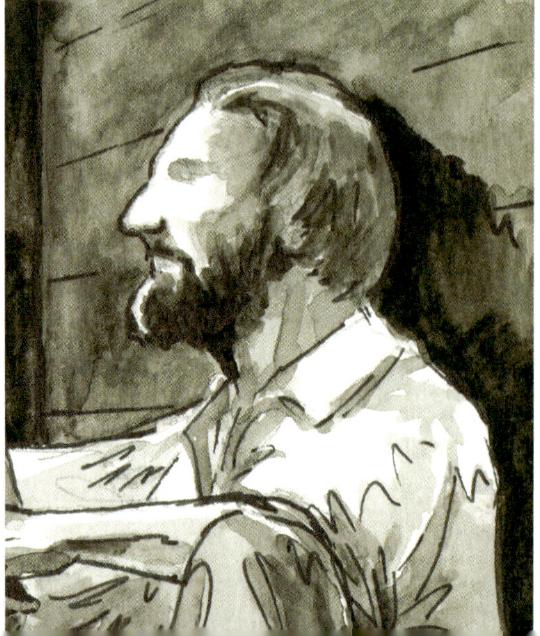

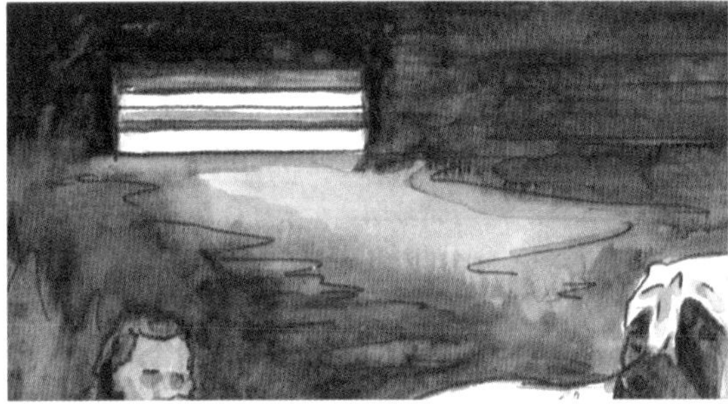

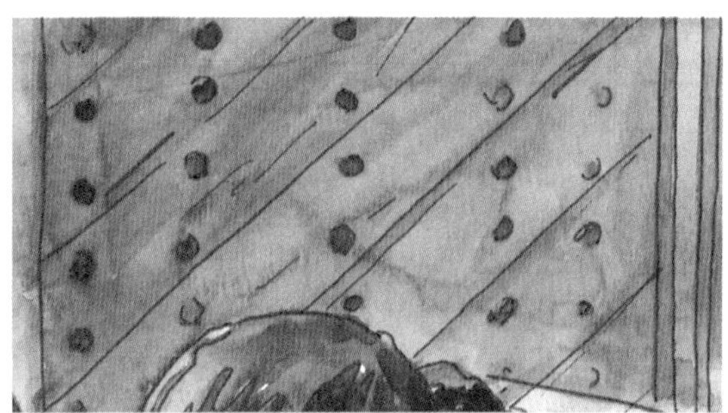

context for the observer. Speaking of the window bar (which may have been a single, horizontal bar, not vertical, slatted ones),[15] light pours through the window horizontally toward Joseph, again using directional angles to lead viewers and suggesting rays of light and hope.

In the image of Hyrum blessing his infant son, Joseph F. Smith, I placed the participants in the upper, main portion of Liberty Jail. The large, riveted door behind Hyrum and Mary is familiar to many who have visited historic Liberty Jail.

In the scene, Hyrum places his right hand on his infant son, as his wife Mary holds him. I thought this a more intimate and familial trio than if Joseph and Hyrum were holding the babe. Mary was not well, as her sister Mercy indicated, and I wanted her face to show strain and suffering. Hyrum also looks slightly haggard and worn, while infant Joseph F. sleeps soundly during the blessing.

Behind Hyrum is a figure that can represent either Joseph Smith or a guard, watching over the blessing. I will leave that up to you as the viewer to decide.

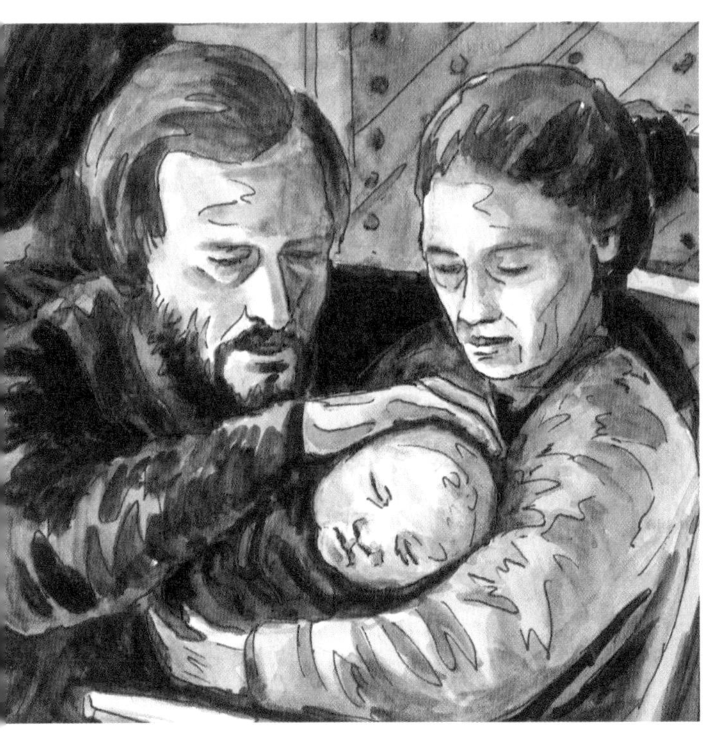

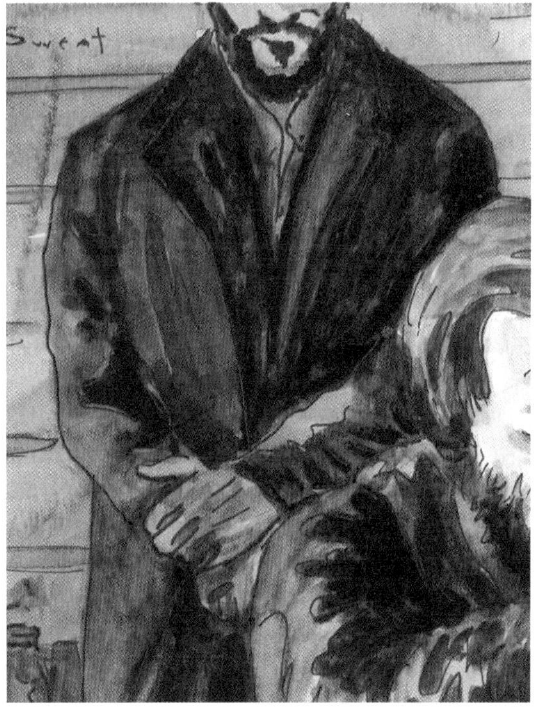

AN APPLICATION

The way Doctrine and Covenants 121 reads today can cause us to miss an important application of how small offerings of love can catalyze large revelations from above. Section 121 contains excerpts from a letter Joseph Smith wrote on 20 March 1839. The section opens with Joseph's heart-wrenching plea, "O God, where art thou?" (see Doctrine and Covenants 121:1), followed by his queries about how long he and the Saints must endure these unlawful sufferings before the Lord intervenes. In our excerpted and edited edition of the letter in Doctrine and Covenants 121, after Joseph's pleas come the comforting words of the Lord, "My son pease be unto thy soul thine advirsity and thy afflictions shall be but a small moment"[16] (see 121:7). It's almost as if Joseph pleads in prayer, and then the divine reassurance comes immediately as an answer. However, the original letters offer us an insight into the actual catalyst for the revelatory words from God.

In the original letter, after asking, "O God, where art thou?," Joseph writes for *four more pages* of issues from Missouri. Then he informs, "We received some letters last evening one from Emma one from Don C[arlos] Smith and one from Bishop Partridge all breathing a kind and consoling spirit we were much gratified with there contence [contents] we had been a long time without information and when we read those letters they were to our ~~soles~~ <souls > as the gentle air, <is> refreshing."[17] Then, because of the effect from "the voice of a friend," Joseph writes, "and when the hart is sufficiently contrite and <then> the voice of inspiration steals along and whispers my son pease be unto thy soul thine advirsity and thy afflictions shall be but a small moment."[18]

> Kind and consoling words can act as catalysts for the Comforter.

When people are suffering and struggling, we sometimes don't know what to do to alleviate their pain. Indeed, sometimes we can't. One thing we can always do is to take the time to write a heartfelt note, send a sincere email, or type a loving text. Simple expressions of how much we love a person, what they mean to us, why we admire and respect them, how we are feeling with and for them, and any other sincere expression of love, loyalty, and friendship can bring the Spirit into the lives of those who are in pain. Indeed, kind and consoling words can act as catalysts for the Comforter. Who is someone in your life that could benefit today from a simple written expression of love and friendship from you?

AN ANALYSIS

1 Why is it that most of us know the stories about the men in Liberty Jail not being able to stand up in the lower dungeon or their being fed human flesh for meals (both stories may also have dubious origins), but we aren't aware of stories about pets and blessings in the jail?

2 From the sources cited in this background, it is evident Joseph Smith loved his dog. Although animals are not sealed into the covenant family of Abraham, I have to ask, Will we have pets in heaven? (see Revelation 5:13).

3 Hyrum Smith may have blessed Joseph F. Smith in Liberty Jail. We are told in Doctrine and Covenants 20—our Church's constitution—that if we have children we are to "bring them unto the elders . . . who are to lay their hands upon them in the name of Jesus Christ and bless them" (Doctrine and Covenants 20:70). But what does a formal baby blessing do? How is it different from praying for our children? President Russell M. Nelson told of a time he witnessed a father bless his daughter at church. The dad "gave her a name, and then offered a beautiful *prayer*. But he did *not* give that child a blessing. That sweet baby girl got a name but no blessing! That dear elder did not know the difference between a prayer and a priesthood blessing. With his priesthood authority and power, he could have blessed his infant, but he did not."[19] How do we call on the priesthood to truly bless our children, and what does that look like and mean?

NOTES

1. Search for "Liberty Jail" on lds-general-conference.org.
2. See Alexander L. Baugh, "Joseph Smith's Dog, Old Major," *BYU Studies* 56, no. 4 (2017): 53–98.
3. A. W. Harlan, letter to the editor, 17 February 1888, *Keokuk Daily Post*, publication date unknown, copy in Hawking Taylor Papers, 1837–1890, State Historical Society of Iowa, Des Moines, as cited in Baugh, "Joseph Smith's Dog, Old Major," 59.
4. George A. Smith, Memoirs of George A. Smith, 1817–September 10, 1847, 29, MS 1322, George A. Smith Papers, Church History Library, The Church of Jesus Christ of Latter-day Saints, Salt Lake City.
5. Baugh, "Joseph Smith's Dog, Old Major," 58–59, 61.
6. Baugh, "Joseph Smith's Dog, Old Major," 63.
7. "Letter to Emma Smith, 21 March 1839," 2, The Joseph Smith Papers.
8. "Letter to Emma Smith, 4 April 1839," 2, The Joseph Smith Papers.
9. A. W. Harlan, letter to the editor, 17 February 1888.
10. Baugh, "Joseph Smith's Dog, Old Major," 62.
11. *Saints*, vol. 1: *The Standard of Truth, 1815–1846* (Salt Lake City: The Church of Jesus Christ of Latter-day Saints, 2018), 374.
12. Mercy F. Thompson, "Letter to My Posterity," as cited in Pearson H. Corbett, *Hyrum Smith, Patriarch* (Salt Lake City: Deseret Book, 1963), 201.
13. Edward Stevenson, *Reminiscences of Joseph the Prophet, and the Coming Forth of the Book of Mormon* (Salt Lake City: self-pub., 1893), 41.
14. Alexander L. Baugh, "Was Joseph F. Smith Blessed by His Father Hyrum Smith in Liberty Jail?," *Mormon Historical Studies* 4, no. 1 (Spring 2003): 102.
15. Based on personal discussions with Alex Baugh.
16. "Letter to the Church and Edward Partridge, 20 March 1839," 8, The Joseph Smith Papers.
17. "Letter to the Church and Edward Partridge, 20 March 1839," 7.
18. "Letter to the Church and Edward Partridge, 20 March 1839," 7–8.
19. Russell M. Nelson, "Ministering with the Power and Authority of God," *Ensign*, May 2018, 69.

After Liberty (20" x 14", oil on board, 2019)

AFTER LIBERTY

Timeline: April 1839

Related Doctrine and Covenants Sections: 121–23

A BACKGROUND

Early in the morning on 22 April 1839, a ferryboat docked in Quincy, Illinois. Thousands of Latter-day Saints had taken refuge in the tiny town of Quincy after being driven from the state of Missouri. Dimick Huntington rode down to the Quincy dock to see who had just arrived. As people disembarked the ferry, a certain ragged-looking man in a floppy black hat caught Dimick's attention. As Dimick got closer, the man raised up his head, and Dimick exclaimed, "My God, is it you Brother Joseph?" After months in prison at Liberty Jail and being separated from the Saints, suddenly the Prophet was standing unexpectedly on the east banks of the Mississippi River on the Quincy shore. Dimick said that Joseph "raised his hand and slowed me, saying, hush hush." Joseph asked, "Where's my family?" Dimick told Joseph where they were staying four miles out of town and asked if Joseph wanted to be taken to his parents' house. Joseph said, "No, it would be too great a shock. They are old and cannot bear it," and then specified, "Take me to my family as quick as you can."

Dimick took Joseph through the backstreets of town, cautious because Joseph did not know the "friendly feelings that existed, in Quincy" and "was fearful he might be arrested again." When they arrived, Emma looked out, and immediately recognized her husband as he was dismounting his horse. She burst out and "met him half way to the gate."

These heart-rending details come from a later reminiscent statement by Dimick Huntington. Perhaps the best part of his statement, however, is his detailed description of Joseph after Liberty when he arrived in Quincy. The description is

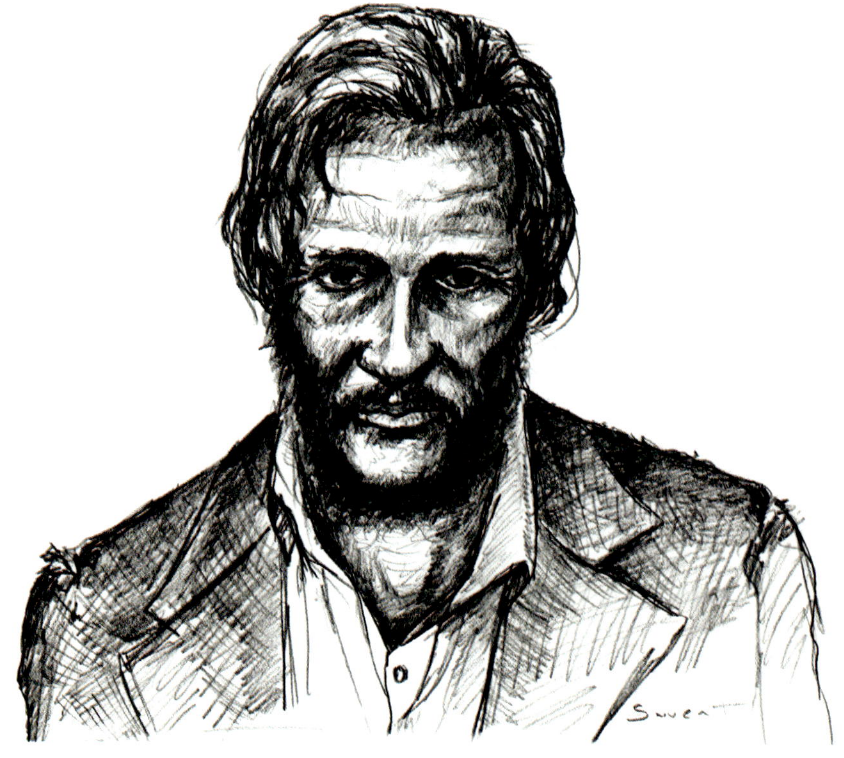

rich and vivid. Dimick remembered that Joseph "was dressed in an old pair of boots, full of holes, pants torn [and] tucked inside of boots." He wore a "blue cloak with collar turned up, wide brim black hat, rim sopped down." He said that Joseph "had not been shaved for some time" and then inserted that Joseph "looked pale and haggard."[1]

The experience at Liberty Jail had been a painfully refining experience for Joseph. One can't help but read accusation, frustration, and condemnation in some of his letters from Liberty Jail. He called George Hinckle "a wolf in sheep's clothing." Reed Peck was compared to Judas, who led Joseph "as the savior was led, into the camp as a lamb prepared for the slaughter." W. W. Phelps was "as one of Job's comforters," and "this poor man who professes to be much of a prophet has no other dumb ass to ride but David Whitmer" and concluded of the Church's traitors, "we sometimes think the devil ought to be ashamed of them."[2] He said the proceedings of the legislature "has damned the state of Missouri to all eternity."[3]

Toward the end of his prison stay, Joseph wrote "we find our [health] wearing away very fast." But one also can read hope, optimism, and courage in his letters during his time in Liberty. He confidently wrote that "Mormonism is truth."[4] Although he was imprisoned, he wrote to the Saints to "let us cheerfully do all things < that> lieth in our power and then may we stand still with the utmost asurance to see the salvation of God."[5] Although he suffered at the hands of religious intolerance, Joseph liberally wrote from prison, "We ~~should~~ ought always to be aware of those prejudices which sometimes so strangly presented themselves and are so congenial to human nature against our nieghbors friends and brethren of the world who choose to differ with us in opinion and in matters of faith."[6] Although the government had treated and trampled on his and other Saints' constitutional rights, Joseph declared, "The constitution of the unitid States is a glorious standard it is founded in the wisdom of God. it is a heavenly banner it is to all those who are privilaged with the sweats of its liberty like the cooling shades and refreshing watters of a greate rock in a thirsty and a weary land. . . . The mormons as well as the presbitarians and those of evry other class and description have equal rights to partake of the fruite of the greate tree of our national liberty."[7]

When Joseph Smith emerged from Liberty Jail, he may have looked haggard and pale, but he surely wasn't defeated. It wasn't in his nature. Joseph would soon lead the Saints to gather again near Commerce, Illinois, and optimistically rename it Nauvoo, the beautiful. There he would reach the zenith of his personal, political, and prophetic powers. There he would reveal some of his most exalting doctrines, such as the redemption of the dead, a Heavenly Mother, God once being a man, and eternal marriage. After Liberty, Joseph seemed more determined than ever to move forward the work which God had called him, no matter the consequences. Liberty didn't ruin Joseph, it refueled him. I had to paint him, symbolizing these ideas and looking as Dimick described him, after Liberty.

AN IMAGE

In my painting, I tried to represent what Dimick Huntington described in his statement. Joseph wears a black, floppy hat. His face is pale, thin, worn, gaunt, and bearded. Joseph's eyes are purposely averted from the viewer and are lined and heavy, almost distant, as though he is reflecting on the unfathomable sufferings and loss in Missouri.

The Prophet wears his blue cloak, thread bare and old, with the collar turned up.

Joseph's pants have holes and are tucked into his boots that are also worn out, as Dimick said.

I also want this image to symbolize the trauma and triumph of trial. The dead tree behind Joseph suggests the loss of something dear in the past (Zion in Missouri). The water and

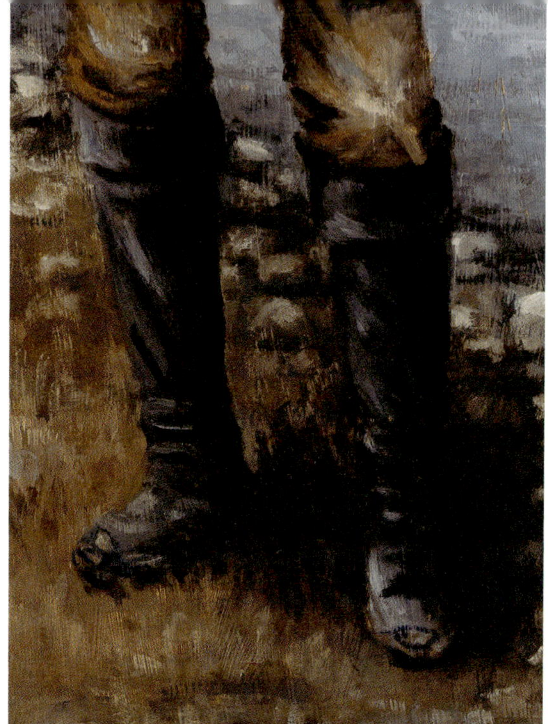

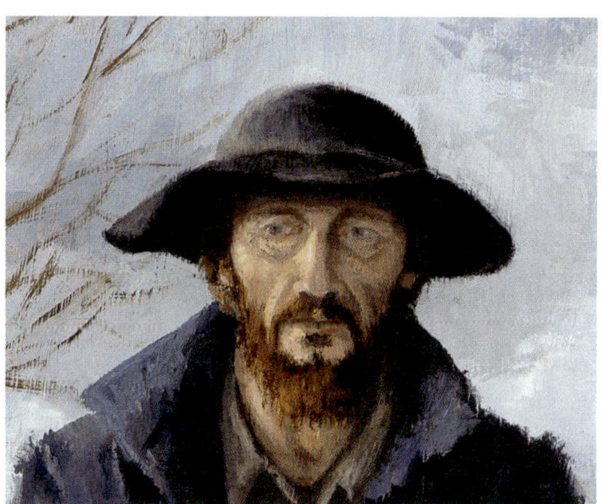

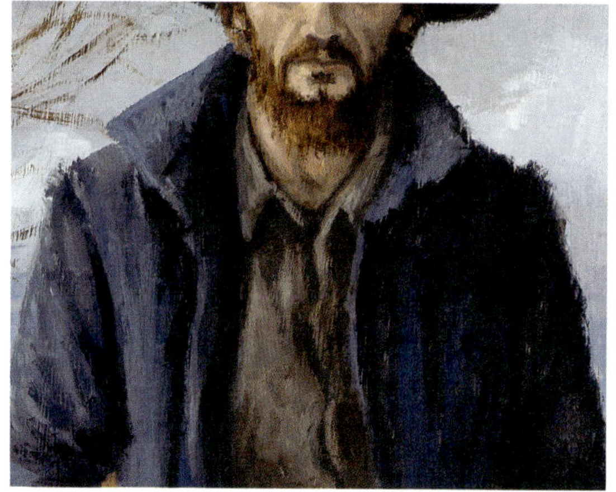

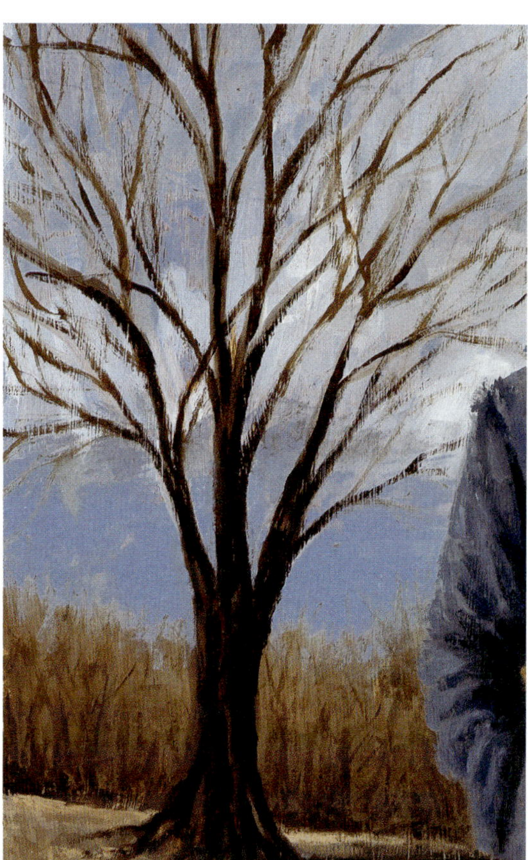

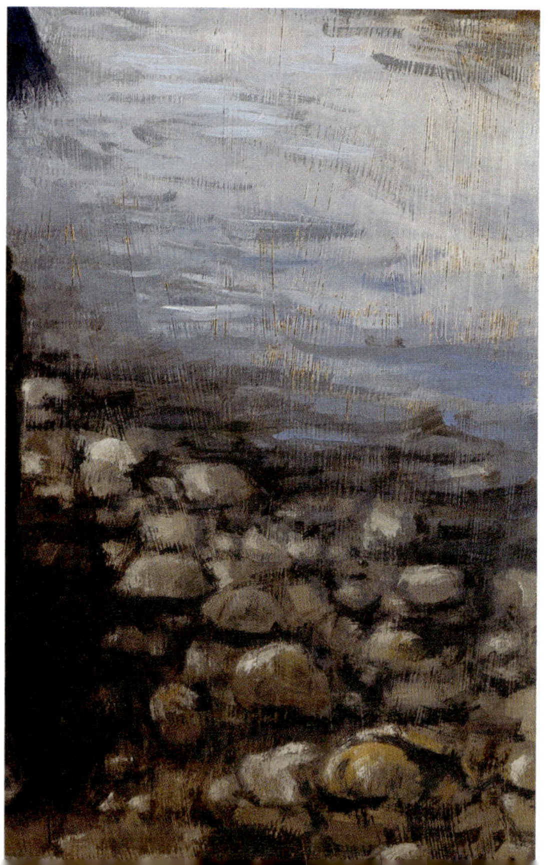

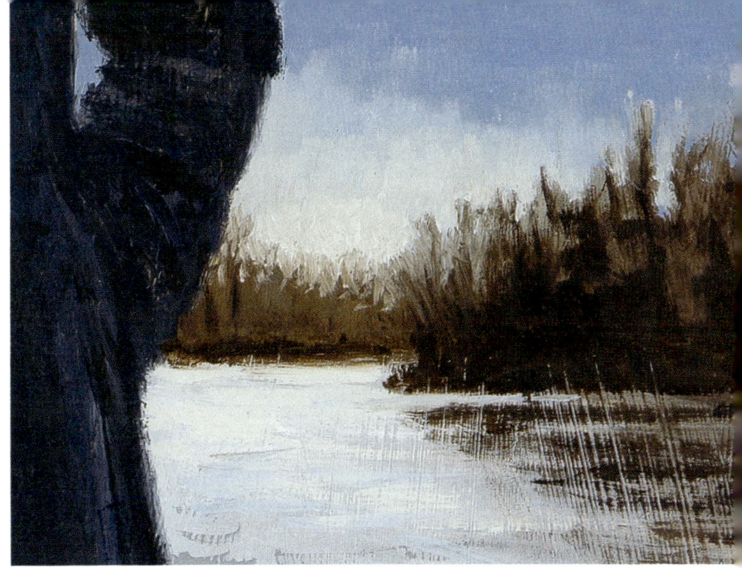

rock-lined shore suggest the difficulties Joseph and the Saints have passed over.

Although haggard, pale, and thin, Joseph stands, ready to take the next step forward in faith. Among the muted earth tones, there's an optimistic yellow glimmer of hope over the clouds on the horizon.

AN APPLICATION

From Liberty Jail, Joseph dictated a letter to the Saints, encouraging them to persevere: "Zion shall yet live, though she seemeth to be dead," he assured them. "The very God of peace shall be with you and make a way for your escape from the adversary of your souls."[8] In those letters, Joseph Smith revealed truths to give us hope and peace and direction during times of trial that are paralleled nowhere else other than perhaps the book of Job. Portions of these letters are canonized today in Doctrine and Covenants 121–23. Elder Jeffrey R. Holland, in his classic talk "Lessons from Liberty Jail," spoke of truths to remember during days of difficulty.[9] The following are ten principles I would share from these poignant Doctrine and Covenants sections that derive from Joseph's experience in Liberty Jail:

The Prophet Joseph Smith was never the same after Liberty. He was different, for good. So are all who faithfully endure difficulty and trial.

1. Remember, this too will pass (121:7; 122:4).
2. Endure well, asking "whats" not "whys" (121:8).
3. Rely on beloved family and friends (121:9).
4. Others of great faith also have trials, and often worse (121:10; 122:8).
5. God's in control and has plans (121:25, 33,122:9).
6. God will repay unfairness—there is a divine law of restoration (121:15–24).
7. Seek the Spirit's insights and an eternal perspective (121:26, 29).
8. Remember that suffering gives experience, and can be for our good (122:7).
9. Hold tightly to your faith and rely on the power of the priesthood (122:9).
10. Cheerfully do everything you can, and then stand still and trust God (123:17).

The Prophet Joseph Smith was never the same after Liberty. He was different, for good. So are all who faithfully endure difficulty and trial. "All these things shall give thee experience, and shall be for thy good. . . . Therefore, hold on thy way, and the priesthood shall remain with thee; for their bounds are set, they cannot pass. Thy days are known, and thy years shall not be numbered less; therefore, fear not what man can do, for God shall be with you forever and ever" (Doctrine and Covenants 122:7, 9).

AN ANALYSIS

1 Why is suffering essential to our mortal experience and eternal progression? In particular, why do the righteous sometimes suffer while the wicked seem to prosper? What is the balance between our preaching that living the gospel will bring you joy and success and help you avoid some of the hardships of life, and the reality that in order to sanctify his people God often allows—and maybe even requires—that they endure difficulty?

2 How do we "remain calm, patient, charitable, and forgiving" during times of suffering, as Elder Holland admonished in his talk on lessons from Liberty Jail?[10] At times, Joseph seems to have struggled with that (casting angry dispersions at dissenters and maligning the state of Missouri in his letters). How do we not do the same?

3 Based on your experience during your own personal times of suffering and sorrow, what would you add to my list of ten principles to remember? If you had to write a letter from your own metaphorical Liberty Jail, what would you say to help those who suffer?

NOTES

1. Dimick B. Huntington statement, circa 1854–1856; CR 100 396, spelling and punctuation modernized. Joseph Smith history documents, 1839–1860 / Materials used by Church historians, 1854–1856, Church History Library.
2. "Letter to the Church in Caldwell County, Missouri, 16 December 1838," The Joseph Smith Papers.
3. "Letter to the Church and Edward Partridge, 20 March 1839," 6, The Joseph Smith Papers.
4. "Letter to Isaac Galland, 22 March 1839," 53, The Joseph Smith Papers.
5. "Letter to Edward Partridge and the Church, circa 22 March 1839," 7, The Joseph Smith Papers.
6. "Letter to Edward Partridge and the Church, circa 22 March 1839," 8.
7. "Letter to Edward Partridge and the Church, circa 22 March 1839," 8–9.
8. "Letter to the Church in Caldwell County, Missouri, 16 December 1838," 7.
9. Jeffrey R. Holland, "Lessons from Liberty Jail" (Church Educational System fireside address at Brigham Young University, 7 September 2008).
10. Holland, "Lessons from Liberty Jail."

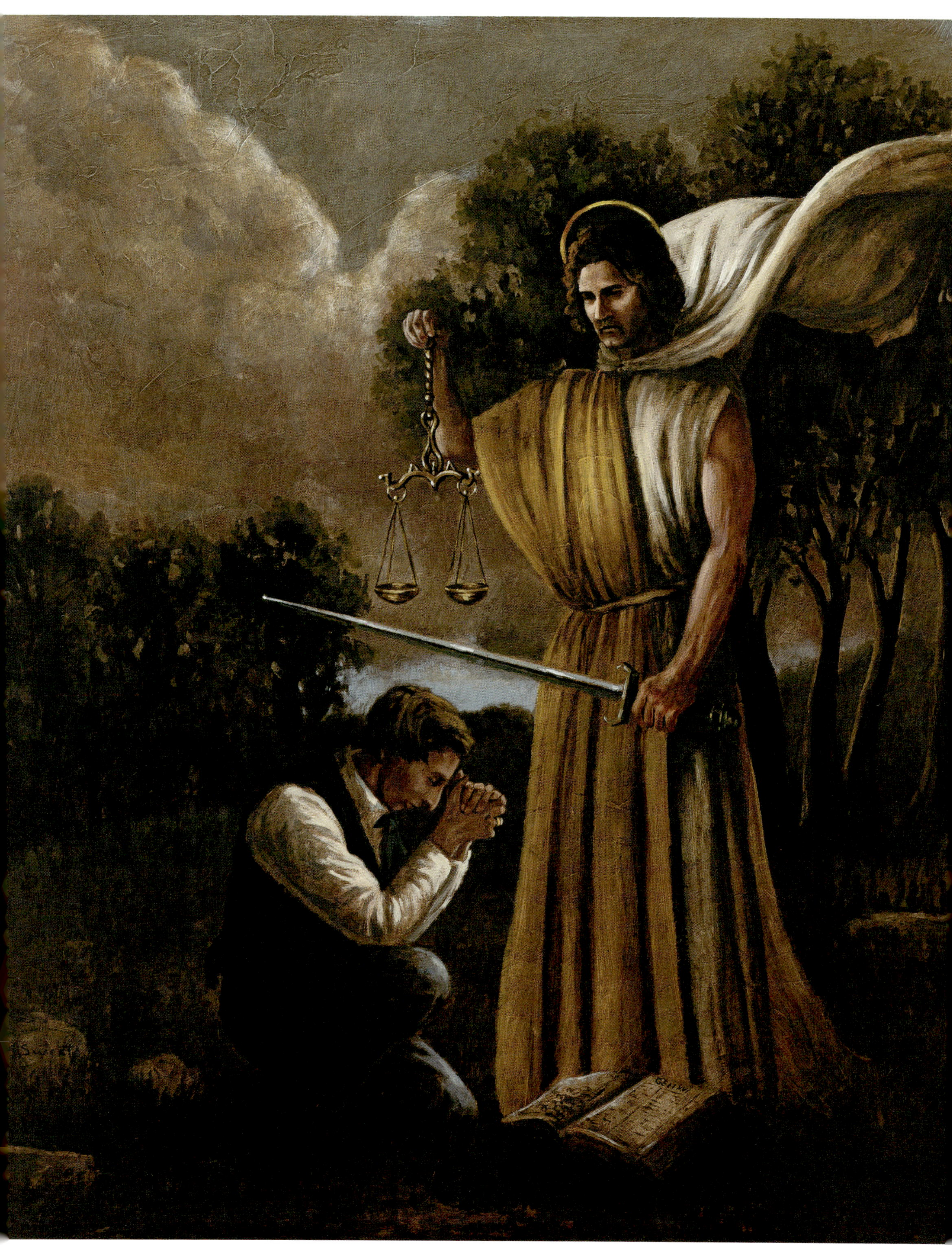

An Angel with a Drawn Sword (28" x 24", oil on board, 2018)

AN ANGEL WITH A DRAWN SWORD

Timeline: circa 1834–42

Related Doctrine and Covenants Section: 132

A BACKGROUND

Joseph Smith possibly married his first plural wife, Fanny Alger, sometime in the mid-1830s.[1] Although the evidence for this marriage is far from conclusive,[2] by available indications this first attempt by Joseph to restore the Old Testament practice of polygamy went disastrously. Emma rejected it as adulterous when she learned of it.[3] Joseph hoped that confiding in Oliver Cowdery would help him lead Emma to understand. Instead, Oliver sided with Emma, accusing Joseph of adultery.[4] Understandably, Joseph pulled back from polygamy. He and others had been burnt by the fire this incendiary practice could cause. Joseph wouldn't marry a plural wife again until 1841 in Nauvoo, when he married Louisa Beaman (or Beman).[5] Joseph's waiting at least five years to implement this revealed practice "showed an uncharacteristic reluctance, hard for one who feared God,"[6] Richard Bushman wrote. What may have moved him forward, despite his reticence?

A Gospel Topics Essay on the subject says, "Joseph told associates that an angel appeared to him three times between 1834 and 1842 and commanded him to proceed with plural marriage when he hesitated to move forward."[7] Brian Hales, historian of Joseph Smith's polygamy, has found twenty different accounts from nine witnesses who give statements and information about this angel who commanded that plural marriage be implemented.[8] None of the statements are directly from Joseph Smith himself nor contemporaries. All are secondhand, reminiscent accounts. The earliest account is from Joseph Robinson in 1853; the latest is from 1905, when Mary Elizabeth Rollins remembered Joseph telling her, "The angel came to me three times between the years of 1834 and 1842 and said I was to obey that principle or he would slay me."[9]

Joseph Robinson, who gave the earliest recollection in 1853, said, "The Lord instead of releas-

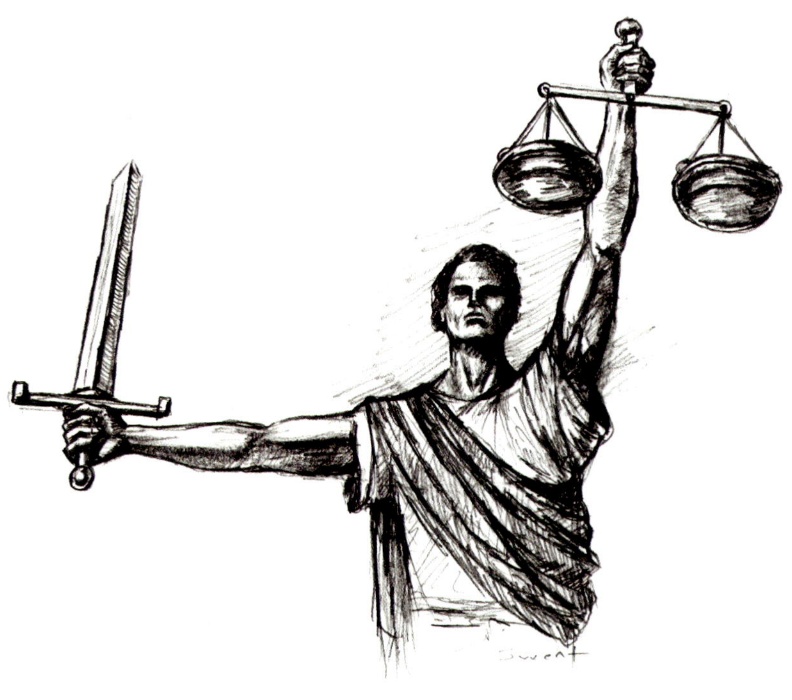

ing [Joseph Smith] from that burden, he sent an holy angel with a drawn sword unto him, saying unto him, Joseph, unless you go to and immediately teach that principle (namely polygamy or plural marriage) and put the same in practice, that he, Joseph, should be slain for thus saith the Lord, that the time has now come that I will raise up seed unto me as I spoke by my servant Jacob as is recorded in the Book of Mormon, therefore, I command my people."[10]

Eliza R. Snow recalled that the Prophet "was himself afraid to promulgate it [plural marriage] until the angel came and stood beside him with flaming sword and bade him do the command of God. Not until then did Joseph enter into polygamy."[11]

In a *Deseret News* article in 1881, Zina Huntington, plural wife of the Prophet, was cited: "Zina D. Young told of Bro. Joseph's remark in relation to the revelation on [plural] marriage. How an angel came to him with a drawn sword, and said if he did not obey this law he would lose his priesthood; and in the keeping of it he, Joseph, did not know but it would cost him his life."[12]

Helen Mar Kimball, also one of Joseph's plural wives, recalled: "This fact [plural marriage] the Lord revealed to His prophet, Joseph Smith, as early as the year 1831. And yet, had it not been for the fear of His displeasure, Joseph would have shrunk from the undertaking and would have continued silent, as he did for years, until an angel of the Lord threatened to slay him if he did not reveal and establish this celestial principle."[13]

Although "the angel" is not identified, nor is it specified exactly when or where it appeared, and though some details differ in what the angel supposedly said, if this was the event that moved forward Joseph's practice of polygamy, it had to be represented visually.

AN IMAGE

I purposely chose to paint this image in an older, glazed, multilayered, almost Baroque style of the seventeenth and eighteenth centuries. Baroque painting is partly known for depicting moments of high religious drama in detail, using chiaroscuro (high contrast of light and shadow) to produce dramatic effects.[14] In this scene the angel has just descended from on high, his cape fluttering in a sense of motion. Although haloed in righteousness, his face is somber and serious, reflecting the seriousness of the message and consequences of its rejection.

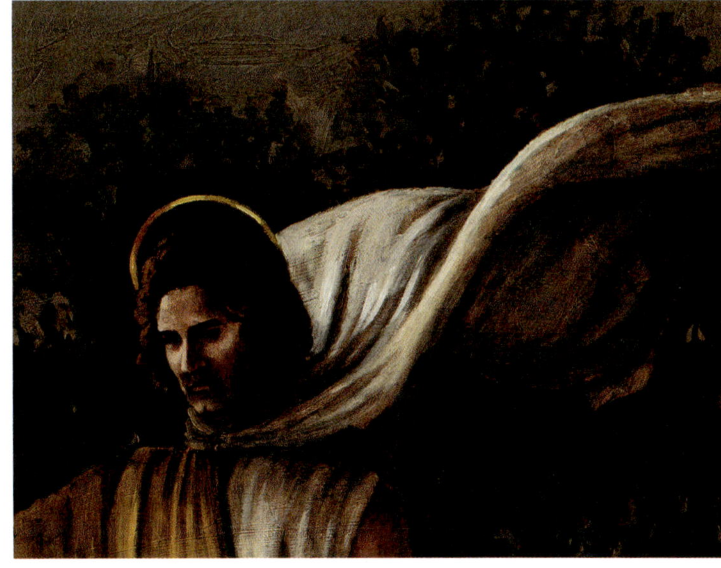

In his right hand, the angel holds a scale over Joseph's head, suggesting impending judgment. The various accounts about the angel use descriptive phrases like "threatening him with

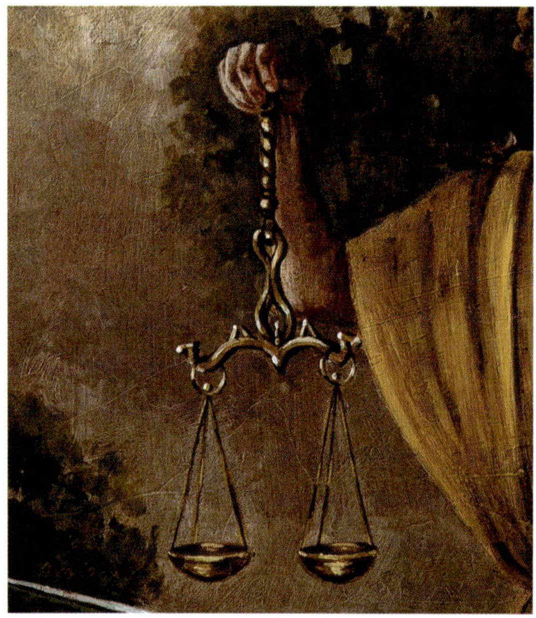

destruction," "threatening to slay him," "he would be slain," "his priesthood should be taken from him," "he should be destroyed," or "lose [your] position and [your] life."[15] I wanted to represent these ideas, and using a symbol seemed the most appropriate way to do so.

In his left hand, the angel holds a drawn sword just over Joseph's head, his arm flexed and bare, hearkening to scriptures that the Lord will "make bare his arm" of power to implement his divine will (see 1 Nephi 22:10–11; Isaiah 52:10; Doctrine and Covenants 133:3).

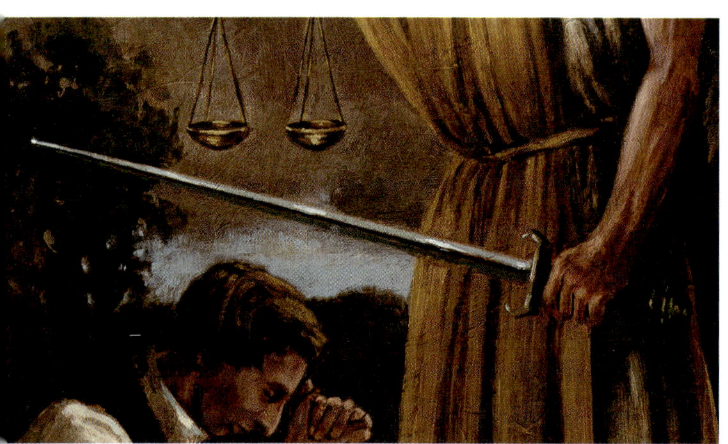

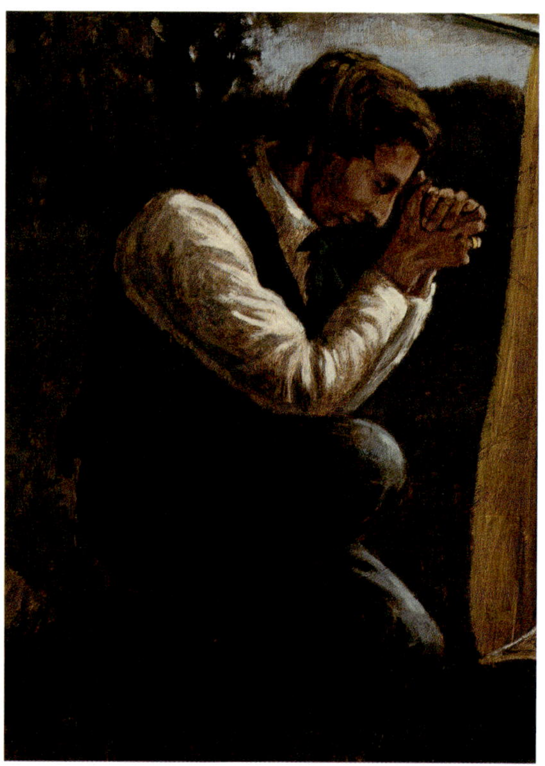

Below the sword, Joseph kneels in humble supplication, his submissive posture suggesting his resignation to the revelation.

At Joseph's feet sits an open Bible, its pages resting open to Genesis 16, where Abraham marries Hagar as a plural wife. It is likely that Joseph first inquired and learned about plural marriage while translating the Old Testament in 1831[16] (see section heading to Doctrine and Covenants 132).

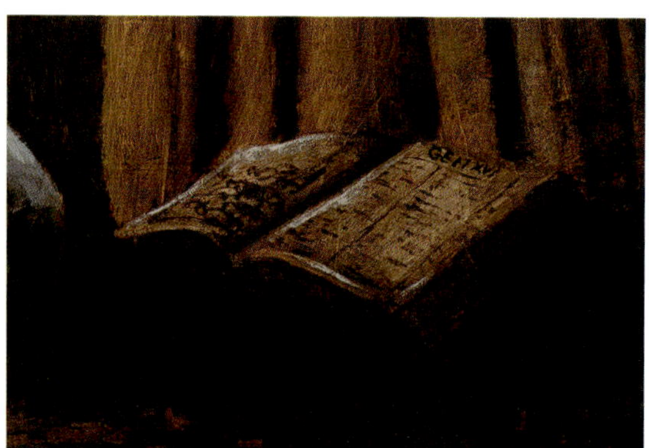

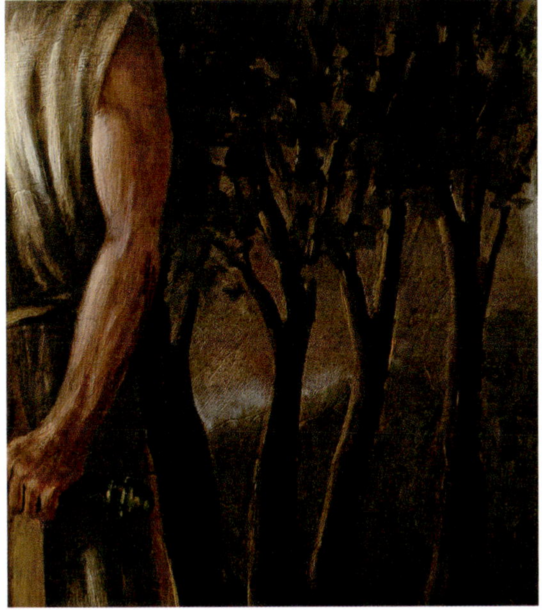

In the scenery behind the angel are trees, representing women to whom Joseph would be married,[17] creating a broad, dynastic family tree.[18]

Over the horizon, dark clouds gather, suggesting the impending storm that implementing plural marriage will bring. There is, however, a hint of blue breaking through the clouds, suggesting optimistic deliverance for Joseph's obedience to this difficult command (see Doctrine and Covenants 132:46, 49).

AN APPLICATION

The heading to Official Declaration 1 says, "The Bible and the Book of Mormon teach that monogamy is God's standard for marriage unless He declares otherwise (see 2 Samuel 12:7–8 and Jacob 2:27, 30)." Plural marriage is not required for exaltation, as modern-day Church leaders have repeatedly taught.[19] Anyone practicing plural marriage today will be subject to Church discipline. Today's law is to believe and implement monogamy.

Although plural marriage is not necessary for exaltation, living the law of sacrifice is. Plural marriage during Joseph Smith's time was often equated with Abrahamic sacrifice (see Doctrine and Covenants 132:50, 59–60). While you and I are not asked to live the law of plural marriage like some of the early Saints, we are told that one of the purposes of this life, ironically (or logically) found in the Book of Abraham, is for God to "prove [his children] herewith, to see if they will do all things whatsoever the Lord their God shall command them" (Abraham 3:25).

Notice the *all* in that verse. *All things.* Think how differently it would read if it said, "to see if they will do *some of the things* the Lord their God shall command them," or "*the convenient things*" or "the *culturally acceptable things.*" No, it's *all things*. That seems to be how God was testing Abraham. Will you do everything I ask you? Perhaps that was also what God was testing Joseph and some early Saints with when he commanded plural marriage. Perhaps that is also what he will test us with, in a different way, today. One of the reasons God asks us to sacrifice is to make manifest what we truly love. *Lectures on Faith* 6:7 famously teaches, "A religion that does not require the sacrifice of all things, never has power sufficient to produce the faith necessary unto life and salvation."[20] Note again the *all* in that statement.

Are we willing to sacrifice all for Jesus and God's kingdom? "He that taketh not his cross, and followeth after me, is not worthy of me. He that findeth his life shall lose it: and he that loseth his life for my sake shall find it" (Matthew 10:38–39).

Will you do everything I ask you? Perhaps that was also what God was testing Joseph and some early Saints with when he commanded plural marriage. Perhaps that is also what he will test us with, in a different way, today.

AN ANALYSIS

1 Some have discounted the accounts of the angel with a drawn sword because those don't seem consistent with how they think God works. Don't events such as Joseph being destroyed or losing his priesthood or life seem unduly coercive and harsh? Can you think of times in scripture where God or angels may seem threatening and punitive to either support this narrative or discount it? What do you think of the accounts of a threatening angel?

2 As mentioned, the angel is never identified. Who might this angel be? Moroni? Or perhaps one of the other "divers angels" Joseph mentions in Doctrine and Covenants 128:21, such as Gabriel or Rafael.

3 How do we balance the Church's emphasis on family first, when implementing certain Church practices or believing certain Church teachings has the potential impact of harming some family relationships? How do we balance Jesus being the prince of peace with statements like this: "Think not that I am come to send peace on earth: I came not to send peace, but a sword. For I am come to set a man at variance against his father, and the daughter against her mother. . . . And a man's foes shall be they of his own household. He that loveth father or mother more than me is not worthy of me" (Matthew 10:34–37).

NOTES

1. "Fragmentary evidence suggests that Joseph Smith acted on the angel's first command by marrying a plural wife, Fanny Alger, in Kirtland, Ohio, in the mid-1830s." "Plural Marriage in Kirtland and

Nauvoo," Gospel Topics Essay, The Church of Jesus Christ of Latter-day Saints.

2. Principal sources for this possible plural marriage to Fanny Alger are Mosiah Hancock, *Narrative*, in Levi Hancock, *Autobiography*, 63, Church History Library; Oliver Cowdery to Warren Cowdery, 21 January 1838, Oliver Cowdery Letterbook, Huntington Library; and Minute Book 2, 12 April 1838, Church History Library. Credit to Andrew Hedges for providing these sources.
3. At Oliver's 1838 membership hearing, David W. Patten said Oliver Cowdery "gave a history of some circumstances respecting the adultery scrape stating that no doubt it was true. He also said that Joseph told him, "he had confessed to Emma." "Minute Book 2," 124, The Joseph Smith Papers. Brian C. Hales writes, "Emma did not believe the ceremony was valid and concluded the relationship was adulterous." "Fanny Alger," Joseph Smith's Polygamy (website).
4. When Oliver Cowdery was charged on nine accounts for his Church membership in 1838, one of the charges was for "insinuating that [Joseph Smith] was guilty of adultery." Editors for the *Joseph Smith Papers* write, "Testimony from George W. Harris, David W. Patten, and Thomas B. Marsh confirmed that Cowdery had made such insinuations about JS's relationship in Kirtland with a young woman named Fanny Alger." "Journal, March–September 1838," 30, note 54, The Joseph Smith Papers.
5. See "Plural Marriage in Kirtland and Nauvoo." Sources for this marriage include Joseph Bates Noble affidavit, 6 June 1869, Joseph F. Smith Affidavit Books, Church History Library; Wilford Woodruff, Journal, 22 January 1869, Wilford Woodruff Collection, Church History Library; Temple Lot Transcript, Part 3, 432, 436, questions 793, 861. Credit to Andrew Hedges for providing these sources.
6. Richard Lyman Bushman, *Joseph Smith: Rough Stone Rolling* (New York City: Alfred A. Knopf, 2005), 437.
7. See "Plural Marriage in Kirtland and Nauvoo."
8. Brian C. Hales, "Encouraging Joseph Smith to Practice Plural Marriage: The Accounts of the Angel with a Drawn Sword," *Mormon Historical Studies* 11, no. 2 (2010): 55–71.
9. Mary Elizabeth Rollins Lightner, remarks, Brigham Young University, 14 April 1905, L. Tom Perry Special Collections, Brigham Young University, as cited in Hales, "Encouraging Joseph Smith to Practice Plural Marriage."
10. Oliver Preston Robinson ed., *History of Joseph Lee Robinson* (n.p.: History Comes Home, 2007), 27.2, as cited in Hales, "Encouraging Joseph Smith to Practice Plural Marriage."
11. Eliza R. Snow, "Two Prophets' Widows a Visit to the Relicts of Joseph Smith and Brigham Young," in *St. Louis Globe-Democrat* (St. Louis, MO), 18 August 1887, 6, as cited in Hales, "Encouraging Joseph Smith to Practice Plural Marriage."
12. "The Prophet's Birthday," *Deseret News*, 12 January 1881, 2, as cited in Hales, "Encouraging Joseph Smith to Practice Plural Marriage."
13. Helen Mar Kimball Whitney, *Why We Practice Plural Marriage* (Salt Lake City: Juvenile Instructor Office, 1884), 53, as cited in Hales, "Encouraging Joseph Smith to Practice Plural Marriage."
14. See "The Baroque Period," Lumen (website); "Baroque Art," *Encyclopedia of Art*, visual-arts-cork.com.
15. See summary table of angel with drawn sword accounts in Hales, "Encouraging Joseph Smith to Practice Plural Marriage," 65–70.
16. Revelations on plural marriage "emerged from Joseph Smith's study of the Old Testament in 1831." "Plural Marriage in Kirtland and Nauvoo."
17. Trees are sometimes used as a symbol for women in scripture, such as the palm tree called Tamar. See "Palm tree," Bible Study Tools (website). See also Cecilia Haendler, "Trees as Male and Female: A Biblical Metaphor and Its Rabbinic Elaboration," http://www.lectio.unibe.ch/15_1/pdf/haendler_trees_as_male_and_female.pdf.
18. "Joseph did not marry women to form a warm, human companionship, but to create a network of related wives, children, and kinsmen that would endure into the eternities." Bushman, *Joseph Smith: Rough Stone Rolling*, 440.
19. See Bruce R. McConkie, *Mormon Doctrine*, 2nd ed. (Salt Lake City: Bookcraft, 1966), 578–79; Charles W. Penrose, "Peculiar Questions Briefly Answered," *Improvement Era*, September 1912, 1042; James R. Clark, comp., *Messages of the First Presidency of The Church of Jesus Christ of Latter-day Saints*, 6 vols. (Salt Lake City: Bookcraft, 1965–75), 5:329; Marcus B. Nash, "The New and Everlasting Covenant," *Ensign*, December 2015, 41–47. See also Brian C. Hales, "Does Exaltation Require Polygamy?," Joseph Smith's Polygamy.
20. *Lectures on Faith* (Salt Lake City: Deseret Book, 1985), 7:9, 75–76.

PART THREE

ILLINOIS

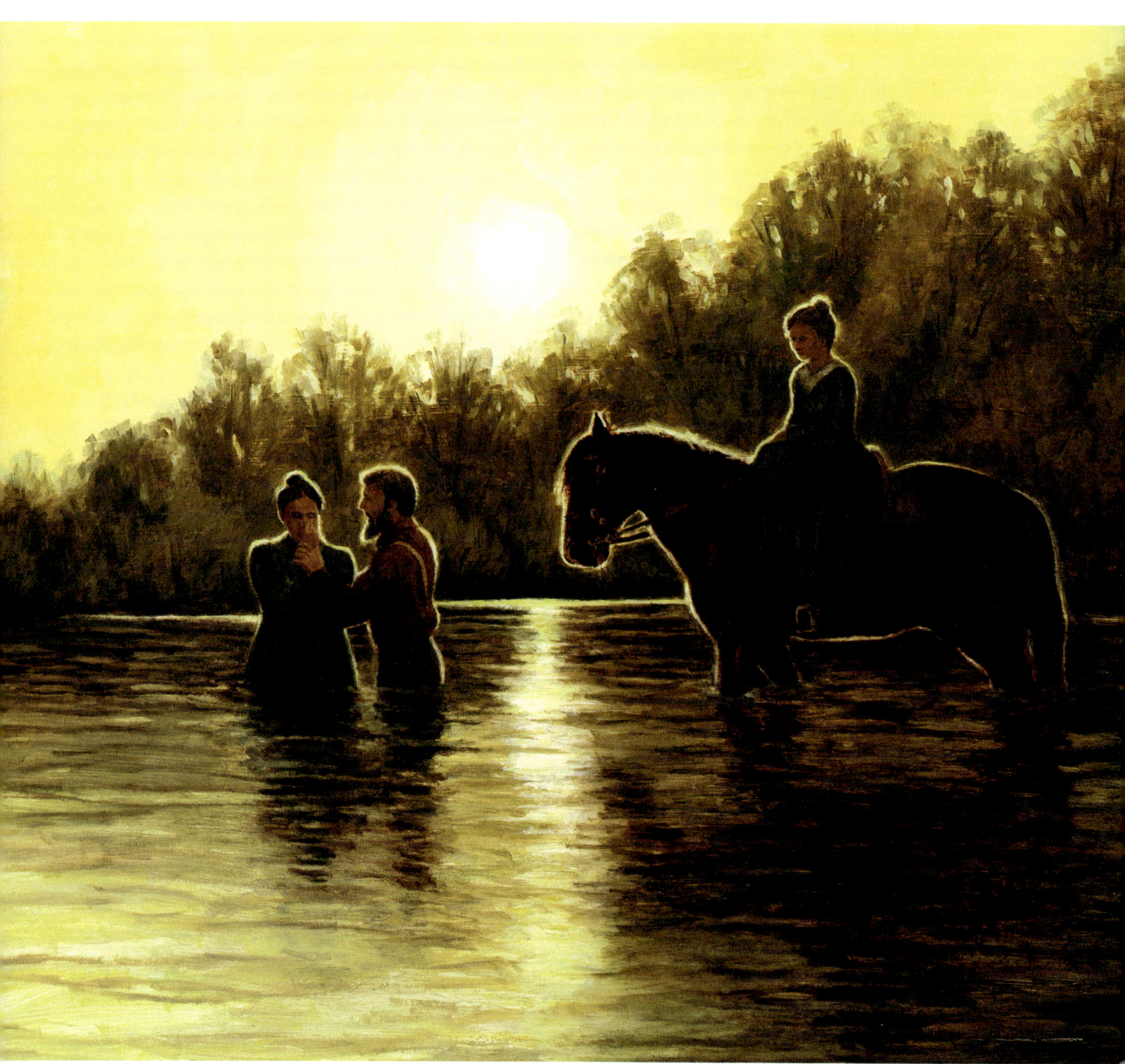

Jane Neyman and the First Baptism for the Dead (20" x 24", oil on board, 2019)

JANE NEYMAN AND THE FIRST BAPTISM FOR THE DEAD

Timeline: Summer 1840

Related Doctrine and Covenants Sections: 127–28

A BACKGROUND

In the hot, muggy summer of 1840, Joseph Smith first preached the revolutionary doctrine of baptism for the dead at the funeral sermon of Seymour Brunson, his bodyguard and friend. In the congregation that day was a woman named Jane Neyman, whose teenage son, Cyrus, had died without being baptized into the Church. Likely referring to Jane, one person later remembered that Joseph "saw a widow in that congregation that had a son who died without being baptized, and [said] . . . that this widow should have glad tidings."[1] Joseph then taught the doctrine of baptisms for the dead, citing 1 Corinthians 15:29, and told the Saints they could do the same for their deceased ancestry.[2]

Joseph concluded, "I have laid the subject of baptism for the dead before you[;] you may receive or reject it as you choose."[3] Jane chose to accept it and act upon it. Sometime after the funeral sermon, [4] Jane invited an elder named Harvey Olmstead to help her and headed down to the Mississippi River. Detailing the event years later, Jane's scribe wrote, "[Jane] then went & was baptized for her son Cyrus Livingston Neyman by Harvey Olmstead." Importantly, the event was witnessed—not by two elders, but by a woman, Vienna Jaques, and on horseback nonetheless! The affidavit of this event says, "Vienna Jaques witnessed the same by riding into the river on horseback to get close so as to hear what the ceremony would be." Harvey Olmstead did not have a prescribed prayer to say for the vicarious ceremony and seems to have created one himself on the spot. Later that night at dinner, when Joseph heard that a baptism had been performed, he asked "what he [Harvey Olmstead] said," and on having it recited to him, Joseph simply responded "that father Olmstead had it right."[5]

Thus, likely the first baptism for the dead was a female being baptized for a male, in a river

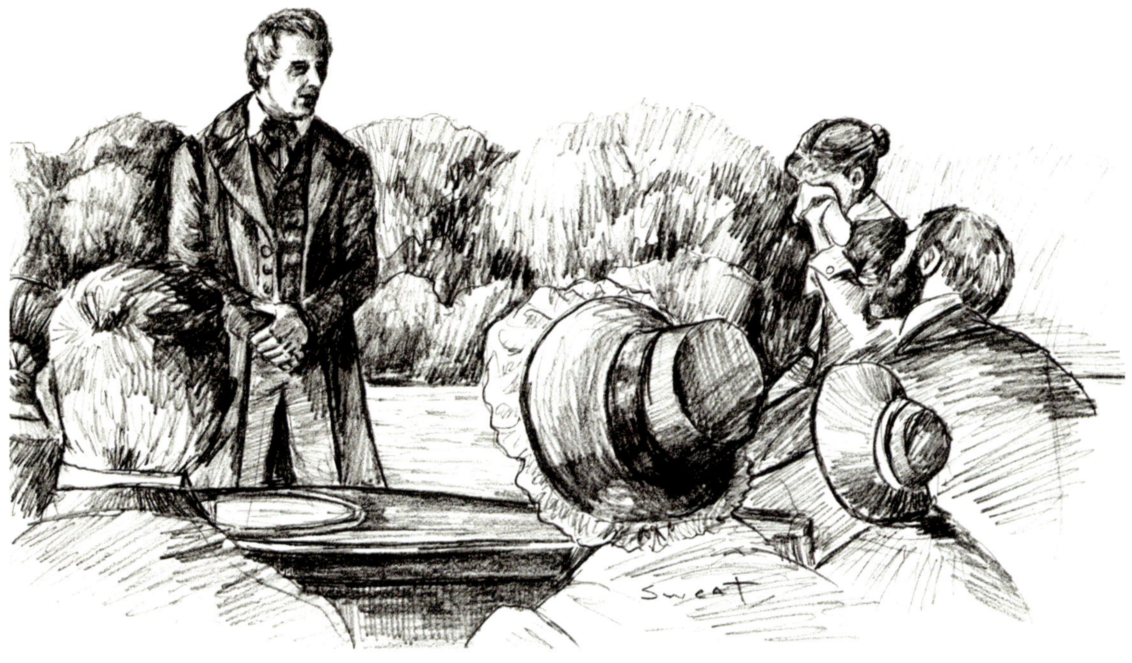

and not a temple, witnessed by a woman on a horse, performed by an elder with a made-up prayer. And you know what? It counted! This rich, atypical, previously undepicted yet seminal moment in Latter-day Saint history had to be created.

AN IMAGE

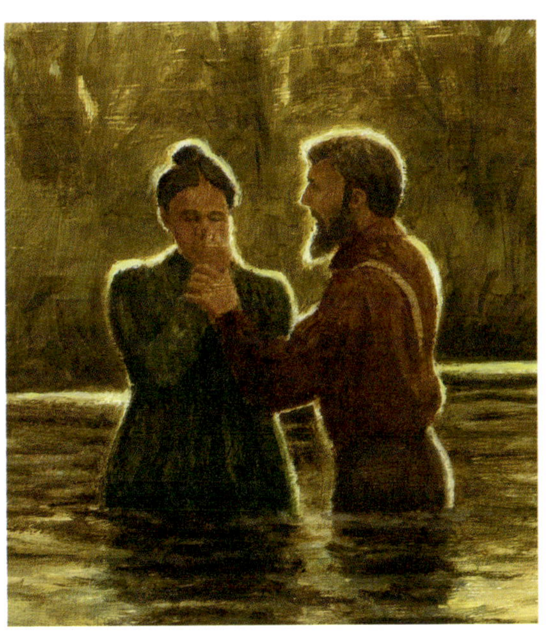

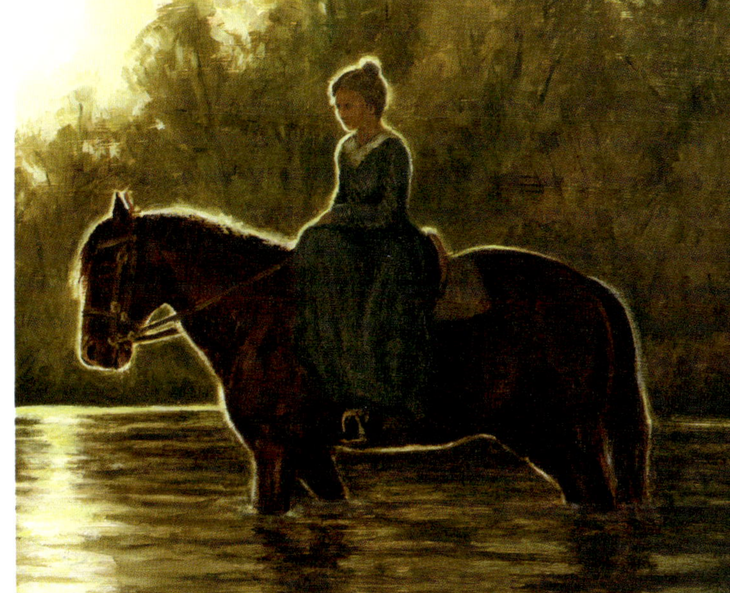

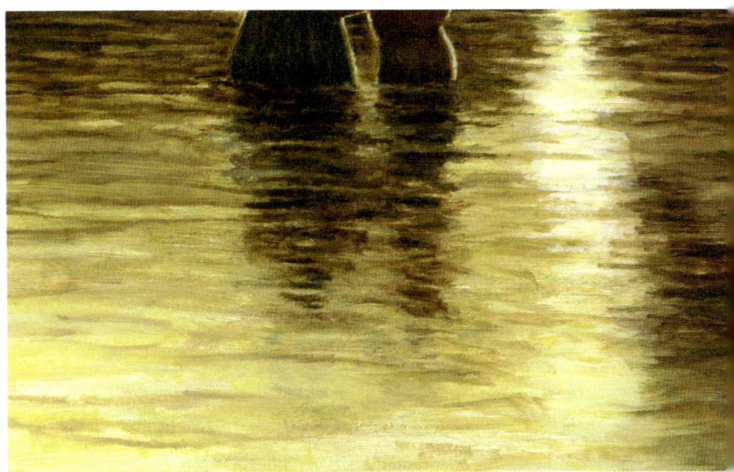

In my depiction of this event, Harvey prepares to baptize Jane, and Vienna looks on, perched sidesaddle on horseback. Compositionally I chose to portray this painting as the sun began to set, flooding images with yellow backlight rim light. There's something to that.

It is not uncommon to see reflections in the water in a spiritual or mystical way, even using them to suggest the unseen spirits or presence of those who are on the other side. I had that in mind with the reflections in this image.

Aside from the color and lighting in this image, you can see a purposeful division of the plane into four quadrants, the sun and its reflection dividing down the center vertically, the river's edge dividing the plane horizontally. The tree line and its reflection act as a deliberate

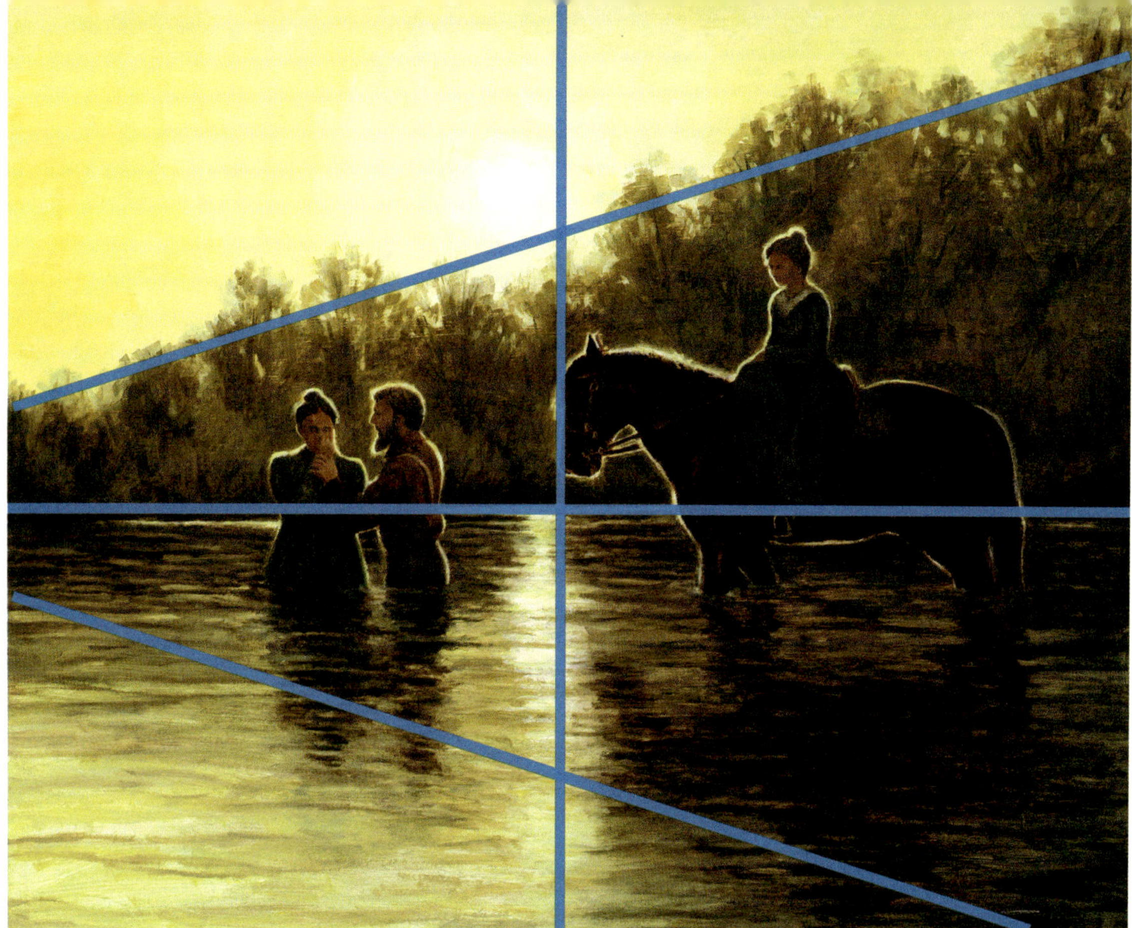

diagonal to pull the viewer broadly from right to left toward the baptism. These are just simple, geometric approaches to creating an aesthetically pleasing, purposeful, and symbolic composition.

AN APPLICATION

As mentioned, the baptism of Jane Neyman for her son Cyrus was unstructured and atypical, yet still applicable. In fact, the doctrines of baptism for the dead, like most doctrines and practices in the Church, have developed slowly and have taken dramatic shifts.[6] Like an old Polaroid photo, complete pictures did not develop immediately but came into clarity over time. For example, Joseph Smith had to quickly reiterate that these baptisms could be done *temporarily* in rivers but that it was an ordinance that belonged to the temple (see Doctrine and Covenants 124:29–32). He also had to clarify that these vicarious baptisms needed to be recorded (see Doctrine and Covenants 127:6; 128:4–7). The theology and purpose of the vicarious baptisms took shape over time, such as our creating a record of ordinances for our dead becoming the modern-day offering of the sons of Levi (see Doctrine and Covenants 128:24). Performing work for the dead became "necessary and essential to our salvation" (Doctrine and Covenants 128:15), creating a welding link between the generations (Doctrine and Covenants 128:18).

The ordinance of baptism for the dead still wasn't yet perfect, however. Not until November of 1841 did the Church began doing *confirmations* for the dead also.[7] It wasn't until April 1845 that Brigham Young gave the directive that men be baptized for men, and women for women.[8] Even in our own day, practices related to work for the dead have shifted and changed. For a long time, ordained priests were not allowed to perform proxy baptisms for the dead. Then, in 2017, the First Presidency announced that young men who are ordained priests can now baptize for the dead.[9] Recently, I was sitting with my wife doing some sealings for the dead in the temple. For whatever reason, I was the only male participant (other than the sealer and two male temple workers), but there were about ten other women, including my wife, in the sealing room. The door cracked open, and one of the temple workers was called out, leaving us with the sealer, one witness, and me as the only male to potentially act as the other witness. We couldn't move forward, and just sat around waiting for another man to show up to witness. I turned to my wife and whispered something like, "I just don't understand why women can't act as witnesses. It's not a duty assigned to any particular priesthood office, is it? I mean, the first baptism for the dead was witnessed by a woman!" No kidding, just a few weeks later, in October 2019 the Church "announced an historic policy change Wednesday morning allowing women, youth and children to serve as witnesses of sealing and baptismal ordinances performed in and out of temples."[10] It was purely coincidental timing, but I take credit!

The Restoration unfolded line upon line, bit by bit, principle by principle, and it is yet unfolding. God gives as we act faithfully, even if we at times act imperfectly. Through his authorized servants, the Lord adapts the practices of his Church to meet changing needs in changing times. He does not give everything at once, lest it overwhelm us. Nor does he always leave things as they are, lest they underserve us. Mistakes are made, from top down, as we strive our best based on our current understanding. The Lord accepts our sincere efforts to do his will, even when things may not be done perfectly. Jane Neyman and the history of baptisms for the dead confirm that these things are so.

The Lord accepts our sincere efforts to do his will, even when things may not be done perfectly.

AN ANALYSIS

1 I mentioned in the application that God does not give us everything at once, but reveals things slowly, line upon line. Why do you believe he does that? Why doesn't he give us everything up front? Why does he allow us to implement incomplete directives in ignorance? How does that approach contribute better to our growth than the alternative, or does it, and why?

2 Joseph quickly corrected some erroneous aspects of baptisms for the dead (no recorder), while allowing others to go on. Why are some supposed "mistakes" allowed to perpetuate for years in the Church and even decades before they are corrected, while others are caught and quickly changed?

3 How can you know the difference between what is an alterable policy or practice in this Church, and what is an unchanging doctrine? For example, is baptism at the age of eight years old an unalterable doctrine or a changeable policy (see Doctrine and Covenants 68:25)? What practices are truly unalterable across all dispensations?

NOTES

1. Sermon delivered at Nauvoo on 15 August 1840 (Saturday), reminiscent account of Simon Baker, Journal History, Church History Library, Book of Abraham Project (website).
2. See *Saints*, vol. 1: *The Standard of Truth, 1815–1846* (Salt Lake City: The Church of Jesus Christ of Latter-day Saints, 2018), 422.
3. Jane Neyman Statements, 1854 November 29, CR 100 396, Joseph Smith history documents, 1839–1860 / Materials used by Church historians, 1854–1856, Church History Library.
4. There appears to be some discrepancy for when the actual baptism occurred. In Jane's sworn statement given in 1854 of the event, the date of 13 September is given related to Joseph's sermon about Seymour Brunson, which funeral took place on 15 August. On the Jane Neyman statement, added sometime later and written in pencil next to 13 September is "(Aug 15?)." After that date it says, "She then went and was baptized for her son." See Jane Neyman Statements, 1854 November 29.
5. Jane Neyman Statements, 1854 November 29.
6. See R. Devan Jensen, Michael A. Goodman, and Barbara Morgan Gardner, "'Line upon Line': Joseph Smith's Growing Understanding of the Eternal Family," *Religious Educator* 20, no. 1 (2019): 34–59.
7. See note 32 in Alexander L. Baugh, "'For Their Salvation Is Necessary and Essential to Our Salvation': Joseph Smith and the Practice of Baptism and Confirmation for the Dead," in *An Eye of Faith: Essays in Honor of Richard O. Cowan*, ed. Kenneth L. Alford and Richard E. Bennett (Provo, UT: Religious Studies Center, Brigham Young University; Salt Lake City: Deseret Book, 2015), 113–37.
8. Brigham Young, "Speech," 6 April 1845, *Times and Seasons* 6, no. 12 (1 July 1845): 954. Wilford Woodruff later recalled, "When that [baptism for the dead] was first revealed . . . a man would be baptized for both male and female [but] afterward we obtained more light upon the subject and President Young taught the people that men should attend to those ordinances for the male portion of their dead friends and females for females." Journal History, 9 April 1857.
9. See "Church Adds New Opportunities for Youth and Children to Prepare for and Participate in Temples," *Church News*, 17 December 2017.
10. "Women Can Serve as Witnesses for Baptisms, Temple Sealings, President Nelson Announces in Historic Policy Change," *Church News*, 2 October 2019.

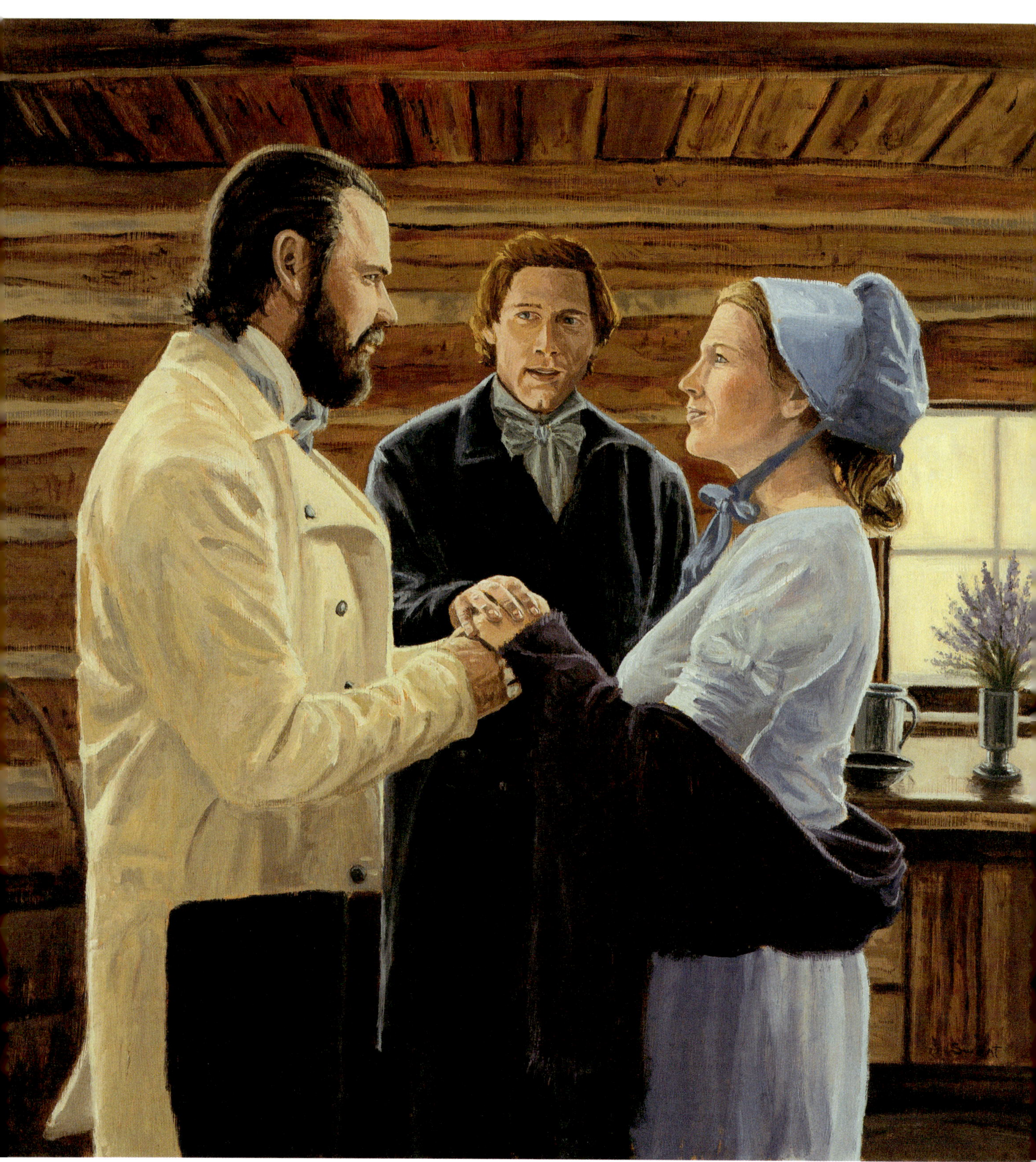

Eternal Marriage: The Sealing of Benjamin and Melissa Johnson (20" x 20", oil on board, 2017)

ETERNAL MARRIAGE

Timeline: May 1843

Related Doctrine and Covenants Sections: 131–32

A BACKGROUND

In mid-May 1843, Joseph Smith traveled southeastward from Nauvoo about twenty-five miles to a small town named Ramus (today's Webster), Illinois. There, a congregation of Latter-day Saints had gathered to hear the Prophet and others speak to them at a stake conference. Joseph's sister, Katherine Smith Salisbury, lived just south of Ramus in a town named Plymouth, Illinois.[1] For this conference, however, Joseph stayed with his good friend, Benjamin "Benny" Johnson, where some of the most important teachings that exist today on eternal marriage took place in the solitude of the Johnson home.[2]

Benjamin Johnson remembered, "The Prophet often came to our town, but after my arrival, he lodged in no house but mine, and I was proud of his partiality and took great delight in his society and friendship."[3] Staying at Benjamin's home on Tuesday evening, 16 May, Joseph called Benjamin and his wife, Melissa, to come sit down and talk. The Johnsons had been married since Christmas Day 1841,[4] not yet two years—still newlyweds. Joseph told them "he wished to marry us according to the Law of the Lord." Benjamin recalled, "I thought it a joke, and said I should not marry my wife again, unless she courted me, for I did it all the first time. He chided my levity, told me he was in earnest, and so it proved, for we stood up and were sealed by the Holy Spirit of Promise."[5]

You have to love it when you crack a joke and the Prophet doesn't think you're funny. You must also love that the words Joseph Smith said at this sealing wound up becoming canonized scripture. William Clayton, Joseph's secretary, recorded Joseph's conversation with the Johnsons on the evening of 16 May 1843. Joseph Smith taught Benjamin and Melissa Johnson that

> except a man and his wife enter into an everlasting covenant and be married for eternity, while in this probation; by the power and authority of the Holy Priesthood; they will cease to increase when they die, that is, that they will not have any children after the resurrection; but those who are married by the power and authority of the Priesthood in this life, and continue without committing

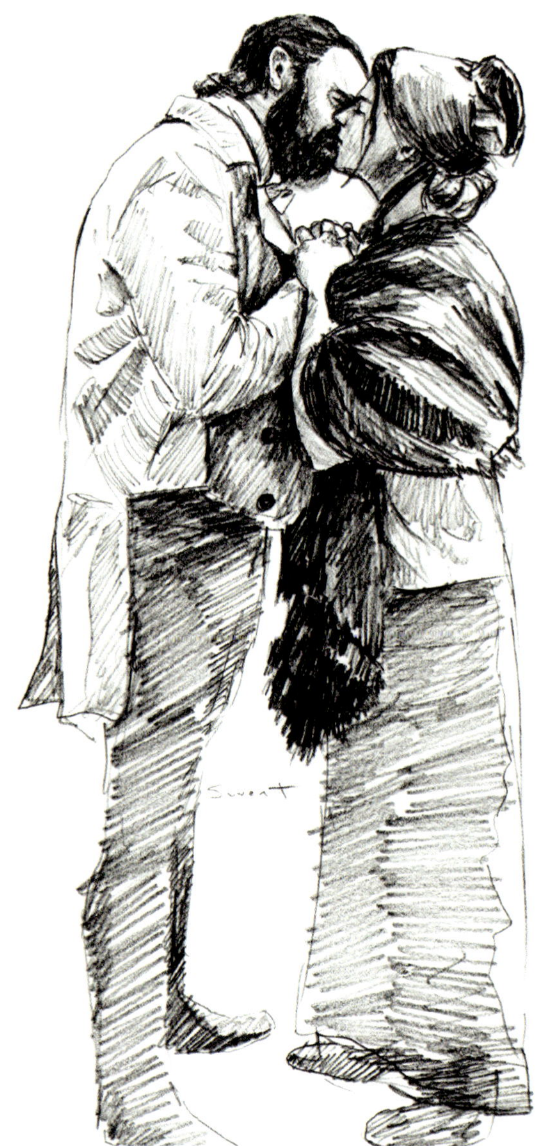

> the sin against the Holy Ghost, will continue to increase and have children in the celestial glory. . . . In the celestial glory there are three heavens or degrees, and in order to obtain the highest, a man must enter into this order of the Priesthood, and if he does not, he can not obtain it. He may enter into the other, but that is the end of his kingdom, he can not have an increase.[6]

If that last part sounds familiar to you, it is because it is the source material for Doctrine and Covenants 131:1–4. Yes, the doctrine that there are three degrees in the celestial glory and the requisites for eternal increase come from Joseph's sealing sermon to the Johnsons. These words were copied and later added to Joseph's journal history. In 1876, under the direction of President Brigham Young, Apostle Orson Pratt added twenty-six new sections to the Doctrine and Covenants, including these teachings on the centrality of eternal marriage for exaltation and eternal increase to the Johnsons.[7]

As these teachings are so pivotal and ubiquitous to Latter-day Saint doctrine today, I felt this hitherto undepicted scene needed to be painted.

AN IMAGE

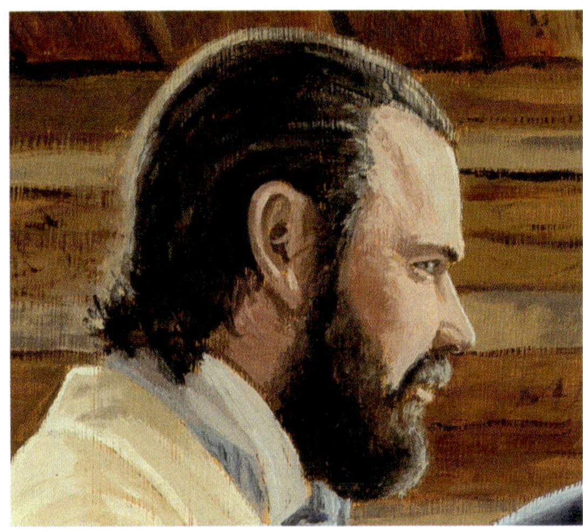

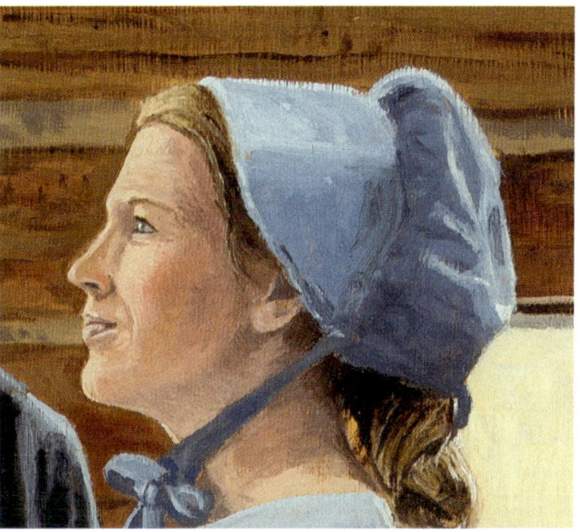

I wanted this image to feel sweet. I wanted a look of love and enlightenment from the idea of eternal marriage captured in the gazes of Benjamin and Melissa.

Joseph happily looks over to Benjamin, his mouth slightly open as he speaks truths about eternal marriage.

Because the sealing took place in their home, without a temple or a prescribed ceremony, I chose to place Joseph's hands on the Johnsons'

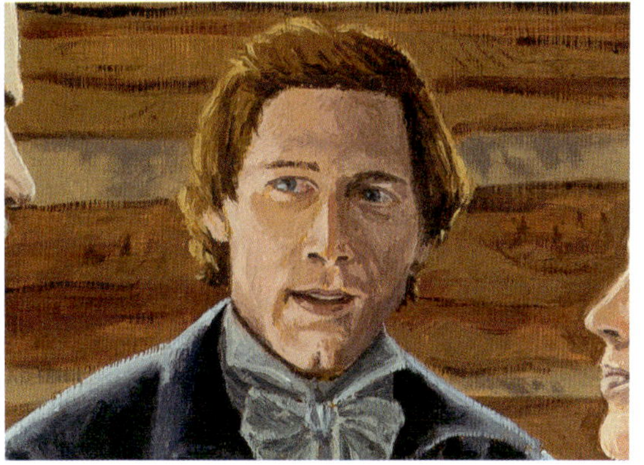

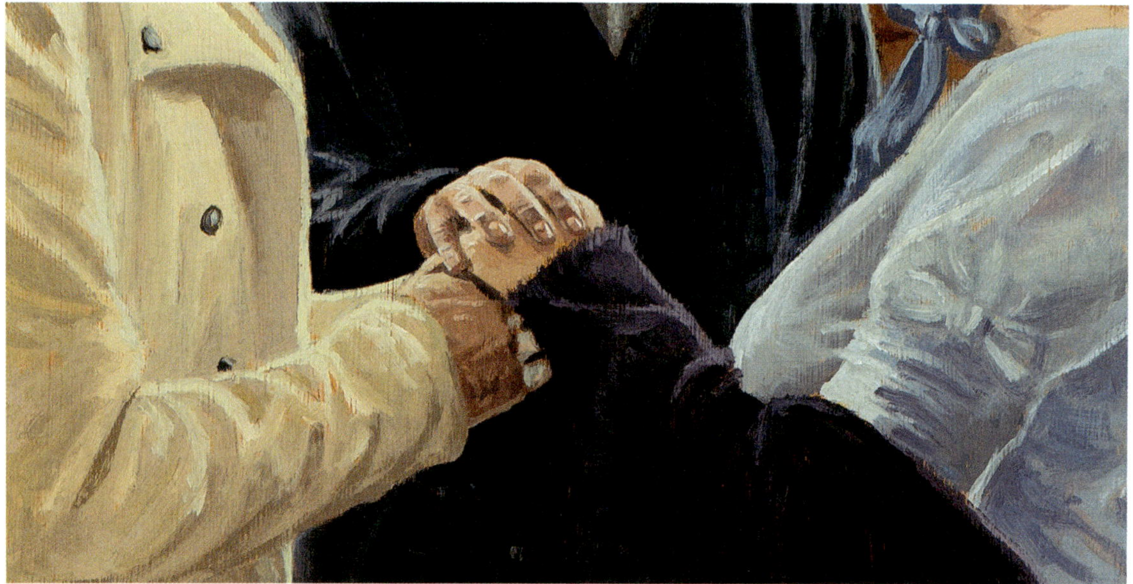

intertwined hands, a symbol of them united in eternal marriage by the sealing power of the priesthood. Alas, there is no mention of these mechanics in any existing documents of which I am aware, so this pose is purely hypothetical but logical.

The sealing took place in the "evening," according to Benjamin Johnson, and it is likely that the sun may have set by then, but I wanted the evening sun coming in through the windows to give natural light to and the feel of hopeful anticipation for this event. On a counter in front of the window is a bouquet of purple wildflowers to symbolize the idea of eternal love and increase.

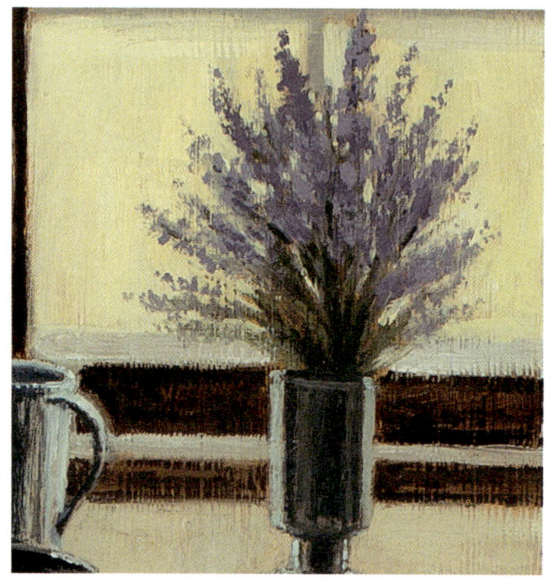

AN APPLICATION

President Russell M. Nelson has taught, "No man in this Church can obtain the highest degree of celestial glory without a worthy woman who is sealed to him. This temple ordinance enables eventual exaltation for both of them."[8] Salvation is between us and God. Exaltation is between us, our *spouse*, and God. Thus, as the Church's *General Handbook* teaches: "One of the requirements for obtaining eternal life is for a man and a woman to enter the covenant of celestial marriage (see Doctrine and Covenants 131:1–4). A couple makes this covenant when they receive the marriage sealing ordinance in the temple. This covenant is the foundation of an eternal family. When faithfully kept, it allows their marriage to endure forever. Ultimately, they can become like God (see Doctrine and Covenants 132:19–20)."[9]

These teachings on the potential for eternal marriage and family bring inexpressible joy to some, yet simultaneously bring deep anguish to others, such as those who come from part-member families, experience divorce, never marry, or identify as LGBTQ+. No matter our marital situation with others, all of us are in control of our covenant situation with God. Church leaders exhort in the *General Handbook*:

> In this life, many people have limited opportunities for loving family relationships. No family is free from challenges, pain, and sorrow. Individuals and families exercise faith in the Lord and strive to live according to the truths He has revealed concerning the family. The Savior has promised that He will help bear the burdens of all who come unto Him (see Matthew 11:28–30).
>
> Heavenly Father's plan of happiness ensures that all His children will have the opportunity to accept His gospel and receive His greatest blessings (see Doctrine and Covenants 137:7–10). All who make and keep covenants with God can experience joy and "peace in this world, and eternal life in the world to come" (Doctrine and Covenants 59:23; see also Mosiah 2:41). God's promise of eternal life includes eternal marriage, children, and all other blessings of an eternal family.[10]

Even for those who are married in the temple, the sealing between a husband and wife seems only a conditional sealing (see Doctrine and Covenants 132:7, 18). We can "make a covenant . . . for time and for all eternity," says the Lord, but if this covenant is not according to "me or by my word, which is my law," these "cannot . . . inherit my glory; for my house is a house of order" (132:18). All covenants that are not "sealed by the Holy Spirit of promise . . . are of no efficacy, virtue, or force in and after the resurrection from the dead" (132:7). Eternal marriage covenants become validated only "when faithfully kept" according to the prophets.[11]

Speaking personally, I have a *promissory* sealing with my wife, but it will only be actualized by our faithfulness. I must earn my wife's love in eternity by the way I show her my love in mortality.[12] We must live so that our eternal marriage is sealed by the Holy Spirit of promise, which secures the initial seal and ensures its blessings.[13] Joseph Smith actually taught Benjamin and Melissa Johnson of *two* sealings. "He said there was two seals in the Priesthood," William Clayton

We must earn our spouse's love in eternity by the way we show them our love in mortality.

recorded. "The first was that which was placed upon a man and woman when they made the covenant & the other was the seal which alloted to them their particular mansion."[14] Thus, as Doctrine and Covenants 132:19–20 describes, "a man" and "a wife" must enter "the new and everlasting covenant" and then have that covenant "sealed unto them by the Holy Spirit of promise," resulting in their being sealed to "their exaltation and glory in all things," having "a continuation of the seeds forever and ever," and "then shall they be gods."

AN ANALYSIS

1 In the last fifty years or so, contemporary society has undergone radical shifts in views on marriage, moving more toward the primary purpose of marriage being to fulfill personal needs, not necessarily societal or eternal ones. This individualistic view of marriage has created unprecedented levels of family instability and fracture.[15] How does our doctrine on eternal marriage change the way you view or approach marriage?

2 Teachings from Doctrine and Covenants 131 and 132 on a man and a woman being sealed in order to be exalted are central doctrines to why the Church does not sanction same-sex marriage.[16] Referencing Doctrine and Covenants 131:1–4 and Doctrine and Covenants 132:19, President Dallin H. Oaks taught, "Eternal life includes the creative powers inherent in the combination of male and female—what modern revelation describes as the 'continuation of the seeds forever and ever.'"[17] Some of the most pressing questions of contemporary society and in the Church, however, are regarding LGBTQ+ equality and rights. Because of the Church's teachings on male-female eternal marriage, some LGBTQ+ members don't feel like they have viable options or places in the Church. President M. Russell Ballard taught, "I want anyone who is a member of the Church who is gay or lesbian to know I believe you have a place in the kingdom and I recognize that sometimes it may be difficult for you to see where you fit in the Lord's Church, but you do. We need to listen to and understand what our LGBT brothers and sisters are feeling and experiencing. Certainly, we must do better than we have done in the past."[18] What can you do to better listen to and understand LGBTQ+ Saints? Accepting the Lord's revealed doctrine on male-female marriage, how can we "do better than we have done in the past" so that LGBTQ+ members feel loved, welcomed, respected, and equally valued in the Lord's restored Church?

3 Doctrine and Covenants 131 mentions that in the celestial glory there are three heavens or degrees. To enter the celestial kingdom, one must be baptized. To be exalted in the celestial kingdom, one must have an eternal marriage. There are two of the possible three degrees. What qualifies someone for the other degree in the celestial kingdom? How does this three-part celestial division work, and why?

NOTES

1. "Younger, Katharine Smith," People, The Joseph Smith Papers.
2. For more about eternal marriage, see R. Devan Jensen, Michael A. Goodman, and Barbara Morgan Gardner, "'Line upon Line': Joseph Smith's Growing Understanding of the Eternal Family," *Religious Educator* 20, no. 1 (2019): 34–59.
3. Benjamin F. Johnson, *My Life's Review: The Autobiography of Benjamin Franklin Johnson*, ed. Lyndon W. Cook and Kevin V. Harker (Provo, UT: Grandin Book, 1997), 85–86.
4. "Johnson, Benjamin F.," People, The Joseph Smith Papers.
5. Johnson, *My Life's Review*, 85–86.
6. "History, 1838–1856, volume D-1 [1 August 1842–1 July 1843]," 1551, The Joseph Smith Papers.
7. See Robert J. Woodford, "The Story of the Doctrine and Covenants," *Ensign*, December 1984, 32–37.
8. Russell M. Nelson, "Salvation and Exaltation," *Ensign*, May 2008, 9.

9. *General Handbook: Serving in The Church of Jesus Christ of Latter-day Saints* (Salt Lake City: The Church of Jesus Christ of Latter-day Saints, 2020), 2.1.2.
10. *General Handbook*, 2.1.
11. *General Handbook*, 2.1.2.
12. "Realize that a sealing ordinance is not enduring until after it is sealed by the Holy Spirit of Promise. Both individuals must be worthy and want the sealing to be eternal. Richard G. Scott, "Temple Worship: The Source of Strength in Times of Need," *Ensign*, May 2009, 45.
13. See "Holy Spirit of Promise," in Guide to the Scriptures (available online). "The Holy Spirit of Promise is the ratifying power of the Holy Ghost. When sealed by the Holy Spirit of Promise, an ordinance, vow, or covenant is binding on earth and in heaven. (See D&C 132:7.) Receiving this 'stamp of approval' from the Holy Ghost is the result of faithfulness, integrity, and steadfastness in honoring gospel covenants 'in [the] process of time' (Moses 7:21). However, this sealing can be forfeited through unrighteousness and transgression." David A. Bednar, "Ye Must Be Born Again," *Ensign*, May 2007, 22.
14. "Journal, December 1842–June 1844; Book 3, 15 July 1843–29 February 1844," [139], The Joseph Smith Papers; see also Clayton, Journal, 16 May and 19–20 October 1843.
15. See Stephanie Coontz, *Marriage, a History: How Love Conquered Marriage* (New York: Penguin, 2006).
16. See, for example, "God Loveth His Children" (2007), churchofjesuschrist.org; "First Presidency Statement on Same-Gender Marriage," 20 October 2004, newsroom.churchofjesuschrist.org.
17. Dallin H. Oaks, "*Two* Great Commandments," *Ensign*, November 2019, 74.
18. M. Russell Ballard, "Questions and Answers" (devotional address at Brigham Young University, 24 November 2017), speeches.byu.edu.

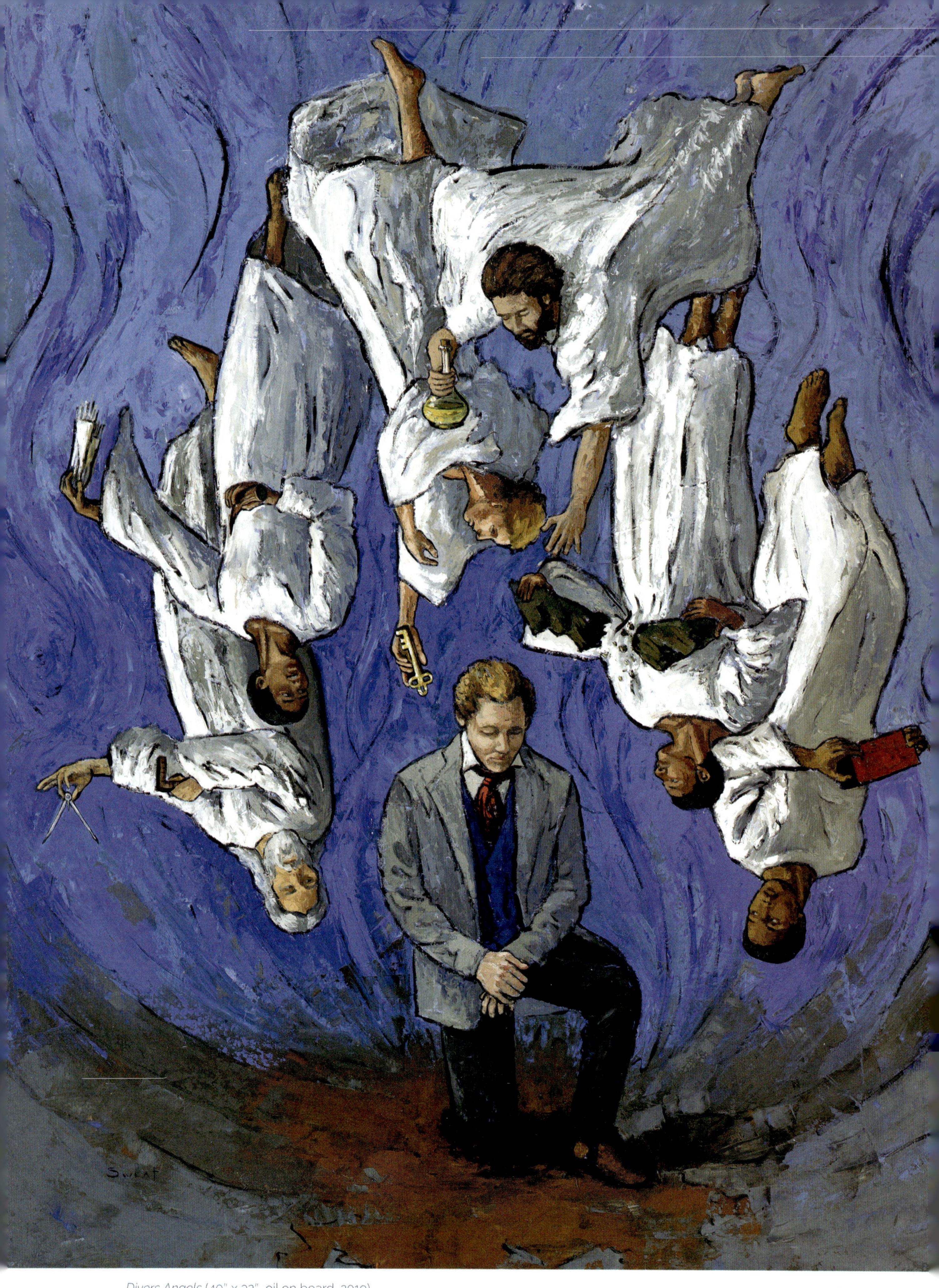

Divers Angels (40" x 32", oil on board, 2019)

DIVERS ANGELS

Timeline: 1829–44

Related Doctrine and Covenants Section: 128

A BACKGROUND

There is a colloquial proverb that says, "If you understand everything, you must be misinformed." Although priesthood authority is perhaps the defining feature of the Restoration, there are aspects of priesthood authority, ordinances, and keys that seem to be more esoteric or even completely unknown. For example,

- Where did we get the authority to perform healing blessings?
- Is a priesthood key of authority needed to build the New Jerusalem?
- How did God reveal the temple endowment to Joseph Smith?

In a now canonized letter that Joseph Smith wrote to the Saints on 6 September 1842, Joseph Smith eloquently described various angelic messengers who had delivered priesthood authority to him. He lists familiar angels such as Moroni, and Peter, James, and John (see Doctrine and Covenants 128:20). But he also lists less familiar, or even completely unknown angels, such as Michael (see "Michael Detecting the Devil"), Gabriel, and even Raphael (see Doctrine and Covenants 128:20–21). Joseph says that each of these angelic visitors came "declaring their dispensation, their rights, their keys, their honors, their majesty and glory, and the power of their priesthood; giving line upon line, precept upon precept; here a little, and there a little" (Doctrine and Covenants 128:21).

What "dispensation," "right," "key," "honor," "glory," or "power" of the priesthood did the angel Gabriel bring to Joseph Smith? Joseph taught us that Adam was Michael and that Gabriel was

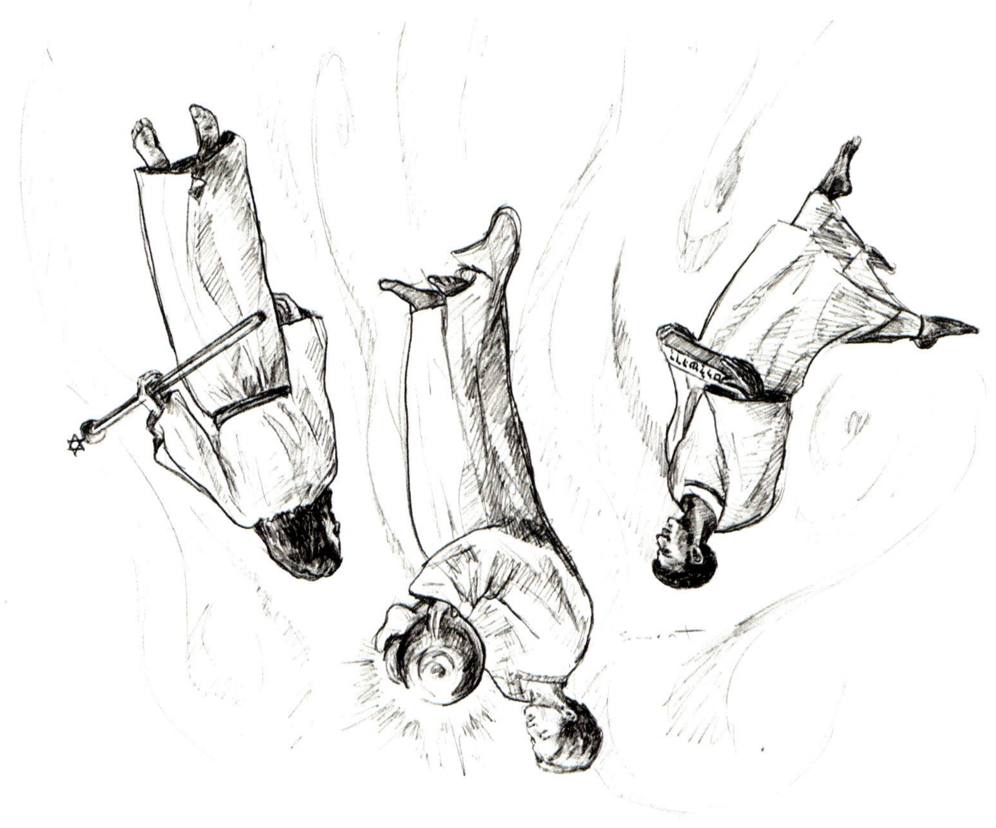

the ancient biblical patriarch Noah, who "stands next in authority to Adam in the Priesthood: he was called of God to this office and was the Father of all living in his day and to him was given the Dominion. These men held keys first on Earth and then in Heaven."[1] Joseph did make one connection between Gabriel and the endowment, albeit tenuous, when he taught in November 1835, "The endowment about which you are so anxious, you cannot comprehend now, nor could the Angel, Gabriel explain it to the understanding of your dark minds." However, this "endowment" had more to do with Joseph Smith's definition of an outpouring of heavenly power to perform miracles such as the "sick will be healed, the lame made to walk the deaf to hear and the blind to see."[2]

Similarly, what "dispensation," "right," "key," "honor," "glory," or "power" of the priesthood did the angel Raphael bring to Joseph Smith? Who even is the angel Raphael? I know of no known statement where Joseph Smith expounds who Raphael may be or what his priesthood-centered mission may have entailed. Raphael is not mentioned in the Old or New Testament but is mentioned in the Apocrypha. The name Raphael means "God heals" or "to heal."[3] True to his name, in the apocryphal book of Tobit, Raphael was sent to simultaneously heal Tobias and a woman named Sara, "And the holy angel of the Lord, Raphael was sent to heal them" (Tobit 3:25). Raphael goes on to teach Tobias how to use a fish for healing (see Tobit chapters 6, 7, and 11, for example). In the Ethiopian Book of Enoch, rediscovered in 1773, Raphael is one of the four key angels of God and "is in charge of all the diseases, and in charge of all the wounds of the sons of men" (Book of Enoch, the First Parable, 40:9).[4] Thus, in early Christian art, Raphael is often shown carrying a fish, a staff, a light, or a small receptacle of oil. One Latter-day Saint commentator theorized that Raphael is associated with the healing angel that troubled the water at the Pool of Bethesda just as Latter-day Saints used to perform baptisms for healing: "By invoking the image of Raphael the healer, Smith emphasized the concept that the temple was a place of physical healing, a sacred space that conveyed an amplified endowment of power, a healing that was once conveyed by one who attended the throne of God."[5] Is Raphael our angel of healing? Joseph Smith seemed to know, but nothing has ever specifically been taught on the subject by other Church leaders.

Thus, this image represents these "divers" (diverse) angels who each restored "their dispensation, their rights, their keys, their honors, their majesty and glory, and the power of their priesthood." This painting depicts those six concepts through unnamed heavenly messengers, diving down from heaven, ready to dispense a symbolic item related to teachings and rituals of the Restoration.

AN IMAGE

Because the timing, purpose, and nature of these angelic ministrations is somewhat esoteric, like other paintings representing angels in this series (such as "The Chamber of Father Whitmer"), I chose to abstract and stylize this painting. Obviously, the first compositional choice made was to make a play on words and show the "divers" angels actually diving down from heaven, ready to dispense their priesthood upon Joseph Smith. Because "divers" means *diverse*, as in many or

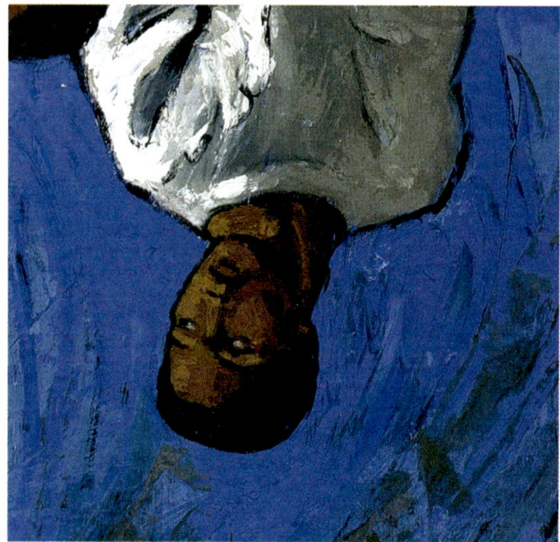

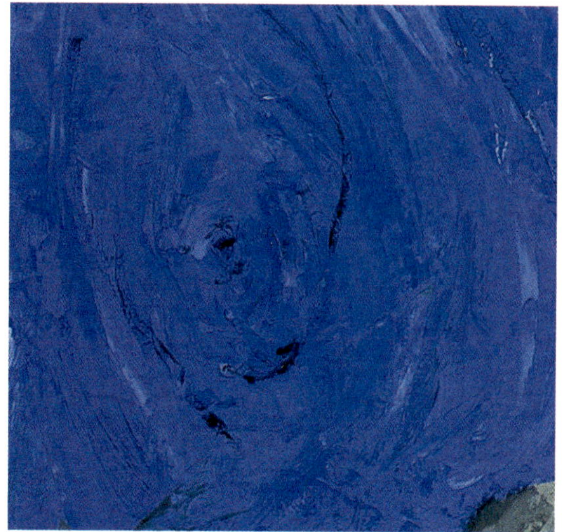

different, I wanted to show angels who represent different nationalities, including African, Islander, Latino, and Asian.

In the painting, the angels are surrounded by a blue background. Vincent Van Gogh once explained to his brother Theo, "I paint infinity, . . . the richest, intensest blue that I can contrive, and by this simple combination of the . . . rich blue background I get a mysterious effect, like a star in the depths of an azure sky."[6] The blue has swirls, similar to Van Gogh's *Starry Night* painting, which suggest the motion and movement of the angels in heaven in bringing about this latter-day work on the earth.

Joseph Smith kneels at the center of the painting, head bowed, as he was the central figure to receive all the dispensed keys from these angels.

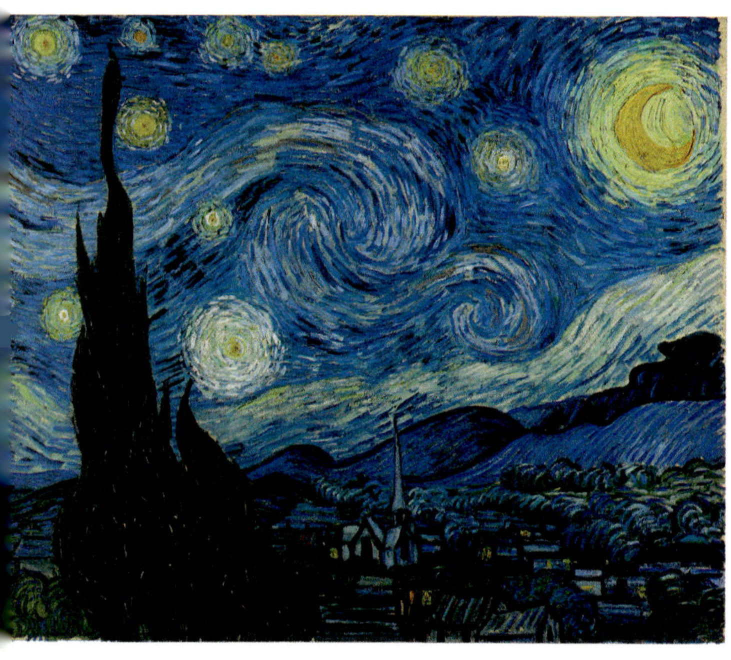

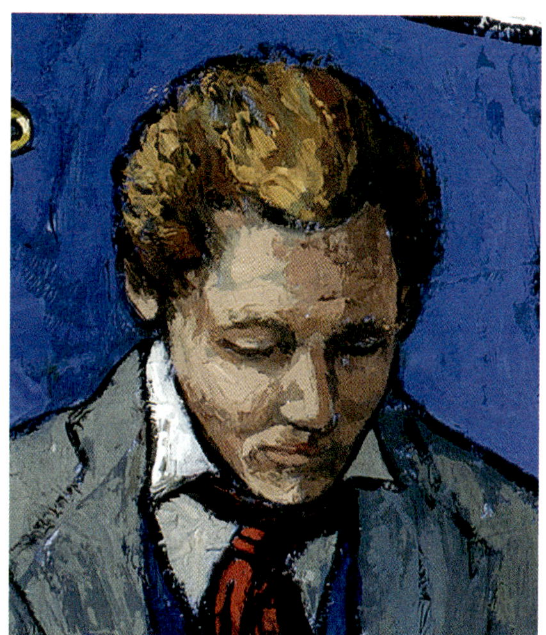

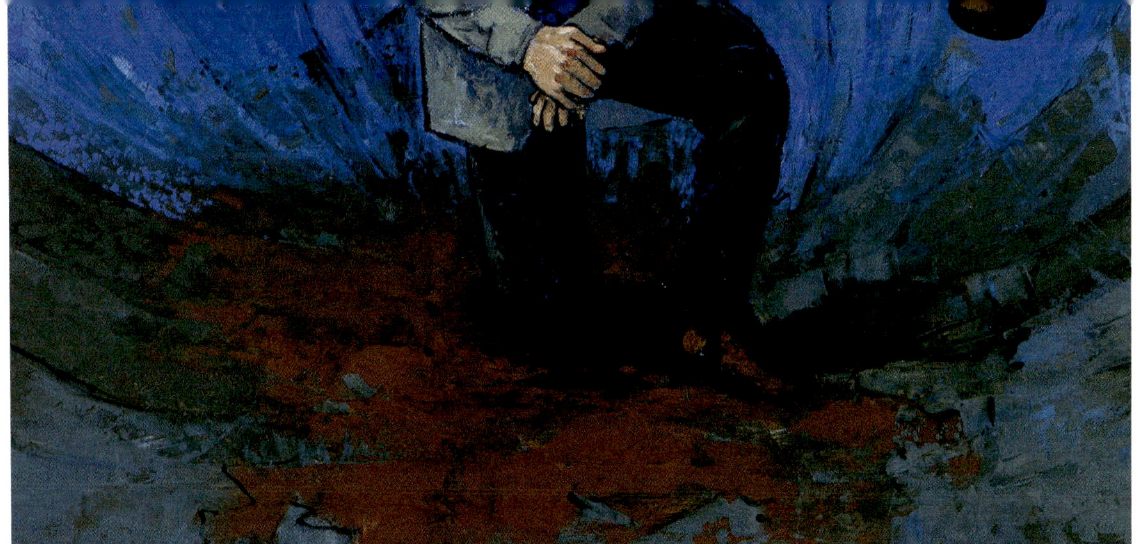

I painted a brown base or ground for Joseph to kneel on, the brown suggesting earth and mortality meeting with the blue of heaven and eternity.

Each angel holds a symbolic item, representing a key or power, an ordinance or ritual, that is part of Restoration theology and practice. From right to left, one angel holds a brick, another breaks apart a mountain, and yet another reaches his hand out toward Joseph as he holds a jar of oil. The angel directly above Joseph extends a key, while the one to its right holds a ram's horn and towel. The last carries a drawing compass and a builder's square. Some of their symbolic meaning may be obvious, while others more uncertain, and for me to explain them in specificity would rob the viewer of some of their own interpretations and insights, which is one of

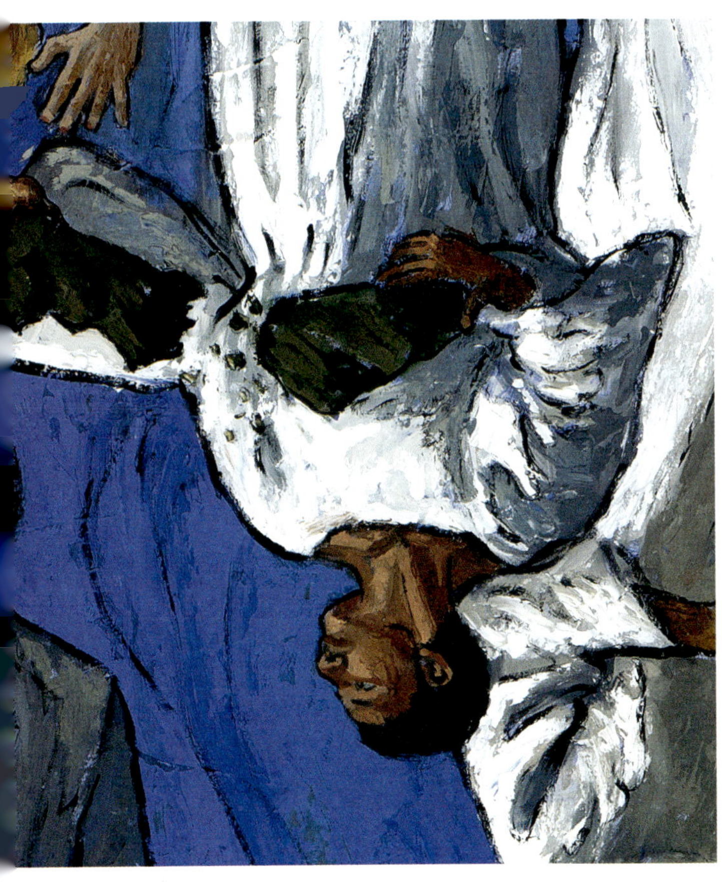

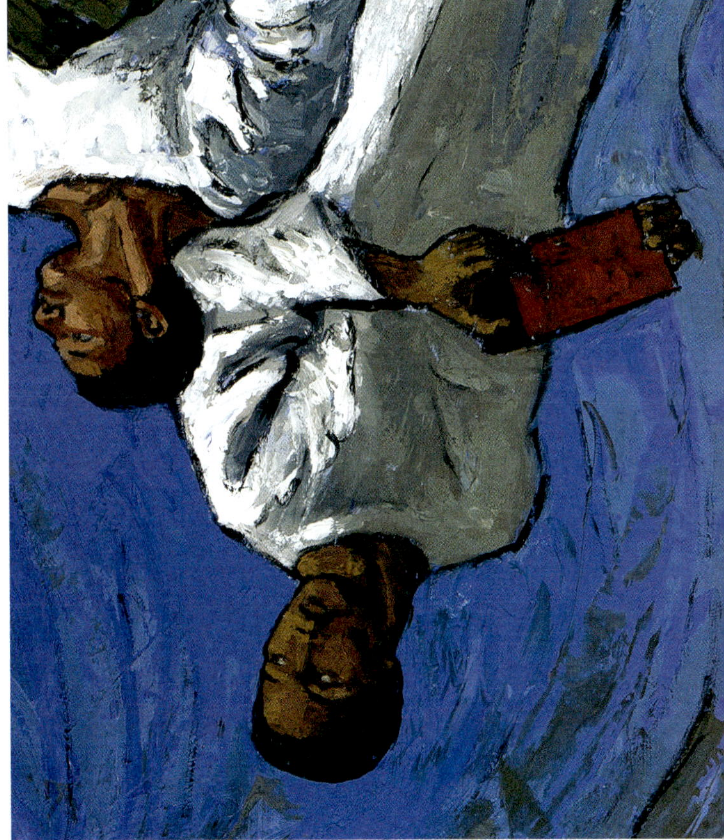

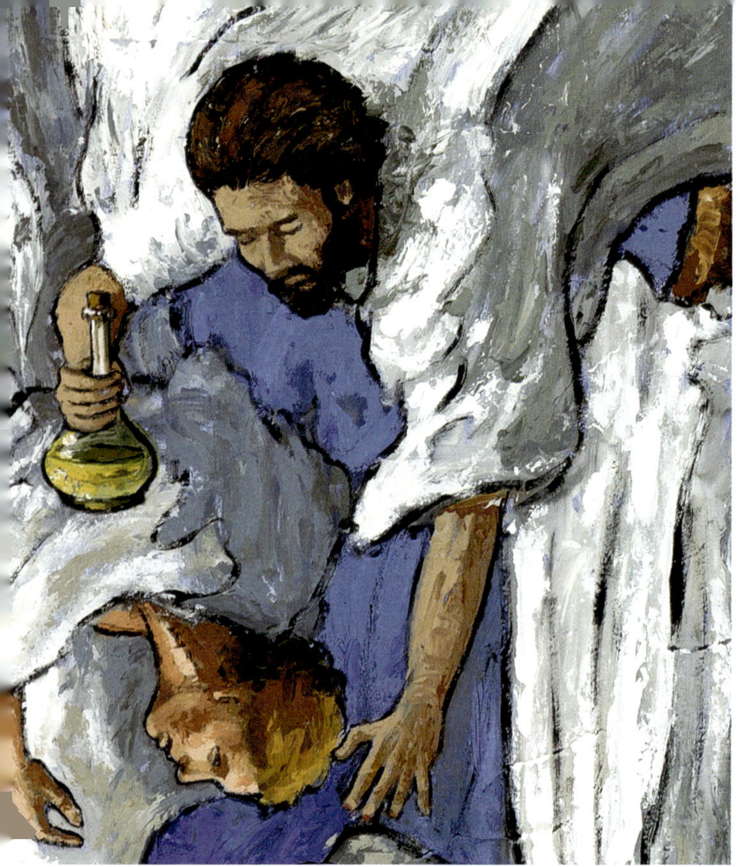

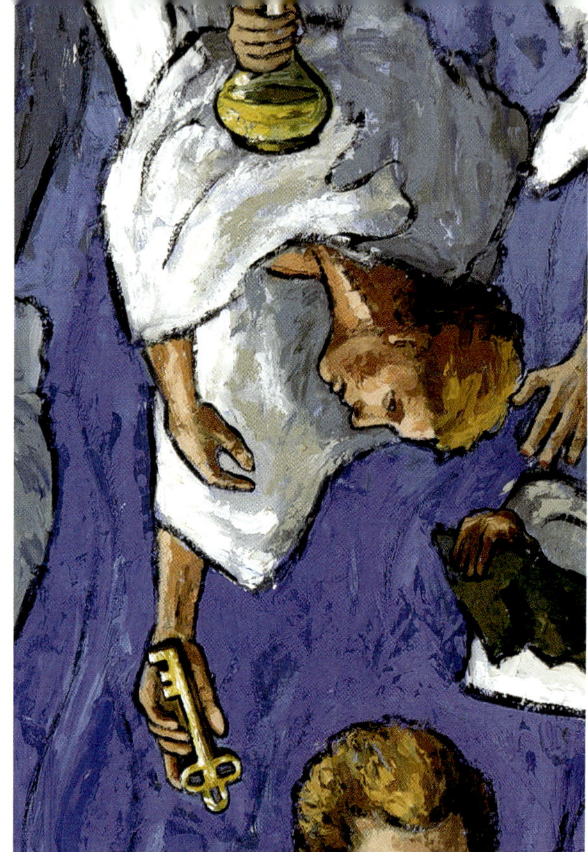

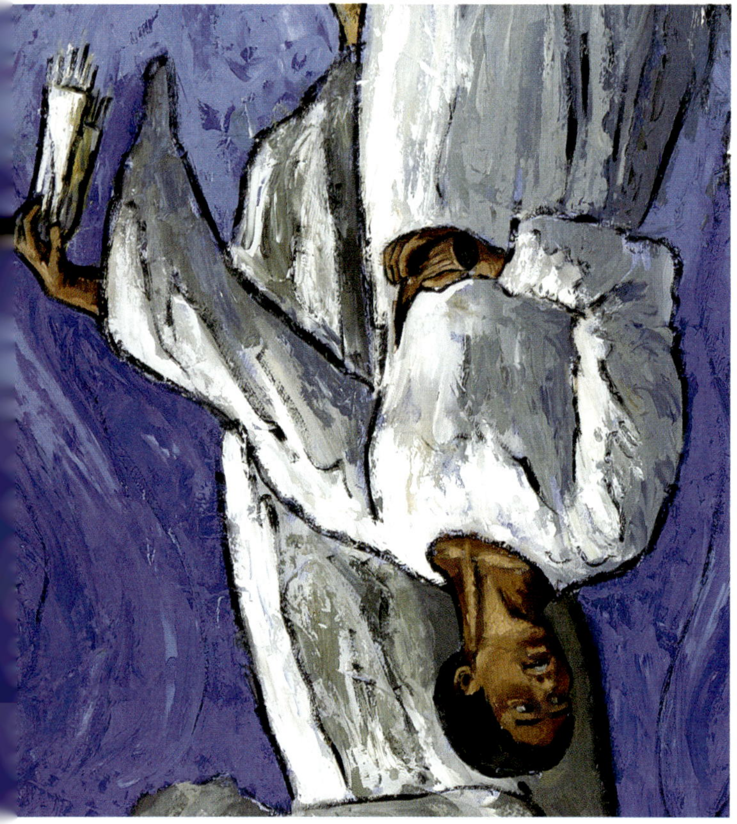

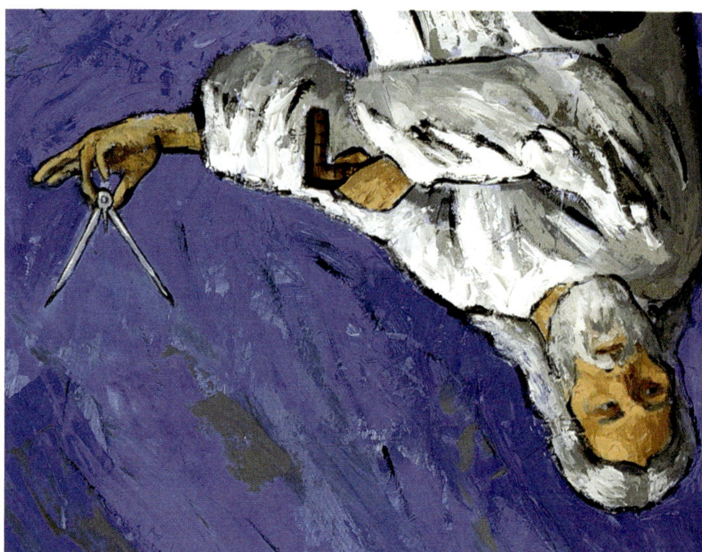

the beauties of art. Like the identity of Rafael or the mission of Gabriel, perhaps some things are better left hinted at but undocumented. As it is already, I've likely said too much. Maybe Joseph felt the same way.

AN APPLICATION

When we say that this Church is "true," we can't possibly mean that this Church is perfectly organized. The organization of the Church has shifted and changed over time and may yet in the future, but it was still "true" in 1830 when we had only a first and second elder and no bishops or First Presidency. The Church isn't "true" because it has perfect teachings, as there are yet "many great and important things pertaining to the Kingdom of God" to be revealed (Articles of Faith 1:9). The Church isn't "true" because it has all the truth, as truth is found in many places in the world outside of the institutional Church. The Church isn't true because it has never made any mistakes, because, as President Dieter F. Uchtdorf said in general conference, there have been times when "leaders in the Church have simply made mistakes."[7] The Church isn't even true just because the Book of Mormon is true. Indeed, there are millions of people who believe in the Book of Mormon but belong to different restoration churches.

What makes the Church "true" is that the Church is *authorized.* It is authorized because heavenly beings gave priesthood keys and authority to Joseph Smith, who passed them on to his subsequent successors in the apostleship, down to the living prophet and apostles today of The Church of Jesus Christ of Latter-day Saints. The Church is "true" because it is authorized to dispense the covenants and ordinances of exaltation, recognized by God. President David O. McKay once taught, "If at this moment each one [of you] were asked to state in one sentence . . . the most distinguishing feature of the Church of Jesus Christ of Latter-day Saints, what would be your answer?" President David O. McKay said, "My answer would be . . . divine authority."[8] President James E. Faust said, "Without priesthood keys and authority, there would be no church."[9] Elder Jeffrey R. Holland said, "The priesthood of God, with its keys, its ordinances, its divine origin and ability to bind in heaven what is bound on earth, is as *indispensable* to the true Church of God as it is *unique* to it and that without it there would be no Church of Jesus Christ of Latter-day Saints."[10]

This idea is important in that it may be helpful for those who begin to think the Church is not true because it has changed some of its teachings, its policies, its programs, or its organization or has made mistakes. The question each of us should ask is, "Do I believe that heavenly beings visited Joseph Smith and dispensed keys of priesthood authority to him to perform the covenants and ordinances of exaltation, and that those keys have been passed on to the current living apostles and prophet?" Keys are the key question. I believe God is doing a great work on this earth to bring about the restoration of all things. I believe God is working through many people, religions, governments, and organizations the world over to bring about his will. I believe truth is to be found in many places and spheres. I believe God loves all his children equally. But I also believe that this is the authorized organization to dispense the exalting covenants of Abraham, which have been restored through diverse angels to God's prophet in this dispensation, Joseph Smith.

The Church is "true" because it is authorized to dispense the covenants and ordinances of exaltation.

AN ANALYSIS

1 President Spencer W. Kimball once taught that we don't have all the keys of the priesthood, such as the keys of resurrection, and Brigham Young taught we also don't have the keys of creation.[11] What other future priesthood keys may need to be dispensed and for what purposes?

2 Address some of the questions posed in the beginning paragraph: Where did we get the authority to perform healing blessings? Is a priesthood key of authority needed to build the New Jerusalem? How did God reveal the temple endowment to Joseph Smith? What other ordinances, rituals, or actions are done in the Church where the source of authority may be unknown or unclear? What ordinances, rituals, or actions are done in the Church where the source of authority is very clear (for example, John the Baptist and the authority to baptize)?

3 I used the definition of the Church being "true" as directly connected to having the recognized priesthood keys to dispense the covenants of exaltation. What other ways might you define what it means for the Church to be true?

NOTES

1. July 1839 report of instructions by Willard Richards, in "History, 1838–1856, volume C-1 [2 November 1838–31 July 1842] [addenda]," 11 [addenda], The Joseph Smith Papers.
2. November 1835 instructions, "History, 1834–1836," 127, The Joseph Smith Papers.
3. "Raphael," Behind the Name (website).
4. *The Book of Enoch: A Modern English Translation of the Ethiopian Book of Enoch* with introduction and notes by Andy McCracken, 59, scriptural-truth.com.
5. Kris Wright, "Situating the Archangel Raphael in Section 128: A Theory," By Common Consent (website).
6. Kathleen Powers Erickson, *At Eternity's Gate: The Spiritual Vision of Vincent Van Gogh* (Grand Rapids, MI: Eerdmans, 1998), 172.
7. Dieter F. Uchtdorf, "Come, Join with Us," *Ensign*, November 2013, 21–24.
8. David O. McKay, in Conference Report, April 1937, 121.
9. James E. Faust, "Where Is the Church?" (devotional address at Brigham Young University, 1 March 2005), 8.
10. Jeffrey R. Holland, "Our Most Distinguishing Feature," *Ensign*, May 2005, 43; emphasis added.
11. Spencer W. Kimball, *Ensign*, May 1977, 49; Brigham Young, in *Journal of Discourses* (London: Latter-day Saints' Book Depot, 1854–86), 15:137.

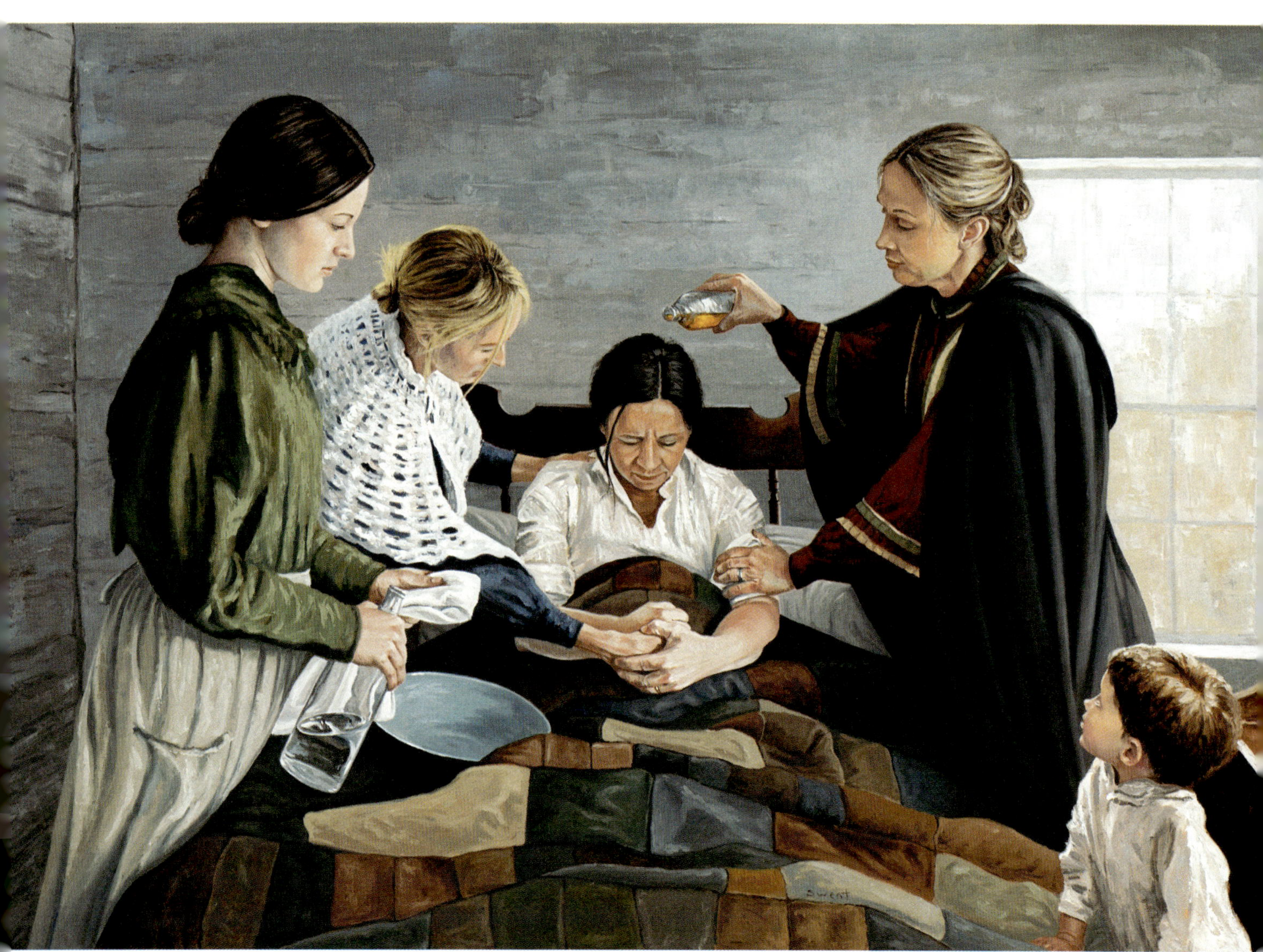

Relief Society Healing (36" x 54", oil on board, 2019)

RELIEF SOCIETY HEALING

Timeline: 1830s–1930s

Related Doctrine and Covenants Sections: 46, 84

A BACKGROUND

In the small town of Mayfield, Ohio, new Latter-day Saint converts Sarah Leavitt and her husband, Jeremiah, tended to their sick, eighteen-year-old daughter, Louisa. So much medical care had been given to Louisa that the family was about to lose their team of horses to pay for more. Despite the treatments, Louisa remained weak, feeble, and bedridden. What to do? Her mother, Sara, recorded:

> I lay pondering on our situation, thinking we should be undone if our team was taken from us, and prayed earnestly to the Lord to let us know what we should do. There was an angel who stood by my bed to answer my prayer. He told me to call Louisa up and lay my hands upon her in the name of Jesus Christ and administer to her and she should recover. I awakened my husband, who lay by my side, and told him to get up, make a fire, and get Louisa up. . . . I administered to her in faith, having the gift from the Lord. It was about midnight when this was done and she began to recover from that time and was soon up and about, and the honor, praise and glory be to God and the Lamb.[1]

This story of a Latter-day Saint woman laying on hands to administer a healing blessing to her daughter is not unique. Through the 1830s and for the next hundred years, Latter-day Saint women actively participated in healing blessings of children, women, and men.[2] For example, in 1838 Mary Isabella Horne's daughter "had taken very ill, and her life despaired of, in fact it seemed impossible for her to get better. The mother of the Prophet, Mrs. Lucy Smith, came and blessed the child and said she should live."[3]

Many saw such healing blessings as evidence that the days of miracles and spiritual gifts had

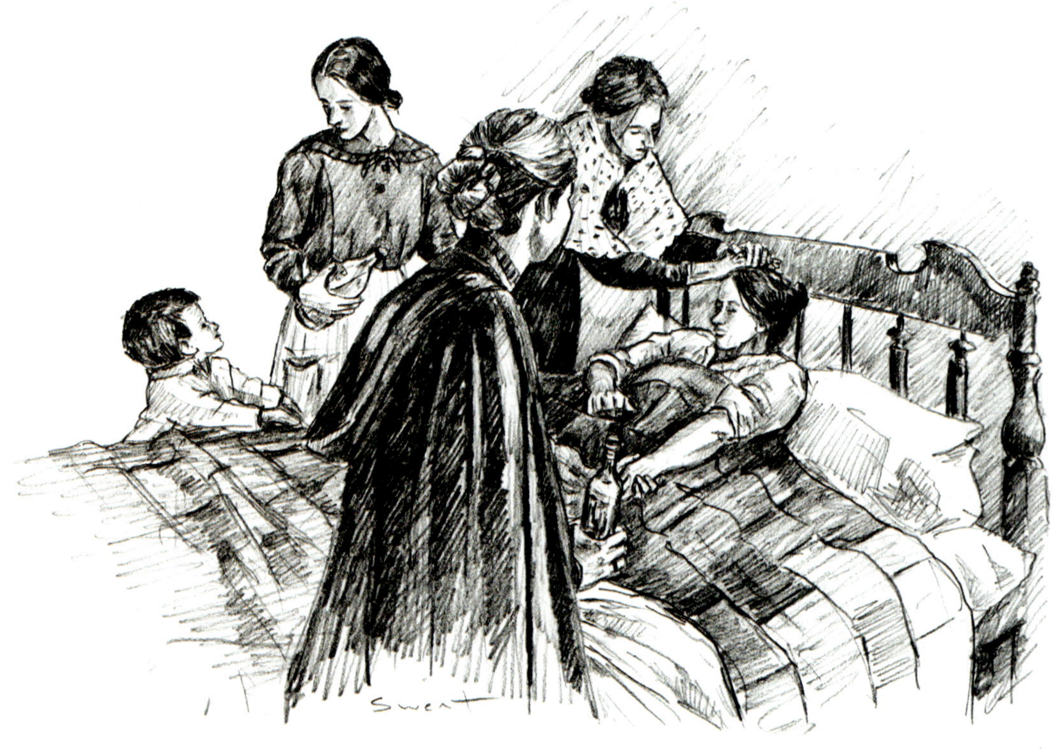

not ceased and were present with the Church.[4] When the Nauvoo Female Relief Society was organized on 17 March 1842 under the Prophet Joseph Smith's direction, he gave several sermons to its members. At one of the meetings of the Nauvoo Relief Society, Joseph Smith spoke on the propriety of women laying on hands to heal the sick at that time. The Prophet read to the sisters from 1 Corinthians 12, a chapter on spiritual gifts. The minutes of that meeting say:

> Pres[t.] Smith continued the subject by adverting [referring] to the commission given to the ancient apostles 'Go ye into all the world' &c.— no matter who believeth; these signs, such as healing the sick, casting out devils &c. should follow all that believe whether male or female. He ask'd the Society if they could not see by this sweeping stroke, that wherein they are ordaind, it is the privilege of those set apart to administer in that authority which is confer'd on them— and if the sisters should have faith to heal the sick, let all hold their tongues, and let every thing roll on. . . .
>
> Respecting the female laying on hands, he further remark'd, there could be no devil in it if God gave his sanction by healing. . . .
>
> Pres[t.] S then offered instruction respecting the propriety of females administering to the sick by the laying on of hands— said it was according to revelation.[5]

The women took heed to his counsel and acted accordingly. At the close of one Nauvoo Relief Society meeting, "Mrs. [Elizabeth Davis] Durfee bore testimony to the great blessing she received when administered to, after the close of the last meeting, by Pres[t.] E. Smith & Councillors Cleveland and Whitney. she said she never realized more benefit thro' any administration— that she was heal'd," adding a quip that she "thought the sisters had more faith than the brethren."[6] At another meeting on 23 June 1842, "Mrs. Chase prophesied that henceforth, if the sisters are faithful, the gifts of the gospel shall be with us, especially the gift of healing."[7]

With the approval and even encouragement of Church leadership and for the remainder of the century, women in the Church performed various healing rituals by virtue of their faith in Jesus. During this time, "many women received priesthood blessings promising that they would have the gift of healing."[8] Elder Franklin D. Richards spoke to members of the Relief Society in 1888 and said, "I wish all the sisters were so faithful that they were healers of the sick, through the power of God."[9] Editors for the book *The First Fifty Years of Relief Society* wrote: "Nineteenth-century Latter-day Saint women particularly cherished the gift of healing, and it became closely associated with their ministry among the sick and needy. . . . Women gave blessings of healing in Nauvoo, during the Saints' trek westward, and in Utah. . . . Joseph Smith's successors as church president, including Brigham Young, John Taylor, and Wilford Woodruff, also encouraged women's use of the gift of healing."[10]

As time passed, women (particularly those who had received their temple endowment)[11] began to wash, anoint, and seal anointings when administering blessings, sometimes in conjunction with their husbands and sometimes with other sisters. Oil was often used to anoint the afflicted part of the body or even given to swallow as part of the blessing.[12] At a time of high infant mortality and questionable medical practices, women would also administer to mothers before childbirth to wash, anoint, and seal an anointing on the expectant mother. Some used a prescribed blessing for childbirth, blessing specific parts of the body to perform their functions properly.[13] Zina D. H. Young told the Cache Valley Relief Society in 1886, "I wish to speak of the great privilege given to us to wash and anoint the sick and suffering of our sex. I would counsel every one who expects to become a mother to have this ordinance administered by some good faithful sister."[14]

At the turn of the twentieth century, however, various factors converged that lessened the emphasis on women performing healing blessings, and eventually contributed to its complete cessation. Progressive Era–health reforms in Utah fostered increased acceptance of and reliance on improved medical care and health practices.[15] A growing emphasis on "scientific rationalism" and away from charismatic gifts became more prevalent among a new generation of Church members.[16] The institutional Church began to distance itself from individual pentecostal spiritual expressions, like speaking in tongues, and moved increasingly toward structure and uniformity.[17] Uncertainty arose about the propriety of women performing the healing rituals that had been previously accepted. Church leaders (male and female) emphasized that women were acting by faith in giving these ministering blessings but not by priesthood office (which office could speak in the name of the Lord)[18] and that these blessings were not considered Church ordinances.[19] Church leaders clarified that the scriptural directive was that "the *elders* of the church, two or more, shall be called, and shall pray for and lay their hands upon them" (Doctrine and Covenants 42:44) and began to emphasize this scriptural pattern and mandate (see also James 5:14). In particular was a newly expressed emphasis that only elders who held the Melchizedek Priesthood had the authority to "seal" an anointed blessing.[20] Thus, by the mid-twentieth century, women's participation in healing anointings and blessings faded as the elders fulfilled this role, and eventually dropped out altogether.[21] Today in the Church, the *General Handbook* directs that "only worthy Melchizedek Priesthood holders may administer to the sick or afflicted."[22]

Although only a few generations removed, the long history of sisters performing healing blessings has largely been forgotten by the modern body of the Church. Because healing was a cherished part of early Latter-day Saint women's practice for one hundred years and because discussions on the role of women and the priesthood in the Church continue today, I wanted to produce an image to celebrate this important period of women's ministry in Church history to help inform the current one. I also wanted to produce a painting of women coming together in unity, in love, in power, and in faith to comfort, care for, strengthen, and minister to each other. One scholar has noted that much religious art depicting women either pits them against one another (like the foolish and wise virgins) or has them as individual, solitary figures. Very rarely are women depicted in a united group.[23] In this image, they are.

AN IMAGE

At the center of the image sits a woman in bed, head bowed in faith, preparing to be anointed for a blessing.

On the far left a younger woman holds the water and towel used to wash her, with a bowl resting below her on the bed.

On the right stands a woman preparing to administer the anointing. She confidently leans

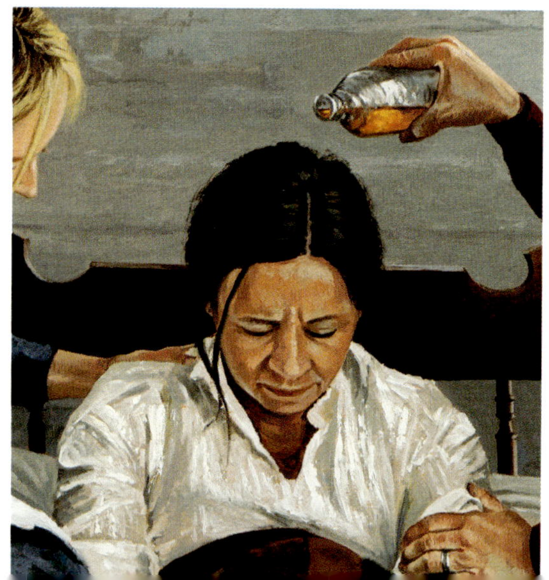

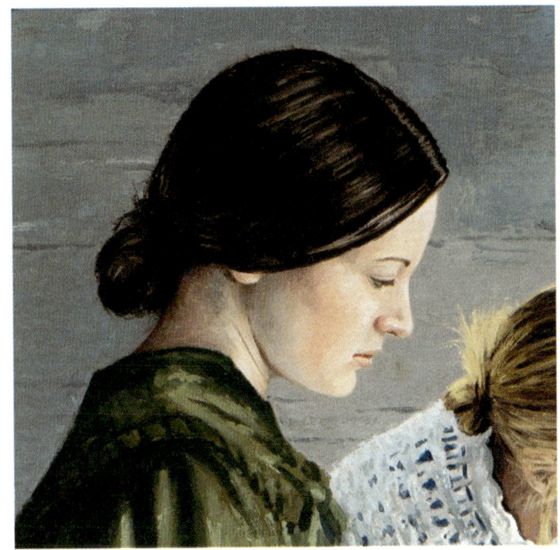

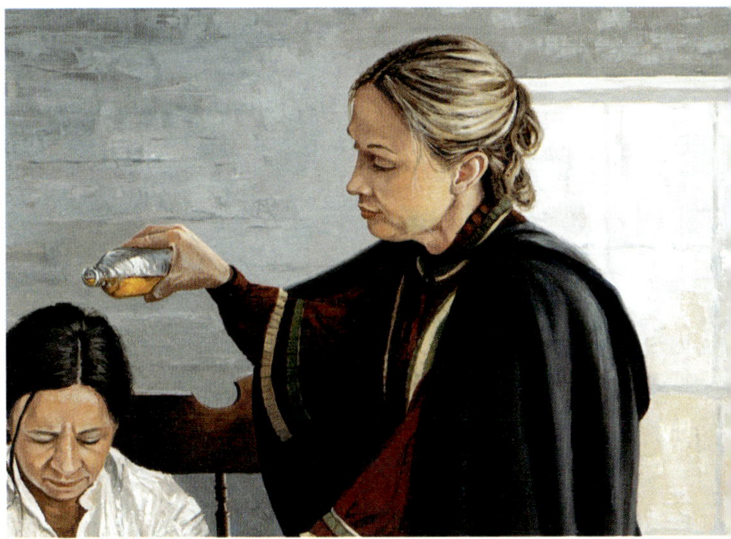

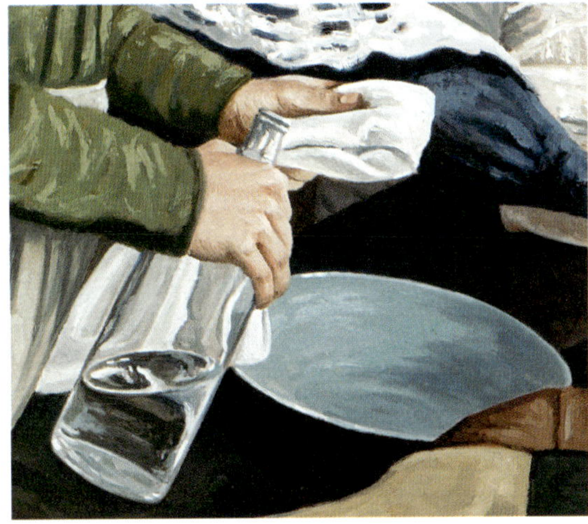

forward, her clothing symbolic of the spiritual power she carries—her winter riding cloak almost acting as a cape connected to supernatural ability.

At the bottom right of the composition stands a little boy (bottom left image), leaning forward to watch what these faithful women are doing to bless his mother, looking up to them both literally and symbolically. Behind him is a cradle preparing to receive a new sibling.

A third ministering woman leans in, her left hand tenderly resting on the shoulder of the sister in need, to offer comfort and consolation. I painted three women performing the blessing because "often three women participated in the healing ritual and used the rhetoric of three to claim healing power." [24] The three women in this image could also be a subtle reference to the three great spiritual gifts—often visually represented as women—of faith, hope, and charity and the spiritual healing these gifts bring into our lives. The woman preparing the washing

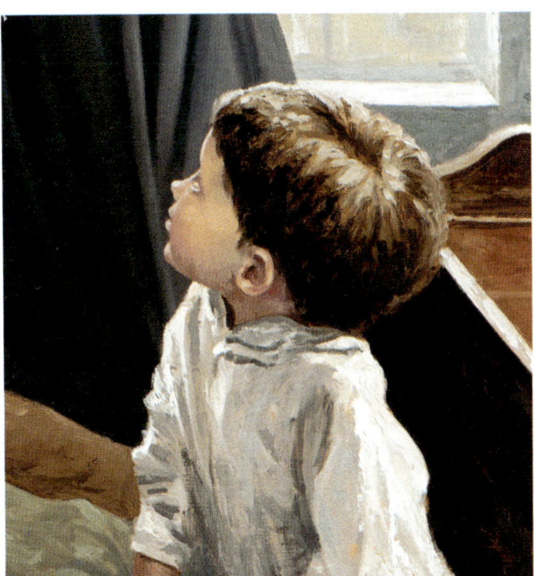

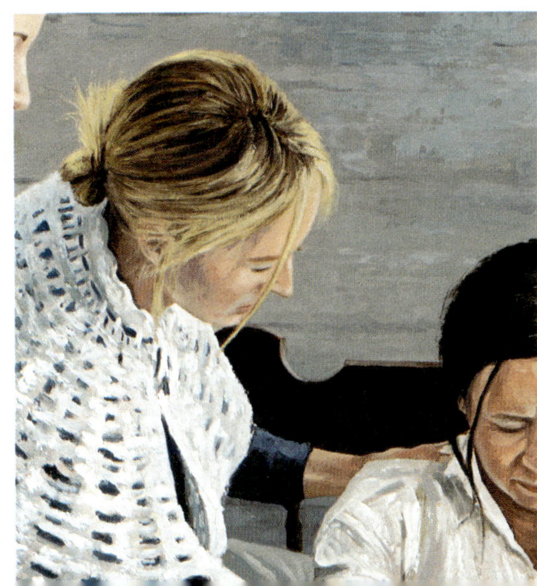

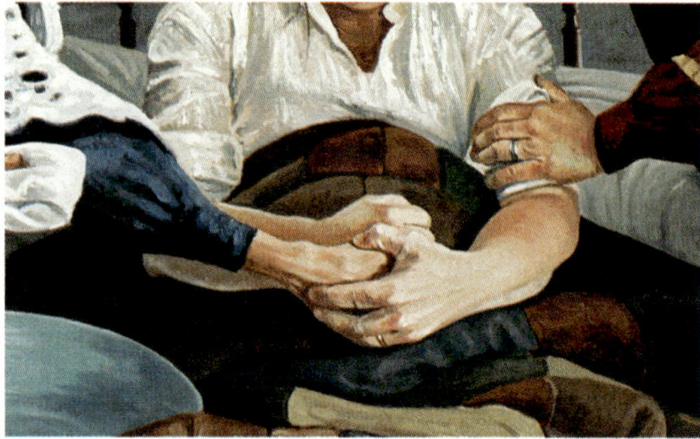

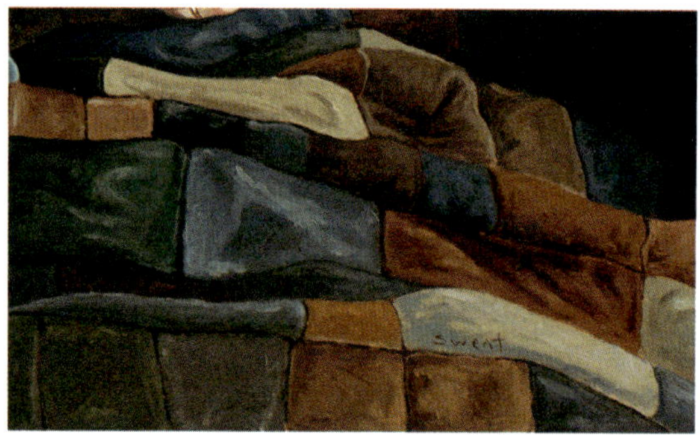

could represent faith, the woman anointing, hope, and the women comforting, charity.

Central to the painting are the intermixed hands in the middle. I love this—hands praying, hands supporting, hands strengthening—and how it symbolizes the unity and care that early Latter-day Saint women experienced in these rituals often associated with their Relief Society ministry.

Compositionally, the angles of the bed form an upward carat (^) toward the central figure, and the position of the heads and hand of the women form a downward angle (v) in the negative space above the central woman, directing the eyes of the viewer and dividing the space in an X shape.

Last, a major visual element of this painting is the quilt. In preparatory compositions, I considered having the blanket as a muted, solid color for ease of painting. However, as quilting is often a symbol of female work and unity, the idea of the quilt itself—different patches, shades, and shapes of fabric stitched together into a cohesive whole—seemed like an important symbol to typify the female body of Christ's restored Church coming together to do his holy work.

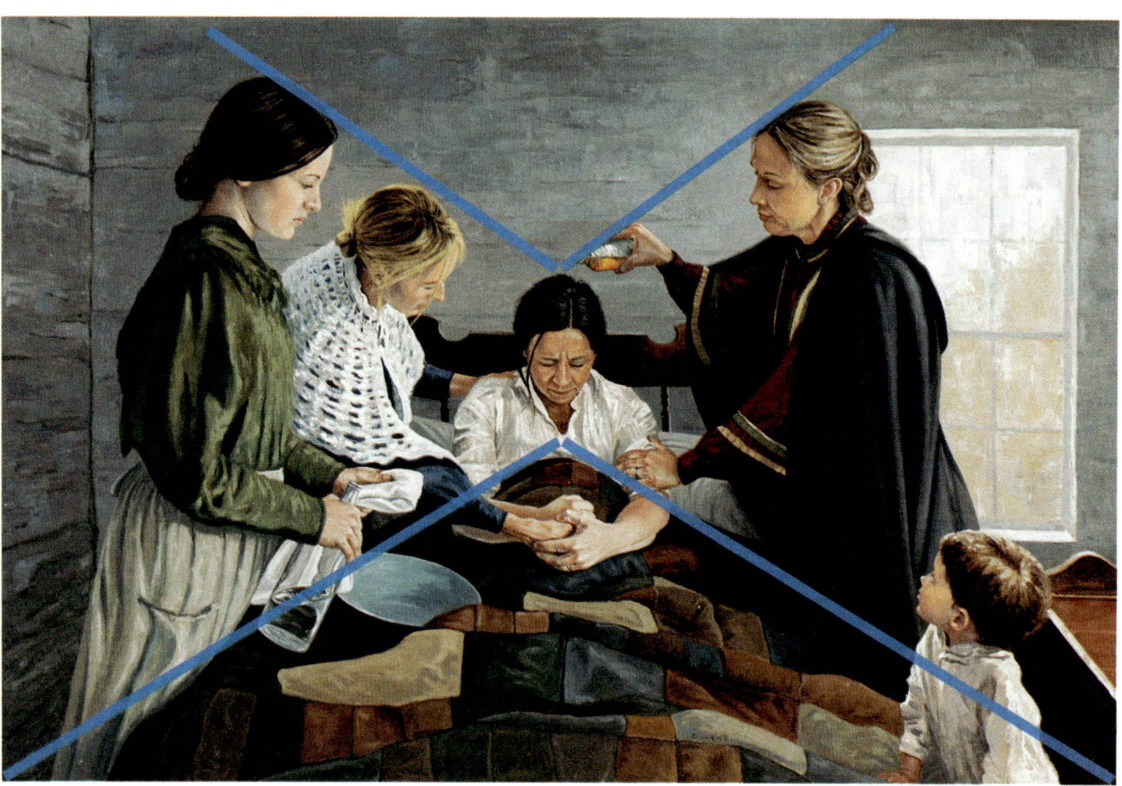

AN APPLICATION

By the later part of the twentieth century, women's participation in healing blessings had almost entirely faded from common Latter-day Saint knowledge and discourse. The cognizance of this lost practice, however, is important because modern Latter-day Saints ask fundamental questions about and emphasize women's connections and claims to priesthood power and authority. Excellent and comprehensive scholarly articles such as Jonathan Stapley and Kristine Wright's "Female Ritual Healing in Mormonism" have had broad scholarly circulation and impact.[25] Popular book publications such as Sheri Dew's *Women and the Priesthood* (2013), Neylan McBaine's *Women at Church* (2014), and more recently Wendy Ulrich's *Live Up to Our Privileges: Women, Power, and Priesthood* (2019) and Barbara Morgan Gardner's *The Priesthood Power of Women: In the Temple, Church, and Family* (2019) have added significantly to the discussion and understanding. In 2014, Elder Dallin H. Oaks gave a landmark general conference talk specifying that women have priesthood power and authority (although not keys and offices), saying poignantly, "We are not accustomed to speaking of women having the authority of the priesthood in their Church callings, but what other authority can it be?"[26] In 2015 the Church published a Gospel Topics Essay on "Joseph Smith's Teachings about Priesthood, Temple, and Women" that addressed many similar female themes, including women and healing blessings. And in the October 2019 general conference, President Russell M. Nelson pleaded with the sisters of the Church: "How I yearn for you to understand that the restoration of the priesthood is just as relevant to you as a woman as it is to any man. . . . Those who are endowed in the house of the Lord receive a gift of God's priesthood power by virtue of their covenant, along with a gift of knowledge to know how to draw upon that power. The heavens are just as open to *women* who are endowed with God's power flowing from their priesthood covenants as they are to men who bear the priesthood."[27]

Something is stirring in the collective consciousness of the Church about women's divine role and influence. To be clear, I am not advocating any particular position regarding women and ordination to priesthood offices with this painting, nor a return to women performing healing blessings. If I am emphasizing anything with this painting, it is to follow current prophetic directives, particularly directives for women to understand how their covenants and the temple endow them with power and authority. This painting celebrates women who know their divine potential and how to call upon the powers of heaven to help accomplish the work of salvation. This is what Relief Society is all about, then and now. I hope you see this and more in this painting.

What I am also advocating with this painting is knowledge, as knowledge brings understanding and power. I believe knowing our past helps us more clearly understand our present and informs our future. As Church leaders continue to guide, teach, and reveal on subjects pertaining to women, spiritual power, covenants, authority, the Relief Society, and the temple, there may be aspects of womanhood and priesthood that will be more fully explored, understood, or resolved. That is what prophets do. As an example, Joseph Smith told his wife Emma that as its president, she could instruct members of the Relief Society to set apart female teachers and deacons as they needed,[28] which the Relief Society instituted in 1868 as officers called "deaconesses."[29] Elder Dallin H. Oaks taught in 2014, "The Lord has directed that only men will be ordained to offices in the priesthood."[30] Are there untapped and uniquely female "appendages" (Doctrine and Covenants 107:5) related to the priesthood (different than male offices such as priest or elder) that have yet to be implemented or revealed in the Church? I don't know. Only time and revelation will tell.

What I do know is that half this Church is female. Personally, I have a wife and four daughters, along with many other female family members and friends who are or will be part of this magnificent Church. I want females to know that they have equal claims to call upon and access God just as any male does. I want the women in my life, in my congregation, in my community, and in this Church to know that they can be endowed with divine power through the holy temple; that the Spirit will be manifest in the lives of and operate with anyone—regardless of gender—who receives it, and that those who receive it will also receive his spiritual gifts as they are called for and expediently granted, such as revelation, prophesy, healing, tongues, faith, working of miracles, and many more (see 1 Corinthians 12; Moroni 10; Doctrine and Covenants 46). I want the women in my life to know that the oath and covenant of the Father pertaining to priesthood ordinances applies equally to women as well as men, and that through those faithful covenants we receive the powers of godliness, even all that God has (see Doctrine and Covenants 84:20–22, 33–40). I want them to know that God loves all his children, regardless of gender or any other category (see 2 Nephi 26:33). I want this image to help promote that knowledge and understanding, no matter where Church teachings pertaining to women and authority may have been in the past, or may go in the future.

Knowing our past helps us more clearly understand our present and informs our future.

AN ANALYSIS

1 It was common knowledge in the early Church that "every person who has faith in Jesus Christ may lay hands on the sick and pray for their recovery."[31] What the Church began to differentiate at the turn of the twentieth century was an elder's office to speak in God's name, and to seal an anointed blessing.[32] What do you think that means? What difference does it make for a priesthood office holder to bless a sick person by virtue of the Melchizedek Priesthood as opposed to a person praying for healing through faith?

2 How can we better teach Church members, both male and female, that women not only have equal access to God's power as men do, but how to draw and call upon that power in their everyday lives, for their families, and for their congregations? How can we better help women to have the mindset of being part of a modern school of the prophetesses[33] through the Relief Society, with the vision that through the temple they are to become future priestesses, and to have the confidence to receive the gifts of the Spirit such as prophecy, healing, visions, minis-

tering of angels, tongues, and faith to perform mighty miracles?

3 As referenced, early Latter-day Saint women viewed themselves with a priestly conferral through their temple endowment. Joseph Smith taught the Relief Society that "he was going to make of this Society a kingdom of priests"[34] and that "the Sisters would come in possession of the priviliges & blesings & gifts of the priesthood,"[35] likely referencing their participation in temple ordinances. In the Old Testament, the only people who were washed, anointed, clothed in ceremonial robes, and allowed to enter the holiest room in the temple that represented the presence of God were kings and priests. Today, all worthy Latter-day Saint adults, men and women, can have that privilege and blessing. How might better understanding the temple endowment inform present discussions related to women and priesthood in the Church?

NOTES

1. Juanita L. Pulsipher, ed., "History of Sarah Studevant Leavitt" (n.p., 1919), Book of Abraham Project (website); see also MS 62, Special Collections, J. Willard Marriott Library, University of Utah, Salt Lake City.
2. For the most comprehensive treatment of this subject, see Jonathan A. Stapley and Kristine Wright, "Female Ritual Healing in Mormonism," *Journal of Mormon History* 37, no. 1 (Winter 2011): 1–85.
3. "A Representative Woman: Mary Isabella Horne," *Woman's Exponent* 11, no. 4 (15 July 1882): 9.
4. See Stapley and Wright, "Female Ritual Healing," 42.
5. "Nauvoo Relief Society Minute Book," 36, 41, The Joseph Smith Papers.
6. "Nauvoo Relief Society Minute Book," 31.
7. "Nauvoo Relief Society Minute Book," 69.
8. "Joseph Smith's Teachings about Priesthood, Temple, and Women," Gospel Topics Essay, churchofjesuschrist.org.
9. Jill Mulvay Derr, Carol Cornwall Madsen, Kate Holbrook, and Matthew J. Grow, eds., *The First Fifty Years of Relief Society: Key Documents in Latter-day Saint Women's History* (Salt Lake City: Church Historian's Press), 552.
10. Derr et al., "Introduction," in *The First Fifty Years of Relief Society*, xxiv.
11. Many early Latter-day Saint women and men saw a connection between women performing healing and washing and anointing blessings for childbirth with their role as priestesses in relation to the temple endowment. For a good summary on this point, see Stapley and Wright, "Female Ritual Healing," 54–58.
12. Stapley and Wright, "Female Ritual Healing," 17.
13. See Carrie Ann King Johnson, "Rhetoric in Mormon Female Healing Rituals during the Nineteenth Century" (master's thesis, Utah State University, 2016), 28–29.
14. Logan Utah Cache Stake, Logan Utah Cache Stake Relief Society Minutes and Records, 1868–1973, Church History Library, vol. 2, 11 September 1886.
15. For a good treatment on the struggle against and eventual acceptance by many Latter-day Saints in Utah of improved medical care in the progressive era, see Benjamin Carter, "Health, Medicine, and Power in the Salt Lake Valley, Utah, 1869–1945" (PhD diss., University of Utah Department of History, December 2012), particularly chapters 2 and 3.
16. According to BYU history professor emeritus Thomas G. Alexander, "Such [charismatic spiritual] experiences were incompatible with the type of scientific rationalism increasingly popular in church circles" at the time. Thomas G. Alexander, *Mormonism in Transition: A History of the Latter-day Saints, 1890–1930* (Urbana: University of Illinois Press, 1986), 305.
17. For a case study of this phenomenon regarding the gift of tongues, see Alan J. Clark, "'We Believe in the Gift of Tongues': The 1906 Pentecostal Revo-

lution and Its Effect on the LDS Use of the Gift of Tongues in the Twentieth Century," *Mormon Historical Studies* 14, no. 1 (2013): 67–80.

18. President Joseph F. Smith taught that a woman could "pray for their sick and to rebuke diseases" as much as a man could, but a man "holding the priesthood, can do it by virtue of this, as well as in the name of the Lord." Derr et al., *The First Fifty Years of Relief Society*, 606. Eliza R. Snow explained in 1883, "Women can administer in the name of JESUS, but not by virtue of the Priesthood." Morgan Utah Stake Relief Society Minutes and Records, 1878–1973, Church History Library, Salt Lake City, vol. 1, 28 April 1883, 88; emphasis in original, as cited in "Joseph Smith's Teachings about Priesthood, Temple, and Women."
19. In 1888 President Wilford Woodruff wrote to general Relief Society secretary Emmeline B. Wells that the "practice that has grown up among the sisters of washing and anointing sisters who are approaching their confinement [labor and delivery] . . . is not, strictly speaking, an ordinance, unless it be done under the direction of the priesthood." As cited in Derr et al., *The First Fifty Years of Relief Society*, 541–42.
20. See Stapley and Wright, "Female Ritual Healing," 45–50, where Joseph F. Smith encouraged women to no longer use the word "seal" when administering to other women but to use the word "confirm" for the blessing.
21. Derr, Madsen, Holbrook, and Grow, "Introduction," in *The First Fifty Years of Relief Society*, xxv.
22. *General Handbook: Serving in The Church of Jesus Christ of Latter-day Saints* (Salt Lake City: The Church of Jesus Christ of Latter-day Saints, 2020), 18.13.1.
23. See Jennifer Champoux, "Wise or Foolish: Women in Mormon Biblical Narrative Art," *BYU Studies Quarterly* 57, no. 2 (2018): 71–93.
24. "Rhetoric in Mormon Female Healing Rituals," 31.
25. Stapley and Wright, "Female Ritual Healing," 1–85.
26. Dallin H. Oaks, "The Keys and Authority of the Priesthood," *Ensign*, May 2014, 50.
27. Russell M. Nelson, "Spiritual Treasures," *Ensign*, November 2019, 77, emphasis in original.
28. "Minutes and Discourses, 17 March 1842," 8, The Joseph Smith Papers.
29. Sarah M. Kimball and Eliza R. Snow, "Duty of Officers of F R Society" [ca. May 1868]; Fifteenth Ward, Salt Lake Stake, Relief Society Minutes, March 1868–May 1869, undated entry, 36–39, LR 2848 32, Church History Library.
30. Oaks, "Keys and Authority of the Priesthood," 50.
31. "Who May Rebuke Disease?" (editorial), *Deseret News*, 8 April 1901, as cited in Stapley and Wright, "Female Ritual Healing," 45.
32. See Stapley and Wright, "Female Ritual Healing," 45–50.
33. Phebe Woodruff, as cited in Derr et al., *The First Fifty Years of Relief Society*, 5.
34. "Nauvoo Relief Society Minute Book," 22.
35. "Journal, December 1841–December 1842," 94, The Joseph Smith Papers.

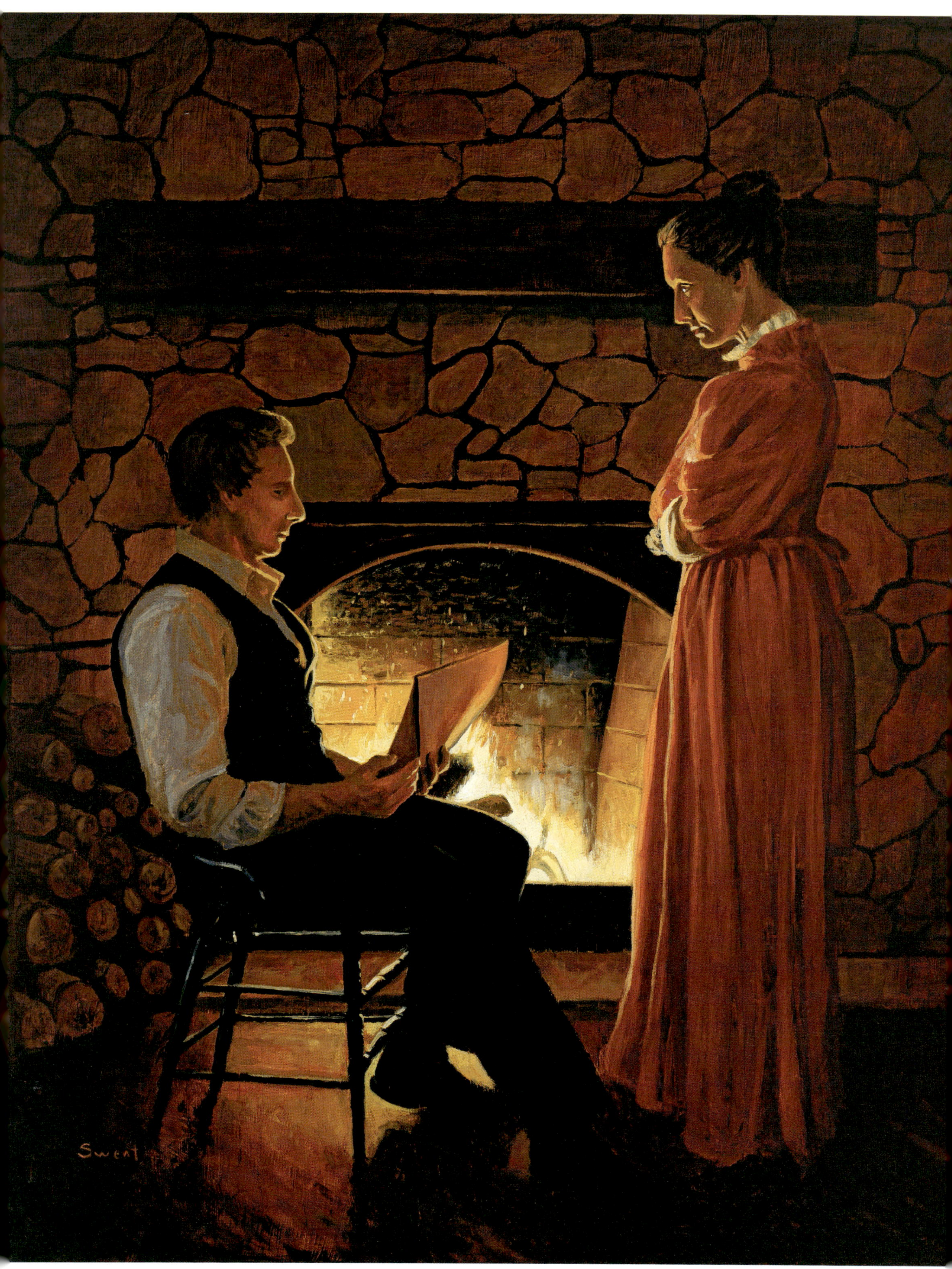

Purgatory (24" x 20", oil on board, 2017)

PURGATORY

Timeline: 12–17 July 1843

Related Doctrine and Covenants Section: 132

A BACKGROUND

In the summer of 1843, tensions ran high between Joseph and Emma Smith over the practice of plural marriage. Editors of *The Joseph Smith Papers* write, "At first aghast at what her husband was doing, Emma eventually agreed to a few of the plural marriages but then pulled back. She oscillated between hesitant submission and outright opposition to the practice."[1]

To help persuade Emma that the revelation on plural marriage was from God, on 12 July 1843 Joseph Smith wrote down the Lord's teachings on eternal and plural marriage. Hyrum Smith took the revelation to Emma to read it to her, hoping it would have a positive effect. When Hyrum returned to Joseph Smith's office, according to William Clayton, "Hyrum replied that he had never received a more severe talking to in his life, that Emma was very bitter and full of resentment and anger."[2] Clayton added in his journal that day that Emma "said she did not believe a word of it and appeared very rebellious."[3]

The next day, Joseph Kingsbury made a copy of the revelation.[4] After noting some business details, Joseph's short journal entry for 13 July simply reads, "I in conversation with Emma most of the day."[5] The difficult nature of that "conversation" needs little interpretation. The writing of the revelation on eternal and plural marriage created a nearly irreconcilable marital struggle. Although Joseph and Emma deeply loved each other, plural marriage had created a wedge between them that they couldn't resolve. Clayton wrote that on 13 July he was called to come into a private room with Joseph and Emma where "they stated an agreement they had mutually entered into they both stated their feelings on many subjects & wept considerable."[6]

Over the next few days, Joseph and Emma made financial agreements, such as deeding Emma sixty city lots and part ownership of the steamboat *Maid of Iowa*,[7] perhaps as a way to ensure a financial stability for Emma if their marriage moved toward separation or divorce, something Joseph may have feared.[8] Four days after writing the revelation on plural marriage, a cryptic entry is found in Joseph's journal for 17 July 1843. It begins with "Mostly at home" and then ends with "4 days last past in [purgatory]."[9] This journal entry is recorded by Willard Richards, and the word for "purgatory" is recorded in shorthand.

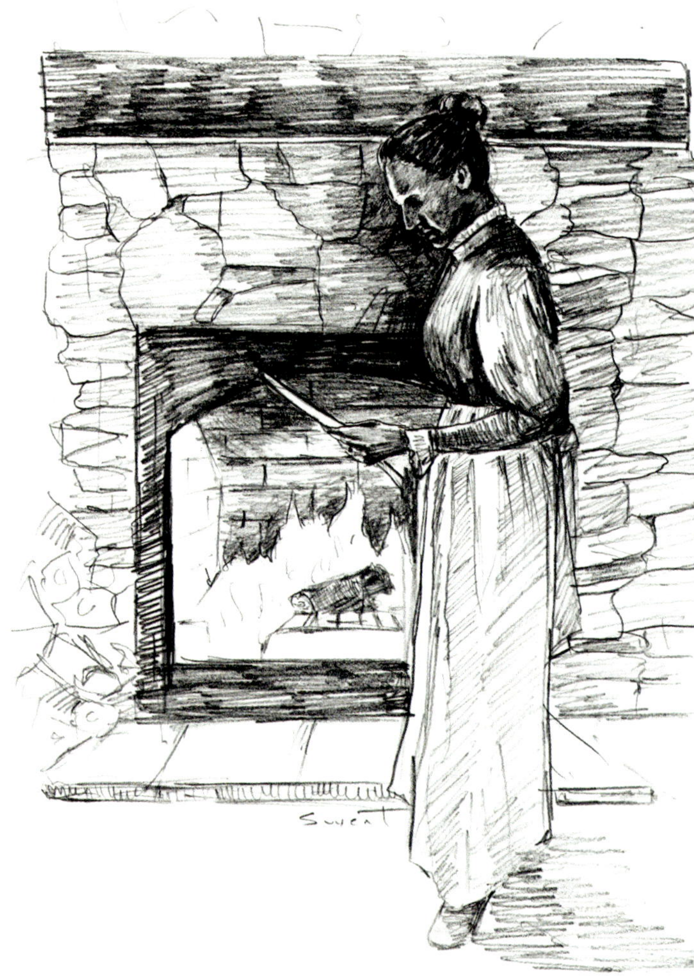

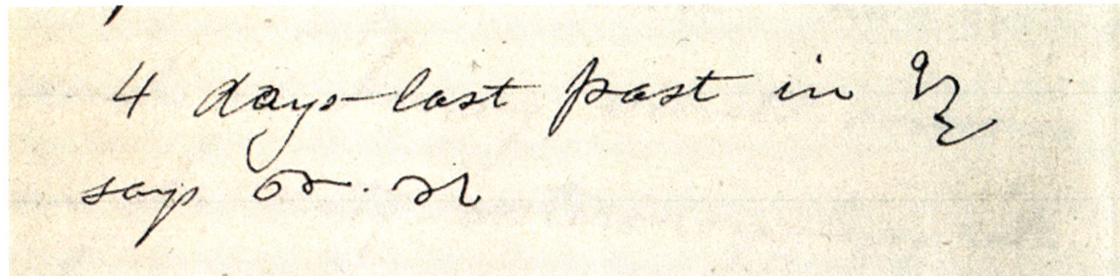
4 days last past in
says

During these four tumultuous days, according to William Clayton, Emma Smith destroyed the original written revelation on plural marriage: "Two or three days after the revelation was written Joseph related to me and several others that Emma had so teased, and urgently entreated him for the privilege of destroying it, that he became so weary of her teasing, and to get rid of her annoyance, he told her she might destroy it, and she had done so."[10]

There are very few artistic images portraying anything to do with Joseph Smith's practice of plural marriage. The few that exist are largely pejorative satire. I felt an image striving to express the difficult struggle caused by the revelation and practice of plural marriage was important, both to further historical understanding and to represent continued difficulty regarding this revelation. Hearkening to the opening essay of this book, I didn't want to paint a John Trumbull. I titled this painting *Purgatory* for a reason.

AN IMAGE

I decided to create this image in low firelight. The high contrast creates drama, and the symbol of a fire communicates understandable tension. The undertones of the painting are a brownish-red, burnt sienna. Typically, a canvas or board is primed and then stained with an under color to give a foundation to work against. That primed color is important as it often bleeds or peeks through various parts of the painting, providing a cohesive tint, in this case a dark brown or red.

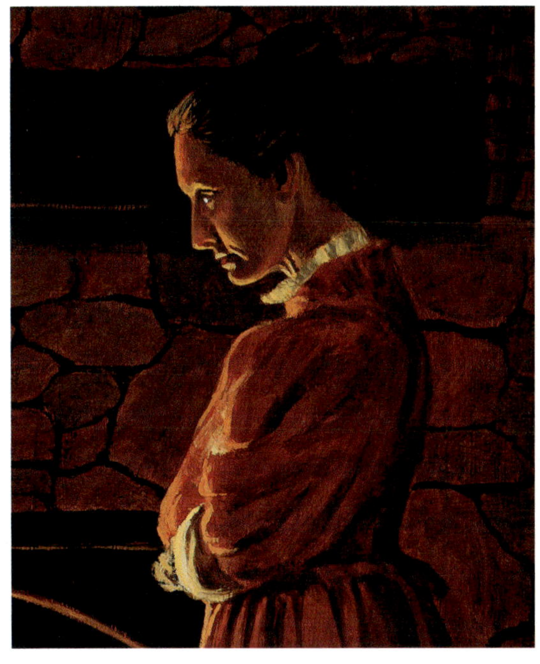

In the image, Emma stands, arms crossed in a defiant yet self-protective posture, her eyes glaring at her husband in both anger and pain.

Joseph sits in a position of submissive resignation, his face pained at the turmoil of following the God he knows and loves while simultaneously wounding his beloved wife because of it.

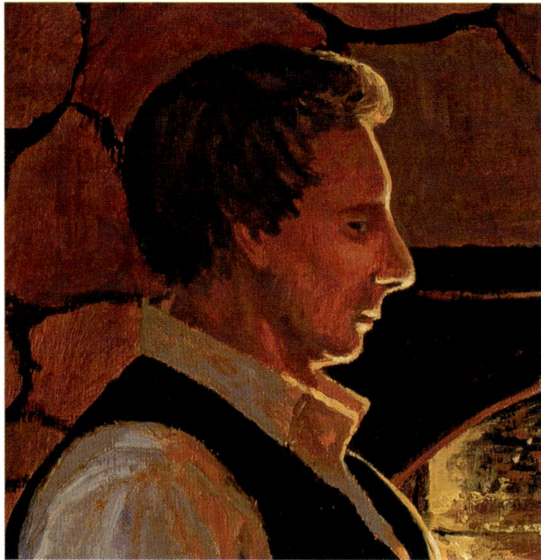

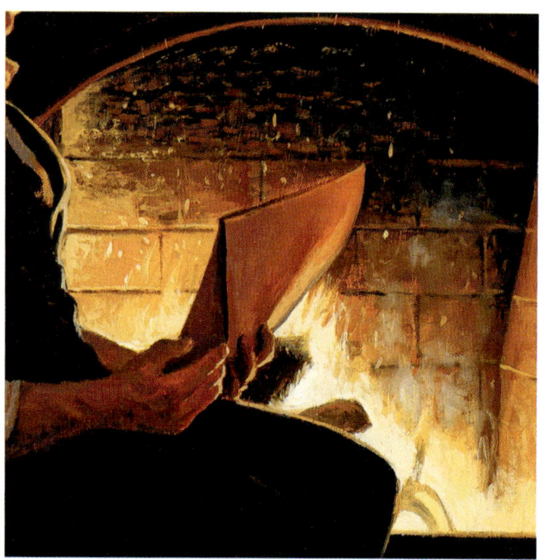

His eves are averted away from Emma, as though he can't look at her directly to face the reality of the revelatory conflict.

One of Joseph's hands holds the revelation. His other hand is slightly upturned as though he is trying to explain the document's content, but to no avail. Behind him, the sparks and embers fly, mimicking Joseph's and Emma's emotions. There are a handful of secondhand sources that claim that the way Emma destroyed the original revelation was by burning it in the fire, although Emma herself later claimed she did no such thing.[11]

Above the fireplace is a large wooden mantle. I included this to symbolize the idea of taking up your cross (see Mark 8:34–35) to sacrifice and follow God. On the left-hand corner, a small cross is etched into the wood to suggest this sacrificial concept, to which Doctrine and Covenants 132 refers (see 132:50, 51, 60).

I painted Joseph and Emma having this tense discussion in front of a large stone fireplace. This would be larger than the fireplace at their Nauvoo homestead where they lived at the time, but I enlarged it purposefully because the stones symbolize the rocky nature of their relationship during these months. I also used the outline of the stones to paint the hidden "purgatory" shorthand between Joseph and Emma.

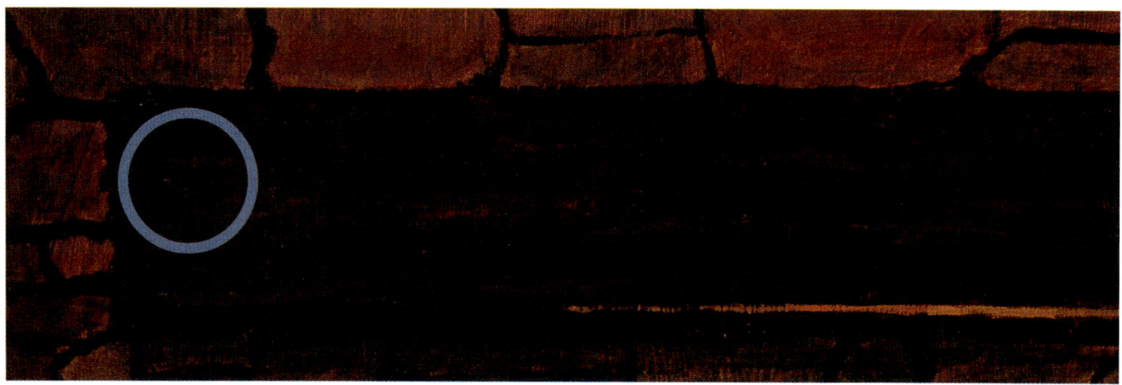

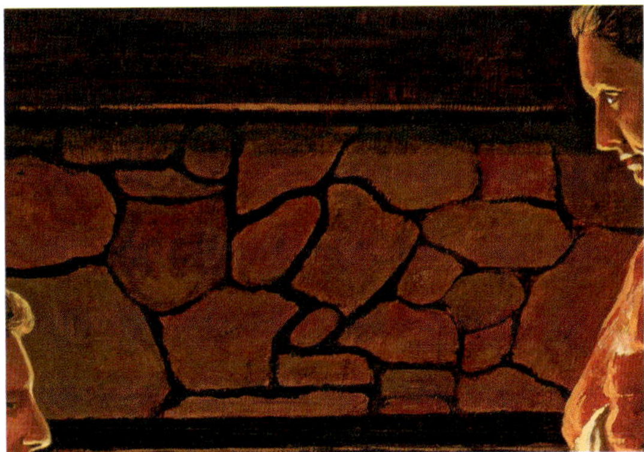

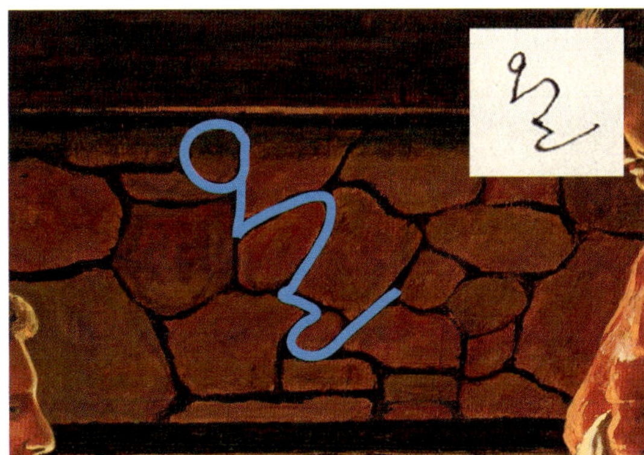

AN APPLICATION

While still providing divine comfort, God's revelations are not always comfortable. Sometimes, "Thy will be done" produces pain, difficulty, sorrow, and struggle. While all are free to come to their own conclusions about Joseph Smith and the early Church's practice of plural marriage, some who have chosen to reject the practice as nondivine do so because of its negative effects in the lives of some of those who lived it. If trouble, sorrow, and pain were the litmus test for the correctness of revelation, however, Jesus would have never atoned; the Apostle Paul would have never preached; the pioneers would have never trekked west; missionaries would not be called to serve; and mothers wouldn't bear or nurse children. Difficulty is not synonymous with nondivinity. Reservations don't negate revelations. While feeling like purgatory, the teaching can yet arise from divine authority.

For some, plural marriage was the worst thing that ever happened to them. For others, however, it was among the best. As Pulitzer prize–winning author Dr. Laurel Thatcher Ulrich explained in her book *A House Full of Females*: "Plural marriage . . . provoked wildly divergent emotions. Augusta Cobb rejoiced [calling plural marriage "glorious"]. Emma Smith raged. Vilate Kimball urged caution. Mother Moon collapsed in despair."[12] We cannot properly nor appropriately interpret through our personal lenses other people's past lived experience. We must allow them to speak for themselves instead of assuming to speak for them. As with monogamous marriage, some loved and were greatly blessed by plural marriage (women and men), others ignored it, while others were hurt by or hated it.

A Gospel Topics Essay on the subject says, "Plural marriage was among the most challenging aspects of the Restoration. For many who practiced it, plural marriage was a trial of faith."[13] That trial continues today, not in practice (because it ceased at the turn of the twentieth century)[14] but in understanding the revelation. As C. S. Lewis once taught, however, about facing difficult subjects:

> If our religion is something objective, then we must never avert our eyes from those elements in it which seem puzzling or repellent; for it will be precisely the puzzling or the repellent which conceals what we do not yet know and need to know. . . . The . . . truth which you do not know and which you need must, in the very nature of things, be hidden precisely in the doctrines you least like and least understand. It is just the same here as in science. The phenomenon which is troublesome, which doesn't fit in with the current scientific theories, is the phenomenon which compels reconsideration and thus leads to

> new knowledge. Science progresses because scientists, instead of running away from such troublesome phenomena or hushing them up, are constantly seeking them out. In the same way, there will be progress in Christian knowledge only as long as we accept the challenge of the difficult or repellent doctrines.[15]

In our lives, there may (or yet will) be "repellent doctrines" that God asks us to reconsider, to accept, to follow, to let go of in faith, even if it produces probationary pain. It is my belief that—while uncomfortable—if we embrace the difficult things that God lays at our feet, we will come to better know, trust, love, and become like him as we humbly become more like little children (see Mosiah 3:19), trusting in the Lord with all our heart and not leaning on our own understanding (see Proverbs 3:5–6). Jesus didn't repel his difficult divine directives. Instead, he consistently said, "Thy will be done" (Matthew 26:42). Joseph Smith and many early Saints who bucked cultural norms and faced the public and private firestorms that resulted from implementing plural marriage didn't repel their difficult divine directives either. The question that remains is, will we?

God's revelations are not always comfortable. Sometimes, "Thy will be done" produces pain, difficulty, sorrow, and struggle.

AN ANALYSIS

1 There are some who claim that plural marriage was altogether a mistake, or perhaps a divinely permissible experiment on Joseph Smith's part, but not God's will. What do you make of that? Could God allow such latitude by his prophets? What historical or scriptural evidence supports this line of thinking, or is contrary to and undermines it? If the revelation was from God and not a mistake, could aspects of its implementation have been erroneous? If so, which? If not, why?

2 How can we better discuss Latter-day Saint plural marriage openly and faithfully? When we skirt around it or defame it to be more socially acceptable, do we do a disservice to Nauvoo and the early Church pioneers who greatly sacrificed to implement it? How do we discuss it if we disagree with it, without trampling on graves? And conversely, how do we discuss it if we agree with it, without sounding like we want its return? How do we honor and respect those who practiced it regardless of where we personally stand with it?

3 Emma Smith's reputation tends to take drastic pendulum swings in Latter-day Saint Church culture and discourse. During Joseph Smith's lifetime, she became almost like a queen in the Church, an "elect lady" (Doctrine and Covenants 25:3). After she refused to follow President Brigham Young and the main body of the Church west to Utah—and eventually affiliated with the reorganized Church (now the Community of Christ)—she was vilified by many Latter-day Saints. So much so that by the early to mid-1900s, we rarely, if ever, discussed Emma in official Church publications.[16] Today,

her reputation in common Latter-day Saint spheres often swings again toward veneration. Why do we tend to either lionize or vilify influential people of the past? Why is it so difficult to see their obvious greatness but also acknowledge any apparent weakness?

NOTES

1. Dean C. Jessee, Mark Ashurst-McGee, and Richard L. Jensen, eds., *Journals, Volume 1: 1832–1839*, vol. 1 of the Journals series of *The Joseph Smith Papers*, ed. Dean C. Jessee, Ronald K. Esplin, and Richard Lyman Bushman (Salt Lake City: Church Historian's Press, 2008), xxx.
2. B. H. Roberts, *A Comprehensive History of The Church of Jesus Christ of Latter-day Saints*, 6 vols. (Salt Lake City: The Church of Jesus Christ of Latter-day Saints, 1930), 2:106–7.
3. William Clayton, Journal, 12 July 1843, Internet Archive.
4. Joseph C. Kingsbury, Affidavit, 22 May 1886, MS 3423, Church History Library.
5. "Journal, December 1842–June 1844; Book 2, 10 March 1843–14 July 1843," 308, The Joseph Smith Papers.
6. Clayton, Journal, 13 July 1843.
7. Clayton, Journal, 15 July 1843: "Made Deed for Vz S.B Maid of Iowa from J. to Emma. Also a Deed to E. for over 60 city lots."
8. Clayton, Journal, 16 August 1843. Discussing the difficulty over Joseph's plural marriages to Emily and Eliza Partridge, Joseph said Emma "would pitch on him & obtain a divorce & leave him."
9. Joseph Smith Papers editors interpret this symbol as Taylor shorthand "p-r-g/j-t-r-y." Note 7 on "Journal, December 1842–June 1844; Book 3, 15 July 1843–29 February 1844," 4, The Joseph Smith Papers.
10. Clayton, Journal, 12 July 1843.
11. See Linda King Newell, "The Emma Smith Lore Reconsidered," *Dialogue: A Journal of Mormon Thought* 17, no. 3 (1984): 89–91.
12. Laurel Thatcher Ulrich, *A House Full of Females: Plural Marriage and Women's Rights in Early Mormonism, 1835–1870* (New York City: Alfred A. Knopf, 2017), 106–7.
13. "Plural Marriage in The Church of Jesus Christ of Latter-day Saints," Gospel Topics Essay, churchofjesuschrist.org.
14. "Plural Marriage in The Church of Jesus Christ of Latter-day Saints" states, "Since President [Joseph F.] Smith's day, Church Presidents have repeatedly emphasized that the Church and its members are no longer authorized to enter into plural marriage and have underscored the sincerity of their words by urging local leaders to bring noncompliant members before Church disciplinary councils."
15. C. S. Lewis, *The Weight of Glory* (New York: Harper One, 2001), 34, and C.S. Lewis, *God in the Dock: Essays on Theology and Ethics.* Walter Hooper, ed. (Grand Rapids, MI: Wm. B. Eerdmans Publishing Co., 2014), 89.
16. Linda King Newell says that "excepting only a few paragraphs in a 1933 *Relief Society Magazine* [a 1978 *Church News* article] marked the first time in nearly a century since Emma's death that any article had appeared on her in an official Church periodical." Newell, "Emma Smith Lore Reconsidered," 89.

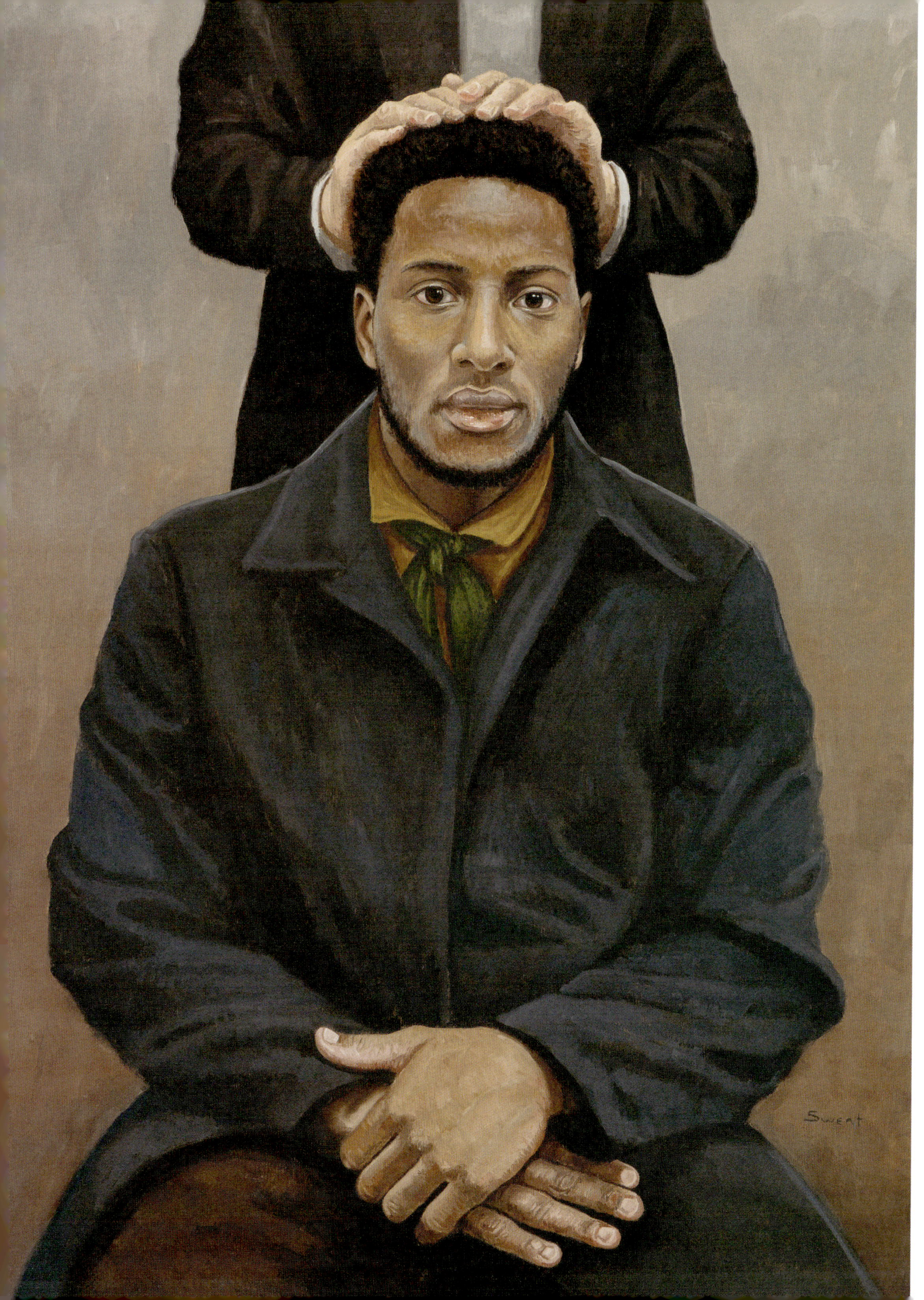
Sweat

THE ORDINATION OF Q. WALKER LEWIS

Timeline: circa 1843–52

Related Doctrine and Covenants Section: Official Declaration 2

A BACKGROUND

At Winter Quarters in the spring of 1847, an eccentric, mixed-race man named William McCary was upset. He was ostracized from the body of the camp and claimed that the reasons were racial. McCary couldn't see (or admit) that it wasn't his ethnicity but more his heresy that were causing the problems—he lead a private schismatic group with suspicions of sexual deviance and claimed he could transfigure into various prophets.[1] President Young clarified to McCary that the suspicion he was facing "has nothing to do with the blood for [from] one blood has God made all flesh, we have to repent [to] what we av lost." Then, as an example that race doesn't affect Church standing or priesthood status, Brigham referenced a luminous example, "We av one of the best Elders an African in Lowell [Massachusetts]."[2] That African American was an elder named Q. Walker Lewis.[3]

Walker Lewis was born in 1798 in Massachusetts. He was "literate, educated, upper-middle class, . . . well connected socially and politically. . . . A very successful barber, Lewis was a radical abolitionist, a prominent organizer of and participant in the Underground Railroad, a Most Worshipful Master of Freemasonry, one of two—possibly three—free black men known to hold the higher priesthood in the 1840's" who "was well known and well respected among [early] Mormon leaders."[4]

How and when Walker Lewis joined the Church is unknown.[5] He was likely ordained to the priesthood by Joseph Smith's brother, William Smith, in 1843–44 when William came through Lowell, Massachusetts, on an eastern states mission. An elder wrote to Brigham Young in 1847, saying that Walker Lewis had been "ordained some years ago by William Smith," although Jane Manning James would later claim Walker was ordained by Parley P. Pratt.[6]

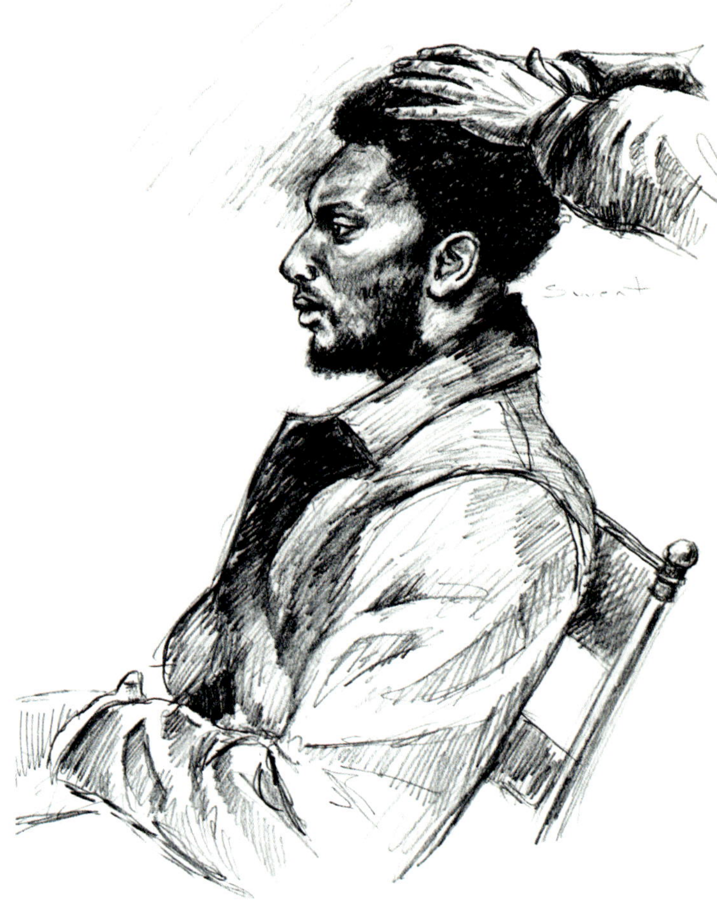

Some Latter-day Saints today are surprised to learn that black men such as Walker Lewis held the priesthood early in Church history, having been taught (or having assumed) that black Latter-day Saints were *always* banned from the priesthood until 1978. However, the Church—early on—was open racially both in terms of membership and priesthood ordination. As a Gospel Topics Essay says, "From the beginnings of the Church, people of every race and ethnicity could be baptized and received as members.

. . . During the first two decades of the Church's existence, a few black men were ordained to the priesthood."[7] Some Church members know about 1841 black convert Jane Manning James, who was faithful for almost seven decades and died in Utah in 1908.[8] Perhaps the best-known black male in the early Church is Elijah Abel, who was ordained a Seventy and participated in some of the Kirtland Temple rituals.[9] Some of the Latter-day Saints' early troubles in Independence, Missouri, derived directly from the Church's proposition to allow free black Latter-day Saints to gather to Zion, contrary to Missouri law.[10]

Although Brigham Young had proclaimed to William McCary and others an open-racial priesthood position in 1847 and complimented black men such as Walker Lewis, his views would soon change. The reasons are muddy and conjectural, but the confluence of a few events appear to have contributed to President Young's altered position. At Winter Quarters, William McCary continued to stray from the Church and started preaching his own brand of doctrine, including secret "sealings" with women through sexual relations, fleeing in the summer of 1847 when he was exposed.[11] In 1846 an elder named William Appleby came through Massachusetts and met Walker Lewis. Appleby, however, wrote a letter complaining to Brigham Young that Walker Lewis's son, Enoch, had married a white Latter-day Saint woman. Young didn't learn about this interracial marriage in the Church until 1847, roughly the same time as McCary's apostasy. Brigham reacted extremely negatively to this news because he held to early American views that black and white races should not intermarry. Coinciding with these events, 1847 is when the first public statements of black men not being allowed to hold the priesthood begin to appear.[12]

Walker Lewis, however, seemed to be unaware of this shifting tide in the Church. He faithfully responded to the call to gather to the Salt Lake Valley and pioneered across the entire country, arriving in Utah by early October 1851.[13] Upon his arrival in Utah, Lewis received his patriarchal blessing from John Smith, the Church Patriarch and the Prophet's uncle.[14]

Lewis gathered to Utah amidst a debate on another major factor that may have also influenced the position on black African priesthood ordination: the hotly debated question of slavery. Although many Church members opposed slavery and Latter-day revelation stated that it was "not right that any man should be in bondage one to another" (Doctrine and Covenants 101:79), there were some Saints who accepted it, bringing some black slaves into Utah Territory. In 1852 the Utah legislature legalized a regulated form of slavery in the territory, "allowing enslaved men and women to be brought to the territory but prohibiting the enslavement of their descendants," among other provisions such as requiring consent before any move and access to education.[15] Apostle Orson Pratt, who served in the territorial legislature, strongly opposed the law, saying the Saints were condemning black people "without receiving any authority from heaven to do so."[16] After the law passed, territorial governor Brigham Young "declared publicly for the first time that people of black African descent could no longer be ordained to the priesthood."[17] In his address, Governor Young said it is up to the Lord to remove this restriction, and that one day God "will have it taken away. That time will come when they [black Saints] will have the privilege of all we have the privelege of and more."[18] Although all of Brigham Young's reasons for implementing the priesthood restriction are not fully known and "Church records offer no clear insights into the origins of this practice" (Official Declaration 2 heading), he spoke of revelation one day ending the restriction.

After traveling across the country and spending less than one year in the valley, Walker Lewis abruptly left Utah in the spring of 1852. The most in-depth article on Walker Lewis theorizes that Utah's legalization of slavery—which law also forbade and punished black and white interracial marriage or sexual intercourse—along with the priesthood restriction on black Africans instigated Walker Lewis's quick exodus from Utah. Walker journeyed back to Massachusetts and reopened his barbershop, never again returning to the Church. He died just a few years later, in October 1856.

Connell O'Donovan, whose in-depth article on Walker Lewis I've referenced, writes: "I see how visionary [Walker Lewis] truly was in hoping and dreaming toward a future far beyond racism, beyond political inequities and ecclesiastical injustices. . . . Hopefully, he no longer remains a mere curiosity, a minor footnote in LDS history. . . . His life was not incidental but central to the solidification of Mormon priesthood denial."[19] "This is a man whose life deserves greater attention," Margaret Blair Young wrote of Walker Lewis, noting that despite his influence, "we have no pictures of him."[20]

I wanted to correct that.

AN IMAGE

Because there are no known photographs or paintings of Walker, I wanted to put an image to his name to honor his legacy and better emphasize this generally lesser-known, but important, aspect of ordaining black men to priesthood offices in early Latter-day Saint history. I painted him, eyes open and gazing directly at the viewer, to also cause us to acknowledge him and to help the viewer reflect on racial issues that likely drove him from the Church.

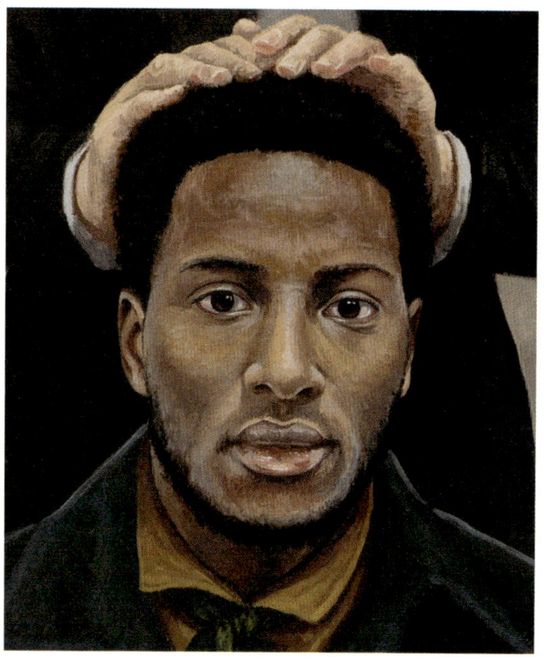

I also purposely cut off the composition to *not* show who ordained him. This is for two reasons: (1) As mentioned, it may have been the Prophet's brother William Smith, or it may have been Parley P. Pratt. Not showing the face of the ordainer acknowledges this historical ambiguity. And (2) more importantly I didn't want the painting to distract from Walker Lewis. Having

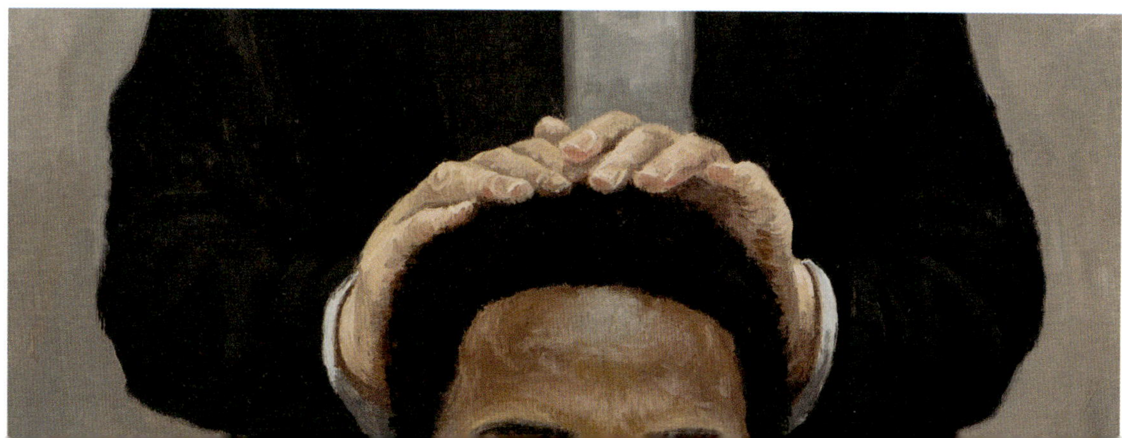

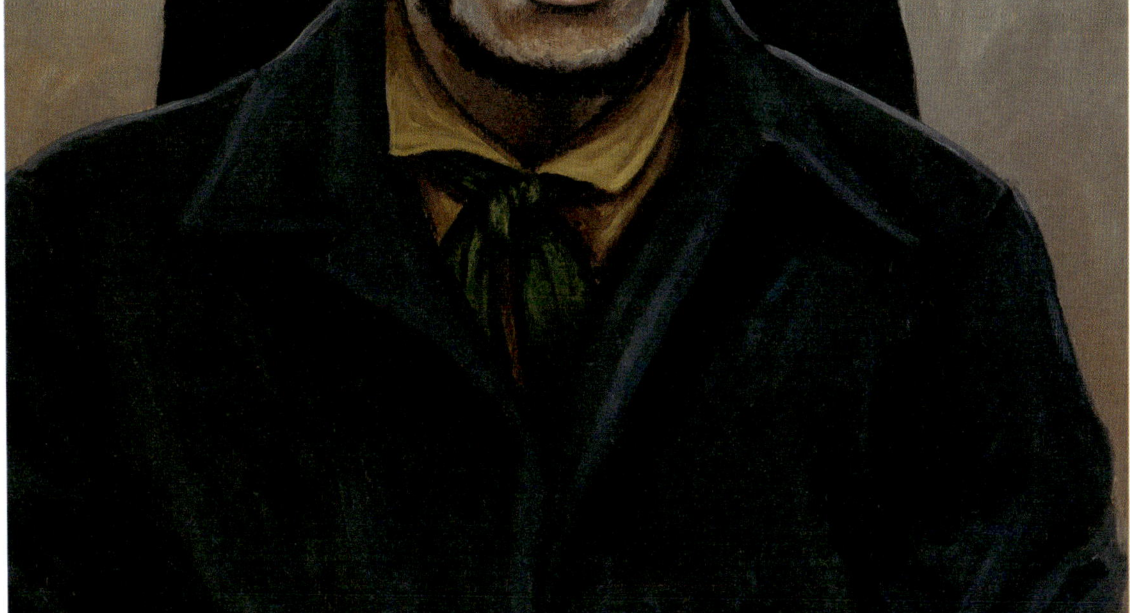

one face, one set of eyes, helps direct the viewer and the image to stay on its central focus. I kept the background devoid of detail to not distract.

I purposely painted the shirt an orange color. I have no idea whether he would or would not have worn such a color, but the yellowish-orange I chose is the complement of blue, the color of his coat, and is visually pleasing. The green of his tie is mixing the yellow-orange of his shirt and the blue of his coat. Hence, another set of artistic decisions that have no historical validation but merely artistic ones.

The last part of the painting I mention are Walker Lewis's hands. I love them, not just because of how they are painted, but more because

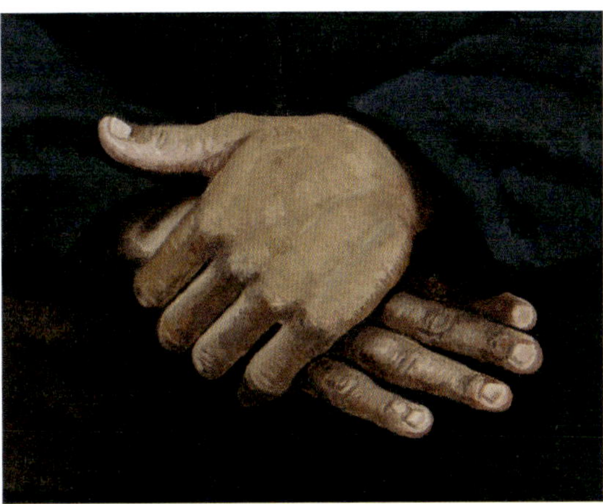

they symbolize a ready willingness to serve the kingdom of God, which he and so many other Saints of color then and now have done.

AN APPLICATION

So what do you do if you are Q. Walker Lewis, or any other man or woman—past, present, or future—who experiences injustice, unfairness, or oppression? How do we have faith in a God that is fair in a world that clearly isn't? Ever since the Fall of Adam and Eve, the world's equity meter has been thrown off-kilter—and is completely broken for some. In his goodness, however, God sent his Son, Jesus Christ, to make at-one-ment for his children to bring things into harmony—an offering of rebalancing, restitution, recompense, and restoration. The basic definition of the word *atonement* means to reconcile or to restore to harmony,[21] to bring things undone back to at-one, to put things in their rightful state, to return things to an unimpaired condition. As our Savior, Jesus takes things in their fallen condition and perfectly repays, reinstates, refreshes, returns, rectifies, redeems, recompenses, and renews. The central premise of Jesus's Atonement is to perfectly right all mortal wrongs. Whether in this life or the next, Jesus will fully restore all things and then some. This restoration of all things (see Acts 2:21) will culminate with the millennial reign of the Savior when this earth will be renewed, when the knowledge of the Lord will cover the earth, when sin and death will be conquered, when God will wipe away all tears (see Revelation 21:4), and when God's will is "done in earth, as it is in heaven" (Matthew 6:10). In other words, *the* Restoration of all things hasn't happened yet. It is a future event.

Until then, as President Russell M. Nelson taught, "we are witnesses to a process of restoration. If you think the Church has been fully restored, you are just seeing the beginning. There's much more to come."[22] Or, as President Dieter F. Uchtdorf asked: "Are you sleeping through the Restoration? . . . In reality, the Restoration is an ongoing process; we are living in it right now."[23] Every action that helps overcome the telestial effects of the Fall contributes to the continued Restoration. The removal of the policy restricting black Africans and priesthood is part of this process. In the 1940s and 1950s, Church leaders began having increased discussions about the Church's policy, seeking for God's inspiration on how to proceed. From Brigham Young onward, Church prophets foretold that the day would come when the policy would be changed, but reportedly felt it was not yet the right time to do so.[24] Then in June of 1978, Church President Spencer W. Kimball received a revelation lifting the priesthood restriction from those of black African ancestry, confirmed by revelation to the First Presidency and Quorum of the Twelve Apostles. In President Kimball's words, "We have pleaded long and earnestly in behalf of these, our faithful brethren. . . . [The Lord] has heard our prayers, and by revelation has confirmed that the long-promised day has come when every faithful, worthy man in the Church may receive the holy priesthood."[25] Since that time forward, worthy members of black African ancestry have received the blessings of the temple and black African men have been ordained to priesthood offices, serving in local and general priesthood leadership positions within the Church. Church leadership, its members, and the world have grown in knowledge and understanding, and thus in 1978 we received more knowledge and understanding, which we have happily received in the process of the ongoing Restoration.

Whether in this life or the next, Jesus will fully restore all things and then some.

AN ANALYSIS

1 How do you answer the question about the Church's restrictions on black Africans and the priesthood and temple? Was it racism, revelation, or a mixture of the two? One person once said to me, "We know why Brigham Young implemented the restriction. It was racism on the part of American society, Church members, and Church leadership." Another posed hypothetically, "If the Church had been restored in Canada, where slavery did not exist, this restriction would not have happened or been an issue. We simply need to acknowledge that racism was the

reason." What is your reaction to those claims? What do factors such as God's will, agency, culture, and knowledge play as they contribute to the process of revelation?

2 One difficult aspect of the restriction of black Africans and priesthood was the explanations put forward to justify the policy—that blacks were not valiant in the premortal life, that they were descendants of Cain or Egyptus, and so forth. A Gospel Topics Essay from the Church says, "Over time, Church leaders and members advanced many theories to explain the priesthood and temple restrictions. None of these explanations is accepted today as the official doctrine of the Church."[26] Elder Jeffrey R. Holland said, speaking of the black priesthood restriction: "I have to concede to my earlier colleagues. . . . They, I'm sure, in their own way, were doing the best they knew to give shape to [the policy], to give context for it, to give even history to it. All I can say is however well intended the explanations were, I think almost all of them were inadequate and/or wrong."[27] Elder Bruce R. McConkie said his own and some other Church leaders' comments about blacks and priesthood were with given with "limited understanding."[28] What do we learn from this history? How do we ensure we don't repeat these mistakes—creating disavowable doctrinal explanations in future decades—for various Church policies and practices in our day? How do we continue to follow God's authorized servants in faith knowing that some explanations for current practices may change in the future, as well as the practices themselves, as the Restoration continues?

3 Although some actions by Church members or leaders in our history have fallen short of gospel teachings, the Church has repeatedly condemned racism.[29] President Russell M. Nelson said, "The Creator of us all calls on each of us to abandon attitudes of prejudice against any group of God's children. Any of us who has prejudice toward another race needs to repent!"[30] President Nelson discussed this topic in a joint statement with leaders of the NAACP. What can we do to build "bridges of cooperation rather than walls of segregation"? How can we "reach out and serve someone of a different background or race"? What "processes, laws, or organizational attitudes regarding racism" can we help to "root out"?[31]

NOTES

1. See Angela Hudson, "William McCary, Lucy Stanton, and the Performance of Race at Winter Quarters and Beyond," *Journal of Mormon History* 41, no. 3 (July 2015): 114–20. See also John Turner, *Brigham Young: Pioneer Prophet* (Cambridge, MA: Harvard University Press, 2012), 221; Connell O'Donovan, "The Mormon Priesthood Ban and Elder Q. Walker Lewis: 'An Example for His More Whiter Brethren to Follow,'" *John Whitmer Historical Association Journal* 26 (2006): 82–83.
2. General Church Minutes, CR 100 318, box 1, folder 52, 26 March 1847.
3. Quack Walker Lewis was named after his maternal uncle, Quacko (Kwaku) Walker. Kwaku means "boy born on Saturday." Blackpast.org.
4. O'Donovan, "Mormon Priesthood Ban," 48.
5. See O'Donovan, "Mormon Priesthood Ban," 64.
6. See O'Donovan, "Mormon Priesthood Ban," 64, 67.
7. "Race and the Priesthood," Gospel Topics Essay, churchofjesuschrist.org.
8. See James Goldberg, "The Autobiography of Jane Manning James: Seven Decades of Faith and Devotion," history.churchofjesuschrist.org.
9. Edward L. Kimball, "Spencer W. Kimball and the

Revelation on Priesthood," *BYU Studies* 47, no. 2 (2008): 9, 15. See also Newell G. Bringhurst, "Elijah Abel and the Changing Status of Blacks within Mormonism," in *Neither White nor Black: Mormon Scholars Confront the Race Issue in a Universal Church*, ed. Lester E. Bush Jr. and Armand L. Mauss (Midvale, UT: Signature Books, 1984), 131, 133.

10. See W. W. Phelps, "Free People of Color," *Evening and the Morning Star*, July 1833, 109.
11. Hudson, "William McCary, Lucy Stanton, and the Performance of Race at Winter Quarters and Beyond," 121–22.
12. O'Donovan, "Mormon Priesthood Ban," 84–85.
13. See O'Donovan, "Mormon Priesthood Ban," 90.
14. See O'Donovan, "Mormon Priesthood Ban," 91.
15. See "Slavery and Abolition," Church History Topics, www.churchofjesuschrist.org.
16. Orson Pratt, Discourse, 27 January 1852, George D. Watt Papers, Church History Library. Quotation edited for clarity; "so" added at end of quotation.
17. *Saints*, vol. 2: *No Unhallowed Hand, 1846–1893* (Salt Lake City: The Church of Jesus Christ of Latter-day Saints, 2020), 182.
18. Brigham Young Addresses, MSD 1234, box 48, folder 3, dated 5 February 1852, Church History Library, Salt Lake City; see also *Deseret News*, 3 April 1852, 2.
19. O'Donovan, "Mormon Priesthood Ban," 100.
20. Margaret Blair Young, "The One We Forgot: Quaku Walker Lewis," 30 September 2012, Patheos (website).
21. "Atonement," in *True to the Faith* (Salt Lake City: The Church of Jesus Christ of Latter-day Saints, 2004), 14.
22. Russell M. Nelson, in "Interview with President Nelson and Elder Stevenson in Chile," Church Newsroom, 30 October 2018, 5:09–6:28, YouTube.
23. Dieter F. Uchtdorf, "Are You Sleeping through the Restoration?," *Ensign*, May 2014, 58–59.
24. Edward L. Kimball, "Spencer W. Kimball and the Revelation on the Priesthood," *BYU Studies* 47, no. 2 (2008): 4–78. See also Armand L. Mauss, "The Fading of the Pharaoh's Curse: The Decline and Fall of the Priesthood Ban against Blacks in the Mormon Church," *Dialogue: A Journal of Mormon Thought* 14, no. 3 (Fall 1981): 10–45, summarized in Armond L. Mauss, *All Abraham's Children: Changing Mormon Conceptions of Race and Lineage* (Urbana, IL: University of Illinois Press, 2003), 231–41.
25. Official Declaration 2 in the Doctrine and Covenants.
26. "Race and the Priesthood."
27. Jeffrey R. Holland, interview, 4 March 2006, transcript from PBS broadcast *The Mormons*, pbs.org.
28. Bruce R. McConkie, "All Are Alike unto God" (Church Educational System Religious Educators Symposium, 18 August 1978), speeches.byu.edu.
29. See, for example, "Race and the Church: All Are Alike unto God," 29 February 2012, newsroom .churchofjesuschrist.org. See also Peggy Fletcher Stack, "Black Mormons Applaud as LDS Church Condemns White Supremacy as 'Morally Wrong and Sinful,'" *Salt Lake Tribune*, 15 August 2017.
30. "President Nelson Shares Social Post about Racism and Calls for Respect for Human Dignity," 1 June 2020, newsroom.churchofjesuschrist.org.
31. Russell M. Nelson, Derrick Johnson, Leon Russell, and Amos C. Brown, "Locking Arms for Racial Harmony in America: What the NAACP and The Church of Jesus Christ of Latter-day Saints Are Doing Together," *Medium* (Religion), 8 June 2020.

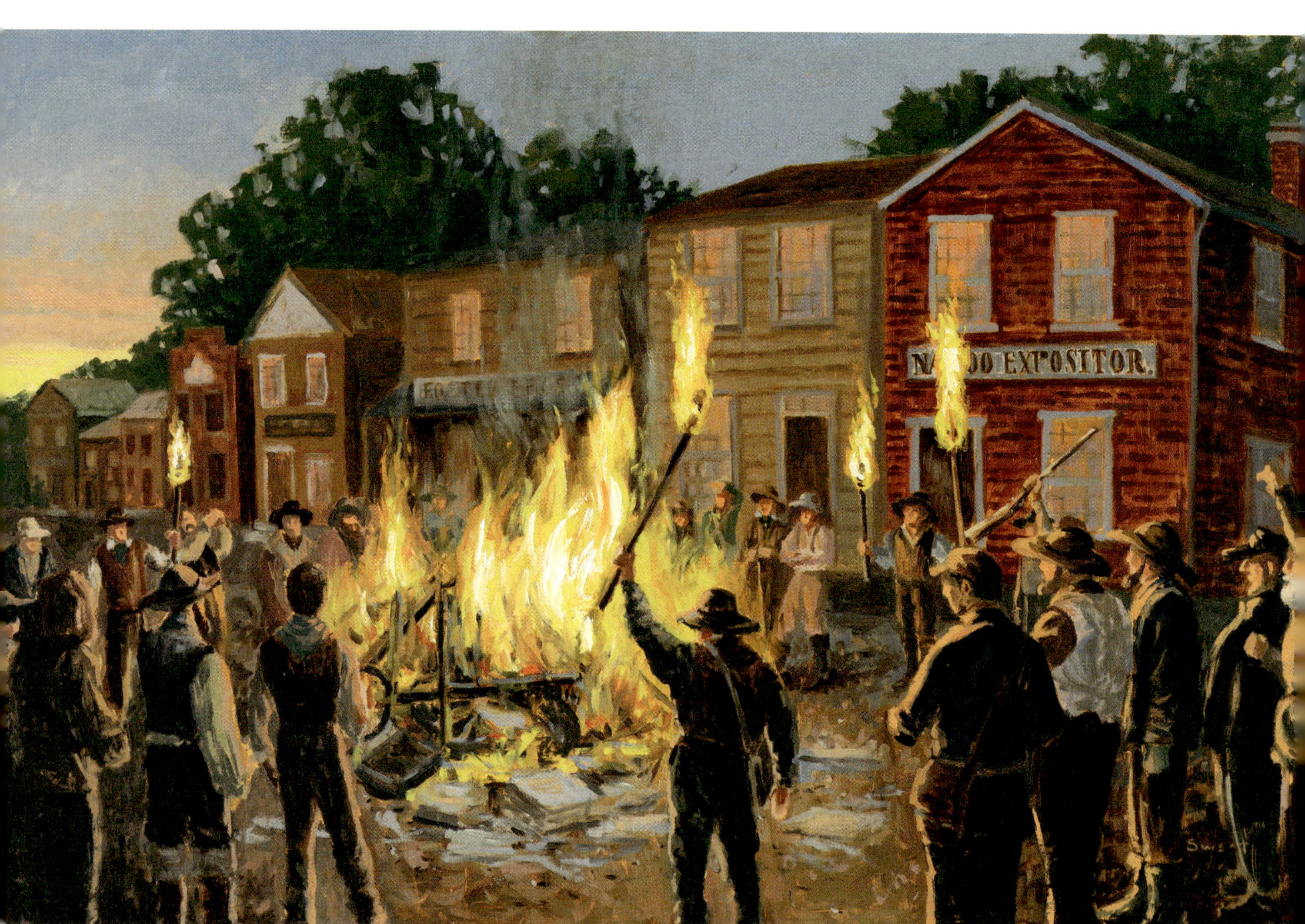

Destruction of the "Nauvoo Expositor" (15" x 24", oil on board, 2019)

DESTRUCTION OF THE "NAUVOO EXPOSITOR"

Timeline: June 1844

Related Doctrine and Covenants Section: 135

A BACKGROUND

On an unseasonably cold June evening in Nauvoo, a fire roared—not a fire to give warmth and light but a bonfire that would eventually lead to bullets and death. In the middle of Mulholland Street, stacks of papers and a printing press burned, and hundreds of tiny metallic pieces of printer's type scattered in the road flickered in the firelight. A hundred men who caused the flames cheered, believing they had just done right. The "riot" that burned this newspaper, however, was not caused by a lawless mob but instead was led by the city marshal and major general of the Nauvoo Legion, acting under the direction of the Nauvoo city council and its mayor, Joseph Smith. What led to this inflammatory event that would ultimately lead to the Prophet's arrest and death?

In the months prior, a faction of Latter-day Saints had grown disaffected with Joseph Smith's leadership of the Church. William Law, Joseph Smith's counselor in the First Presidency, had been removed from his office in January 1844 and was excommunicated in April.[1] His brother, Wilson, was excommunicated the same day. Another set of brothers, Chauncey and Francis Higbee, had also been excommunicated—Chauncey in the spring of 1842 for immoral conduct with multiple women[2] and Francis in May 1844 for apostasy.[3] Yet another set of brothers, Robert and Charles Foster, also had a falling-out with Joseph Smith between January and June of 1844, primarily over business dealings and unfounded claims of polygamous proposals to Robert's wife.[4] Robert Foster was excommunicated the same day as the Laws "for unchristianlike conduct."[5] These men felt that Joseph Smith had become corrupt and that their civil and religious liberties were being trampled on by Joseph's excesses of power.[6]

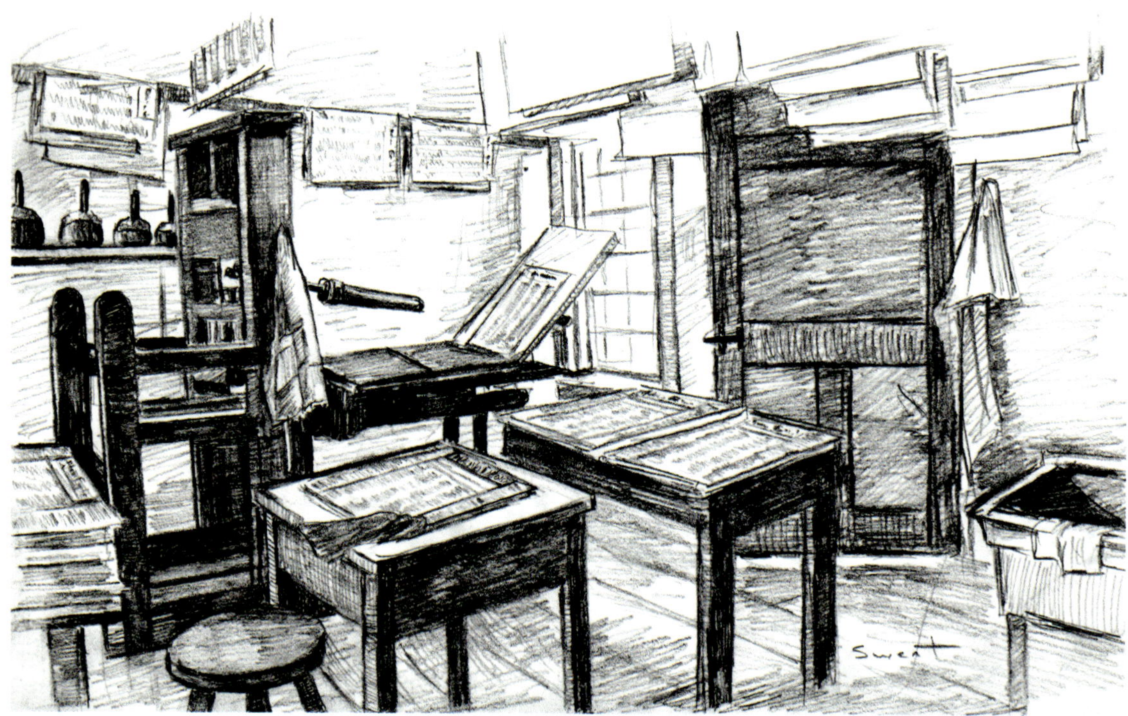

By March 1844, these men and others became principal leaders in a subversive, organized conspiracy against Joseph Smith.[7] On 24 March 1844, Joseph preached a sermon at the temple where he said he had been informed "that Wm. Law. Wilson Law. R[obert] D. Foster. Chaunc[e]y L. Higbee. & Joseph [H.] Jackson had held a caucus, desig[n]ing to destroy all the Smith family in a few weeks."[8] By one account, at one of the conspiratorial meetings Francis Higbee caused everyone present to swear an oath on the Bible "for the destruction of Joseph Smith and his party."[9]

In April Joseph tried to meet with Robert Foster to repair what damages he could, but without success.[10] Robert Foster and the Law brothers were excommunicated by members of the Quorum of the Twelve and high council, but without the accused being able to defend themselves, an action that enraged them and which they said was inconsistent with the Church's governing laws. On 28 April, the Laws, Fosters, and Francis Higbee formed their own church based on the premise that Joseph Smith was a fallen prophet.[11]

By May, William and Wilson Law, Robert and Charles Foster, and Chauncey and Francis Higbee, along with a man named Charles Ivins, purchased a printing press and sent out a prospectus that they were to publish a newspaper called the *Nauvoo Expositor*.[12] On Friday, 7 June 1844, they published their one and only edition. "We are earnestly seeking to explode the vicious principles of Joseph Smith," they printed. They railed against plural marriage as "abominations and whoredoms," Joseph's "attempt at Political power," his false "doctrine of *many Gods*," and his supposedly corrupt financial dealings, "the doctrine of unconditional sealing up to eternal life," saying that they, the writers, were "constrained to denounce them [Joseph and other Church leaders] as apostates." Francis Higbee called for people to gather in strength to "sweep the influence of tyrants and miscreants from the face of the land." While some of the items they listed were true, such as Joseph Smith's private practice of plural marriage or his doctrines of many Gods (from the King Follett funeral discourse), their use of inflammatory rhetoric, character accusations, and threats caused even the publishers of this paper to address the concern, "Will you bring a mob upon us?"[13]

In one of those ironies of history, the one thing Joseph Smith hoped would avoid mob action against him and the Saints was the very thing that brought it on. The next day, Saturday, 8 June, Joseph met with the city council to confer on what actions should be taken, and Joseph "made a Long speech in favor of having an ordinanc[e] to suppress Libels &c in Nauvo[o]."[14] On 10 June, the city council met again. Joseph's journal says:

> investigati[n]g the Merits of the Nauvoo Expositor. Laws. Higbe[es] Fosters &c—— Council passed an ordinance concerni[n]g Libels and for other purposes. also issued an order to me to dest[r]oy the Nauvoo Expositor establis[h]ment. as a nuisanc[e]—— I immediately ordered the marshal to dest[r]oy it without delay. at the same issued an order to Jonathan Dunham. acting Major Gen Nauvoo Legi[o]n.— to assist the Marshall with the Legion if calld upon so to do.— and about 8 o clock the Marshall repo[r]ted. that. he had removd the press. type— & pinteed [printed] pape[r]s— & fixtures into the street & fired them. this was done ~~by~~ because of the Libellus character of the paper.— in slanderi[n]g the Municipality of the city.— the possey consisting of some hundred retur[ne]d with the Marshal— in front of the Mansion— & I gave them a short address told them they had done right. that they had executed my orders— requi[re]d of me by the city council. . . . the speech was loudly greeted by 3 cheers— 3. times.

The historic journal entry then ends with an ominous threat: "Francis M. Higbee and othe[r]s made some th[r]eats which will appear in duee course of Invstigatin [investigation]." It closes with a literal yet emblematic statement of a chill in the air: "East wind very cold & cloudy."[15]

The following day, 11 June, William Clayton wrote that "Foster threatens vengeance" and that "several of them said that the Temple shall be thrown down Joseph['s] house burned & the printing office torn down. F[rancis]. M. Higbee threatened hard."[16] That same day Francis Higbee rode to the county seat of Carthage and filed charges against Joseph and Hyrum Smith and other city leaders for destruction of property and inciting a riot.[17]

Upon hearing the news over in a neighboring town called Warsaw, a newspaperman named Thomas Sharp published in his paper on 12 June, "War and extermination is inevitable! Citizens ARISE, ONE and ALL!!!—Can you stand by, and suffer such INFERNAL DEVILS! To ROB men of their property and RIGHTS, without avenging them. We have no time for comment, every man will make his own. LET IT BE MADE WITH POWDER AND BALL!!!"[18]

Outraged enemies of the Church responded to Sharp's cry and began to gather in Carthage and Warsaw after the destruction of the *Expositor*. Ultimately, Joseph and Hyrum Smith would submit to the charges against them in Carthage, and on 27 June an organized and angry mob would storm the jail where they were held and murder the Prophet and Patriarch. The burning of the *Nauvoo Expositor* fanned the flames that brought Joseph and Hyrum to Carthage, leading to their untimely deaths.

AN IMAGE

In this image, the *Expositor* press and papers are burned in the middle of Mulholland Street as a group of men look on, led by city marshal John Greene. I am uncertain whether they destroyed or burned the press, but I added it to the flames to form a more cohesive narrative image.

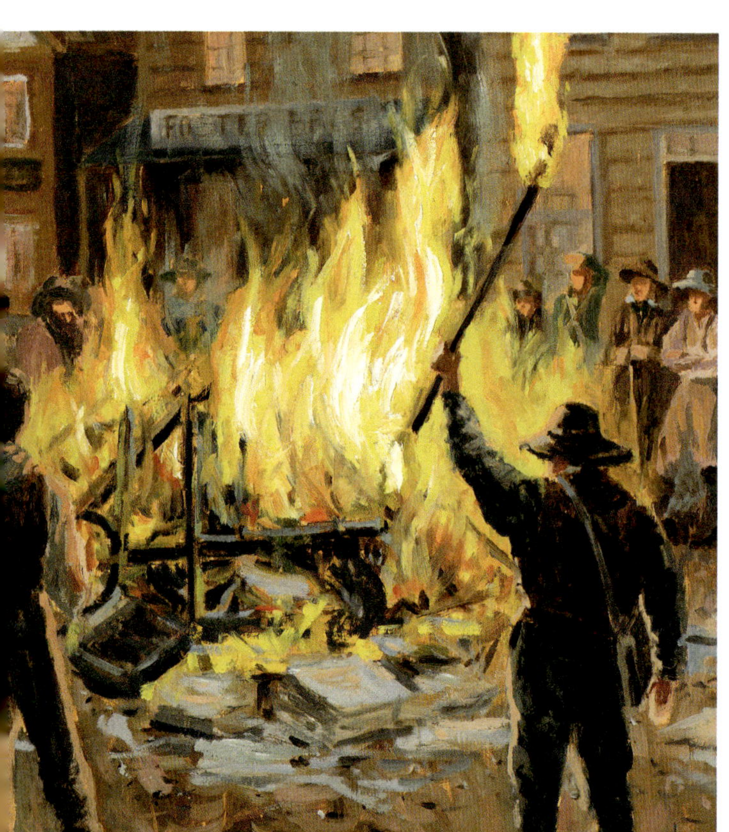

The *Expositor* building, which was located on the second floor, sits to the right of the frame, a prominent sign advertising its new business. This sign likely never existed but was added (using the font from the masthead of the actual *Expositor* paper) because a viewer needs to have sufficient visual information to construct the scene. Having the sign queues up the narrative and is another example of why art can be true to the essence of history but not literal history.

Here is a photograph of the actual *Expositor* building,[19] located on the same lot where a current furniture store operates on 1275 Mullholland Street.

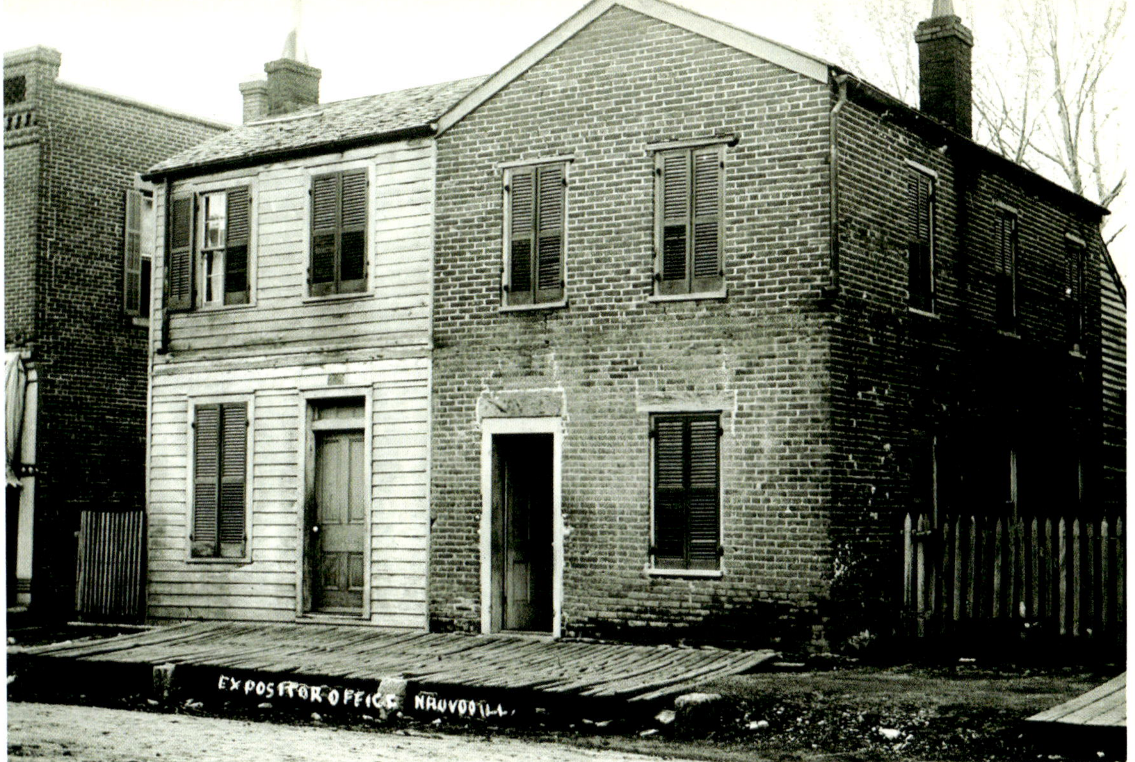

The men in this painting are purposely painted without much detail—just suggestions of figures and clothes in a few brushstrokes—their infamous anonymity highlighted and bathed in the orange and red highlights from the fire they created.

Over in the distance, a setting sun not only gives a nod to the destruction happening by 8 p.m., as reported, but also gives a symbolic signal that the sun will set on the life of the Prophet Joseph Smith.

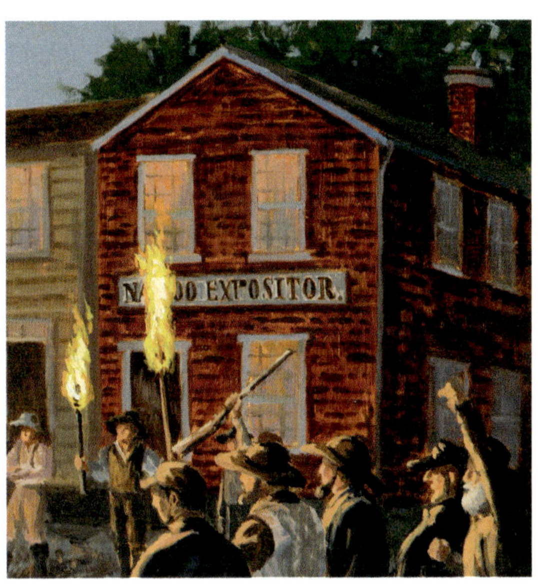

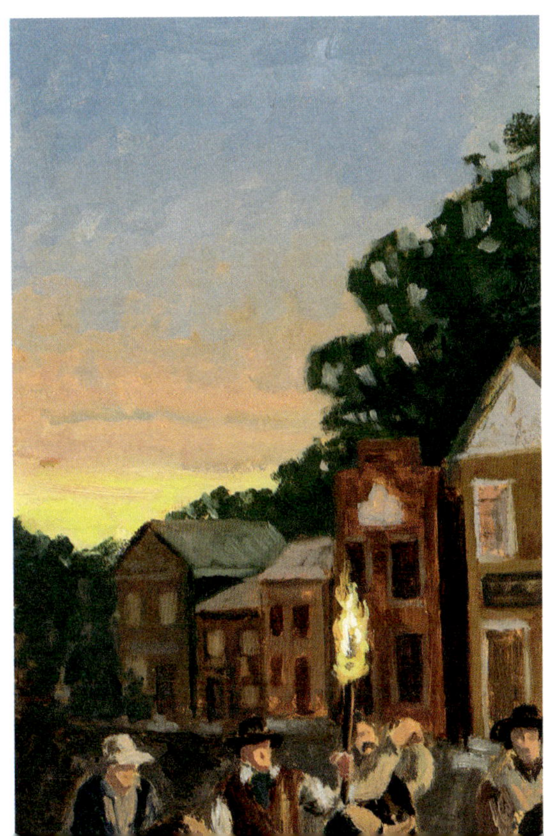

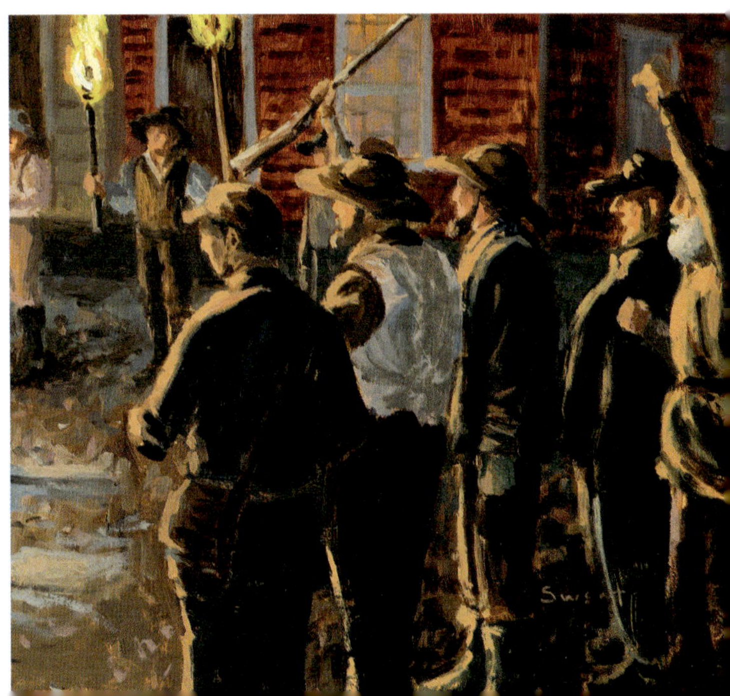

AN APPLICATION

It is easy to look back on the past with 20/20 hindsight and say what should or should not have been done. It is similarly tempting to judge the actions of those in the past by today's standards. In modern American society, freedom of the press is sacrosanct, and reading of Joseph Smith ordering the destruction of a critical rival press grates against our twenty-first-century constitutional sensibilities. However, Elder Dallin H. Oaks drew on his legal expertise to research[20] the legality of the Nauvoo city council's actions in destroying the *Expositor*, writing:

> The city council of Nauvoo was very concerned about that press and felt that it would raise mobs to come to Nauvoo and destroy the city and murder the inhabitants. They, as government officials, had a very legitimate concern. They debated what to do about it. They read Blackstone, which was a major source of law on the frontier. In Blackstone's commentaries on law, it says that the government officials had authority to destroy a nuisance. And they felt that the press was a nuisance. After two days of debate (this was not a sudden thing, and opposition was heard in the council), they finally decided to abate, which is to destroy, a nuisance.
>
> Mormons have generally apologized—including official Mormon historians—for the destruction of the newspaper, deeming it an interference with freedom of the press, a sacred American Constitutional right. The problem with that, I found as I researched this according to the law of Illinois and the United States in 1844 (the year this took place), was that the freedom of the press in the First Amendment did not apply to state action or to city action at that period. It only came to apply to state action or city action by the amendments adopted after the Civil War, the 14th Amendment, and it was so declared by the United States Supreme Court in the 1930s in a 5-4 decision. Well, if it took the United States Supreme Court 100 years to declare that the freedom of the press protected the press against city or state action, [I can easily sympathize with] the people that struggled with that issue in 1844 in Illinois, a time when history shows us a lot of newspapers were destroyed on the frontier, mostly along abolitionist issues, pro-slavery or anti-slavery. It seems to me like it's pretty extreme to say that Joseph Smith and his associates were violating the freedom of the press by what they did. They debated for two days, they fell back on Blackstone, they had no other precedents, and they thought it was legitimate to abate a nuisance, including a newspaper that they thought could bring death and destruction upon their city.
>
> It's hard for us to imagine [sympathy] today, but I don't think it's fair to judge the 1844 city officials—including Joseph Smith—by our refined notions of law and public policy in this day.[21]

Let us pray that our future posterity will first try to understand us and our times before they judge us too harshly and that therefore we will extend the same historical charity to people from the past whom we now study.

The tendency to judge the past based on the values of the today is called "presentism."[22] All of us are guilty of presentism to one degree or another, particularly when it comes to national, Church, or family history. For example, we read about how many early Latter-day Saints didn't consider it necessary to strictly follow the Word of Wisdom until the twentieth century, and we can't fathom how they considered themselves faithful. We discover that great-grandpa had Navy tattoos, and we wonder why he didn't follow the prophet. While not justifying any of those actions, our first position should be to try to understand the people and their context before we criticize their views or behavior. Historian Matthew Grow has likened learning history to traveling. He said:

> The "ugly American" tourist currently conjures up images of individuals refusing to learn even the rudiments of a foreign language while rudely demanding in English to know the way to the nearest McDonald's.
>
> An "ugly" historical traveler judges the past solely based on our own standards; is impatient with historical actors without trying to understand their own circumstances and motivations; and refuses to learn enough to make sense of that history.[23]

One day, our children, grandchildren, great-grandchildren, and others will look at us through lenses with which we cannot now conceive. Their cultural eyewear will be colored with a tint that will shade everything we do in a different light. How will they view things we consider acceptable and commonplace today, things like driving gas-powered cars, certain medical treatments, fast food, social media, our culture of individual self-fulfillment, or even playing football? The irony is that even as I write those hypotheticals that future generations may criticize, I too am blinded by my own culture to see where we may be ignorant and amiss. Let us pray that our future posterity will first try to understand us and our times before they judge us too harshly and that therefore we will extend the same historical charity to people from the past whom we now study.

AN ANALYSIS

1 If you were Joseph Smith, what would you have done with the *Expositor*? Playing hypotheticals is impossible, but do you think worse results would have occurred for the Latter-day Saints in Nauvoo had the city council let the paper continue to be published? Was there a better way to fight back or overpower it? If so, what? How does the modern Church respond to attacks in the press or public, and what can we learn from that example?

2 The *Expositor* criticized Joseph Smith's attempts to mix politics and religion. There are many today who do the same whenever the Church speaks out on political matters. Why is mixing politics and religion almost inevitable? Why does the Church affirm its "right as an institution to address, in a nonpartisan way, issues that it believes have significant community or moral consequences or that directly affect the interests of the Church."[24] Why do you think this should be encouraged or avoided?

3 What is the role of freedom of the press regarding Church matters? Modern Americans often claim we want "transparency," but where do we draw the line? Do we truly want our medical histories published for all? Our personal finances? Our therapy sessions? What about our confessions to bishops, or marks on our Church records? Modern "Nauvoo Expositors," like MormonLeaks (now the "Truth & Transparency

Foundation") claim to serve the public good by promoting transparency in religious institutions (through reporting things such as clergy leaders who don't report sexual abuse cases to police) but also by leaking Church financial documents. What do you think? Do they help, hurt, or achieve something in-between? What is the line of transparency and individual or institutional privacy?

NOTES

1. "Law, Wilson," People, The Joseph Smith Papers.
2. See Andrew H. Hedges, "Joseph Smith, Robert Foster, and Chauncey and Francis Higbee," *Religious Educator* 18, no. 1 (2017): 88–111.
3. "Higbee, Francis Marion," People, The Joseph Smith Papers.
4. See Hedges, "Joseph Smith, Robert Foster, and Chauncey and Francis Higbee," 88–111.
5. "Journal, December 1842–June 1844; Book 4, 1 March–22 June 1844," 91, The Joseph Smith Papers.
6. Lyndon Cook writes that William Law's "motives for apostasy appear to have stemmed from a perception (real or imagined) that his civil and religious liberties were being threatened within the Mormon community." "William Law, Nauvoo Dissenter," *BYU Studies* 22, no. 1 (1982): 70.
7. Conspirator names are listed in "Verbal Statement of Dennison Lott Harris with Annotations," 15 May 1881, Joseph Smith Foundation (website).
8. "Journal, December 1842–June 1844; Book 4, 1 March–22 June 1844," 48.
9. "Verbal Statement of Dennison Lott Harris with Annotations." See also *Saints*, vol. 1: *The Standard of Truth, 1815–1846* (Salt Lake City: The Church of Jesus Christ of Latter-day Saints, 2018), 527–28.
10. "Journal, December 1842–June 1844; Book 4, 1 March–22 June 1844," 84–85.
11. See Hedges, "Joseph Smith, Robert Foster, and Chauncey and Francis Higbee," 88–111.
12. "Nauvoo Expositor," Church History Topics, churchofjesuschrist.org.
13. Excerpts from the *Nauvoo Expositor* as cited in Fair Mormon (website).
14. "Journal, December 1842–June 1844; Book 4, 1 March–22 June 1844," 149.
15. "Journal, December 1842–June 1844; Book 4, 1 March–22 June 1844," 151.
16. Clayton, Journal, 11 June 1844; see also JS, Journal, 11 June 1844, as cited in "Journal, December 1842–June 1844; Book 4, 1 March–22 June 1844," 151, note 437.
17. Joseph I. Bentley, "Road to Martyrdom: Joseph Smith's Last Legal Cases," *BYU Studies Quarterly* 55, no. 2 (2016): 40.
18. "Unparalleled Outrage at Nauvoo," *Warsaw Signal*, 12 June 1844, 2.
19. Nauvoo Expositor building, Digital Collections, BYU Library, Religious Education Collection.
20. See Dallin H. Oaks, "The Suppression of the *Nauvoo Expositor*," *Utah Law Review* 9, no. 4 (Winter 1965): 862–903.
21. "Elder Oaks Interview Transcript from PBS Documentary," 20 July 2007, newsroom.churchofjesuschrist.org.
22. Merriam-Webster.com, s.v. "presentism."
23. "10 Questions with Matthew J. Grow and R. Eric Smith, 27 February 2018, *From the Desk of Kurt Manwaring* (blog).
24. "Political Neutrality," newsroom.churchofjesuschrist.org.

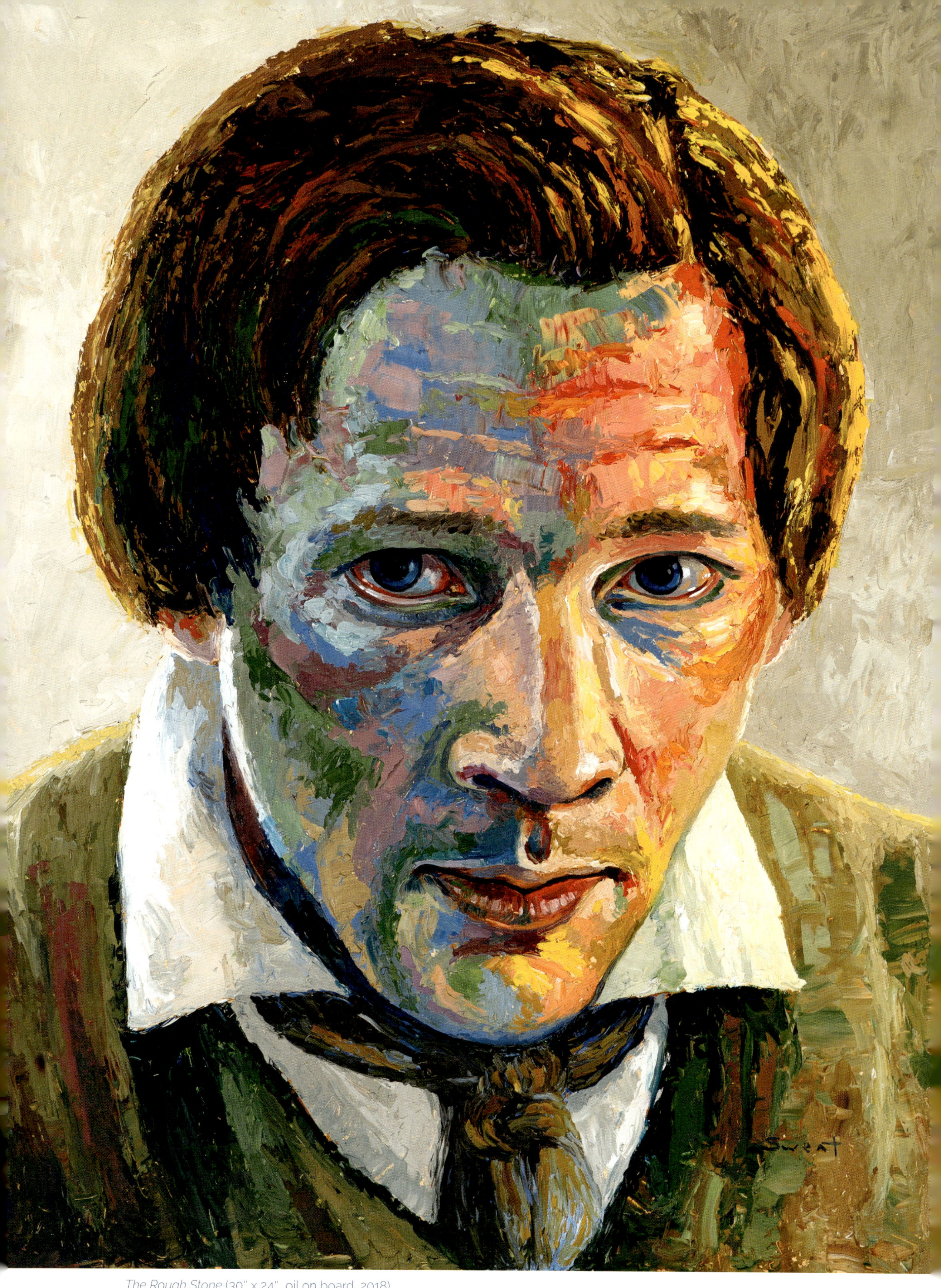

The Rough Stone (30" x 24", oil on board, 2018)

THE ROUGH STONE

Timeline: 1805–44

Related Doctrine and Covenants Sections: 1–135, 137

A BACKGROUND

In 1967, Brigham Young University religion professor Ivan J. Barrett wrote a landmark book, *Joseph Smith and the Restoration.* It was intended for undergraduate students taking Church history classes at BYU. I was not alive in 1967, let alone reading Dr. Barrett's book. I first encountered his text as a missionary in 1995, poring over its pages and hoarding the book from my mission's library, holding on to it for months after I had finished reading so I could refer back to it. That book helped ignite a deep fire in my soul about the prophetic mission of Joseph Smith. After reading Barrett's book, I wrote home to my mother, asking her to send me any books on Joseph Smith she could. Over the months that followed I read *Joseph Smith the Prophet* by Truman G. Madsen, *Discourses of Joseph Smith* by Alma Burton, *Brother Joseph* by Kay Briggs, and *Teachings of the Prophet Joseph Smith* by Joseph Fielding Smith, among other classics. I still have those texts today, highlighted and earmarked, notes spilled all over the margins in my twenty-year-old handwriting. They helped me learn who Joseph Smith was.

Or did they?

There is a remarkable review of Ivan Barrett's book in the spring 1968 edition of *BYU Studies*. After praising the text as "exceptionally commendable," the reviewer, University of Utah associate institute director Reed C. Durham, writes how Barrett argues in the text that religion teachers should only emphasize the "fire and enthusiasm" of past Saints and "not delve into, analyze, or critically introduce any distasteful, suspicious, or questionable areas of church history that in any way will hinder the accomplishment" of seeing past Saints at their best. Durham then writes an open question about this approach: "From my own personal experience in teaching Church history to college students, I

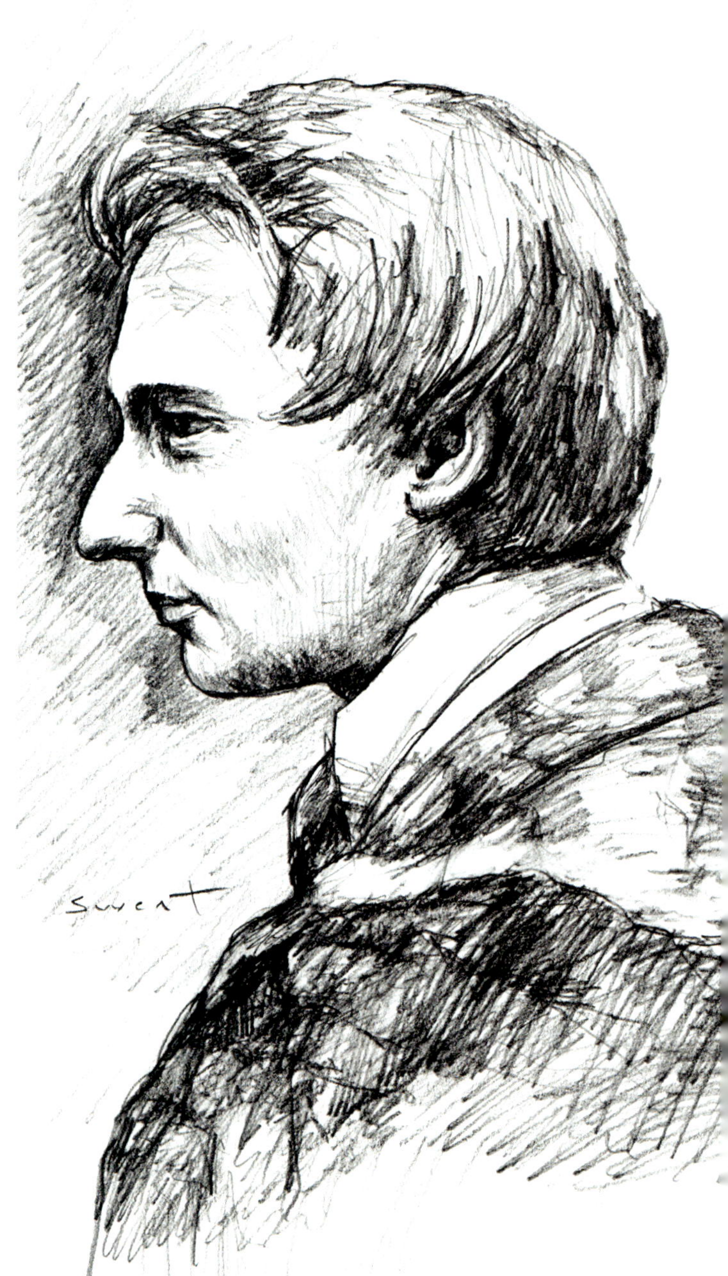

have asked myself the question as to whether in the long range look the student should be exposed to both approaches—the stated guidelines and their opposites—but, of course, in an atmosphere of faith. Can there be learning and profit by also seeing men and women at their worst in Church history? Can knowing the despair, the humanness, the 'real-down-to-earth-like-me-ness' do anything positive for my students? . . . Can the student and I profit by having an honest, 'no holds barred,' 'we search after the truth' attitude? I seriously wonder which of the two approaches is the more negative or positive in the long run. Time and experience may reveal this to us."[1]

Time and experience have revealed that in the decades since *Joseph Smith and the Restoration*, a segment of Saints have read overly glossy versions of Church history and whitewashed profiles of Joseph Smith, resulting in negative consequences. In some portrayals, Joseph sometimes takes on an almost mythological status, like a Greek god among mere mortals. What we see is not a real person but more of a caricature that has been created through reverential Church curriculum, cinema, folklore, and images. Although he was a handsome man, paintings of him over time have almost turned him into a supermodel. Compare some of Sutcliffe Maudsley's profiles of the Prophet from life—with his large convex nose and protruding Nauvoo belly—with some popular modern portraits. Images and hagiographies that airbrush away Joseph's wrinkles are understandable, and in a way commendable, but also can be problematic. When some learn that Joseph didn't always act nobly, they feel slightly betrayed and can wonder if they really know him. The internet has exacerbated this experience as blog posts, podcasts, websites, and social media have pushed lesser-known and sideline histories of Joseph Smith, which were typically kept in the confined corners of scholarly research, forefront into the mainstream.

In 2005, Columbia historian Richard Bushman (assisted by Jed Woodworth) wrote a seminal biography of Joseph Smith, *Rough Stone Rolling*, which took the opposite approach of Barrett's *Joseph Smith and the Restoration*. Bushman—a believing Latter-day Saint—openly discussed various sides of Joseph without trying to criticize or convert. Likely anticipating some blowback by Church members for this approach, Bushman wrote in the introduction to the book, "What I can do is to look frankly at all sides of Joseph Smith, facing up to his mistakes and flaws." Bushman also wrote, "Covering up errors makes no sense in any case. Most readers do not believe, nor are they interested in, pure perfection. . . . We want to meet a real person. . . . Smith called himself a rough stone."[2] Bushman received both positive and negative reception to his book, and some of the negativity came from more conservative Church members and educators who exhibited what Bushman characterized as "a kind of unbending stiffness that denies the realities."[3] As time has passed, however, Bushman's more open style has been validated in its modern embrace by institutional approaches to Church history.[4]

BYU scholar Spencer Fluhman said that one benefit to those who take a more unvarnished attitude is that "they get comfortable with the human side of Church experience. They come to see past Saints and leaders alike less as cardboard superhero cutouts—larger than life but two dimensional—and more like real people. For some, this humanizing view of past Saints makes them more compelling, not less. Instead of unreachable icons of piety or spirituality, they seem somehow more relatable in their humanity, somehow more usable as actual examples for struggling Saints like you and me."[5] It appeals to authors and Saints such as Neylan McBaine, who writes, "I am suspect of tidy history and squeaky clean people."[6]

Most religious leaders, while brilliant and inspired, are also complicated and flawed. Sometimes in our reverence for their genius, we varnish over imperfections. But it's the very shadows that make highlights shine. It's three-dimensional textures that make us want to move in closer and extend our hand to touch something. It's a rainbow of color—the reds and the blues, the yellows and the greens—with all their symbolic meaning that makes things richer and more vibrant. And in my scholarly study of Joseph Smith, he is a colorful man. I wanted to create a portrait of Joseph Smith that was a little different and attempted to express these ideas through paint.

AN IMAGE

This portrait of the Prophet Joseph Smith symbolically represents the various aspects of his character, a self-described "rough stone"—the varied warm and cool colors, painted thick and coarse with my palette knife, all coming together into a cohesive whole.

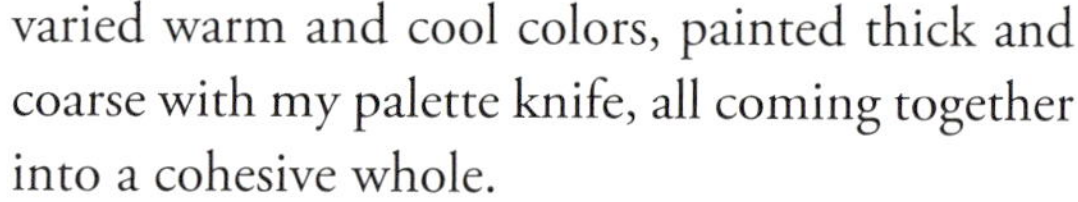

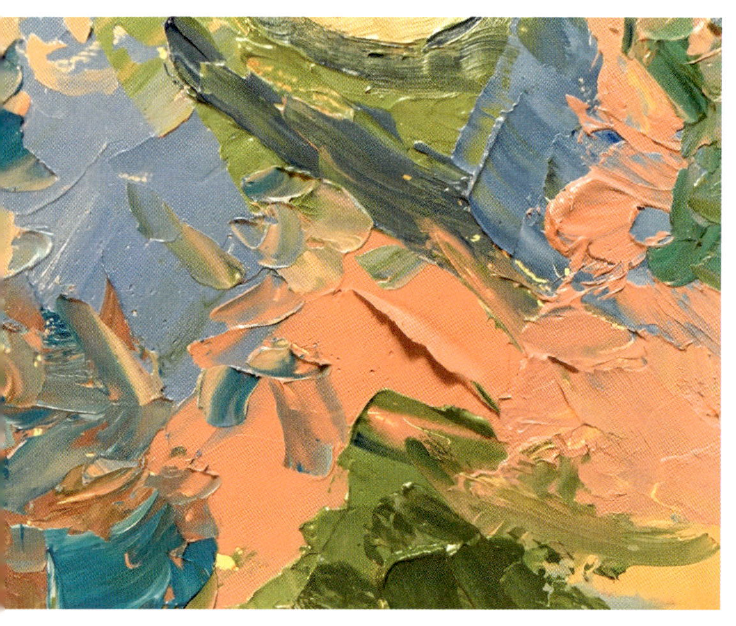

Joseph's mouth is surrounded by yellow, orange, pink, blue, purple, green, tan, and red, the bright colors of his nature and disposition that contributed to him being the right instrument through whom God could speak in these latter days.

I painted his eyes with my brushes as opposed to my palette knives. I wanted his blue eyes to look intently and directly at the viewer as if Joseph has just asked an important question—one the viewer must reconcile. One cannot conveniently overlook Joseph Smith. His bold claims and character call out to anyone who crosses his path, causing us to consider the source of his achievements and his impact upon history and humanity.

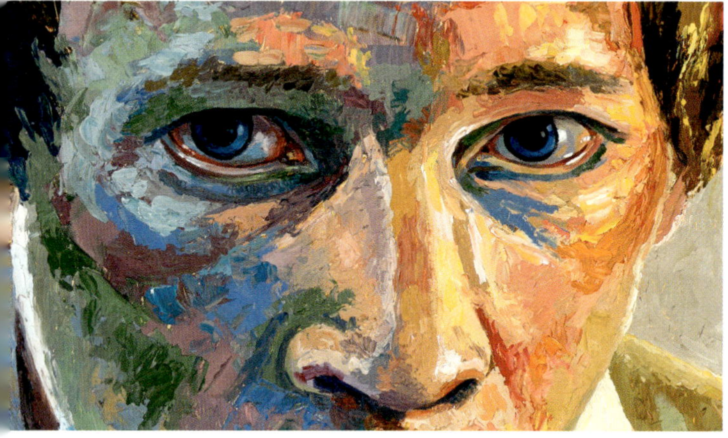

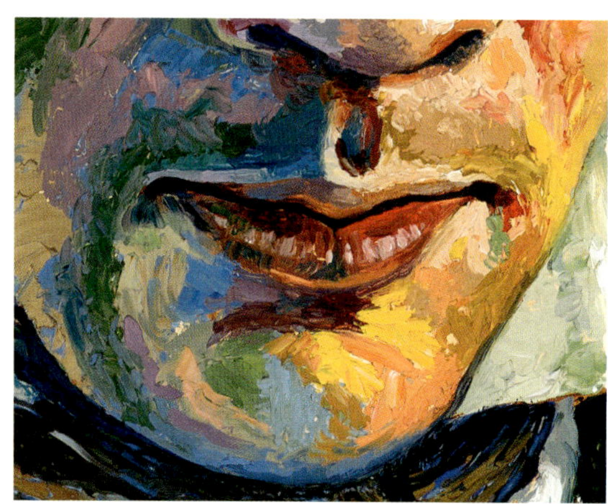

AN APPLICATION

The monumental undertaking of the publication of the Joseph Smith Papers Project opens a new window, or at least an enlarged one, into the life of Joseph Smith. As stated in their introduction to *Journals, Volume 1*, "The publication of his papers will permit readers to observe the origins of this resilient religious culture and throw light on the achievements—and the complexity—of its intrepid founder. . . .These volumes provide essential resources for the study of Joseph Smith's life and times."[7]

The difficulty, however, is that very, very few Latter-day Saints have ever read a volume of *The Joseph Smith Papers*, let alone many or all available volumes. They are, in the stated goal of the Church Historian's press who created them, meant to be primary sources for scholars on the life and teachings of Joseph Smith. If you've looked at the sources for this book, you've seen hundreds of times where I've called upon and benefited from the *The Joseph Smith Papers* in seeking to explain Joseph Smith or early Church history.

An interesting question I've asked myself is, "What would we learn about Joseph Smith if *The Joseph Smith Papers* were our only source to know him by?" What if we forgot all the secondary and tertiary commentary, the selective sampling of statements, the devotional biographies, the doctoring by critics and apologists alike, and threw it all out, starting fresh? What if we took a cue from Christian author Phillip Yancey's classic, best-selling Christian book *The Jesus I Never Knew*? In it, Yancey tries to put away everything he's learned about Jesus in his youth, in church sermons, and throughout his Bible college years, and then explores Jesus as though he had never met him, using only the New Testament as his source to form conclusions. It's a delightful read. Applying the same technique, when we peel off generational varnish, what do we learn about Joseph Smith from analyzing the primary texts themselves? Although, as editors for the *Joseph Smith Papers* themselves write, "extensive as the papers of Joseph Smith are, they do not afford readers unobstructed access to his mind and heart,"[8] I believe it nonetheless would afford Latter-day Saints a deeper understanding and better informed perspective of the Prophet. Just take one volume—such as *Journals, Volume 1*—and read it all the way through. I've done that, and it's extremely insightful. There's something freeing about reading the actual, raw source yourself. Perhaps you've experienced that a little in the extensive original quoting I've done herein.

Admittedly, the *Papers* at times can be dense and tedious reading, but the editorial work is top-notch, the primary documents are untainted by later interpretation, and the hidden gems are invaluable. While it's tough sledding at times, it also is a commentary on the level we are actually willing to go to deeply learn about Joseph Smith. How much do we want to get to know *primary* Joseph Smith before any slant, including my own in this book? I don't expect people to read every volume (I haven't even done that yet, and I'm a Church history professor. What can I say? Legal and business records just aren't calling out to me), and maybe not even one volume all the way through, but why not? At minimum, searching josephsmithpapers.org and becoming familiar with the web version and resources available should be the least we can do. There's no excuse from those who love and want to learn about the Prophet.

If you're afraid of what you might find—that perhaps you will read something that doesn't fit the Restoration framework you've created—I would hearken to Joseph Smith's own mantra, referenced in the introduction: "Mormonism is truth."[9] To quote the influential thinker and author Yuval Noah Harari, "It takes even greater courage to admit ignorance and venture into the unknown. Secular education teaches us that if we don't know something, we shouldn't be afraid of acknowledging our ignorance and looking for new evidence. Even if we think we know something, we shouldn't be afraid of doubting our opinions and checking ourselves again. . . . Questions you cannot answer are usually far better for you than answers you cannot question."[10]

Throughout this book, I have sought to present important, underdepicted events in the history of The Church of Jesus Christ of Latter-day Saints for those very reasons.

I have purposely chosen paintings that are important but at times also uncomfortable. Images such as Joseph looking in a hat or wrestling with William or arguing with Emma are not mantle pieces or images you will likely ever see in the *Ensign.* At the same time, I've painted images of the First Vision and marriage sealings and angels descending to Joseph that may be. I hope this art and the discussions that accompany them have helped you more broadly learn about and more deeply appreciate God's servants and saints as they really were.

I am eternally grateful for my belief that Joseph was a prophet, but I am also deeply grateful that I know he was also a man. Seeing his humanity doesn't lessen my belief in his prophetic role—it increases it. It shows me that God will work through imperfect people who are doing their very best to follow him. I've seen that in Joseph, I've seen it in other men and women from Church history, I've seen it in modern Saints today, and I've seen it in myself. I hope these paintings, and your increased efforts to study about and learn from Joseph Smith, will do the same for you. There is yet so much to learn.

AN ANALYSIS

1 What have you learned about Joseph's character, his strengths, and his weaknesses that have helped you to better understand, know, or appreciate him? What have you learned about how Joseph Smith grew line upon line in his understanding of the gospel, the Restoration, and the purposes of God? What do you believe about his prophetic teachings and claims? Why?

2 What are your thoughts about Bushman's *Rough Stone Rolling* approach to Church history versus Barrett's *Joseph Smith and the Restoration* approach? Do you like to learn about Joseph's errors, failings, and shortcomings, or would you prefer to focus on his accomplishments, strengths, and achievements?

3 Each generation is a product of its times, has prophets for its times, and has pedagogy for its times. What mistakes do you think we are we making today in how we educate the Church about Joseph Smith and Church history that may cause problems a few generations from now? How can we correct it?

NOTES

1. Reed C. Durham, "Book Reviews: Ivan J. Barrett, *Joseph Smith and the Restoration*," *BYU Studies* 8, no. 3 (1968): 345.
2. Richard Lyman Bushman, *Joseph Smith: Rough Stone Rolling* (New York City: Alfred A. Knopf, 2005), xix–xx.
3. Richard Lyman Bushman, *On the Road with Joseph: An Author's Diary* (Midvale, UT: Greg Kofford Books, 2007), 55.
4. The Joseph Smith Papers Project, the narrative Church history *Saints*, the Gospel Topics Essays, *Revelations in Context*, and Church Educational System courses such as Foundations of the Restoration are indicators of this claim. Additionally, Elder M. Russell Ballard gave a landmark talk in February 2016 to Church Educational System employees in which he said: "Our curriculum [in the past], though well-meaning, did not prepare students for today. . . . More than at any time in our history, your students also need to be blessed by learning doctrinal or historical content and context by study and faith accompanied by pure testimony so they can experience a mature and lasting conversion to the gospel and a lifelong commitment to Jesus Christ. . . . [Provide] faithful, thoughtful, and accurate interpretation of gospel doctrine, the scriptures, our history, and those topics that are sometimes misunderstood." "The Opportunities and Responsibilities of CES Teachers in the 21st CenturyS" (worldwide Church Educational System training broadcast, 26 February 2016).
5. J. Spencer Fluhman, "Faith in the Past: Church History in an Information Age" (address to LDS Business College, 11 November 2014), ldsbc.edu.
6. Neylan McBaine, *Women at Church: Magnifying LDS Women's Local Impact* (Salt Lake City: Greg Kofford Books, 2014), 6.
7. Dean C. Jessee, Mark Ashurst-McGee, and Richard L. Jensen, eds. *Journals, Volume 1: 1832–1839*, vol. 1 of the Journals series of *The Joseph Smith Papers*, ed. Dean C. Jessee, Ronald K. Esplin, and Richard Lyman Bushman (Salt Lake City: Church Historian's Press, 2008), xv, xxxv, xli.
8. *JSP*, J1:xxxviii.
9. "Letter to Isaac Galland, 22 March 1839," 54, The Joseph Smith Papers.
10. Yuval Noah Harari, *21 Lessons for the 21st Century* (Spiegel & Grau: New York, 2018), 212.

EPILOGUE

Tomorrowland: The Future of Latter-day Saint Art

When Disneyland opened in 1955, a key component of the park was an area called Tomorrowland. It was meant to provide a glimpse into the potential future of technology, space exploration, inventions, science, communication, transportation, and the like. It provided a blueprint of possibilities.

But along the way, Tomorrowland got stuck in the past. Like a professor who gives a training on "active student learning" through an hour-long monologue, Tomorrowland failed to live up to its own name. Within a few decades it became dated. As one writer summarized: "Tomorrowland is meant to represent the future. . . . [However], by [the 1980s], park guests were jokingly referring to the area as 'Yesterdayland.' . . . Today, Tomorrowland in Disneyland is the park's biggest eyesore."[1]

Similarly, Latter-day Saint art can be at risk of failing to live up to its own identity. Since the turn of the nineteenth and through the twentieth century, Latter-day Saints have enjoyed a rich history of visual arts. Our people and artistic heritage have been forged and blessed by masters like Dan Weggeland, C. C. A. Christensen, John Hafen, James Harwood, LeConte Stewart, Cyrus Dallin, Avard and Leo Fairbanks, Mary Teasdel, Minerva Teichert, Arnold Friberg, Alvin Gittins, and so many more. As we look to the future of Latter-day Saint art, we should build off this masterful momentum but not expect to stay in the same trajectory as its pioneering predecessors. The Church of the early 1900s is very different from the modern Church of 2020. Think how ill-suited it would be if Church programs and curriculum had stayed the same. Why, then, should our artistic subjects and expressions? We must be attentive that Latter-day Saint art doesn't suffer the same fate as Disney's Tomorrowland, becoming stuck in a past aesthetic that worked for its time but doesn't appeal to a modern, changing, growing, international Church. If we remain in the artistic past, we may shut off the very thing that could potentially define Latter-day Saint religious art—not any particular style *but a willingness to embrace an eclectic aesthetic as a representation of the Church's global mission to learn, embrace, and express truth.* Brigham Young said, "'Mormonism,' so-called, embraces every principle pertaining to life and salvation, for time and eternity. No matter who has it. If the infidel has got truth it belongs to 'Mormonism.' The truth and sound doctrine possessed by the sectarian world, and they have a great deal, all belong to this church."[2]

Brigham's mantra can apply to the future trajectory of Latter-day Saint art. Truth is expansive, innovative, and diverse, not limited, static, and narrow. Let's remember this in the art we produce and promote in the next century, because if we assume a closed posture with our art as an institution and a body, we will likely stunt our own growth and possibilities as we strive to fulfill President Kimball's "Gospel Vision of the Arts."[3] As the ongoing Restoration continues, and many great and important things pertaining to the kingdom of God are yet to be revealed (see Articles of Faith 1:9), there are also many great and important paintings yet to be created.

Innovator and designer Angela Oguntala expressed this concept in her TED talk: "In the same way our visions inspire us, they can also start to limit us. If we hear the same narratives over and over again and if we see the same visuals over and over again, then that becomes our scope of possibility. That becomes our benchmark for what we believe is good—and what's not. So today I want you to think about your assumptions about the future because there are just so many different futures and alternatives out there. And if we choose to be more curious about them, then they will make us rethink what's possible."[4]

The relationship of Church art and truth is symbiotic. Art is always a reflection of the culture in which it is a created, but art also influences and changes the culture which it inhibits. Art can be, and often is, an engine of knowledge, understanding, and emotion, and therefore action, change, and growth. We can use artistic platforms (and herein I am including all the various artistic disciplines) as a vision of what can and should be. Indeed, we must.

We must show earthly realities and heavenly possibilities. Because whatever art we produce, will be.

A popular phrase in promoting social change has been the mantra: "You can't be what can't see."[5] Regarding religious art, we could modify that phrase to be "you can't know what you aren't shown." We need more art, of more subjects, in more diverse mediums and styles, teaching more truth. I hope that some of the subjects in this book will be reinterpreted by other artists, in their diverse and unique approaches, to both educate and innovate in ways that my expressions of these events cannot due to my limitations as an artist. Diversity in artistic expression is a catalyst for broader understanding. We need to produce it, promote it, patronize it, and purchase it—because, as scholar Terryl Givens wrote in 2007, "it is likely that in another generation, 'Mormon art' will be the focus of the church's most creative energy and a potent element in shaping a rapidly transforming Mormon culture."[6]

Artist J. Kirk Richards gave these remarks at the opening of the 2019 International Art Competition at the Church History Museum in Salt Lake City:

> In an increasingly global church and with a critical mass of women's voices, our challenge will be to open our canon of imagery, encouraging a diversity of depictions both of the divine and of the lived faith experience. Opening the canon may largely fall on the shoulders of correlation committees, but there are things you and I can do. As artists, we can be inclusive in our imagery. As patrons and curators, we can expand the edges of our time worn circles of artistic comfort. We can examine the art on our walls and ask ourselves, would this be welcoming to a visitor, or to a Latter-day Saint from a background different from my own? There is such an immensely beautiful diversity within our lived faith, and we can embrace it through our artistic choices.[7]

Using truth as our foundational aesthetic, we must produce and embrace varied styles, subjects, and expressions as the Church grows, diversifies, and changes. We must continue to explore historical and scriptural events that have never been depicted, or that should be redepicted through new lenses. Through Latter-day Saint religious art, we must show the historical past of its members, their lived present, and also their potential future—things as they really were, really are, and are to come, because that is "truth" (see Doctrine and Covenants 93:24; Jacob 4:13). We must use art to give expression to our unique, rich, and expansive theology—something that the arts are uniquely qualified to communicate. We must show earthly realities and heavenly possibilities. Because whatever art we produce, will be.

NOTES

1. Eric Diaz, "Why a New Tomorrowland Is Long Overdue at Disneyland," 29 August 2019, nerdist.com.
2. Brigham Young, "Building the Temple—Mormonism Embraces All Truth," 8 April 1867, in *Journal of Discourses* (London: Latter-day Saints' Book Depot, 1854–86), 11:371.
3. Spencer W. Kimball, "The Gospel Vision of the Arts," *Ensign*, July 1977, 2–5.
4. Angela Oguntala, "Changing the World," TED Radio Hour, 12 April 2019, National Public Radio (website).
5. See Milbrey W. McLaughlin, *You Can't Be What You Can't See* (Cambridge, MA: Harvard Educational Press, 2018). See also "'You Can't Be What You Can't See': Making Tech Careers a Reality for Women," *The Guardian*, 27 February 2017.
6. Terryl Givens, *People of Paradox: A History of Mormon Culture* (New York: Oxford University Press, 2007), 338.
7. J. Kirk Richards, "The Future of Latter-day Saint Art" (address at awards ceremony for the 11th International Art Competition of the Church of Jesus Christ of Latter-day Saints on 14 March 2019), jkirkrichards.wpcomstaging.com/.

AFTERWORD

A Painting from Concept to Creation

People sometimes ask me how long it takes to *paint* a painting. However, they rarely ask how long it takes to *create* a painting, and there's a difference. The time it takes to lay down paint is often overshadowed by the hours spent coming up with and composing ideas. Painting and creation are not synonymous terms.

This is why I've always enjoyed seeing the creative process of other artists—the behind-the-scenes production. I sometimes enjoy the bonus features on movies that show the work and decisions that went into creating a movie as much as the movie itself. Podcasts like *Song Exploder* that take apart songs layer by layer fascinate me and help enhance my appreciation of music. In that spirit, this afterword traces a painting, *The First Visions*, from concept to creation. Artists each have their own systems and approaches, but this example is emblematic of my process for most of the images in this *Repicturing the Restoration* book.

Each painting in this series began with identifying something that wasn't typically (or ever) depicted in a Restoration scene. In this case, the First Vision is one of the most often depicted artistic events by Latter-day Saint artists. But in my research and teaching of the First Vision, I noticed there were key elements in the various historical accounts that were not often depicted in paintings: the fire from heaven, Satan, the Father and Son not appearing simultaneously, many angels in the grove, and the idea of it being a *vision* (heaven opening up to Joseph's mind).

COMPOSITIONAL SKETCHES

Once I formulate ideas such as this, I begin with compositional sketches. The purpose of these sketches is to start fleshing out how to approach the scene by laying down major shapes, groupings, and perspectives. I am not worried about detail and do not reference any models or photographs, but I want to try to bring out generally what I am thinking to see how it may work. These sketches are done fairly quickly. This was my first compositional sketch for *The First Visions*.

Herein you see a hint of the grove of verti-

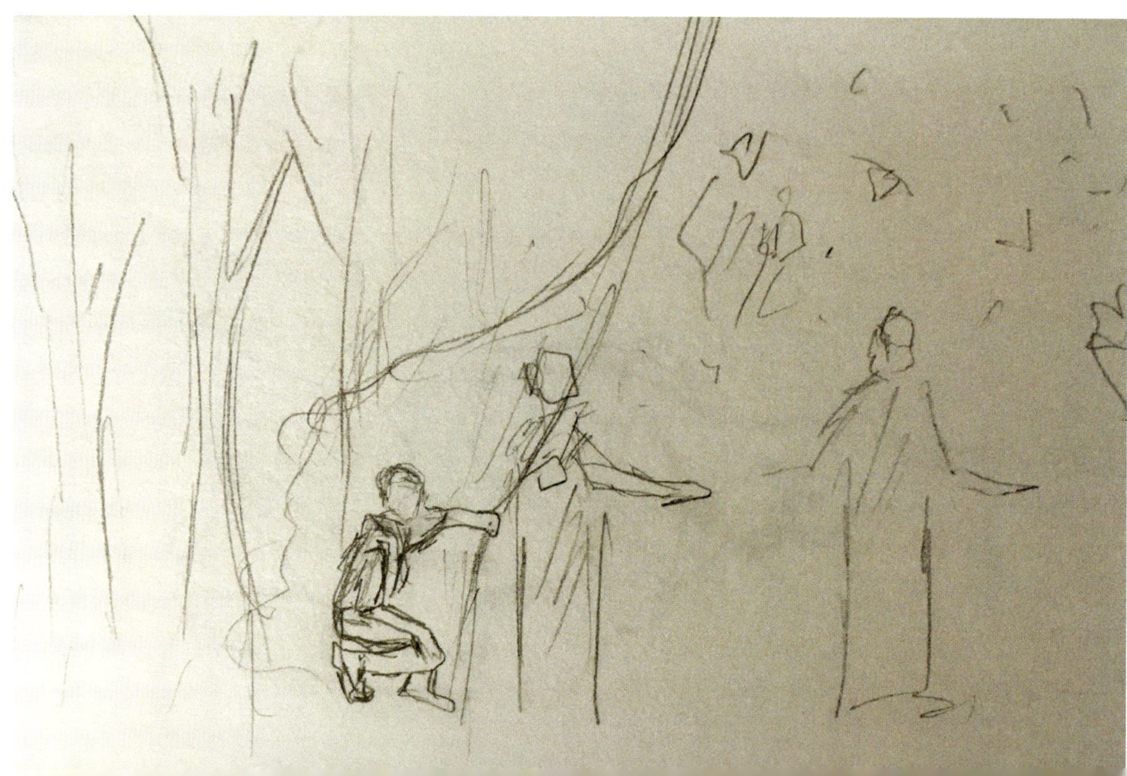

cal trees on the left, but the major element is a dividing curtain midway through the composition, and kneeling Joseph is pulling the curtain of the mortal veil back, ready to peer into heaven where he sees the Father and Son and a grouping of angels behind them. The left half of the image would have been the grove, and the right half behind the curtain, heaven. I like this idea of pulling back the veil (and still may pursue a painting like this one day) but was unhappy with the placement of God and Jesus. I wanted them higher and not side by side. It also didn't allow me to depict the fire as I desired, and I was worried that the curtain would be too abstract a concept. So I sketched out another version.

Again, there is a dividing line idea between the grove and heaven, this time cutting diagonally through the scene. Diagonals are visually pleasing, and I liked the grouping of angels as a halo. Also, the Father and Son are higher above Joseph. Yet this composition still wasn't quite sending the message of one being appearing, and then another. The typical side-by-side view of God and Jesus wasn't doing it for me. So a third compositional sketch followed.

You can see a progression from compositional sketch one, two, and now to three. The dividing line is now cutting diagonally the other direction, and I am using the fire instead of a curtain to visually divide the scene and space. The Father appears first in front of the Son, as Jesus is yet descending, conveying the idea that one appeared and then another shortly thereafter, as the records say. The fire now envelops Joseph, as Orson Pratt wrote, as though he's been pulled into a heavenly vision. Notice at the ground I sketched Joseph lying on his back too—like the vision was taking place in spirit and his physical body was lying on its back, as he said he was when he came to after the vision closed. I cut that out of the final idea as it was too confusing (this is very Paulish, "whether in the body

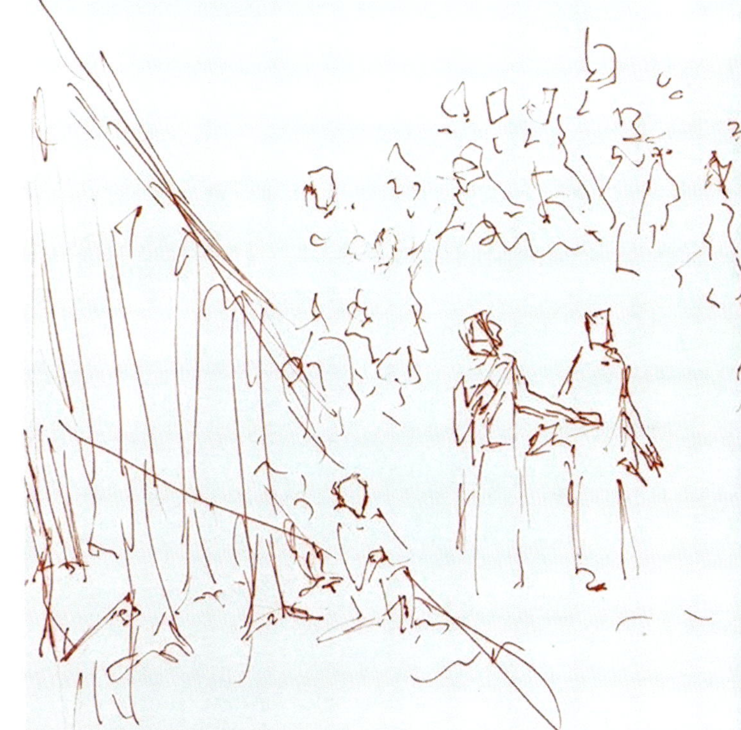

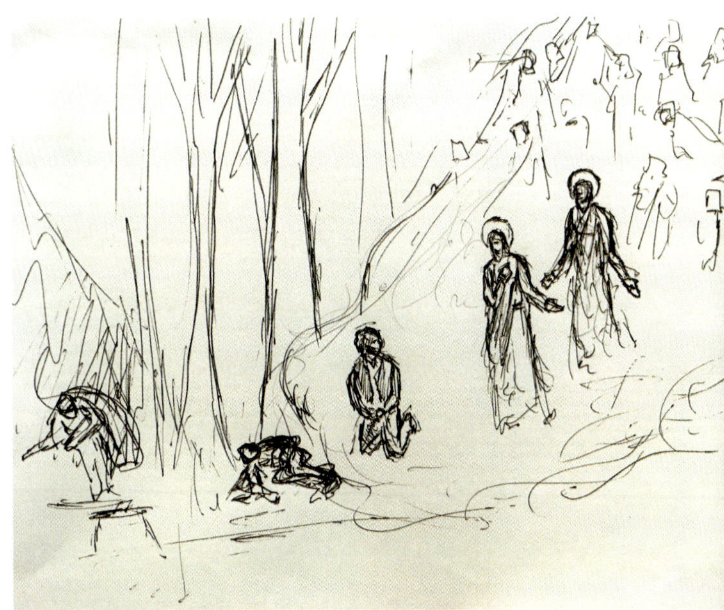

[or out], I cannot tell," see 2 Corinthians 12:2. But visually it made it feel like *two* Josephs were there. Weird!). I also sketched in Satan in the left corner fleeing. I liked this general composition because it successfully conveyed the new, typically undepicted elements that I had imagined. My next step was to start moving forward by photographing models.

PHOTOGRAPHING REFERENCE MODELS

I can paint from memory and imagination, but I am also a very retinal artist, meaning I can re-create in paint well what I see in life. My eyes naturally perceive contrast and color and can triangulate for proportion and balance. For these reasons, I like photographing models for key figures in my paintings. How to find and photograph a fourteen-year-old boy having a vision? I was in my ward's Young Men presidency at the time I created this image, in charge of the teachers quorum (fourteen-year-olds), and we were planning our quorum's weeknight activities. Problem solved! I asked the boys, "How would you like to do an activity where we study and talk about the First Vision accounts and then you guys model as Joseph Smith for one of my paintings?" They were all for it. What good boys! I told them to bring simple button-up shirts and khakis and vests or overshirts to give a general visual vibe, and they dug through their pioneer-trek clothing and showed up ready to go.

I am fortunate that Mark Mabry, the photographer for the popular *Reflections of Christ* series, is one of my very good friends and happened to be in my ward at the time and that his son Mark Mabry III was one of my teachers-quorum boys, so Mark came to help direct the photo shoot. We set up a backdrop and lights in a random room in our ward building and got to work.

This pose—leaning slightly away and looking over his shoulder, showing a little fear, looking up to the right part of the scene—fit my composition best, so I worked and picked from this series of shots with this great young man, Ryan Hafen. Here was the final picture I chose to use for the painting.

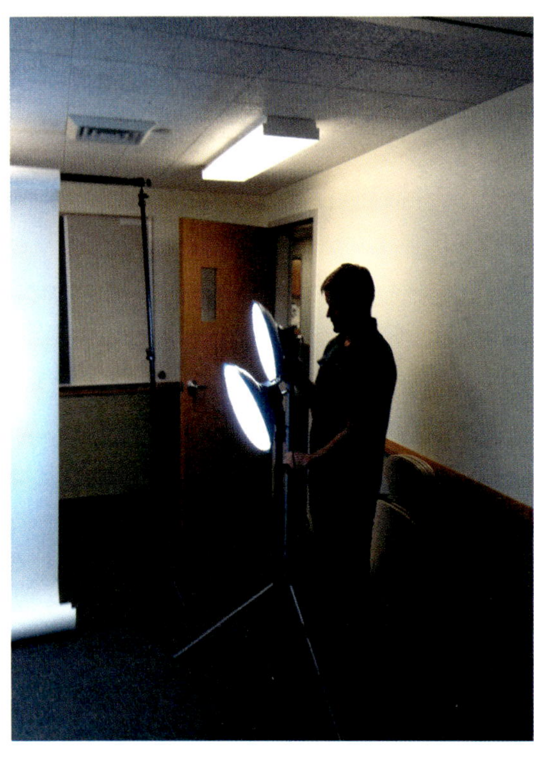

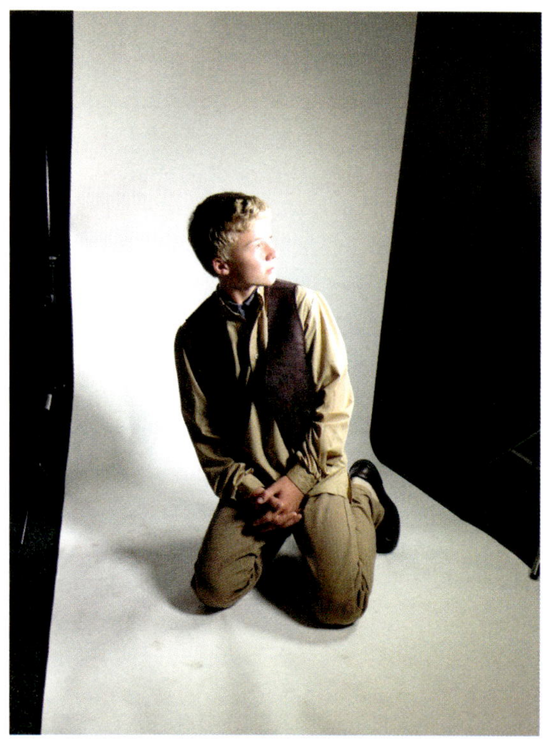

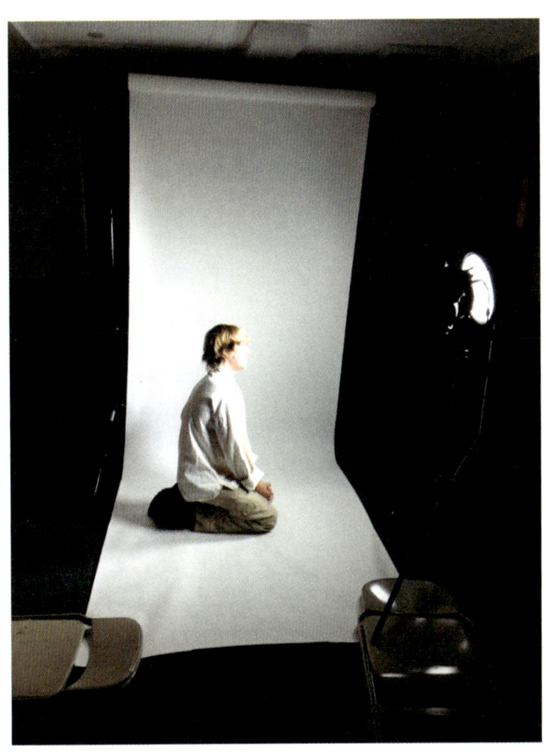

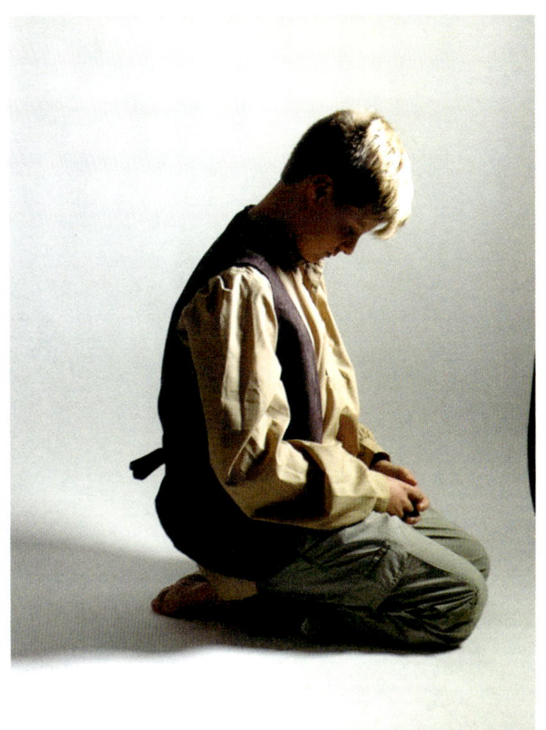

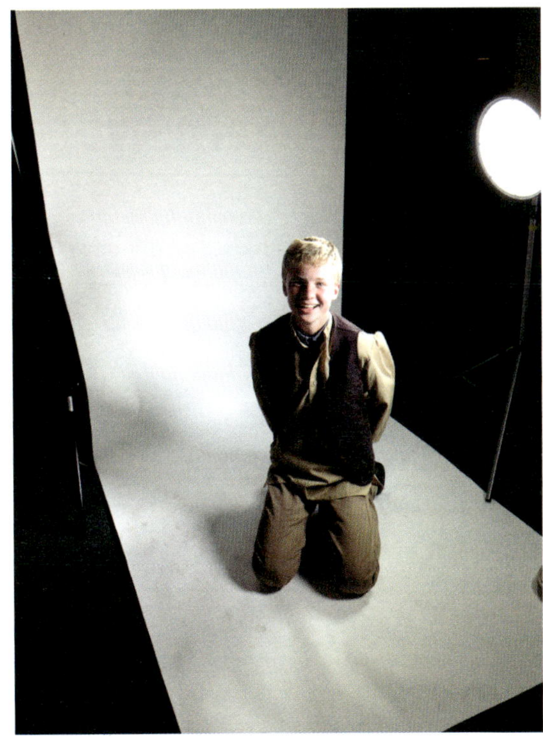

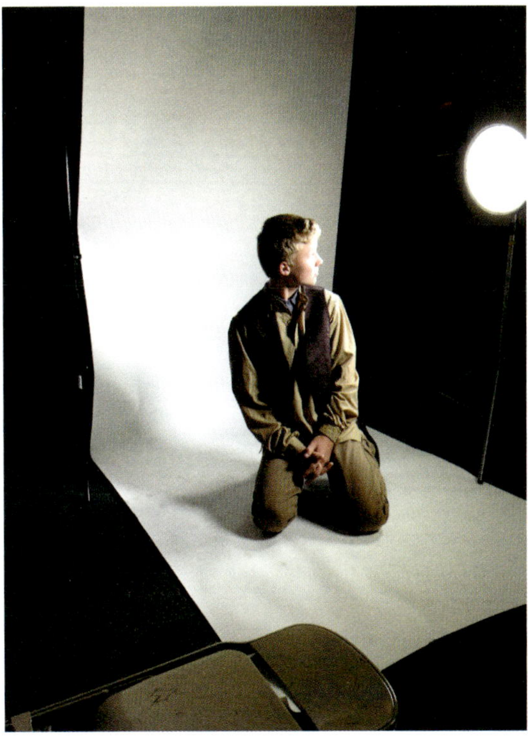

For the images of the Father and the Son, Mark Mabry was generous and sent me some of his unpublished photographs from his *Reflections of Christ* series to look through and find poses and head shots that matched ones for the Father and Son I had sketched. I chose this for the Father's body (middle, left), although digitally I would later replace the head with the head from another photograph looking the other direction and change the left arm reaching upward.

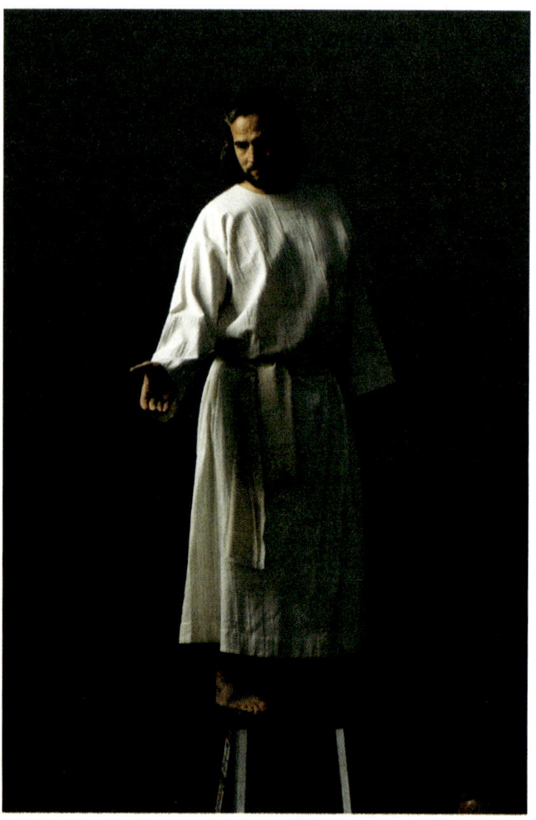

I chose this pose for the Son (below, right):

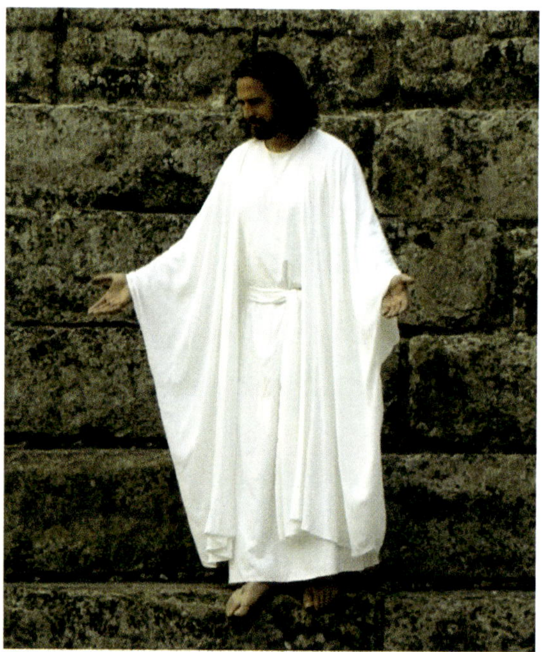

I wanted images of the Sacred Grove that were in early spring. Frankly, I could have photographed most any grove of trees from back east in early spring, or pilfered images from Google to use as a reference point. However, I was lucky to be traveling on a teaching assignment to the New York area in the early spring and was able to spend time in the Sacred Grove to photograph. Here I am in front of the replica Smith log home with my wife, Cindy, the Sacred Grove behind us.

It was perfect timing. The leaves were just starting to come out (so symbolic to me). Here are a few of the grove pictures I took.

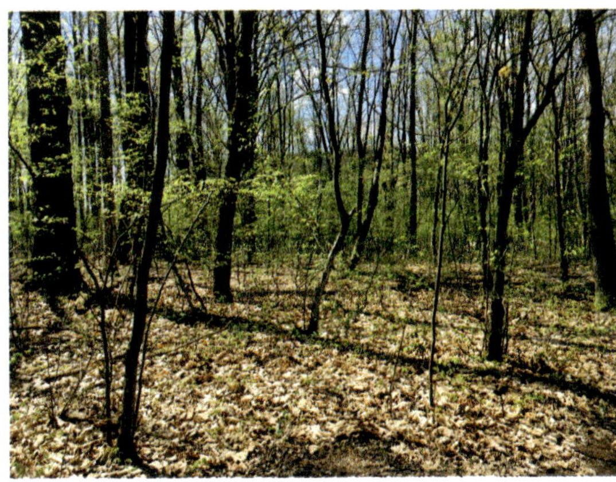

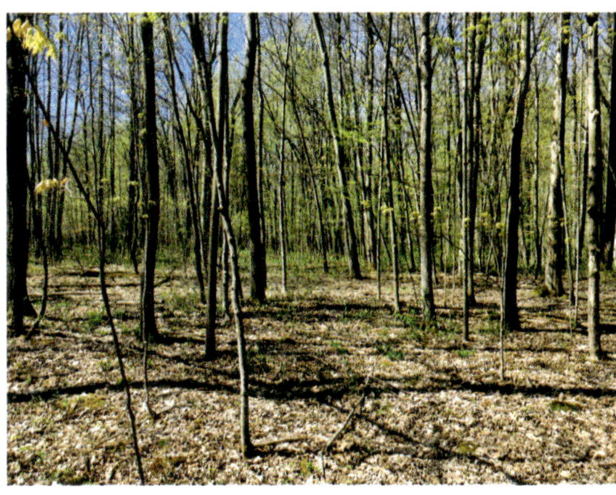

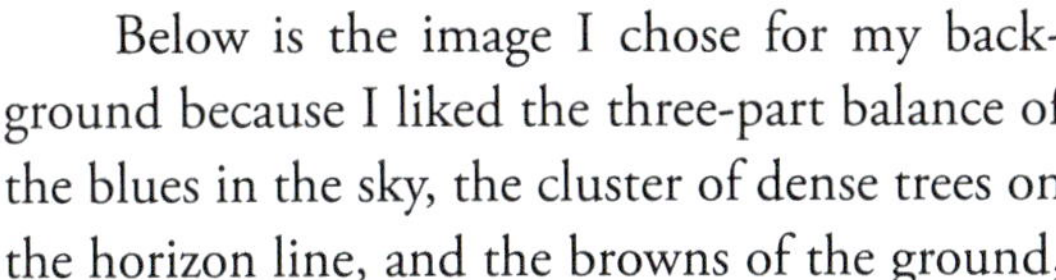

Below is the image I chose for my background because I liked the three-part balance of the blues in the sky, the cluster of dense trees on the horizon line, and the browns of the ground, which opened up where I could place Joseph. It balanced best visually, with strong, vertical, dark tree lines.

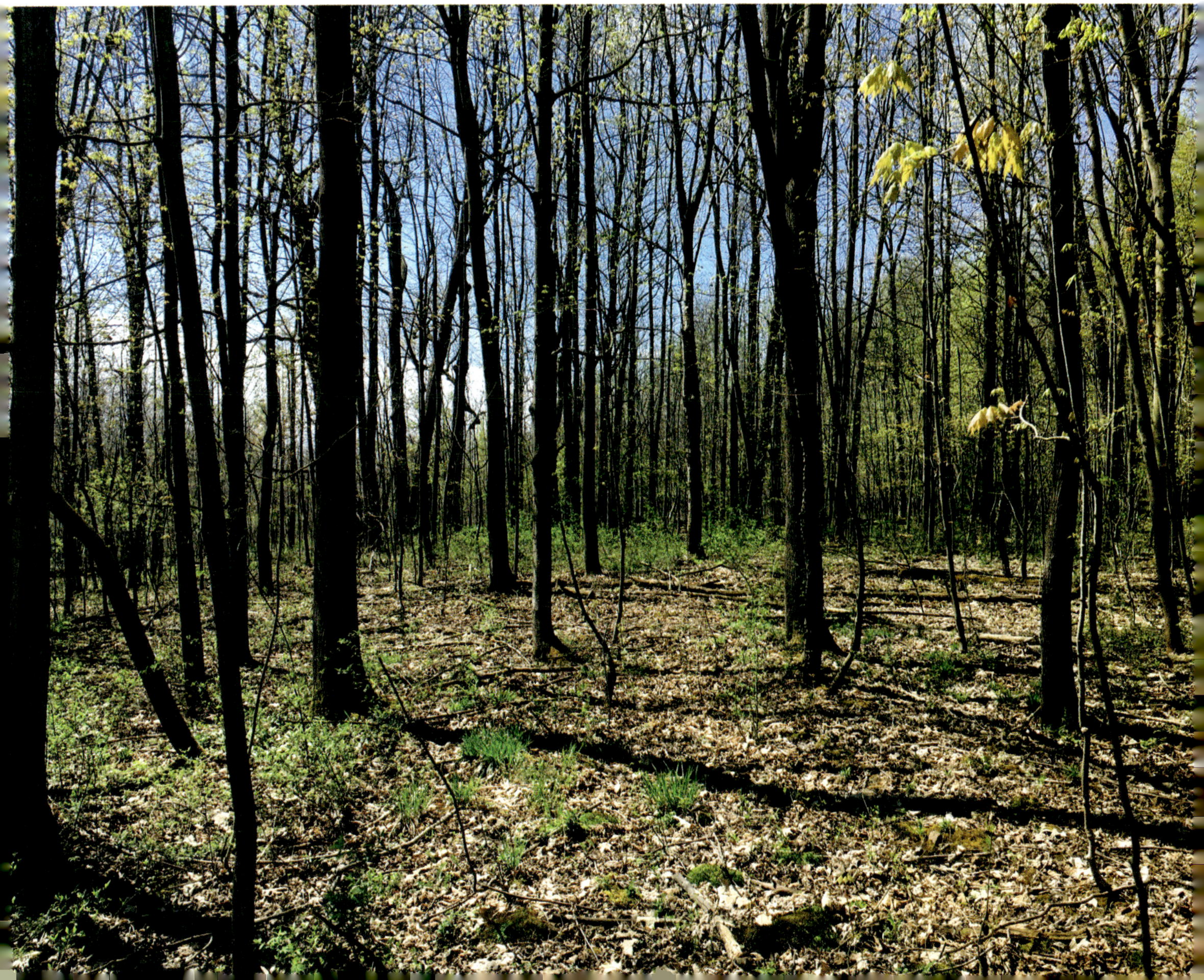

PHOTOSHOP AND SURFACE PREPARATION

With these elements photographed and ready, I took the images onto a layered photo editing and drawing software on my computer to place key elements. In the layered image, you will see that I move and cut and adapt digitally, such as adding more to the sky to make room for the angels, adding a different arm and head onto the Father to turn toward the Son, and tilting Joseph back a hair more. I added some random images of fire to get a visual feel for what the flames could look like, and placed a Googled image of a crowd into the background to give visual suggestion for the

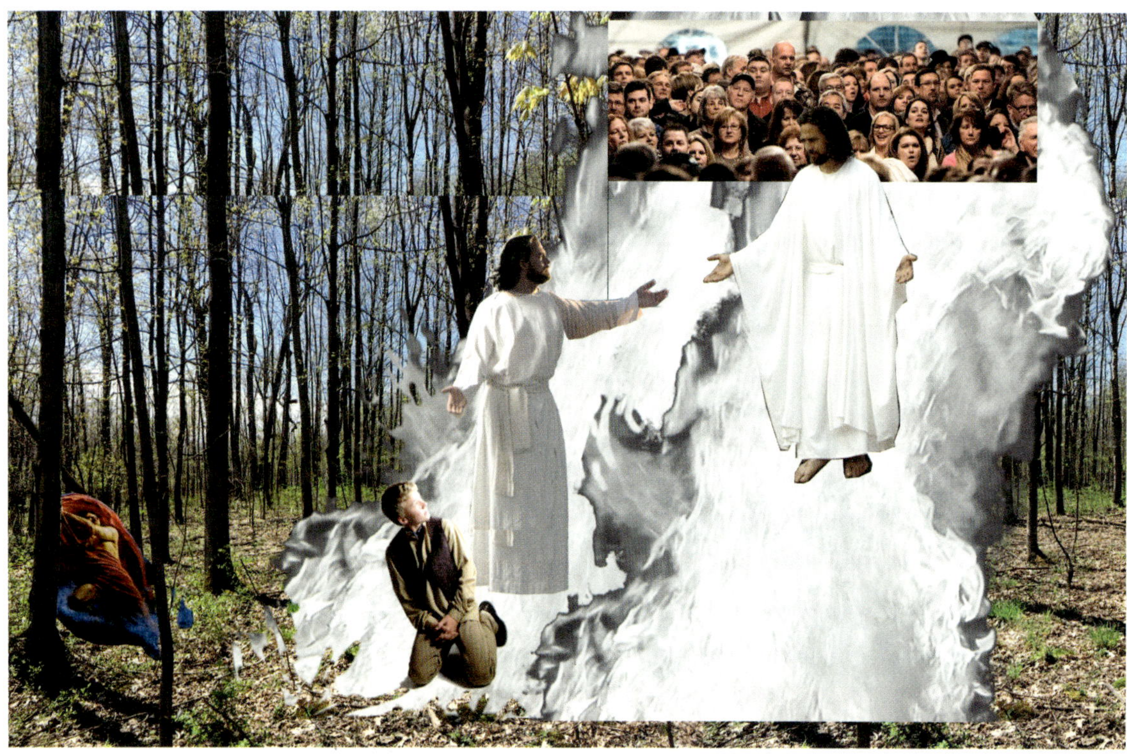

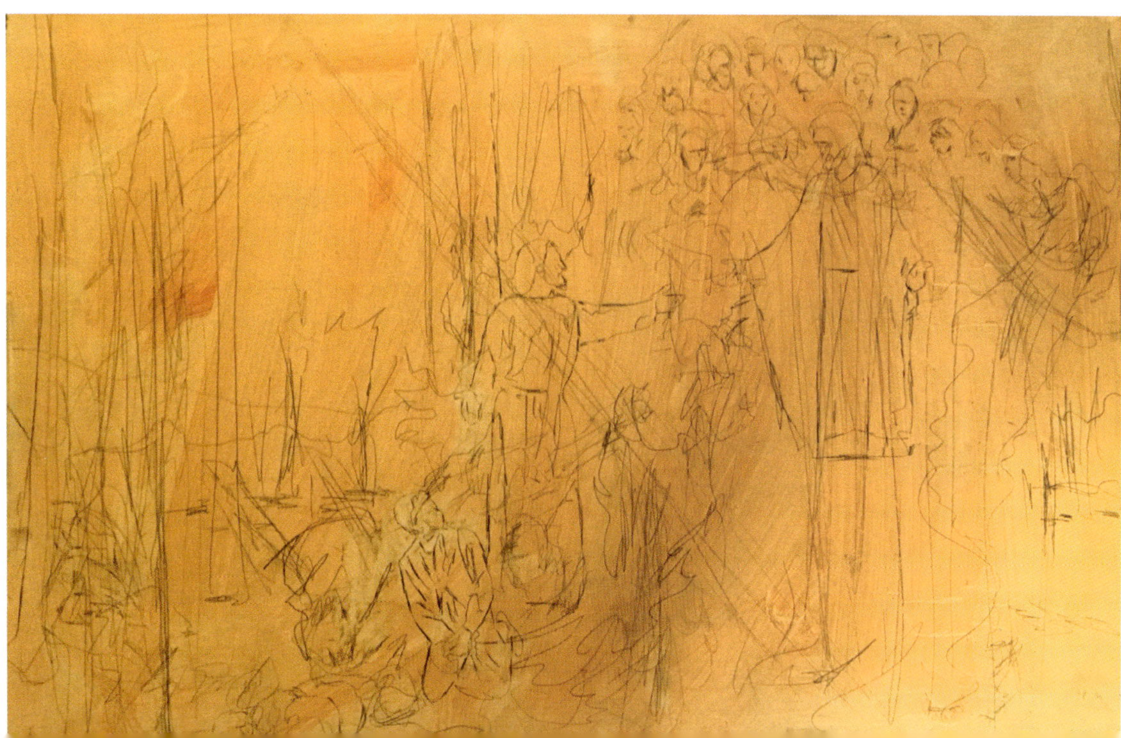

heads of the angels. In an homage to Carl Bloch, I cut his Satan out of his classic painting of Jesus casting out the adversary for a reference to adapt.

Next, I prepared my painting surface. I like painting on board, typically a one-quarter Masonite, as it is how I was trained and allows a firmer surface than canvas for sanding and palette knife work. I cut the board to the size and dimensions I want to paint (painting size varies based on purpose and approach). The board was then gessoed (primed white) and stained with a midtone brown. When the stain has dried, I used a simple number two pencil to draw the figures onto the board, using the digital composition as a reference.

PAINTING THE IMAGE

After the image was composed and drawn on the stained board, I began to lay down paint. I first used a thinned, dark paint to outline the pencil in oil-painted lines so they visually stand out and don't get lost as I paint. From there, the colors started to go down. I typically paint in layers, moving from the background to the foreground. Not only is it often practically necessary to do this, but the human eye can pick up subtle layering, so working from back to front helps create a feeling of depth. For example, in this painting I first laid down the blue sky and horizon line greenery, the base ground, then the fire. Afterward I began to lay down the figures and foreground. Below is the painting well along, yet in process, missing the trees and some details.

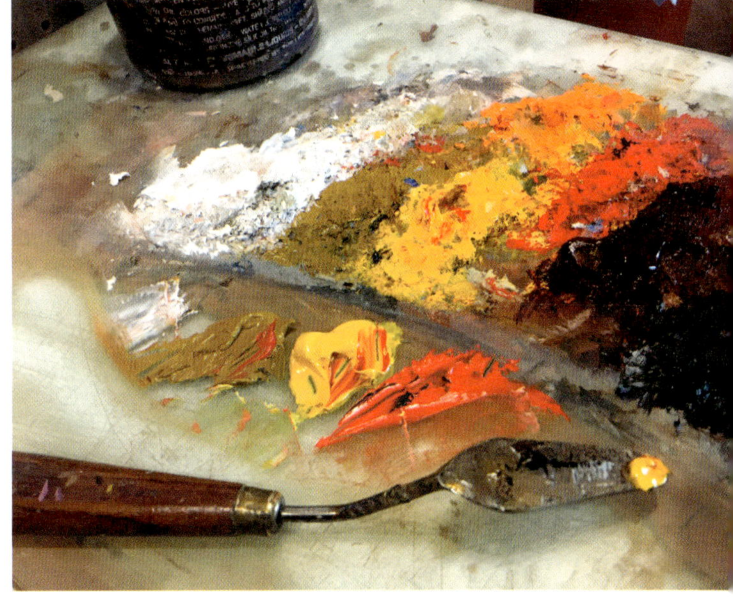

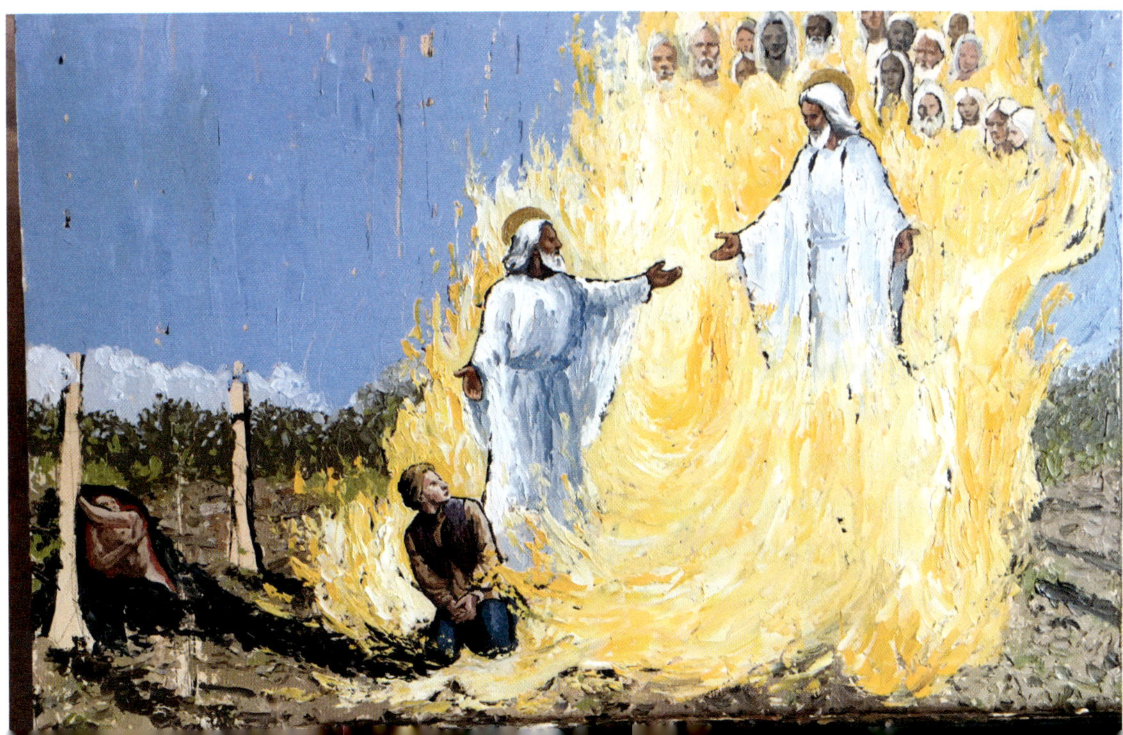

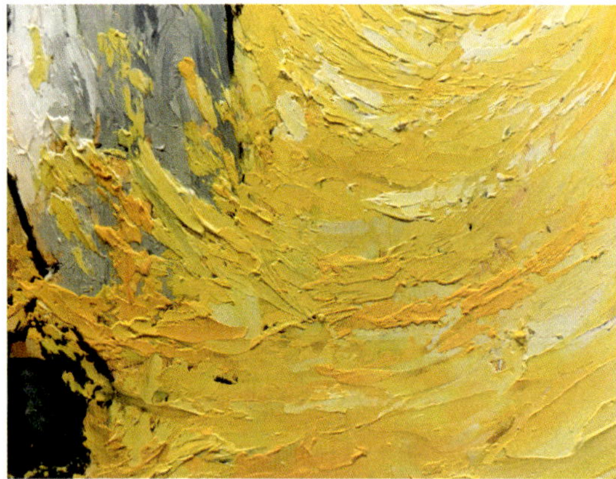

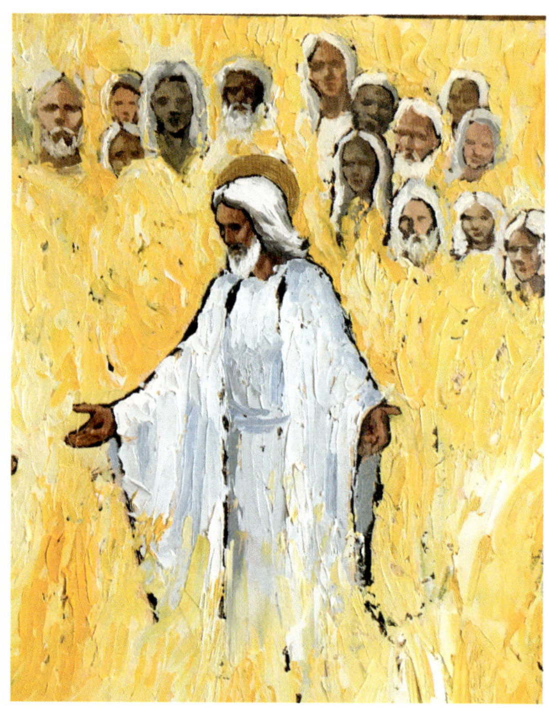

I painted nearly this entire painting with my palette knife (some parts of the faces were done with typical paintbrushes), mixing paint and picking it up on the back edge of the knife, then pressing it down onto the board.

The palette knife forces me to lay down thicker paint and to use bolder, more energetic and decisive artistic strokes rather than dabble indecisively.

Some compositional decisions are made while you paint. For example, originally, I had only a handful of angels behind the Savior.

However, it felt empty and lacking. The thought of angels crowding in and filling the space and overflowing the scene was preferable, so more angels were added.

Weeks later, after the palette knife work with its thicker paint dried, I went back and re-outlined the major figures with a darker outline using a brush. This is simply a stylistic approach,

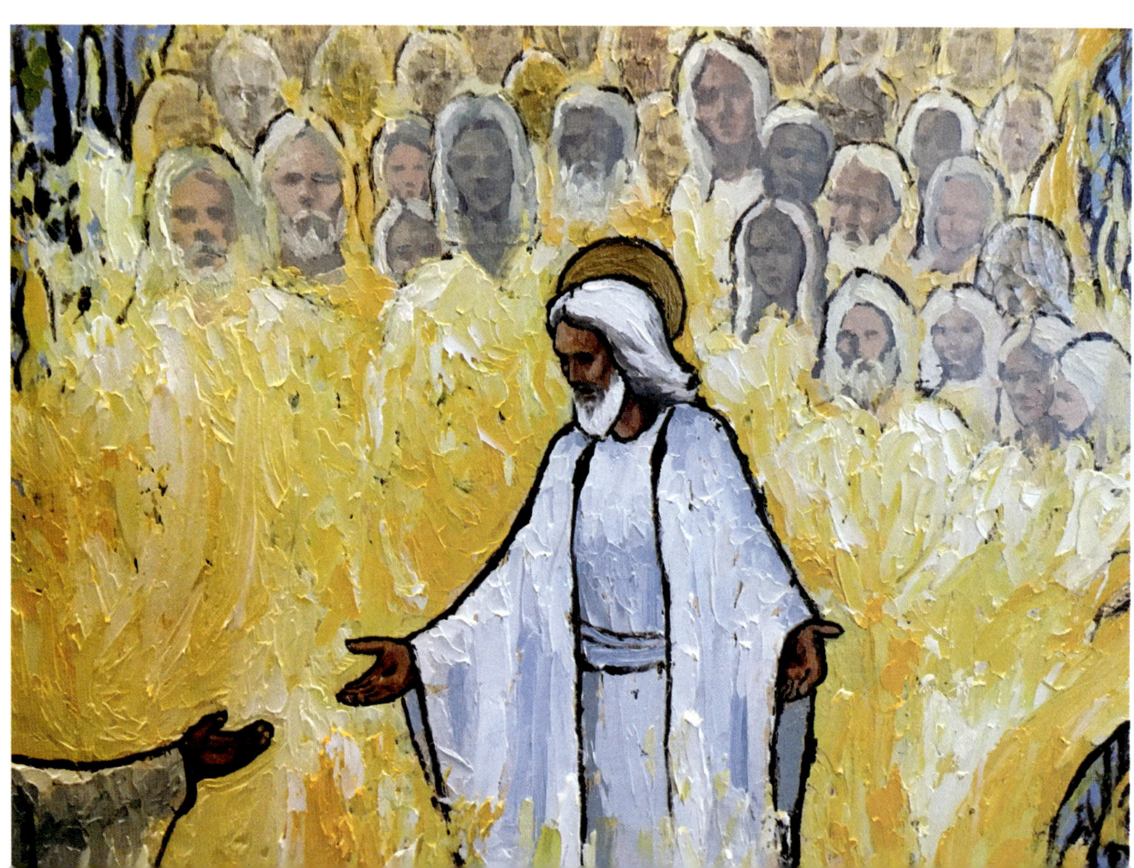

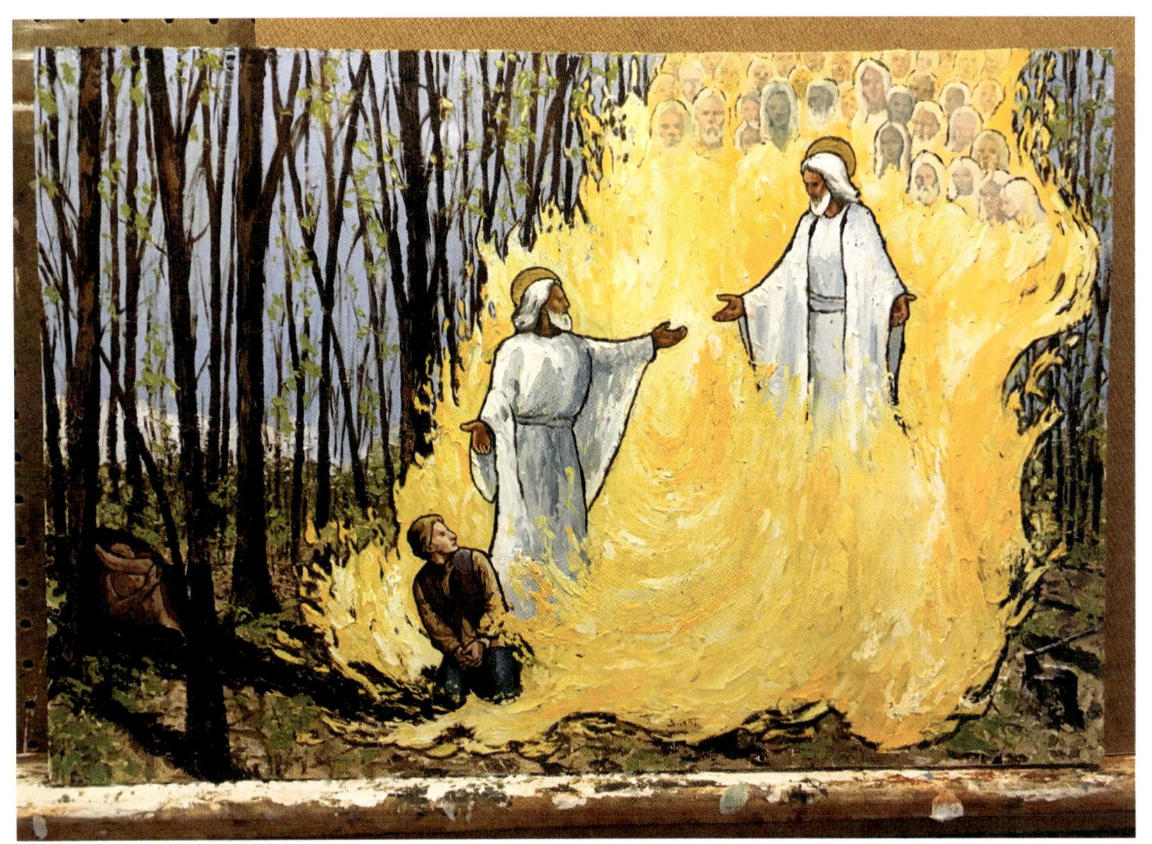

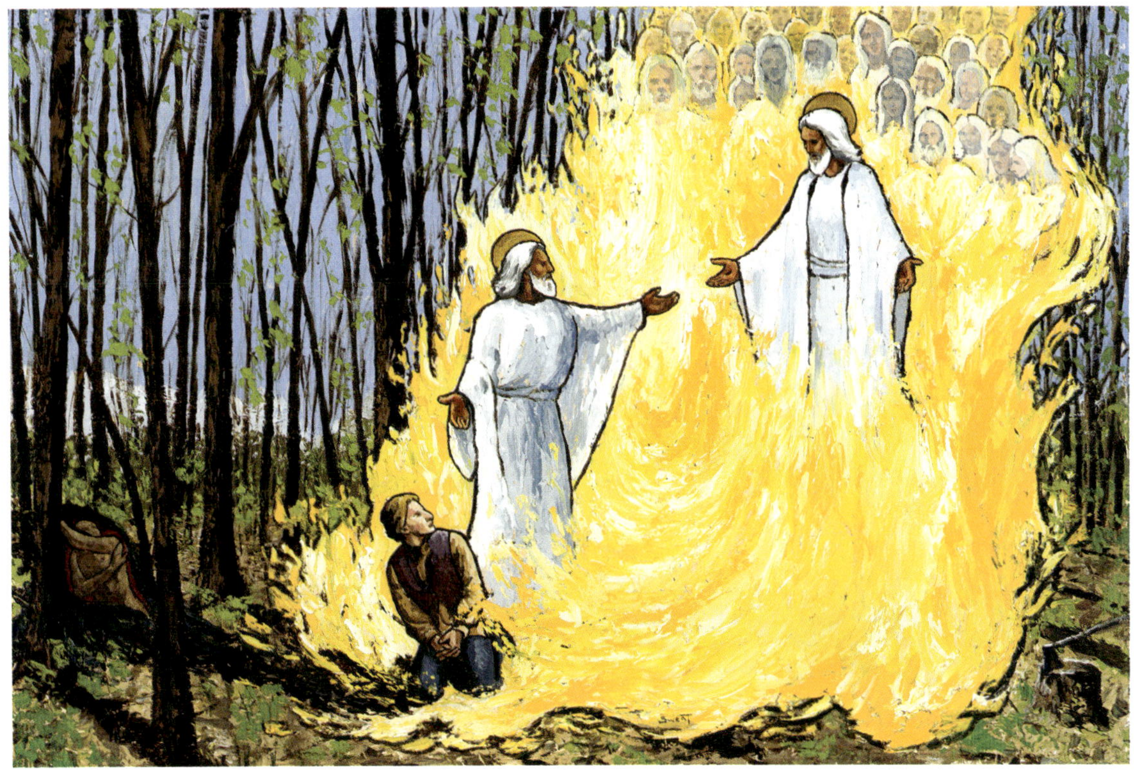

but one I enjoy, particularly in a First Vision image because it hearkens to early stained-glass images of the First Vision, one of the first artistic mediums used to depict the event. Here is the final painting, drying on my easel.

The last step was to take the original painting to a photographer who specializes in high-resolution, color-accurate capturing and reproduction. Most paintings in this *Repicturing the Restoration* series were photographed by Heath Brown at Masterlab in Midvale, Utah. He does excellent work, and I've relied on his skills for years. The high-resolution digital file is then used for reprinting, such as for the images in this book and for paper prints.

And there you have it, a painting from concept to creation!

THE CONCEPT OF CREATION

The process of creating a painting such as this is often more complex, difficult, and maddening than some might assume. You must fight through doubt, discouragement, and frustration, exercising patience and faith (at least I do). Yet there is something innately spiritual and rewarding in creating something from start to finish—to have something in your mind and then bring it into existence by organizing elements and energy. President Dieter F. Uchtdorf spoke eloquently about this innate godly pull to make things:

> The desire to create is one of the deepest yearnings of the human soul. No matter our talents, education, backgrounds, or abilities, we each have an inherent wish to create something that did not exist before.
>
> Everyone can create. You don't need money, position, or influence in order to create something of substance or beauty.
>
> Creation brings deep satisfaction and fulfillment. We develop ourselves and others when we take unorganized matter into our hands and mold it into something of beauty. . . .
>
> You may think you don't have talents, but that is a false assumption, for we all have talents and gifts, every one of us. The bounds of creativity extend far beyond the limits of a canvas or a sheet of paper and do not require a brush, a pen, or the keys of a piano. Creation means bringing into existence something that did not exist before—colorful gardens, harmonious homes, family memories, flowing laughter.[1]

I hope sharing the background process of this image from concept to creation might inspire you to use your skills to create something, whether that's a beautiful yard, a successful business, a website, a piece of furniture, a podcast, or your own piece of art. Take that spiritual creation forming in your mind, plan out its details and tasks, and bring it to temporal life (see Moses 3:5). The process and product will bless your life and the lives of those around you. Now, go on and create something!

NOTE

1. Dieter F. Uchtdorf, "Happiness, Your Heritage," *Ensign*, November 2008, 118–19.

ACKNOWLEDGMENTS

Large and long-term projects such as this involve many pivotal people, without whom the final product would not be the same or even exist at all.

I am indebted (literally) to the Religious Studies Center (RSC) at Brigham Young University for an initial grant to fund the materials costs involved to produce some of these paintings. I thank Thomas Wayment, former publications director at the RSC, for his initial interest in this project, along with the current director, Scott Esplin, for shepherding it through to completion. Thanks to Devan Jensen and his editorial team at the RSC, including Shirley S. Ricks and Meghan Rollins Wilson, for improving and refining the final manuscript. Thanks to Emily V. Strong for creating the beautiful typesetting, graphics, and layout for this visually rich book. And thanks to Brent Nordgren at the RSC for overseeing the business matters and overall production. At Deseret Book, I express thanks to my product director, Lisa Roper, for her support and guidance with this dual-label publication, and also to the reviewers from Deseret Book's board and the RSC for their improvements in the text.

I am grateful to each of my BYU colleagues. I, indeed, am lucky to learn from each of their extensive historical, doctrinal, and scriptural expertise, and I acknowledge the collective wisdom I've gleaned from them and put in the concepts illustrated and discussed into this book. In particular, I am grateful to my colleagues Michael MacKay and Gerrit Dirkmaat, whose invitation to illustrate the Book of Mormon translation for their book *From Darkness unto Light* acted as the impetus for this entire project. I also am indebted to the many historians and researchers whom I cite throughout this text, and especially those involved in producing *The Joseph Smith Papers*, which I relied upon heavily.

I am grateful to the professors at the University of Utah art school who gave me my foundational artistic training, particularly John Erickson, Paul Davis, and Brad Slaugh. I also acknowledge the Springville Museum of Art and their curatorial staff for selecting and showing some of the paintings from this series in their annual Spiritual and Religious Art show over the past seven years, spurring added interest and support. As I have sought inspiration for this project, I have also been edified by my association with many in the Latter-day Saint arts scene, including those involved with the Center for Latter-day Saint Arts and the Mormon Arts Foundation. I am grateful for the encouragement I've received from J. Kirk Richards throughout this project, someone I consider a friend, and one whose artwork continually inspires me in my own.

Many friends, family members, and students also agreed to pose as key models in paintings, whom I thank: Kate Allen, Paul Allen, Alex Baugh, Ryan Hafen, Lauren Hales, Zac Hales, Rachel LeBaron, Mark Mabry, Tara Mabry, Spencer McQueen, Michael Shelton, Cindy Sweat, Truman Sweat, students in the 2018 BYU Church History Travel Study program, and many random missionaries in Nauvoo dressed in time-period costume at Church pageants who posed for photographs.

And, of course, my immediate family is closely involved in all I do. My children come visit and talk with me as I paint, are interested in the images I am producing, and even sometimes help lay down the initial color layers. Above all, I am completely beholden to the love of my life, my wife Cindy, for twenty-three years of love, encouragement, and support of my artistic and literary endeavors. She was married to me before I ever decided to major in art in college, get a PhD, become an author or religion professor, and she has supported me through it all. She has seen up close and knows intimately the lows, frustrations, effort, pain, and failure that have come over many years before any highs, breakthroughs, inspiration, opportunities, or successes ever happen. Without her I would have given up long ago. With her love by my side, I feel I am able to do what God wants me to do. When it became apparent that my life's direction would be to become a full-time religious educator and not a full-time artist, I wrote in my personal journal on 2 January 2000: "I simply want to use my talent to the best of my capacity and not bury it . . . [and to] touch other people with my ideas." I'm thankful to all who have helped me realize this desire, and I hope this project has, in some way, touched your life for good.

INDEX

Page numbers in *italics* refer to images.

A

B

C

D

E

F

G

H

I

J

T

U

V

W

Y

Z